How to Make the World *Your* Market

The International Sales and
Marketing Handbook

How to Make the World *Your* Market

The International Sales and Marketing Handbook

Herman J. Maggiori

BURNING GATE PRESS
LOS ANGELES

HOW TO MAKE THE WORLD YOUR MARKET: THE INTERNATIONAL SALES
AND MARKETING HANDBOOK
© 1992, Herman J. Maggiori. All rights reserved.

For information address:
Burning Gate Press
P. O. Box 6015
Mission Hills, CA 91395-1015
(818) 896-8780

FIRST EDITION

LOC # 91-73712
ISBN   1-878179-06-3

ACKNOWLEDGEMENTS

The author's heartfelt thanks are extended to the many people who have helped in the writing of this book.

Foremost among these is my wife, Dee, a professional writer and editor who closely edited my manuscript, tightened up my occasionally verbose prose, and put every word on her computer. Her encouragement to start the task of putting into readable form 35 years of export and international operations experience and carrying it to its conclusion, was invaluable.

In addition, my appreciation for help and encouragement goes to: my publisher, Mark Kelly, who saw merit in the original short manuscripts and gave insightful advice and suggestions for improvement; William A. Marshall, a consultant for A. N. Deringer Freight Forwarders, Stratford, Connecticut, who provided many of the export shipping forms and helpful shipping advice; Susan Berry of the Hartford, Connecticut District Office of the Department of Commerce, who provided information on Commerce's export assistance and export control programs; Barry Tarnef, technical director of CIGNA Property & Casualty's Specialty Lines/Loss Control Services, for permission to use CIGNA materials on insurance and export packing; Mr. Robert Adamsky of Chase Bank, Bridgeport, Connecticut, for export collection documents, and Thomas A. Farrelly, President of Thomas A. Farrelly Associates, Trumbull, Connecticut, for his invaluable help in defining Incoterms 1990.

All of the above have contributed to helping make this volume possible, and to fostering a vitally needed interest in exporting.

Contents

How to Make the World *Your* Market

The International Sales and
Marketing Handbook

INTRODUCTION

If you've toyed with the idea of marketing your company's products overseas and adding "International, Inc." to your company's name—this is the right time to do something about it.

If you have wondered how companies get started in exporting and become multinational entities whose products are household names—THIS BOOK IS FOR YOU! Read on.

In today's world of high-tech products, super-fast air travel, fax machines and overnight-mail and package delivery to just about any part of our planet, doing business in foreign countries is no longer a dream or a hardship. It is a reality attested to by thousands of small and large American manufacturers and their counterparts in many foreign countries who are exporting their goods and services and making profits for their companies by selling in countries some of them never knew existed a few short years ago.

With faster lines of communication and transportation, products made by a small company in West Virginia are being shipped regularly to a manufacturer in Hong Kong who uses them as important components in his products. A mid-western U.S.A. producer of household items regularly makes life easier for thousands of Latin American housewives who may never have known that such efficient time and labor-saving devices existed until that company started looking into sales beyond the borders of the United States. Many thousands of useful products made in America and in demand around the world are now being exported all over the globe.

Services too, can be exported. Many small U.S. companies are now entering the global market-place with services such as architectural design, quality systems for manufacturing entities, information technology, accounting and financial services and food and restaurant services, and a host of other services. Foreign markets welcome these and thousands of other U.S. products and services. Exporting makes good business sense!

Exporting is not something for large corporations only. Any business, large, small, or medium can become involved in this exciting and profitable area of commerce—not only to make profits, but also to realize its full growth and expansion potential. Often a small company can have a trading edge over a large one because of its ability to react more quickly to an opportunity for business, or to go after a smaller "deal" which larger companies would label as "to small to bother with."

In addition, many foreign companies are anxious to work with small American companies, considering them to be an entré for their products into the super-U.S. market. The global economy continues to expand, constantly creating more opportunities for those involved in international trade.

What Exports can do for American Companies and the United States

Recent figures published by the Department of Commerce show that U.S. exports in 1990 rose to a new record of $389.3 billion, an increase of 8 percent over the $364 billion reached in 1989. In 1988, U.S. exports totaled over $322 billion, an increase of 30 percent over the previous year. Of the 1990 total, 80 percent were manufactured goods, 11 percent agricultural products and 9 percent mostly mineral fuels and crude materials. This strong "boom" in exports, along with a slower pace of imports, improved our trade-deficit to $108.7 billion, the lowest since 1983, and also made large contributions to America's economic growth. They also helped ease the effect of the 1990-91 recession which hit many areas of the country. Exports also made significant improvement in the profits of the estimated 100,000 American companies who took advantage of the dozens of burgeoning overseas markets in all parts of the world, notably in Europe, Canada, the Pacific Rim countries and Mexico. The year 1991 is also off to a good start with January exports of $34.5 billion, the second highest month on record.

What has this meant for many companies in a wide range of industries? The Department of Commerce analysis of 1990 export totals shows that U.S. exports have increased about 76 percent since 1986. Foremost among the many industries which have benefitted from this strong increase in this period are:

Small manufactured goods................Up 145.9%
Electrical Machinery.........................Up 133.1 %
Aircraft...Up 99.4%
Computers and Office Machines.......Up 69.5 %
Cars and Trucks................................ Up 6 1.4%
Machine Tools.................................. Up 23.0%

Many other industries registered significant increases in exports and, as a whole, the United States showed a remarkable drop in imports. Machine tool imports dropped by 50 percent. Many companies showed exports totaling as much as 30-40 percent and more of their total sales.

While the undervalued U.S. dollar has played an important role in this surge of exports, making American goods and services less costly in foreign markets, another strong factor has been the revitalization, higher productivity rates, and lower production costs of many U.S. factories.

Current productivity has been growing almost three times as fast as in the late 1970s when exports were also growing steadily. Many economists, forecasters and international organizations are predicting that U.S. exports will grow approximately 50 percent faster than imports through the rest of this decade.

There has been no better time in recent years than NOW to consider exporting your products and do something positive about making the world your market.

As this is being written at the end of 1991, we must, in addition to the rapidly increasing world population, consider the recent startling turn of events in the East European countries and in the former U.S.S.R. These will eventually add greatly to the number of available markets for U.S. exporters and will have a great impact on the world's economy.

The Soviet Union, (or whatever it will be called as further events unfold) presents a consumer market of 280 million people, equal to the United States and Canada. An additional 140 million people make up the total market of the former Communist East European countries. Although these populations are included in the total world figures, they have not been an effective part of the world trade arena for most U.S. companies.

Before rushing off with brief case and order book in hand be aware that they are not yet markets as we know them, and won't be for some time to come. However, now *is* the time to take a cautious look at what you might be able to offer in terms of goods and services, and to look for the correct relationships in each of the countries which will eventually need an enormous range of consumer and industrial goods and all types of services. If you work now toward gaining a foothold for the future, you have a better chance of succeeding when free-market economies are finally established. This will only come after each country has developed and implemented:

- New banking systems for currency conversion and control.
- Up-to-date communication networks
- Workable distribution systems
- De-centralized, market-focused economies
- Managers and workers who understand and accept the free-enterprise system.

This increasing population and the political and socioeconomic changes in the former Communist world present a potential world-wide export market with staggering opportunities for profits and growth. For every $1 billion in U.S. exports, 22,000 jobs are created. In 1989 merchandise exports accounted for nearly seven million jobs in the United States. America needs to continue to strengthen its economy and provide more jobs for American workers.

So Why Don't More Companies Export Their Products and Services?

Many feel it is too much trouble to get involved in exporting, or that it is too costly to do business with overseas customers. Others feel they are doing well enough in the U.S. market, so why bother?

While it is true that there are differences in selling to overseas markets, and that the U. S. marketplace is large and profitable for many companies, it is also a fact that the domestic marketplace is increasingly becoming the target of many foreign competitors. Many sectors are shrinking for U. S. manufactured products. Those foreign competitors are exporting!

U. S. manufacturers cannot continue to sit back and let foreign manufacturers gain increasing shares of their markets. They must be on the lookout for additional markets in which they can sell their products so that they can continue to grow. Believe it—there are many good markets overseas for American products and services.

After reading what exports have done for our country and thousands of U. S. companies who have decided to export their products, you should at least, take a look at whether or not your company can join the multitude of those who contributed to the impressive statistics cited above.

What You Will Learn from This Book

While some of the basic strategies which have resulted in successful sales in the U. S. market may be used in selling to overseas markets, there are many different and fundamental elements which must be understood and implemented in order to become a successful exporter.

It is the intent of this text to explore and define these elements, and to illustrate how they are all vitally important components in formulating and implementing a profitable global sales and marketing plan.

We will explore and explain such factors as: making a full commitment to your export program; assessing the exportability of products; identifying and researching foreign markets; evaluating local competition in chosen markets; locating, appointing, and evaluating overseas distributors and agents; offering favorable financing on overseas sales and getting paid for them.

It is our aim to help you through these and the various other steps required to implement an export sales program for your company. This can be accomplished in several individual phases, or on a more accelerated basis, depending upon how fast or how slowly you wish to proceed, and what your company's resources will allow.

Following the guidelines offered in this book can change the course of your business life, and will undoubtedly have a desirable impact on your profits. Chances are good that you'll decide exporting is the way to go. Good! If so many others can do it, why not you?

Let's look at everything you want and need to know about exporting, from how to get started, to getting paid for what you sell. It could be the most important business step you've ever taken.

Chapter 1

TAKING A LOOK

Before making a definite decision to export, it is important that you take a look at your present business. Are you adequately supplying your domestic customers with products and services? What is the outlook for your business (or your industry)? Is it growing? Slacking off? Static? Could you continue to satisfy the demand for your products if you started making some foreign sales? Could you do so from your regular production, or would you have to add manufacturing capability? If foreign sales really started to grow, do you have adequate resources to increase your manufacturing equipment, capital and personnel? Would the profit generated by initial overseas sales be sufficient to help you increase your commitment to export? Would the profit cover the cost of increasing staff to handle export sales and starting a full fledged export department? Consider too, how exporting will affect your company's growth and profitability.

Look at Your Product

If you are satisfied with your answers to most of the above questions, you can now begin to think about your product itself. A decade or two ago, the prevailing attitude was that all the world wanted a U.S. made product because it was the best available. Almost any company could be successful in exporting its products without expending too much effort. This is no longer true. Today high quality and innovative products are readily available from many worldwide sources, possibly at lower prices or better terms. Today your products must have "exportability" and must do what they have been designed to do as well or better than someone else's.

Herman J. Maggiori

The U.S. government and foreign markets want metric goods
You give an inch... and they won't take it

WASHINGTON, DC—Most SCORE counselors are keenly aware by now that all businesses—large and small—that contract with the federal government must be using the metric system by the end of FY 1992, which is September 30, 1992. This is mandated in the Omnibus Trade and Competitiveness Act of 1988. Federal procurement contracts represent $380 billion in business opportunities. This has far-reaching implications—are your small business government contracting clients capable of making the change? Is your SCORE chapter capable of providing counseling and workshops to assist your clients in their transition? If not, what are you doing about it?

There are other important considerations in metrication that must be considered as well such as dealing with large domestic or multi-national corporations that have switched to metric because of the volume of international sales and manufacturing they do and small businesses themselves getting involved in international trade. "...small businesses [have been] reluctant in the past to adopt metric standards as a part of their operating systems. Continued reluctance will put many business at a competitive disadvantage as the impact of metric change pervades our economy," says the SBA's Metrication Action Plan.

But large businesses, an important customer of small businesses, are increasingly changing to metric. Two independent studies of Fortune 1000 businesses found that:

• 62 percent of all large firms produce at least one metric product;
• 32 percent of total net sales of the firms' products are metric product sales;
• 34 percent of new products use metric designs;
• 28 percent of the firms have formal metric policies;
• 34 percent of the firms provide metric training for their employees;

• 16 percent reported lost sales due to an inability to supply a product in metric version;
• 68 percent felt metric would become the predominant system of measurement in their industry; and
• 50 percent favored mandatory conversion in 20 years.

If small business wants to continue to market itself to America's biggest businesses, it will have to make the change, and the sooner the better. The small business that plans early will have a competitive advantage.

The SBA report continues..."Changing to a predominant use of metric is not without costs, but there are opportunities for savings as well. A simple example is the success story of the U.S. distilled spirits industry. The industry used the metric change as a once-in-a-lifetime opportunity to reduce container sizes. The industry changed from 53 to seven sizes, clearly demonstrating the power of standardization.

"Other examples include an approximate $1 million a year Caterpillar Tractor is saving by ordering steel for its plants in worldwide metric amounts. Metrication has also allowed the farm implement manufacturer John Deere to pare down the number of screw sizes used from 70 to 15, thus increasing efficiency and reducing human error."

A recent SBA Office of Advocacy study revealed that American exports accountable to small businesses are approximately 22 percent. That is a tremendous market share that could all be lost if small business fails to take advantage of metrication. Business America reports that, "Surveys of foreign commercial officers revealed that metric demands create problems or cause U.S. firms to lose sales. For example, a firm in the Middle East couldn't find an American producer

that could sell pipe with metric threads for oil machinery. A European firm had to rewire all electrical appliances because the U.S. standard wire diameters were not sufficient to meet national standards."

Metric conversion does not have to be expensive; in fact, it can be quite manageable. A Department of Commerce official quoted in Business America says, "Industry experience has shown that when a timely decision to use the metric system is made and managed properly, there is negligible additional cost, and employees and suppliers experience little or no difficulty in making the transition. When the metric decision is delayed until competitive pressures force the change, there may well be some waste in product obsolescence due to the unacceptability of inch-based designs that fail to meet international market preferences for metric designs." The official also pointed out that metric conversion costs pale in comparison to lost export sales from failing to use metric standards.

Finally, small businesses must consider the implications of the European Economic Community's Harmonized Tariff System, which is part of Europe-1992. The tariff system stipulates the use of the metric system in product descriptions and measurement data for all customs transactions. Europe represents 320 million consumers, too large a market for big or small business to ignore. Big business is surely gearing up for metrication. Small business must comply in order to remain viable with their large counterparts and the European Community.

A thorough knowledge of your industry and the customers it serves will put you on the fast track to finding out whether or not your product can be successfully exported. You may find out that your competitors are exporting their products, or others in your industry are selling similar products overseas.

You will need to know if your product can be sold "as is," or if it will have to be changed in some way to make it acceptable overseas. Because you have had success in selling your product in the United States, don't assume you'll have equal or greater success selling it in foreign markets. Perhaps you will, but there may sometimes be characteristics of a U.S. made product which make it unacceptable in the same form as it is used in the United States.

Because of local custom, usage, regulations or buying habits, your product may have to be changed a little. For example, some markets require that products be in metric dimension, (see article on previous page courtesy of the U.S. Small Business Administration), operate on a different power supply (220 volts/50 cycles, instead of our normal 110 volts/60 cycles), or be packaged differently.

These factors may dictate making some changes in the product you are selling in the American market. Changes don't always have to be major in nature. Often a small adjustment, a change in color, or an added micro-chip is all that is needed to allow you to sell your product overseas and gain a share in a foreign market. The important thing is to know at the very beginning the differences that exist in product acceptance between domestic and foreign markets.

Basically, you should find out:

1. If your product can be exported as already produced and sold in the U.S.A., or if changes are needed.
2. If changes are needed:
   a. What they are, and why they are necessary.
   b. What costs are involved.
   c. What the impact would be on current manufacturing processes.
   d. What the effect of a and c would be on export selling prices.

Look for Possible Markets

You will need to know if there are foreign markets in which your product can be sold. Most products fit into a specific category: consumer, industrial, scientific, medical etc. You probably have many friends or contacts in your specific industry who make similar, non-competitive products. Undoubtedly some of them are exporting. Talk to them. Find out how their products are accepted in foreign markets. If you belong to an industry group or association, ask the executive secretary for information about the prospects for exporting your product. Many associations have foreign members or an international division which can supply you with valuable information.

You can also visit the U. S. Department of Commerce field office in your area to check the export statistics by product category to individual countries or to certain regions. Check your local public library for business directories which will identify the types of customers who use your product. Find out if the classes of customers who use your product exist in certain foreign countries.

A look at some economic indicators in a few countries, such as gross national product, per capita income and purchasing power statistics will tell you if there would be customers in a position to buy and use your product. If your product is used as a component by OEM's (Original Equipment Manufacturers), check one of the directories of manufacturers to see if their products could use yours as a component.

You may find that in some countries there is only a narrow grouping of potential customers, while in others there could be several categories of users.

Selecting Target Markets

You have taken some good first steps and you know there are places in which your product can be sold and customers who can use them. Since there are over 150 foreign markets from which to choose, and you can't start in all or too many at one time, you should select a small number, perhaps three or four, which appear most interesting to you when you start your preliminary analysis. From these, chose a specific one on which to concentrate. See if it has a lot of potential customers in a fairly compact geographical area.

Much will depend upon your product. If it is one required by large numbers of customers, you should choose from among the most populous countries to make your selection. If your product is a specialized one, your sales in any one country could be limited, so choose several countries from among the more likely prospects. Your goal is to select a couple of the most attractive ones which you will next analyze in depth.

Examining and studying your target markets is a major move ahead, and will really get you more deeply into the international picture. You will have to become more involved with finding out what's happening in the targeted markets and how your product might fit. Find out for sure if the initial look you took at potential markets and at your product can pay off in these markets so you can get started making sales. Now you are ready to enter the world of foreign market research.

The following chapter, *DEVELOPING AN INTERNATIONAL MAR-KETING AND SALES PLAN*, will tell you how to start this market research, and show you how to proceed to each step in your move to become an exporting company.

Chapter 2

DEVELOPING AN INTERNATIONAL MARKETING AND SALES PLAN

The ancient Roman sage Seneca said, "Our plans miscarry because they have no aim. When a man does not know what harbor he is making for, no wind is the right wind."

A business manager must know his goal and the correct course to take to reach it.

Every successful business venture should have a plan based on sound facts, analysis, objectives and goals. The managers of most U. S. companies are well aware of the many factors and forces they must contend with in the everyday conduct of business. They know how and where to promote their products, the channels of distribution through which they are bought, stocked and sold, and the motivating and buying habits of consumers across the country. They know and understand the many U.S. laws, rules and regulations which govern their activities and strategies in the daily conduct of their respective businesses.

In addition to this, it is a normal practice for them to formulate precise business or action plans in writing whenever they enter a new phase of their operations, begin a new project, introduce new products or enter into an expansion program. They plan each move, writing down each step to be taken, to implement whatever the new phase of their business might be. They will plan for every action to be taken to ensure no element is overlooked.

Initiating such an exciting venture as an export sales and marketing operation requires a detailed and meticulously thought-out course of action which will state objectives and outline in detail each step to be taken to achieve them. Having made an initial commitment to "take-a-look" at the possibility of exporting, senior management should now agree to give its support and lend company resources to formulating and carrying out an action plan.

Constructing an Action Plan

The basic plan should be put together in such a way that it will plot an exact course to be taken. Each step should be followed until the objectives are reached.

Many elements to be included are shown in the sample plan which follows. As you make your own plan, try to anticipate any problems which could arise as you contemplate market entry strategies. You don't want to be caught unaware in a tricky situation and not have a policy to take care of it.

Most plans will include the elements in our illustration, but variations or additional steps can be made or added depending upon your specific goals, company policies, products or services.

Each step of the sample action plan presented below is explained in fullest detail in the succeeding chapters of this book. Following such a plan will guide you from the very start of export operations to the establishment of a full-fledged foreign sales and marketing division.

THE ACTION PLAN

I. Objectives

    A. Determine if the company should initiate an export sales and marketing operation.

    B. Determine if the company's product(s) are exportable.

    C. Choose and explore selected target markets to determine if there are potential users of the product.

    D. Perform in-depth market research and study enabling the company to penetrate overseas markets if A to C provide affirmative results.

    E. Establish eventual worldwide distribution and sales of the company's products at a profit.

II. Plan of Action

  A. Start Preliminary Market Research
    1. Check industry and public library sources for U.S. export statistics and destinations of same or similar products.
      a. Select some target markets to study.
      b. Identify, analyze and rank target markets by potential.
      c. Determine specific potential customers within target markets.

  B. Perform Detailed Target Market Analysis
    1. Check for import restrictions in targeted markets.
    2. Examine available representation and distribution methods.
    3. Socio-cultural factors affecting trade.
    4. Check for U. S. legislation affecting exports to targeted markets.
    5. Investigate competition, U. S. and local.

  C. Establish Market Selection Criteria
    1. Determine size of market in selected countries.
    2. Fix priorities for market entry.
    3. Establish strategies for market penetration.

  D. Decide on Type of Representation Needed in Each Market
    1. Distributor or agent.
    2. Research needed to locate distributor or agent candidates.
    3. Write introductory letters to potential candidate.
    4. Produce a standard form of distributor or agent contract (see samples on pages 142–159 and 163–173).

  E. Decide How to Organize For Exporting
    1. Direct or indirect exporting.
    2. Management and operating details.
    3. Identify and establish system of allocation of company resources and support functions for export operations.
    4. Staff required— administrative and operating
      a. Clerical.
      b. Documentation.
      c. Packing and shipping.
    5. Establish a time table for competition of each task in action plan.

  F. Develop a Marketing Plan

1. Define the "market" in each country.
   a. Who the customers are.
   b. How you will approach, motivate and sell to them.
2. Develop a profitable pricing structure.
3. Develop a distributor/agent training program
4. Implement basic sales policies—terms, conditions, warranties, returns etc.
5. Request distributors/agents to submit their proposed marketing plan.
6. Decide on the number of markets to be penetrated and establish a time table.

G. Decide on Methods of Market Penetration
   1. Advertising
      a. Develop concept, appeal and content to present products and company in best light.
      b. Determine item "a" in context of the several markets intended to penetrate (each could be different).
      c. Organize product literature—English or foreign languages.
      d. Investigate media available.
      e. Determine space and production costs.
   2. Investigate trade show participation.
   3. Other promotional activities
      a. Investigate possible free publicity in:
         Trade journals (write articles on product)
         Editorial comment in "New Products" sections
         New literature available
         Announcements of entry into export markets
         Announcements of appointments of foreign distributors/agents
   4. Direct sales approach
      a. Where no representation can be obtained.
      b. Correspondence or direct visitation.
   5. Personal visits to markets.
      a. Estimate costs and time out-of-office.
      b. Plan itineraries: markets to visit, time in each.
      c. Coordinate with distributor-search, appointment, evaluation,

attendance at or participation in foreign trade shows or trade missions, visits to potential major customers.

H. Generate an Estimated Sales Forecast
   1. By country and/or market (by month/year)
I. Develop an Operating (expense) Budget (month/year)
J. Establish Distributor/Agent Evaluation Program

No matter how you put together your action plan, or how many elements you include in it, you should consider it your "rules of the game," your basic policy to be followed to gain entry to the best potential overseas markets.

Insofar as possible, stick to the plan so you don't stray from your course. However, as you progress, be flexible and aware of changing conditions in foreign markets which may require you to alter your course to some degree. As indicated earlier, the following chapters will guide you through each element and step of the action plan and help you to build a solid export sales and marketing business.

Chapter 3

DIFFERENCES BETWEEN DOMESTIC AND INTERNATIONAL MARKETS AND RESEARCH

Before you begin an analysis of target markets, you should first understand some of the basic differences between domestic and international markets and the manner in which international market research should be approached.

The United States is a homogenous market operating in one basic culture, customs area, and language (despite wide variations in some local accents). It also has similar local, state and federal laws and regulations, social and economic mores, and industrial and commercial development. Because of these factors, research findings can be extended over large regional areas of the country. The international marketer meanwhile, is faced with over 150 different potential marketplaces, each working under very different and dissimilar social and economic customs, regulations, languages (often dozens of different ones within the country itself), restrictions, customs tariffs, currencies and distribution channels.

It is, therefore, impossible to extend without reservation, market research data for one foreign market over an entire region or group of countries. For example, Colombia is not like all other South American countries. In fact, Colombia by itself, by virtue of its mountainous geography, climatic variations, and the long distances which separate its major cities, is almost literally four or five separate markets, each of which must be studied carefully and usually handled by different distributors. Even the people who inhabit these widely-separated areas are different from those in other parts of the country.

Other countries, such as India, have a wide diversity of cultures, religions, languages and distribution methods ranging from primitive bazaars to ultra-modern shopping malls and supermarkets. Even Europe and its "Common Market" cannot be treated as one marketplace in considering distribution channels, distributor or sales contracts, or the appropriateness of products for sale in a particular country. Many European countries have very different labor laws affecting distributor contracts, and a variety of building and electrical codes which could affect the sale of your products by requiring their conformity to local specifications. Since the people in each country are different, there are also different buying habits which can affect the labeling, packaging and sale of your products.

There are also many differences among the various markets to be penetrated, and basic and fundamental research must be employed to uncover those differences and apply them to your planning at the very beginning of your market studies.

An international market research function within the international sales department can be initiated with the international manager and an assistant doing the basic research, analysis, and evaluation, or it can be done with a full-fledged market research unit made up of several full-time people. The later method can be utilized and its cost justified if the company has already enjoyed a significant amount of export business, and now wants to enter into more significant areas of research and analysis of established markets, or wishes to explore many new markets.

However, since we are dealing with a start-up export sales project, and the primary objective will be to obtain basic information about one or more target markets which may also lead to some initial sales, the market research functions required to attain this goal can be carried out more economically by the person in charge of the project with some secretarial and clerical assistance.

An overall view of some of the major world markets will already have been gained when you first decided to look into the possibility of exporting your products. If an experienced international executive has been hired to establish the export function, he can call upon that experience in the initial steps of researching some target markets.

For purposes of this discussion, let us assume the person designated to start an export function does not have any experience and needs to know how to go about researching the countries selected as initial target markets. Some of the factors which should be considered include some of the same data obtained in your first exercise, "Looking For Possible Markets." These include, population, gross national product, per capita income, industrial and commercial development, government and fiscal stability, market trends, growth, and conditions.

At this point you can take a look at several markets, but you should select one of them to be explored in depth. The next step is to select the factors in each of these markets which sell your product. If it is an automotive product, find out how many vehicles (on and off the road) are registered in the country. This will tell you if it is a worthwhile market in terms of volume.

If your product is a pharmaceutical or medical product, determine the number of hospitals, doctors or other professionals in the country who might need your medical instruments and equipment, service or supplies. If you want to sell industrial products or components, examine the market for the number of factories producing products locally which require your machinery or components. This research will tell you who your customers are, how your products are used, and will give you an idea of the overall consumption of your products.

You will also need to know if there is local competition and the degree to which local products compare with yours. Find out if they are comparable in quality, price and performance. Are any U.S.A. or foreign competitors exporting their products into the target markets? How are these products sold, distributed and used?

A Good Example

Here's how one new-to-export company in the Northeast "took a look" at some markets to see if the product was right for them and if there were customers there who could use and buy their products.

The company, a manufacturer of automotive lead-acid battery-making equipment had a flourishing domestic business selling its equipment to U.S. lead-acid battery manufacturers, among them the component-manufacturing divisions of some large automotive manufacturers.

One of these had manufacturing facilities overseas which included a unit making automotive batteries. A few of the battery production units "found their way" to one of its overseas facilities where, after making a few modifications to the system, they were put into use. Because the systems were the latest state-of-the-art, solid-state, electronic, modular, systems which gave lead-acid batteries their initial or "formation" charge, they literally revolutionized the industry. They made formation charging systems currently (no pun intended) in use appear to be like high school science projects. They also had the capacity of increasing production by a large magnitude, made the batteries more efficient, and cut the formation cycle-time by more than one half.

The favorable reaction of the one overseas company to the systems caused the management of the manufacturer to wonder if they could be sold in volume in other foreign markets. They found that their units used in the one foreign location had been modified to accommodate local power supply, but otherwise were perfectly adaptable to local market usage.

The first look showed them that their product could be exported and used overseas by making only minor, inexpensive changes. They also discovered that batteries themselves were not exported because of their very nature—very heavy with lead plates and heavy outer case, so their shipping costs compared to the low unit value, would make exporting prohibitively expensive.

In addition, it would be dangerous and costly to ship batteries with acid already in the cases. This meant that automotive lead-acid batteries were almost exclusively manufactured in the overseas markets in which they were to be used. It followed then, that there must be a large number of battery manufacturers overseas who would be perfect customers for the new formation charging systems.

Further research led them to the conclusion that such manufacturers would be found in countries which had a large number of registered vehicles and those which had large automotive production plants. New cars need batteries; older cars need replacement batteries.

To determine which countries these were, they consulted an excellent automotive industry report published annually by Johnston International Publishing Corporation, publisher of *Automobile International.* This report gives yearly vehicle production totals for the top 30 manufacturing countries around the world. The figures are broken down by cars, trucks and buses. Another section of the report details world vehicle registrations; in effect a world census. Data for this section is compiled annually from statistics and estimates sent to the Transportation Equipment Division of the U.S. Department of Commerce by U.S. Foreign Service Posts and the United Nations. Data is presented by ten world regions, then broken down by countries within each region. The researcher can look at numbers for 129 countries and select those which are the top vehicle producers and those with the highest population of motor vehicles.

The battery equipment company ranked the top 15 countries for population and the top ten for production. They then chose one country in Europe (Germany), and one in South America (Brazil) as target markets to research in-depth. At that time Germany ranked first in Europe and third in the world in vehicle production and population. Brazil ranked ninth in world population and tenth in vehicle production.

Choosing these two countries as target markets enabled the company to establish a comparison between a highly sophisticated, affluent, developed market and a less-developed, comparatively poor one with stringent import restrictions, but with a burgeoning industrial base and potentially high volume of users for the company's systems.

The next move was to find out who the potential customers were in each market. The state in which the company was located maintained an Export Development Office with a good library of directories and other research materials. With one telephone call to that office, they were able to obtain within a few days the names and addresses of every lead-acid battery manufacturer in the two countries. From the directory they were also able to determine the relative size and financial position of each company, and were thus able to pinpoint those whom they might want to contact by letter.

At the same time the above research was being conducted, not only in Germany, but in all of Europe as well as South America, a search was also made in the same directory for manufacturers of "rectifiers," which is the generic name for battery formation charging systems.

This was important because it had to be determined if there was competition in the local market, the relative size of any competitors, and the nature of the competing product. In this case, it was determined there was only one likely competitor in Europe (Switzerland) and none in South America who made anything similar to the American Company's system.

After completing this phase of the research, the manufacturer concluded that there was definitely a market for its product, and that there were many potential customers ranging from small to large battery manufacturers who produced large quantities for both the vehicle manufacturing and replacement markets. The manufacturer also realized that, luckily, there was very little competition!

The company was now closer to saying "Yes, we can and will export our systems!"

CAUTION

Not every company will have the good fortune to find ready markets with lots of customers and little competition. You must be thorough enough in this initial research to arrive at realistic conclusions. If your findings are not as resoundingly positive, you can still consider exporting. In either case, however, you now have to go the full route of doing a more extensive market research which will apply, not only to the target market, but also to all markets you hope to penetrate.

The Detailed Market Analysis

Many companies will go ahead with an export sales program at this point because the target markets look so enticing. If you've come this far and you're still thinking positive about exporting because the initial study of your target market(s) was favorable, you're taking a real chance of failing if you don't do a more in-depth, detailed analysis of the market(s). You need this further in-depth analysis of several more market factors so you will be fully aware of all the marketing conditions which could affect your business.

In the introduction to this chapter we touched on some of the reasons why international markets differ from domestic markets. We also noted that research applied to one foreign market cannot usually be applied to others.

These differences, relating to socio-economic customs, local regulations, languages, restrictions on importing, geography and other methods of distribution, have to be explored in depth for each market.

They are so very important, that only by having a complete understanding of all these factors as they relate to your market can you hope to be successful in your export sales and marketing program.

Important Market Factors

In studying your markets, you will be looking at many factors which do not exist in the domestic market. Don't let this intimidate you. There are many places and ways to find the information you need, often at little or no cost to you. Because of the nature of foreign markets, you will not have to go into the quantitative market research done for the U. S. market such as surveys, questionnaires, polls, media or advertising agency analysis, or other audit surveys. You will, however, have to concentrate more on many foreign market conditions which can be unstable and subject to unanticipated changes or adjustments depending upon current economic, financial or political situations. So, your research will necessarily be qualitative in nature.

Be sure to include at least the following additional elements in your market studies:

Tariff and Non-Tariff Barriers To Trade

One of the less pleasant facts of life every exporter will surely face is that many countries erect barriers to trade, both tariff and non-tariff. The exporter must be aware of what they are in each market, and how they will affect his ability to export to a given market and the effect they could have on the volume of sales he might obtain. In extreme cases, some restrictions could keep you out of a market completely. These barriers to trade can consist of several different things.

High Customs Duties (Tariffs)

A duty is charged by all countries on imported products according to their value (ad valorem), the quantity (or weight), or a combination of both. In most cases, the duty is a reasonable percentage of the invoice value of the goods, thus not adding significantly to the landed cost. Some countries, however, will impose inordinately high duties in order to protect home industries producing the same or similar products, thus making the imported product too costly for any appreciable volume to be obtained by the exporter. For example, one U.S. manufacturer of a computer-based graphic arts system was effectively closed out of the Brazilian market because duties levied to protect Brazilian computer manufacturers amounted to 154% of the system's value compared with only 4% in the United Kingdom! That exporter knew from earlier research that there was a market in Brazil for his systems, but fortunately, he did go further with his research and uncovered this very strong barrier to trade before he went to the great expense of traveling to the market to establish distribution, etc.

There are many ways to enter a market other than by direct export sales. These include local assembly or manufacturing, joint ventures or licensing. These and other subjects will be treated in another book on Establishing Foreign Operations.

To find out what duties apply to your product, you should obtain the tariff number under which your product is classified. Most countries use the Brussels Nomenclature found in the tariff schedules published by the International Customs Tariffs Bureau in Brussels, Belgium. Copies of these schedules can be found in most Department of Commerce field offices. Since tariffs change frequently, you should be sure you are working with the latest, current schedule.

Although your research may give you current tariff levels for your product and give you an indication of whether they are reasonable or too high, you should always double check your finding with the appropriate consulate of the country in the United States. At a later date, after you have found and worked with a prospective distributor or agent in the country, ask him to investigate the tariff schedule to verify your information. It frequently happens that a product can be classified (legally) under a different number at a lower customs duty, thereby making the product more attractively priced in the market. Always check to be sure your product is classified under the most advantageous tariff schedule number.

Quotas

Quotas are limitations on the quantity or value of certain products which can be imported into a give market. These limitations are usually for a specific time-period, or in its extreme application, may be imposed permanently or even to the total exclusion of the item.

When quotas are placed on a product, it does not necessarily mean that the product cannot be imported into a country, unless the quota is exclusionary. It usually means that any item being imported in excess of the quota may be allowed, but at a higher-than-normal duty.

Import License

Licenses are used by foreign countries for a variety of reasons. If a country has a quota system on certain products, the government may require the importer to obtain an import license as a method to divide the quota equally or proportionately among registered importers. Import licenses are usually issued for a specific monetary and unit value and are valid for a specified period of time.

Other reasons why some countries require import permits include using them to keep track of exports for statistical purposes, to regulate the level of imports, or even to give some importing firms preference over others by not issuing licenses to those firms the government may wish to exclude from importing certain products.

Exchange Permit

If a country has a shortage of hard-currencies, it usually must control the outflow of such currencies, and does so by requiring importers to obtain an exchange permit. In effect, it is another type of import license and some countries require an importer to obtain both. The volume of imports and flow of hard-currency can thus be effectively controlled. When the shortage is acute, the issuance of permits and licenses will be restricted to what the government will decide are essential imports. Be extra careful about countries which require import licenses and/or exchange permits. Do not ship anything unless your customer has sent you bonafide copies of these documents with his order. You could be left "holding the bag" for payment, or with your shipment refused entry.

Product Restriction

These may or may not be government-decreed restrictions, but nevertheless could keep you out of the marketplace. For example, foreign utility companies, (light and power, telephone and natural gas) have the right to impose certain standards on all products both domestic and imported. Therefore, your product must conform to the standards set by these companies as in the case of food or drug laws and safety standards passed by local legislation.

You can consult with the Department of Commerce field offices, foreign consulates in the U. S. or foreign Chambers of Commerce with U. S. offices to find out more about the above-mentioned restrictions, or to find out about any others which may be in force in any given country. Other restrictions (or barriers) to trade could include special taxes on imports, product labeling, very weak patent or trademark regulations, anti-trust or restrictive trade-laws, or any number of other restrictions which may be dreamed up by local governments.

These are but a few examples of trade restrictions and how they can affect your ability to do business in foreign markets. You must be constantly on the lookout for any or all of these. Talk to everyone you can about the subject of trade barriers or restrictions. This is information you need to have and you should not leave it to chance that there will be no restrictions in the markets you choose to enter.

Distribution Methods

One of the more startling differences between U.S. and foreign markets is the way products are bought, sold, stocked, and serviced in foreign countries. Very important factors in the sales success of a product are the channels used to sell to end-users. You must know the prevailing methods of distribution and sale in each market and determine if these are compatible with your product.

Very often, distribution as we know it in the United States and in some of the more developed countries, may not be the way sales are made in your target markets. Prime examples are the still centrally-directed but rapidly changing markets of the former U.S.S.R., Eastern Europe and the People's Republic of China where you must deal primarily with state trading companies which control and handle all imports. Some of the African countries employ marketing and distribution techniques which are still in the early stages of development, for example, street vendors selling a wide range of products are very common. These and other unusual (to us) sales and distribution techniques are found in many of the so-called LDCs (Less Developed Countries). As countries develop their economies and infra-structure, so too, do distribution methods improve and come closer to the types of distribution channels familiar to the United States.

However, even in some of the fully-developed countries of Europe, Asia and elsewhere, the ways in which many products are imported, stocked and resold, can seem strange. While you will, in many places find distribution as we know it, be on the look-out for the differences that could cause problems. If distribution and sales techniques are different, you must find out exactly how they differ and how your type of product can be sold in a given market. Once you have determined the existing channels and methods of distribution in various markets, you will go on to find distributors and agents overseas who will be of great help to you in learning exactly how to promote and sell your products under sometimes vastly different approaches and systems. This subject will be discussed in great detail in the Chapter 13 on Selling and Promoting Products Overseas.

Socio-Cultural Factors

One of the market factors most overlooked by newcomers to exporting is the impact which societal and cultural differences have on the conduct of business in overseas markets. You must realize at the very start that no matter in which part of the world you will be dealing, you cannot assume that the people with whom you come into contact will react in the same way as people in the United States. There are differences due to the varied societal patterns and cultural lifestyles. It is important that you learn how cultures differ from your own and how you can and should incorporate that knowledge into your business thinking and planning to assure your success in the marketplace.

Not being aware of the way people in a given market react to a wide variety of business, ethical, political, religious and economic elements could, at the very least, cause you great embarrassment, or, in the worst-case scenario, loss of good business opportunities.

Take nothing for granted. Look into all aspects of a country's and people's culture to find out what makes them what they are. Find out what motivates them—what turns them off about you or your company, and most of all, your product. Among the many socio-cultural factors you should study are:

Business Practices and Manners

Americans are known world-wide for their fast-paced, direct, to-the-point, (and almost aggressive) business manners. Many foreign (non-American) business people are quite the opposite and have an intense distaste for our usual approaches to a business relationship. An enormous amount of business has been lost by American businessmen who have not bothered to find out before going abroad how to "make a deal;" how his overseas counterpart conducts business, and how he prefers to deal; what motivates him; and yes, even what turns him off!

Let's look at some of the factors which influence European and other foreigners working with Americans. While most European executives probably seem to be more like Americans than executives in other regions around the world, there are many differences, and Europeans differ from one another because they live and work in different countries and cultures. A common denominator among most foreigners however, is that there must be a feeling of trust between them and the person with whom they are dealing. The best written agreement in the world is of no importance if there is not a strong feeling of trust—a feeling that what you say is true—that you will do what you promise—and that you are presenting your company and your product in a truthful and realistic light. Don't use the hard sell!

American Informality will often offend the sensibilities of non-Americans. European and many other overseas business men are quite conscious of social "class," and their professional standing in their communities. Based on their position in society, they observe certain styles of behavior which are often much more formal than Americans are used to. An American who is not conscious of this ingrained formality will find himself or herself socially unacceptable, and unacceptable as a business associate.

Learn what the social rules are in each country and observe them scrupulously. Your counterparts will observe you carefully and will appreciate your knowing the right things to do and say. They'll know you're serious about wanting to do business with them. Your consciousness of their etiquette will add to the feeling of trust they are looking for when listening to your business presentation.

You must also be aware of how you dress when calling on foreign business people. In Europe, conservatism is the rule. Gray or dark blue suits are best. Brown, in current fashion trends is considered informal and too sporty for business or even for more formal social events. In other countries, it is smarter not to try to dress as the natives do. In Latin America, don't wear a guayabera, the long, open-necked white shirt worn outside the trousers, or a safari suit in Africa or Asia.

In the warm, tropical countries of Latin America, and Southeast Asia, wear what you would normally wear during the hot summer months at the office or to a business meeting. Wear a tie and don't take it or your jacket off unless others at the meeting have done so. Then, politely ask if it is alright for you to do so.

Wear good fitting, well-tailored clothing to project a neat, prosperous image of yourself and your company. Forego ostentatious jewelry; and in Arab countries, don't wear visible religious jewelry. In some Islamic countries it is against their laws to display Christian or Jewish religious items.

Attitude

Attitude is another cultural characteristic which has strong influence on the way business is conducted in many countries. There are many different attitudes which influence the way people in various cultures carry on their business dealings with "outsiders." Among these varying attitudes is how they feel about time.

Americans want to make their business presentations quickly and succinctly, close the deal, and move on to the next prospect. Not so in most other countries, even to the matter of keeping appointments on time. In many cultures, for example in the Middle East, Latin America, and some parts of Asia, it is not considered rude for your counterpart to keep you waiting, although he expects that you, as an American, will be punctual. Time is not all that important to most non-Americans, so do not feel insulted if you're kept waiting.

When you are finally ushered into your prospect's office, don't expect to get right down to business. You will probably be offered a coffee or a soft drink. You should not refuse it as it may, in many countries, offend your host's spirit of hospitality.

It is also his way of "setting the scene" for the oncoming business discussion. He will want to chat with you for a while to find out a little about you (as you should about him). He will want to learn about your company and its relative position in your industry, and hear your views on a variety of subjects, usually not related to the business at hand. This is another way to start building up that "trust" mentioned earlier. You'll have plenty of time to discuss business, and you'll find the going much easier and more pleasant after the introductory session.

Language

Language is a factor which obviously cannot be overlooked. Don't assume that all business people in a country speak English. Outside of the United States, only about four percent of the world claims English as its mother tongue. Many others however, speak English well enough to carry on some basic business dealings with an American. Because you can carry on a conversation in English, don't assume that your counterparts think in English, or understand the subtleties of the English language well enough not to become confused or misunderstand some of your intentions. Even if they have been educated in the United States, they will probably still think and react in their own language and according to their own customs and culture.

Obviously, an international marketer cannot learn the languages of every country with which he is working, but he should have at least a good basic knowledge of one or more of the major world languages—Spanish, German, French or Italian. By studying a foreign language, you will also learn something about the country's cultural heritage, its art, aesthetics, music, folklore and religion—all of which will be of great value in understanding your foreign colleagues and the marketplace itself.

You should know also that there are many countries in which more than one language is spoken, and this is an important factor because, as indicated above, language equates to a culture, so if more than one language is spoken, by large segments of the population, there will be more than one culture in those countries. This is a very important matter to consider when you are planning your sales strategies. Examples of countries where this multi-language, multi-cultural factor is very important are the following:

Switzerland has distinct regions where the German, Italian, French and Romansch languages are predominant, although many habitants of each region are multi-lingual. But you will note in each the strong Germanic or Latin cultural influences which will have a bearing on how you will conduct your business and sell your products.

Belgium has two well-defined regions, one French—the other Flemish-speaking. The Latin French and the Low-German Flemish are notably different cultures, and there are also strongly diverse political divisions between the two.

Canada has a similar situation in the almost-total separation of the Province of Quebec from the English-speaking parts of the country. This separation, apart from its political ramifications, has generated many changes in the way business is done in the country, including the packaging, sales, and advertising of products.

India is probably the most diverse country in the world, not only because there are some 200-to 300 languages spoken, but also because there are dozens of religions practiced including major ones such as Hinduism, Buddhism, Jainism, Sikhism, and Muslim. It is important in dealing with Indian business people to understand how the multitude of languages and religions working together affect all aspects of their daily lives, and will influence how you conduct your business in the different regions of the country.

Spain has a population which speaks Spanish, Basque and Catalán. The people are not only different in language, but also in their unique social, political and economic backgrounds, and you must learn to work and act differently with each group. Moreover, in many, many countries you will find regional language differences (dialects) which often sound nothing like the mother tongue.

South and Central America. From Mexico to Chile and Argentina (excluding Brazil where Portuguese is spoken, and Haiti where the language is French or French-patois), the principal language is Spanish. However, despite the commonality of the basic language, the way the language is spoken, written, and used can vary widely in the 21 countries of Latin

America. Much is different also in the culture and attitudes of each of these countries. Your advertising, promotion, packaging, product markings and other sales appeals will have to be carefully planned and implemented with each country in mind rather than with a regional approach.

Africa as a continent is extremely diverse. Although it is basically divided into English-French-Arabic-speaking countries, with Portuguese used in Angola and parts of Mozambique and Afrikaans in South Africa, there are hundreds of tribal languages spoken up and down the entire continent. This makes for a polyglot of cultures, attitudes, religions, technologies and social structures. Study and work with each market separately.

Do try to learn some of the languages of some of your markets. Even if you don't become fluent, your contacts and colleagues will appreciate any attempt you make at even a few key words in their language. It can make a big difference in the way you are treated and how you are accepted. Remember too, you are competing in many markets with experienced international executives from other countries, many of whom are fluent in at least two or three languages other than their own. Some can even boast of fluency in six or eight! Give yourself a break in competing with them and learn some language, other than your own.

Marketing Methods

The ways in which products are sold in many foreign countries often differ greatly from the way in which those same products are sold in the United States. Marketing of consumer products can be especially susceptible to local preferences and needs. For example: many consumer products are sold in the United States in large packages. In foreign countries, dealers as well as housewives have limited shelf or storage space, so they do not like to stock or purchase large-sized packages, especially if there is no price advantage. In addition, many shoppers do not have automobiles at their disposal to go to suburban shopping areas, (if they exist in a given market), or even to carry home a large shopping done in nearby stores. They must shop at small local stores within walking distance to their homes.

Since this means a housewife has to shop more than once a week, she normally prefers products in smaller packages. The way some items are packaged therefore, can mean more or fewer sales for imported products.

Education and Literacy

The Educational and Literacy level of the general population. While statistics of this sort are sometimes out-of-date, they will, nevertheless, give you a good indication of the general level of education country-wide and, by checking several years' figures, you can determine if the levels of education and literacy are growing or declining. You can then decide upon the level of sophistication of your marketing and promotional appeal to a particular market. Your advertising and packaging should be aimed at the degree of accomplishment of these two factors.

Population size by age groups

This is an important piece of data if you want to sell products aimed at teenagers or older people. You need these data to learn if there would be a market for your products used by a particular age group.

Disposable Income

The level of Disposable Income is an important indicator because your research will show if purchasing power is rising, and along with it, the standard of living. To the marketer, this means there is income available to spend on other than the basic items of food, housing and clothing. This "extra" income will then create a demand among this segment of the population for many products not previously affordable, thus making it a possibly very attractive market for you.

There is never an end to doing detailed market studies if you want to increase your exports and market shares. All of the market factors and indicators are dynamic and rarely, if ever, static. Governments rise and fall, as do birth and death rates; economic changes can occur very quickly; restrictions to trade come and go; tastes can change over a period of time. You must be personally aware of the dynamics of your markets at all times.

Don't despair though. This will become increasingly easier as time goes on and you develop your overseas distributor or agent networks. They will be your eyes and ears, and will forewarn you of many changes of which you must be aware. Meanwhile, you will be learning many useful, informative and interesting facts about many parts of the world.

Export Licensing

Although this subject is not actually a part of your detailed market analysis, you must know if the U. S. government places any restrictions on shipping your products overseas. Therefore, it is important to have thorough knowledge about the U.S. requirement that exports of all U.S.-made products be subject to export licensing. This could be considered a barrier to trade, akin to those discussed earlier in this chapter. If the United States Export Control Administration denies an export license to ship certain products to certain countries, then the exporter is, in fact, prevented from doing business in those countries. But hold on. All is not as grim as it may seem!

The underlying reason for the export license requirement is to restrict the shipment of strategic items to some or all countries, i.e. those which may be in short supply in the U.S. or which are considered vital to our national security and defense. For example, the latest state-of-the-art main frame computers useful in the design and production of aircraft weapons or other materiel of war, would not be granted an export license for shipment to any Communist countries, or certain others on the administration's prohibited list.

In Part 370 of the export regulations is a list of all foreign countries, except Canada, separated into seven "country groups" designated by letter symbols, Q, S, T, V, W, and Z.

Part of the regulation is the Export Commodity Control Listing (ECCL) and description of products which require a validated export license (see definition of licenses). Each listed product carries an ECCL number to identify it. This number is necessary not only when applying for a license, but it is also to be inserted in the appropriate place on an export document called the Shippers Export Declaration. (The full subject of export documentation will be treated at length in a later chapter, but because of its importance in the export licensing mechanism, it is introduced here.) This document must accompany every export shipment, and is sent to the export carrier at the time of export. It is then filed with the U. S. Customs Department. It is mandatory that on the "Export Dec," the exporter enters a description of the goods being shipped and notes in the appropriate boxes the ECCL number and the type of export license under which the described products are being shipped.

There are two basic types of export licenses—a General License or a Validated export license. The great bulk of exports can be made utilizing a General License There are about 20 classifications of General Licenses, the most common being, General Destination (G-DEST) depending upon the product and the destination of the goods if the commodities are not on the ECCL list, and are destined for a country for which a validated license is not required. No authorization is required for using a general license, and no document is issued. The designation G-Dest is then entered on the "Export Dec." Some other general license designations include: General License GIT, intransit shipments; General License GLV, shipments of limited value; General License G-COM, certain shipments to cooperating companies; General License GUS, shipments to personnel and agencies of the U. S. government; General License GTE, temporary exports, e.g. products being shipped to an overseas trade show which will be returned to the United States at the show's end, no later than one year after export. Keep in mind that it is your responsibility to check the export regulations to be sure your product and the destination to which it is being shipped does not require a validated license. Be sure to look in the regulations under special provisions which may preclude your use of a general license.

Validated export licenses present a very different set of problems. If your study of the regulations show you do, in fact, need a validated license, it is absolutely mandatory that you have such a document in hand before you make a single export shipment. A special application form, and often certain other supporting documents, are required to be completed and sent to the International Trade Administration Office of the Department of Commerce. If the product to be exported is of a high-technology, the license may also require approval of the Department of Defense. The latter passes on the merits of granting a license only after Commerce has given its approval. Nevertheless, Defense may deny a license.

In addition, either Commerce or Defense may send your application to the Coordinating Committee on Multilateral Export Controls (COCOM). This committee is made up of all the NATO countries (except Spain and Iceland) plus Japan. Each member nation has basically the same export

Herman J. Maggiori

FORM BXA-629P
(REV 3 88)

U.S. DEPARTMENT OF COMMERCE
BUREAU OF EXPORT ADMINISTRATION

STATEMENT BY ULTIMATE CONSIGNEE AND PURCHASER

GENERAL INSTRUCTIONS – This form must be submitted by the importer (ultimate consignee shown in Item 1) and by the overseas buyer or purchaser, to the U.S. exporter or seller with whom the order for the commodities described in Item 3 is placed. This completed statement will be submitted in support of one or more export license applications to the U.S. Department of Commerce. All items on this form must be completed. Where the information required is unknown or the item does not apply, write in the appropriate words "UNKNOWN" or "NOT APPLICABLE." If more space is needed, attach an additional copy of this form or sheet of paper signed as in Item 8. Submit form within 180 days from latest date in Item 8. Information furnished herewith is subject to the provisions of Section 12(c) of the Export Administration Act of 1979, 50 USC app. 2411(c), and its unauthorized disclosure is prohibited by law.

1. Ultimate consignee name and address

Name

Street and number

City and Country

Reference (if desired)

2. Request (Check one)

a. ☐ We request that this statement be considered a part of the application for export license filed by

_____

U.S. exporter or U.S. person with whom we have placed our order (order party)

for export to us of the commodities described in item 3.

b. ☐ We request that this statement be considered a part of every application for export license filed by

_____

U.S. exporter or U.S. person with whom we have placed or may place our order (order party)

for export to us of the type of commodities described in this statement, during the period ending June 30 of the second year after the signing of this form, or on _____

3. Commodities

We have placed or may place orders with the person or firm named in Item 2 for the commodities indicated below:

COMMODITY DESCRIPTION	*(Fill in only if 2a is checked)*	
	QUANTITY	VALUE

4. Disposition or use of commodities by ultimate consignee named in Item 1 *(Check and complete the appropriate box(es))*

We certify that the commodity(ies) listed in Item 3:

a. ☐ Will be used by us (as capital equipment) in the form in which received in a manufacturing process in the country named in Item 1 and will not be reexported or incorporated into an end product.

b. ☐ Will be processed or incorporated by us into the following product(s) _____
(Specify)

to be manufactured in the country named in Item 1 for distribution in _____
(Name of country or countries)

c. ☐ Will be resold by us in the form in which received in the country named in Item 1 for use or consumption therein.

The specific end-use by my customer will be _____
(Specify, if known)

d. ☐ Will be reexported by us in the form in which received to _____
(Name of country(ies))

e. ☐ Other *(Describe fully)* _____

NOTE: If Item d is checked acceptance of this form by the Office of Export Licensing as a supporting document for license applications shall not be construed as an authorization to reexport the commodities to which the form applies unless specific approval has been obtained from the Office of Export Licensing for such reexport

(Reproduction of this form is permissible, providing that content, format, size and color of paper are the same)

Please continue form and sign certification on reverse side.

USCOMM DC 88 24141

Statement Required in Support of License Application

EXPEDITE SHIPMENTS BY COMPLETING THIS FORM CORRECTLY
FOLLOW THESE SPECIFIC INSTRUCTIONS

1. Ultimate Consignee must be person abroad who is actually to receive the material for the disposition or use shown in Item 4. A bank, freight forwarder, forwarding agent, or other intermediary is **not** acceptable as an ultimate consignee.

2. Check box "a" if this is a single transaction, and give the name of person or firm in the U.S. with whom order was placed.
Check box "b" if this is a continuing relationship that is likely to involve a series of orders for the same types of commodities for the same end-user and same end-use. Give the name of the person or firm in the U.S. with whom the orders will be placed.

Show earlier but not later termination date than June 30 of the second year after the signing of this form, if desired.

3. Describe commodities in detail wherever possible, giving particulars such as name, basic ingredients, composition, type, size, gauge, grade, horsepower, etc. Descriptions should be broad enough, however, to include all commodities to which the statement applies.

4. Check "a", "b", "c", "d", and "e", as appropriate, and fill in the required information.

Explanation of how to fill in Statement by Ultimate Consignee/Purchaser

5. Complete both "a" and "b".

6. Supply any other information not appearing elsewhere on the form such as other parties to the transaction.

7. Name all persons, other than employees of consignee or purchaser, who assisted in the preparation of this form.

8. This item is to be signed by both the ultimate consignee and the purchaser if the purchaser is not the same as the ultimate consignee. Only an official of the ultimate consignee named in Item 1, and/or official of the purchaser should complete this item. These must be responsible officials who are authorized to bind the firms of the ultimate consignee and purchaser to the commitments in this statement. Be sure to sign in ink, and type or print the name and title of the person signing, as well as the name of the purchaser firm if the purchaser has signed the statement.

9. This Item is reserved for use by U. S. exporter where additions, corrections, or alterations appear on the form.

THIS FLAP SHOULD BE DETACHED BEFORE SUBMITTING FORM.

Explanation of how to fill in Statement by Ultimate Consignee/Purchaser

40

5. Nature of business of ultimate consignee named in Item 1 and his relationship with U.S. exporter named in Item 2.

a. The nature of our usual business is _____
(Broker, distributor, fabricator, manufacturer, wholesaler, retailer, etc.)

b. Our business relationship with the U.S. exporter is _____
(Contractual, franchise, exclusive distributor, distributor, wholesaler, continuing and regular individual transaction business, etc.)
and we have had this business relationship for _____ years.

6. Additional information (Any other material facts which will be of value considering applications for licenses covered by this statement.)

7. Assistance in preparing statement (Names of persons other than employees of consignee or purchaser who assisted in the preparation of this statement.)

8. CERTIFICATION OF ULTIMATE CONSIGNEE AND PURCHASER (This item is to be signed by the ultimate consignee shown in Item 1 and by the purchaser where the latter is not the same as the ultimate consignee. Where the ultimate consignee is unknown, this item should be signed by the purchaser.)

We certify that all of the facts contained in this statement are true and correct to the best of our knowledge and belief and we do not know of any additional facts which are inconsistent with the above statement. We shall promptly send a supplemental statement to the person named in Item 2, disclosing any change of facts or intentions set forth in this statement which occurs after the statement has been prepared and forwarded. Except as specifically authorized by the U.S. Export Administration Regulations, or by prior written approval of the U.S. Department of Commerce, we will not reexport, resell, or otherwise dispose of any commodities listed in Item 3 above: (1) to any country not approved for export as brought to our attention by means of a bill of lading, commercial invoice, or any other means, or (2) to any person if there is reason to believe that it will result directly or indirectly, in disposition of the commodities contrary to the representations made in this statement or contrary to U.S. Export Administration Regulations.

Ultimate Consignee	Purchaser
Signature in ink _____ (Signature of official of ultimate consignee)	Signature in ink _____ (Signature of official of purchaser firm)
Type or print _____ (Name and title of official of ultimate consignee)	Type or print _____ (Name and title of official of purchaser firm)
Date _____	Type or print _____ (Name of purchaser firm)
	Date _____

9. CERTIFICATION FOR USE OF U.S. EXPORTER in certifying that any correction, addition, or alteration on this form was made prior to the signing by the ultimate consignee and purchaser in Item 8.

We certify that no corrections, additions, or alterations were made on this form by us after the form was signed by the (ultimate consignee) (purchaser).

Type or print _____ (Name of exporter firm)

Sign here in ink _____ (Signature of person authorized to certify for exporter)

Type or print _____ (Name and title of person signing this document)

_____ (Date signed)

The making of any false statement the concealment of any material fact, or failure to file required information may result in denial of participation in U.S. exports. Notarial or governmental certification is not required.

FORM BXA-629P (REV. 3-88)

USCOMM-DC 88-24147

Reverse Side of Statement by Ultimate Consignee/Purchaser

41

Herman J. Maggiori

UNITED STATES DEPARTMENT OF COMMERCE
BUREAU OF EXPORT ADMINISTRATION
P.O. Box 273, Ben Franklin Station
Washington, DC 20044

THIS LICENSE AUTHORIZES THE LICENSEE TO CARRY OUT THE EXPORT TRANSACTION
DESCRIBED ON THE LICENSE (INCLUDING ALL ATTACHMENTS). IT MAY NOT BE
TRANSFERRED WITHOUT PRIOR WRITTEN APPROVAL OF THE OFFICE OF EXPORT
LICENSING. THIS LICENSE HAS BEEN GRANTED IN RELIANCE ON REPRESENTATIONS
MADE BY THE LICENSEE AND OTHERS IN CONNECTION WITH THE APPLICATION FOR EXPORT
AND IS EXPRESSLY SUBJECT TO ANY CONDITIONS STATED ON THE LICENSE, AS WELL AS
ALL APPLICABLE EXPORT CONTROL LAWS, REGULATIONS, RULES, AND ORDERS. THIS
LICENSE IS SUBJECT TO REVISION, SUSPENSION, OR REVOCATION WITHOUT PRIOR NOTICE.

APPLICANT CONTROL NUMBER: C445798

EI DUPONT DE NEMOURS & CO INC   PURCHASER:
REMINGTON ARMS DIV/ATTN L MCCREARY
1007 MARKET STREET
WILMINGTON, DE 19898

ULTIMATE CONSIGNEE: INTERMEDIATE CONSIGNEE:
GLASER TRADING CO
WARTSTR 12
WINTERTHUR, SWITZERLAND

COMMODITIES: TOTAL
    QTY DESCRIPTION   ECCN   PRICE

    2 M/870 12 GA., 5-SHOT, 20" REPEATER EXTRA   5998 $181
      BARREL

                                         TOTAL: $181

PROCESSING CODE: CM

THE EXPORT ADMINISTRATION REGULATIONS REQUIRE YOU TO TAKE THE FOLLOWING ACTIONS
WHEN EXPORTING UNDER THE AUTHORITY OF THIS LICENSE.

    A. RECORD THE EXPORT COMMODITY CONTROL NUMBER IN THE BLOCK
       PROVIDED ON EACH SHIPPER'S EXPORT DECLARATION (SED).

    B. RECORD YOUR VALIDATED LICENSE NUMBER IN THE BLOCK
       PROVIDED ON EACH SED.

    C. PLACE A DESTINATION CONTROL STATEMENT ON ALL BILLS OF LADING,
       AIRWAY BILLS, AND COMMERCIAL INVOICES.

RIDERS AND CONDITIONS:

    1. DISTRIBUTION OR RESALE OF THE COMMODITIES LISTED ON THIS LICENSE IS

Sample of a Validated U.S. Export License

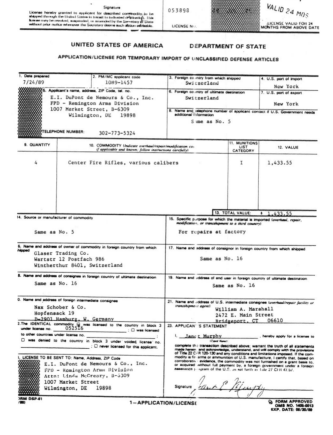

SEAL _Sara T. Hunter_

Signature

License hereby granted to applicant for described commodity to be shipped through the United States in transit to indicated destination. This license may be revoked, suspended, or amended by the Secretary of State without prior notice whenever the Secretary deems such action advisable.

053898

LICENSE No.

'89 AUG -1

VALID 24 MOS

LICENSE VALID FOR 24 MONTHS FROM ABOVE DATE

UNITED STATES OF AMERICA   DEPARTMENT OF STATE

APPLICATION/LICENSE FOR TEMPORARY IMPORT OF UNCLASSIFIED DEFENSE ARTICLES

1. Date prepared	2. PM/MC applicant code	3. Foreign country from which shipped	4. U.S. port of import
7/24/89	1089-1457	Switzerland	New York
5. Applicant's name, address, ZIP Code, tel. no.		6. Foreign country of ultimate destination	7. U.S. port of export
E.I. DuPont de Nemours & Co., Inc. FPD – Remington Arms Division 1007 Market Street, B-6309 Wilmington, DE 19898		Switzerland	New York
		8. Name and telephone number of applicant contact if U.S. Government needs additional information	
TELEPHONE NUMBER: 302-773-5324		Same as No. 5	

9. QUANTITY	10. COMMODITY (Indicate overhaul/repair/modification cost if applicable and known; follow instructions carefully)	11. MUNITIONS LIST CATEGORY	12. VALUE
4	Center Fire Rifles, various calibers	I	1,433.55
	13. TOTAL VALUE:		$ 1,433.55

14. Source or manufacturer of commodity	15. Specific purpose for which the material is imported (overhaul, repair, modification), or transshipment to a third country)
Same as No. 5	For repairs at factory
16. Name and address of owner of commodity in foreign country from which shipped	17. Name and address of consignor in foreign country from which shipped
Glaser Trading Co. Wartstr 12 Postfach 986 Winterthur 8401, Switzerland	Same as No. 16
18. Name and address of consignee in foreign country of ultimate destination	19. Name and address of end user in foreign country of ultimate destination
Same as No. 16	Same as No. 16
20. Name and address of foreign intermediate consignee	21. Name and address of U.S. intermediate consignee (overhaul/repair facility or transshipment agent)
Nax Schober & Co. Hopfensack 19 D-2901 Hamburg, W. Germany	William A. Marshall 2472 E. Main Street Bridgeport, CT 06610

22. The IDENTICAL commodity ☒ was licensed to the country in block 3 under license no. 052516 : ☐ was licensed to other countries under license no. _____ ☐ was denied to the country in block 3 under voided license no. _____ : ☐ never licensed for this applicant.	23. APPLICANT'S STATEMENT
	I, ___Janet Murphy___, hereby apply for a license to (Type Name) complete the transaction described above; warrant the truth of all statements made herein and acknowledge, understand, and will comply with the provisions of Title 22 CFR 120-130 and any conditions and limitations imposed. If the commodity is for arms or ammunition of U.S. manufacture, I certify that, based on corroborative evidence, the commodity was not furnished on a grant basis to, or acquired without full payment by, a foreign government under a foreign assistance program of the U.S. as set forth in Title 27 CFR 47.67.
24. LICENSE TO BE SENT TO: Name, Address, ZIP Code E.I. DuPont de Nemours & Co., Inc. FPD – Remington Arms Division Attn: Linda McCreary, B-6309 1007 Market Street Wilmington, DE 19898	Signature _Janet E. Murphy_

FORM DSP-61 (88)

1–APPLICATION/LICENSE

FORM APPROVED OMB NO. 1405-0013 EXP. DATE: 06/30/89

Application for Special Type Export License

43

Herman J. Maggiori

License Expires:
7-18-93

SEAL

Kerry C. Davis

Signature

License hereby granted to applicant for described commodity to be permanently exported from the United States. This license may be revoked, suspended, or amended by the Secretary of State without prior notice whenever the Secretary deems such action advisable.

4 63820

LICENSE NO.

'90

LICENSE VALID FOR 24 MONTHS FROM ABOVE DATE.

UNITED STATES OF AMERICA   **DEPARTMENT OF STATE**

APPLICATION/LICENSE FOR PERMANENT EXPORT OF UNCLASSIFIED DEFENSE ARTICLES AND RELATED UNCLASSIFIED TECHNICAL DATA

1. Date Prepared	2. PM/MC Applicant Code	3. Country of Ultimate Destination	4. Probable Port of Exit from U.S.
7/13/90	1089-1457	W. Germany	New York

5. Applicant's Name, Address, ZIP Code, Tel. No.

E.I. DuPont de Nemours & Co., Inc.
FPD – Remington Arms Divsion
1007 Market Street, D-6309
Wilmington, DE 19898

6. Names, agency, and telephone numbers of U.S. Government personnel (not PM/MC) familiar with the commodity

None

7. Name and telephone number of applicant contact if U.S. Government needs additional information.

Same as No. 5

TELEPHONE NUMBER: 302-773-5324

8. QUANTITY	9. COMMODITY *(follow instructions carefully)*		10. MUNITIONS LIST CATEGORY	11. VALUE
	X Hardware	☐ Technical Data		
79	Center Fire Rifles, x various calibers		I	33,893.95

Application for Special Type Export License

44

controls as the United States and acts on export license applications in much the same way. COCOM's role is also to prevent controlled products from being diverted to restricted countries.

In a large number of cases however, validated export licenses are granted, and so long as the exporter follows all the rules, there should be no problem.

Although the Omnibus Trade and Competitiveness Act of 1988 (Public Law 100-418) attempts to make export controls less burdensome to exporters by reducing some of the administrative requirements and reducing the list of controlled technology products, it is incumbent upon the exporter to be aware of the provisions of the Export Control Act and how it might prohibit exports of his product to his targeted markets.

Enforcement of Export Controls

Don't ever try to get away with shipping a product without a validated export license if you know, or even suspect, one may be required. And don't even think of diverting such a shipment through an authorized country into an unauthorized one. You will get caught! The Department of Commerce has an Office of Export Enforcement, (and yes, they even have armed agents in various foreign countries from which diversion is likely to take place). Also assisting the department is COCOM, mentioned above which has a large stake in controlling the destination of strategic and sensitive products.

The penalties for infractions of these regulations are quite severe, and range from heavy fines, confiscation of the offending shipment, to imprisonment and/or the loss of all export privileges. Obey the rules! You don't want to lose it all after working so hard to set up your export program.

Other Legislation Affecting Exports

Aside from the U. S. Export Licensing Regulations, there are some other U. S. laws which can affect your export marketing efforts. Foremost among these are:

Sherman Antitrust Law

The Sherman Antitrust Law forbids competing U.S. companies from acting together to fix prices, and restrains agreements on profit markups, price differentials, and collusion in bidding. Some of the provisions of this Act were amended by the Clayton Act, which, in turn, was amended by the Robinson-Patman Act.

All of this legislation can affect your strategies and plans with respect to pricing, channels of distribution, promotion and product marketing. In addition, antitrust and restraint of trade practices in the European Common Market are controlled by the Treaty of Rome (Articles 85 and 86). In most cases, if you follow the letter and spirit of these laws as they relate to interstate trade in the United States, you will not run into any trouble in conducting your export business.

The Foreign Corrupt Practices Act

As we saw in the above section on socio-cultural factors, there are many ways in which foreign businessmen conduct their businesses which are, to say the least, strange to Americans. Another one which is not seen much in American business, but which is common in many countries or cultures, is the asking for and acceptance of bribes as a condition of doing business with you or for other "favors." This can range from very substantial payoffs to a government official who can approve an otherwise forbidden import, to a small payment to a bank clerk or to a custom's worker who can move your paperwork to the top of the pile so you will be paid faster or your shipment cleared ahead of others. None of these officials or workers consider the payments illegal or wrong. Many of them are sadly underpaid on their jobs and look for the "mordida," "baksheesh," or "squeeze" to augment a meager salary.

The U. S. government however, feels a bribe by any other name is still a bribe, and in the early 1970s the Foreign Corrupt Practices Act was passed to put a stop to some very blatant examples of bribery to some high government officials in several foreign countries including the then-Shah of Iran. The law covered just about anything that could be considered a bribe from money, to vacations, to "women."

Many overseas business people cannot understand what all the fuss is about. To them, this "activity" is perfectly natural. In fact, many foreign governments support their nationals who go after large contracts, which usually require large bribes, by offering various kinds of "subsidies" to the company involved so they can be assured of making the sale.

As an indication of the common acceptance of "corrupt payments," the United States is the only country among all industrialized societies which has a law barring them. Many countries continue to consider such payments legal and even tax-deductible as a business expense. Will you lose overseas business if you obey our law and don't provide "baksheesh" to get an order? Some say yes, the U. S. loses many millions of dollars a year; yet many others who have out-and-out refused to make such payments have still gotten the order at normal prices. Probably the truth is that a substantial amount of business is lost. Only your own ethics and morality can tell you how you should handle this matter.

Sources for International Market Research

As noted earlier in this chapter, much of the methodology used in researching the United States market cannot be used, (at least not without a great deal of adaptation) in foreign markets. At the very least, even when scaled back to some degree, such methods will be extremely costly when applied to overseas markets. Also, it can be difficult, or even impossible, to conduct research projects overseas on the scale to which we are accustomed in the United States. Many of the types of data accumulated in domestic market research would not be useful in evaluating foreign markets. Therefore, much time, effort and money would be wasted.

There are however, many and valuable primary and secondary sources available to the international market researcher, much of it obtainable at little or no cost. For example, a great deal of important data on foreign markets is available from U. S. government sources at no charge, or at a very nominal cost. There are many specialists employed by the federal government in the Department of Commerce, Department of State and the Department of Agriculture who can supply much useful and accurate data including identifying specific business opportunities, prospective customers and leads to locating foreign distributors or agents.

The International Trade Administration of the Commerce Department can lead you to excellent sources of a wide range of market information since it has many country desk officers in Washington, D.C. The United States and Foreign Commercial Service (U.S.and F.C.S.) maintains international trade specialists in about 126 locations overseas who have intimate knowledge of the economic, commercial and industrial life of the countries in which they serve.

Some of the specific data which can be obtained in cooperation with Commerce, the US&FCS and other government agencies includes: Export Statistics Profile (ESP) which show product exports to many countries. If your product is not covered in the ESP, obtain either Custom Statistical Service (also from Commerce), Foreign Trade Report FT410 from the U. S. Bureau of the Census which gives the value of U. S. exports to about 160 countries of approximately 4500 U.S.products, Export Information System Data Reports (from the Small Business Administration), or Annual World-wide Industry Reviews (from the Department of Commerce).

International Economic Indicators is a quarterly report of data on the economies of several European countries, Canada and Japan. It covers about 68 economic indicators and shows trends since 1970. It is useful for detailed analysis of the economic situations in major industrial countries (from Superintendent of Documents, Washington, D.C. 20402).

Agricultural Exports

The Department of Agriculture has a wide range of services and information available through its Information Division, and the Foreign Agricultural Service. It publishes a monthly magazine, *Foreign Agriculture* which supplies news, background information, feature articles, and reports and analysis of conditions affecting U. S. Agricultural Exports. Write to the Department of Agriculture for a current listing of available materials.

There are several more publications which will give you excellent economic background and market trends for each country as well as sources of competition, domestic industry and foreign sources of imports. Among them are: *Market Research Reports, Overseas Business Reports,(OBR), Trade Lists, World Trade Directory Reports (WTDR), Country Market Surveys (CMS), Country Trade Statistics,* and *International Market Research Surveys (IMRS).*

IMRs and CMSs will also provide channels of distribution and end-user sections, cultural and business differences and practices.

In addition, they will also provide information on tariff and non-tariff barriers to trade, and will indicate if there are U.S. export controls affecting exports to the country covered in the reports.

Small Business Administration

In addition to the wealth of information available from the U.S. Department of Commerce, consider the offerings of the U.S. Small Business Administration (SBA). The SBA is now in an excellent position to help small businesses enter and succeed in the global marketplace by offering counseling and advice from international experts, training sessions, and a variety of publications designed to assist smaller companies explore the potential and possibilities of exporting.

Some specific programs are now in place to ease the new or potential exporter onto the path of success.

1. The *Export Information System* (XIS) is an export/import database of trade information on 2,500 product categories. Reports are available showing the performance of markets of these 2,500 product categories in overseas markets. Reports created from this data bank will give potential exporters information on:

a. Whether there is an overseas market for their product.

b. What the trends have been in these markets.

c. What competition they will encounter in specific country markets.

Data in the database is organized according to Standard International Trade Classification (SITC) statistics supplied by the United Nations on about 2,500 products reported by over 60 countries which account for over 85% of world trade.

XIS was designed and is administered by the Georgia Small Business Development Center, and is sponsored by the SBA which makes XIS available nationally to its clients.

2. The *Export Services Center* (ESC) now featured at campuses of many State universities is funded by statewide Small Business Development Centers. An ESC offers the resources of the university in which it is located, for example, library services, computer center, data banks, trained students and faculty expertise. In addition, the State Economic Development Department, international departments of major banks, and volunteer executives from the SERVICE CORPS OF RETIRED EXECUTIVES (SCORE), and ACTIVE CORPS OF EXECUTIVES (ACE) both sponsored by the SBA, all offer their assistance and cooperation without charge or obligation.

3. The *Export Legal Assistance Network* (ELAN) is a program in which lawyers who have knowledge of export-related matters volunteer to provide confidential initial legal consultation, *free of charge* to companies making their first entry into the export market. Such assistance can consist of helping the client understand basic contractual tax and regulatory requirements as they relate to starting-up export operations. ELAN's aim is to make you feel comfortable with the legal aspects of exporting. Contract your local SBA Office for details.

4. *Financial Assistance*

a. Export Revolving Line of Credit Program offers a credit line up to 36 months. Loans must be used only to finance labor and materials for manufacturing or wholesaling for export, to develop foreign markets, or to finance foreign accounts receivable.

b. International Trade Loans provide long-term financing to help small business compete more effectively and to expand export markets. SBA offers guarantees on loans made by private lenders to finance U.S.-based facilities or equipment for producing goods or services for export.

5. Small Business Administration's co-sponsorship with the Department of Commerce of the *Matchmaker Trade Delegation Program* designed to match small businesses with prospective agents and distributors overseas. The SBA will provide up to $750 of financial support for up to ten qualified companies attending a specific *Matchmaker* trade delegation. Full details of the program are available from your local SBA office.

6. SBA also offers a regional *International Calendar of Events* on a monthly or quarterly basis. These calendars show dates and locations of export seminars, lectures, business forums and meetings on foreign trade opportunities.

World Population Series (Department of the Census)

This will give you demographic social and economic data including population, age, etc. to help identify potential markets. Also, contact the Data Evaluation Branch of the Department of the Census for more in-depth Country Demographic Profiles giving data on population size, age, breakdown, growth, fertility and mortality rates, education, literacy and economic activity.

SBA Field Offices

Regional Offices marked with an asterisk

Agana, GU	El Paso, TX	Omaha, NE
Albany, NY	Ft. Worth, TX	Phoenix, AZ
Albuquerque, NM	Fargo, ND	Pittsburgh, PA
Anchorage, AK	Fresno, CA	Portland, OR
* Atlanta, GA	Gulfport, MS	Providence, RI
Augusta, ME	Harlingen, TX	Reno, NE
Austin, TX	Harrisburg, PA	Richmond, VA
* Bala Cynwyd, PA	Hartford, CT	Rochester, NY
Baltimore, MD	Hato Rey, PR	Sacramento, CA
Billings, MT	Helena, MT	St. Croix, VI
Birmingham, AL	Honolulu, HI	St. Louis, MO
Boise, ID	Houston, TX	St. Thomas, VI
* Boston, MA	Indianapolis, IN	Salt Lake City, UT
Buffalo, NY	Jackson, MS	San Antonio, TX
Camden, NJ	Jacksonville, FL	San Diego, CA
Cape Girardeau, MO	* Kansas City, MO	San Francisco, CA
Casper, WY	Las Vegas, NV	Santa Ana, CA
Cedar Rapids, IA	Little Rock, AR	* Seattle, WA
Charleston, WV	Los Angeles, CA	Shreveport, LA
Charlotte, NC	Louisville, KY	Sioux Falls, SD
* Chicago, IL	Lubbock, TX	Spokane, WA
Cincinnati, OH	Madison, WI	Springfield, IL
Clarksburg, WV	Marquette, MI	Springfield, MA
Cleveland, OH	Marshall, TX	Springfield, MO
Columbia, SC	Melville, NY	Statesboro, GA
Columbus, OH	Miami, FL	Syracuse, NY
Concord, NH	Milwaukee, WI	Tampa, FL
Corpus Christi, TX	Minneapolis, MN	Tucson, AZ
* Dallas, TX	Montpelier, VT	Washington, DC
* Denver, CO	Nashville, TN	West Palm Beach, FL
Des Moines, IA	Newark, NJ	Wichita, KS
Detroit, MI	New Orleans, LA	Wilkes-Barre, PA
Elmira, NY	* New York, NY	Wilmington, DE
Eau Claire, WI	Oklahoma City, OK	

Check the appropriate telephone directory under "U.S. Government" for telephone numbers.

SBA Regional Offices

Region 1
Boston

For Maine, New Hampshire, Vermont, Massachusetts, Rhode Island and Connecticut
60 Batterymarch, 10th Floor
Boston, MA 02110

Region II
New York

For New York, New Jersey, Puerto Rico and the Virgin Islands
26 Federal Plaza - Room 29-118
New York, NY 10278

Region III
Bala Cynwyd

For Pennsylvania, Delaware, Maryland, Virginia, West Virginia and Washington, D.C.
One Bala Cynwyd Plaza, West Lobby
231 St. Asaphs Road
Bala Cynwyd, PA 19004

Region IV
Atlanta

For North Carolina, South Carolina, Georgia, Florida, Mississippi, Alabama, Tennessee and Kentucky
1375 Peachtree Street, N.E.
Atlanta, GA 30367

Region V
Chicago

For Ohio, Indiana, Michigan, Illinois, Wisconsin and Minnesota
230 South Dearborn Street, Room 510
Chicago, IL 60604

Region VI
Dallas

For Louisiana, Arkansas, Texas, Oklahoma and New Mexico
8625 King George Drive, Bldg. "C"
Dallas, TX 75235-3391

Region VII
Kansas City

For Missouri, Kansas, Iowa and Nebraska
911 Walnut Street, 13th Floor
Kansas City, MO 64106

Region YIII
Denver

For North Dakota, South Dakota, Colorado, Wyoming, Utah and Montana
99918th Street - Suite 701
Denver, CO 80202-2395

Region IX
San Francisco

For California, Arizona, Nevada, Hawaii, Guam, Trust Territories and American Samoa
450 Golden Gate Avenue - Box 36044
San Francisco, CA 94102

Region X
Seattle

For Oregon, Washington, Idaho and Alaska
2615 4th Avenue, Room 440
Seattle, WA 98121

Check the appropriate telephone directory under "U.S. Government" for telephone numbers.

Background Notes

This is a series of studies issued by the U. S. State Department (available for most countries at $2.00 for a single issue, or $34.00 for an annual subscription.) Each issue gives a population, geographic, government and economic profile of each country and details its imports and exports, major trading partners, gross national product, growth rate and many other data of use in evaluating a country's prospects as an importer of your products.

For a more complete list of publications, reports and services available from U. S. government agencies, consult your local Field Office.

Trade Opportunities Program
TO MAKE CONTACTS

Our Trade Opportunities Program (TOP) can send you new sales leads electronically— every day!

You don't always have to send your sales personnel to Buenos Aires or Bonn to scout out customers. Now you can receive up-to-the-minute leads from around the world every workday —without leaving your office.

If you're looking for foreign sales, TOP has the lead you need:

> √ **direct sale requests**
> √ **representation offers**
> √ **investment opportunities**
> √ **licensing partners**
> √ **joint venture partnerships**
> √ **project bids**
> √ **foreign government tenders**

Prescreened TOP leads are gathered daily by U.S. Commercial Officers in 65 foreign countries. The leads list the products or services requested, Standard Industrial Classification Code, and product specifications. Names and contact information are included so you can respond directly to the overseas buyer.

Quick and affordable, this service can lead to substantial export orders while saving you the expense of establishing a market presence overseas. U.S. companies of all sizes can find international customers through TOP:

" TOP has been a useful tool for our company in obtaining trade leads worldwide. Not only do they put you into contact with leading distributors worldwide, but they are an excellent barometer of demand for American products overseas. "

Mr. Stuart Hagler
President
Myriad International Corp.

Dallas, Texas

U. S. DEPARTMENT OF COMMERCE • INTERNATIONAL TRADE ADMINISTRATION • U.S. AND FOREIGN COMMERCIAL SERVICE

Reprinted by permission

TOP leads are printed daily in leading commercial newspapers, some of which are published nationwide. They are also distributed through commercial electronic database services and our *Economic Bulleti7l Board,* where they are maintained for 21 days. Additional sources of TOP information include regional, industry, and trade publications; trade associations; and state development agencies. Every day, TOP leads are also sent electronically to the U.S. Department of Commerce's 68 district and branch offices throughout the United States.

Start lining up your leads now:

❏ **For more information on the Economic Bulletin Board,** call us at 202/377-1986. To subscribe, call 703/487-4630.

As you follow your leads, you may wish to use a related service, our World Traders Data Reports, for background intformation on your overseas customers.

Our TOP leads put you in business!

Reprinted by permission

Agent/Distributor Service
TO MAKE CONTACTS

Exporters! Qualified representatives are out there, and our Agent/Distributor Service will help you find them.

Looking for overseas representatives to expand your business and boost your export sales? Use our Agent/Distributor Service (ADS), and we'll locate, screen, and assess agents, distributors, representatives, and other foreign partners for your business.

If your firm is small and new to export, or if you don't have resources for research or overseas travel, this service is for you. Through ADS, we provide an easy, economical, quick-access opportunity to enter profitable new markets. That's why U.S. exporters come back to ADS:

> " This program has served as our main source in locating qualified representatives in foreign markets."

> Sam D. Haan
> International Sales Manager
> Vermeer Manufacturing Company
> Pella, Iowa

Start by contacting your nearest U.S. Department of Commerce district office. We'll verify your product's marketability, help you prepare product literature packages, and have your product information sent overseas to be reviewed by commercial specialists in the country you've targeted for export. These specialists locate and contact potential agents and distributors, evaluating them in terms of their interest and capability.

You get a list of up to six of the best qualified and most interested contacts, along with appropriate comments and relevant information, such as a guide to local agent practices. Normal turnaround time is 60 to 90 days.

That's not all! We provide valuable follow-up services, including guidance in writing correspondence, making agreements, obtaining local business practice information, and requesting background reports.

ADS is available in most countries. Contact your nearest Commerce district office now so our specialists can start looking for your overseas business representatives.

Don 't wait for agents to find your ads — let our ADS find your agents!

U. S. DEPARTMENT OF COMMERCE · INTERNATIONAL TRADE ADMINISTRATION · U.S. AND FOREIGN COMMERCIAL SERVICE

Reprinted by permission

Export Contact List Service
TO MAKE CONTACTS

Find overseas business prospects through our Export Contact List Service.

Thousands of foreign companies interested in doing business with U.S. firms make up a database of international business contacts available through our Export Contact List Service (ECLS). These names have been accumulated over a period of years at trade promotion activities carried out at U.S. embassies and other posts around the world. And that's just the beginning.

We screen each company and develop a business profile for it. The profile includes name, product or service, telex, telephone, key contact, year established, number of employees, and relative size. Profiles are updated in our Commercial Information Management System (CIMS).

The right contacts for you may already be on our lists, which include:

- √ agents
- √ importers
- √ manufacturers
- √ retailers
- √ wholesalers
- √ distributors
- √ licensing partners

- √ advertising agencies
- √ service companies
- √ marketing firms
- √ banks
- √ state trading and procurement agencies

Many of the companies are buyers of commodities, raw materials, machinery, retail goods, specialty items, and other products and services.

Our ECLS puts mailing lists, labels, or profiles at your fingertips — saving you timeconsuming and costly in-country research. Ideal for building direct-mail campaigns or locating specific customers, our lists let you closely target business prospects by type of firm, import interest, country, and other variables. Government agencies, trade associations, banks, and other organizations are also included.

Take advantage of this economical and effective service today. Contact your nearest U.S. Department of Commerce district office. We'll provide you with complete information on the program and its costs, along with the material you need to start contacting your best overseas business prospects.

Our Export Contact List Service puts you in touch with the world!

U. S. DEPARTMENT OF COMMERCE • INTERNATIONAL TRADE ADMINISTRATION • U.S. AND FOREIGN COMMERCIAL SERVICE

Reprinted by permission

Herman J. Maggiori

 USA ★

Foreign Market Research
TO FIND & ASSESS YOUR MARKETS

Get the vital data you need quickly — through our Foreign Market Research and Trade Statistics services.

Your exporting success could depend on how well you know your target market. But you probably don't have on-staff resources for expensive, time-consuming investigations. Turn to the export information experts. Through our Foreign Market Research and Trade Statistics services you can get just what you need to plot your best overseas sales strategies.

"As a new-to-market small business, the market research information provided by US&FCS assisted us in our decision to make a firm commitment to enter export markets."

Robert E. Sanner
President
CIVCO Medical Instruments Co., Inc.
Kalona, Iowa

Foreign Market Research

The quick and easy way to investigate your overseas sales potential, our Foreign Market Research provides in-depth market data on selected products and industries in countries offering the best opportunities for U.S. goods. This convenient research service helps you select new markets, analyze market conditions, formulate selling strategies, and enter promising foreign markets.

Market Research answers your questions with reliable data collected by professional U.S. embassy staff and in-country market research firms thoroughly versed in local trade conditions. This information is continually sent to U.S. Department of Commerce district offices throughout the United States via our international computerized Commercial Information Management System (CIMS).

U. S. DEPARTMENT OF COMMERCE • INTERNATIONAL TRADE ADMINISTRATION • U.S. AND FOREIGN COMMERCIAL SERVICE

Reprinted by permission

Using the data in CIMS and other sources, we can compile concise, customized reports profiling exactly the export markets that interest you. Reports covering an industry or country — available in print or on diskette — provide the wide range of detailed information you need to export profitably. They may include:

√ best-selling products
√ competitive analyses
√ market access
√ top imports
√ end-users
√ trade barriers
√ market size

√ market characteristics
√ market outlook
√ industry outlook
√ economic trends
√ trade events
√ government regulations

Trade Statistics

Need up-to-date statistics? With electronic access to United Nations and U.S. Bureau of the Census trade information, we can quickly compile trade statistics to answer your most pressing questions, such as:

❑ **Which 10 countries were the top importers of my product last year?**

❑ **How much did each import?**

❑ **Which countries are increasing or decreasing imports of my product, and at what rates?**

❑ **Which countries provide my strongest foreign competition in each of the foreign markets?**

Trade statistics covering 173 countries are available up to the five-digit SITC Rev I level. Data is available from 1962 on, and can be provided in dollar value, quantity, unit value, growth rate, market-share percentage, and other for'ms for months, quarters, years, or our popular S-year groupings.

With our help, you can avoid getting bogged down with exhausting research in voluminous trade statistical tables. Contact your nearest U.S. Department of Commerce district office. We'll work with you to formulate a search tailored to your exact specifications and let you know the cost range in advance.

We do the research you make the sales!

Reprinted by permission

World Traders Data Reports
TO FIND & ASSESS YOUR MARKETS

We'll screen your foreign customers and prospective agents with our World Traders Data Reports.

You're an exporter, not a gambler. Naturally, you want to invest in sound transactions with reputable clients, but how can you check out customers half way around the world? That offer from Japan looks promising, but you just don't know anything about Miharu Imports, Inc.

Screen your customers with our World Traders Data Reports (WTDR). A special service for exporters, the WTDR program provides thorough, confidential background reports on potential foreign trading partners — including buyers, distributors, agents, and retailers.

WTDRs assess your potential customer's reputation and recommend whether to conduct trade with the firm and on what basis. U.S. businesses of all sizes use WTDRs to take the gamble out of exporting:

> *"We have used the WTDR program for many years and will continue to use it as our main source of information in the final process of qualifying new, potential foreign clients. This information has been invaluable to us as a small business."*

Jeffrey Else
International Sales Director
MID-A-MAR Corp., Ltd.
Cedar Rapids, Iowa

> *"Very beneficial in researching the credit worthiness of companies in the international marketplace, from marketing representatives to copartners."*

Ronald A Kissinger
Manager
International Business Development
E-Systems, Inc.
Greenville, Texas

U. S. DEPARTMENT OF COMMERCE • INTERNATIONAL TRADE ADMINISTRATION • U.S. AND FOREIGN COMMERCIAL SERVICE

Reprinted by permission

Crucial information about your new trading partner is provided by WTDR in a convenient one- to three-page format:

√ product lines
√ number of employees
√ capitalization
√ bank and trade references

√ sales volume
√ reputation
√ key officers or managers

Your WTDR may also include:

√ subsidiary/parent relationships
√ recent news items about the firm
√ the firm's U.S. customers

√ operational problems
√ activities of prominent owners
√ branch locations

All information is current — 12 months old or less.

Up to date and reliable, each report is developed from on-the-spot research by private firms or U.S. embassy staff and local contacts, who can get accurate background data from firms that might hesitate to respond to commercial credit agencies. Your identity is held in confidence — the foreign firm does not know who requested the report. You'll find this service especially valuable in countries with no major credit-reporting firms or where business information is closely guarded.

That's not all! Your WTDR qualifies as one of the reports required for obtaining Foreign Credit Insurance Association coverage. And you can use this service not only to screen new customers but to check up on the distributors, dealers, and agents you engage overseas.

To order your WTDR, contact your nearest U.S. Department of Commerce district office. Simply supply the name, address, and other identifying information about your prospective foreign customer. We'll check our international computerized Commercial Information Management System (CIMS) to see if current WTDR information relating to your request is already on file. If it is available, the information is provided to you in a printed report. If not, a request is sent to the U.S. embassy or consulate in the country where the firm is located. Turnaround time is 45 to 90 days for most countries.

Orders must include your firm's name, address, telephone number, and contact. The fee for a WTDR is the same in all countries, but is subject to periodic change. Contact your nearest Commerce district office for current fees and a list of countries covered by this program. WTDRs are generally available worldwide. Exceptions include Soviet Bloc nations and some countries where commercial information is readily available from local mercantile credit reporting agencies.

Don't gamble — Use WTDRs and be sure!

Reprinted by permission

Matchmakers
TO PROMOTE YOUR PRODUCTS

Matchmaker Trade Delegations pave your way to new export markets.

Matchmaker Trade Delegations "match" you with potential agents, distributors, and joint venture or licensing partners. We do the background work — evaluating your product's potential, finding and screening contacts, and handling logistics. You follow up with an intensive trip filled with face-to-face meetings with prospective clients and in-depth briefings on the economic and business climate of the countries visited. We offer:

√ prescreened prospects interested in your product or service
√ in-country publicity
√ convenient sales avenues
√ business appointments scheduled for you through the U.S. embassy or consulate
√ thorough briefings on market requirements and business practices
√ interpreter services

Matchmakers help small and medium-sized companies meet export sales objectives efficiently and economically. We generally target major markets in two countries and limit trips to a week or less so you can interview the maximum number of good candidates with a minimum of time away from the office. You also have the advantage of group-rate hotels and airfare, as well as on-the-spot U.S. embassy support.

" It is hard to imagine a better program for small to mid-sized companies to be involved in than Matchmaker!"

John G. Richardson
General Manager
James Alexander Corp.
Blairstown, New Jersey

If your firm is new to export or new to market in the countries scheduled for visits, and if U.S. content represents 51 percent of the finished value of your products, Matchmakers could be your answer. Contact your nearest U.S. Department of Commerce district office for details.

Let Matchmakers pave your way to profits!

U. S. DEPARTMENT OF COMMERCE • INTERNATIONAL TRADE ADMINISTRATION • U.S. AND FOREIGN COMMERCIAL SERVICE

Reprinted by permission

Interested in Establishing Export Representation in Overseas Markets? Consider This Exceptional Opportunity.

The **Matchmaker Program** was developed by the U.S. Department of Commerce to help U.S. firms explore new overseas markets for their products and services. While Trade Specialists located throughout the United States provide guidance on export regulations, overseas Commercial Officers work to identify the best possible "match" for the marketing interests of participating companies.

A limited number of potential host countries are selected each year, based on results of global surveys and recommendations of our overseas commercial staff. Studies of each selected market then suggest specific themes. Each theme includes end user sectors which provide good opportunities for introduction of U.S. products. Once a Matchmaker is scheduled, a market brief is prepared to provide information and guidance for U.S. firms planning to enter that market.

Matchmaker participation is reserved for executives with authority to sign agency and distribution agreements. U.S. Foreign Commercial Service Officers stationed in the market will evaluate the companies' marketing prospects and develop appropriate private individual appointments for each firm. Specific focus is placed on the establishment of commercial representation links between U.S. exporters and overseas agents and distributors qualified to handle their products and services. Matches are also made when joint ventures or licensing agreements

can best serve U.S. interests. A Matchmaker event takes place in an appropriate business facility. Often, a small booth is used to provide office space for the participant to meet in a comfortable and professional setting.

A portion of each Matchmaker event is usually open to walk-in trade. A variety of group functions will be scheduled to further highlight the importance of the event and to introduce the participant to the market. The U.S. Department of Commerce facilitates your participation as far as possible not only by establishing these forums on a cost effective basis, but also by arranging reasonably priced hotel accommodations and advising best air fare on U.S. carriers when appropriate.

Program Provides
1. Detailed briefing by Foreign Commercial Service Officers and other industry experts.
2. Arrangements for individual business appointments.
3. Promotion of participants' products/services to distributors and representatives.
4. Open sessions with selected and matched key distributors/agents and other types of commercial contacts, tailored to meet the specific objectives of the delegation participant.
5. Publication of an official catalog for use by the overseas industry prior to, during and after the visit.
6. Arrangement of an official reception at which participants may meet socially with local business and government leaders.

7. Arrangements for support staff to assist participants.
8. Assistance in evaluating a representative/joint venture and/or licensing arrangement.

Instructions for Participation
To confirm your participation, the documents listed below must be received by the Department of Commerce. Deadlines are specified in the accompanying literature. Please read carefully the Conditions of Participation which list the responsibilities of the U.S. Government and the participant.
1. Participation Agreement (ITA4008): Complete and sign.
2. Participation Fee: Send the total amount now, payable to U.S. Department of Commerce/ITA. On the face of the check, please write Matchmaker Trade Delegation (location) .
3. Marketing Data Form (ITA-466P): Please pay particular attention to the section on your objectives and the description of your product.
4. Catalog Page: The U.S. Department of Commerce will print and distribute an official brochure containing information provided by you on the company and its products. You provide a maximum of 250 words describing your company and expertise.
5. Sales Literature: Please send 25 copies or sets of your company's sales literature for use in pre-show promotion and to aid in locating and matching appropriate contacts for you.

The accompanying literature specifies deadline dates, participation fee and appropriate Project Officer contacts for this event.

Reprinted by permission

63

Conditions of Participation Matchmaker Trade Delegations

A. Matchmaker Delegation Defined
Overseas event planned. organized and led by Department of Commerce officers which bnngs groups of U S businesspersons representing new to export or new to market firms into contact with agents, distributors, licensees, franchisees or joint venture partners for the purpose of establishing representation in the countries visited

B. Criteria
Firms that participate in a Trade Delegation must use the visit to promote only products or services which, in the judgement of the Department, meet one of the following criteria.
1. Manufactured or produced in the United States
2. If manufactured or produced outside of the United States, the product or service must be marketed under the name of a U.S. firm and have U.S. content representing at least 51 percent of the value of the finished good or service.
The Delegation will be composed of decision-making executives from each of a limited number of companies. Each representative must be a director or senior officer of the participating company with authority to negotiate representation agreements.

C. Within limits of available resources, the U.S. Department of Commerce agrees to:
1. Select a product or service category and an overseas itinerary which offer potential for export development. Selection will be based upon market research and consultation with the Foreign Commercial Service posts in the country selected to be visited and with key trade associations and companies in the industry to be promoted
2. Provide each Delegation member with available market research relevant to the products and services to be promoted for all countries that will be visited.
3. Where appropriate. or upon request. conduct a general briefing for members prior to departure from the United States regarding commercial and economic conditions in the country to be visited. If a briefing in the United States is not practicable. the briefing will be held at the first overseas stop on the itinerary. An in depth briefing by U.S. Commercial Officers at Foreign Service posts will be conducted in each country visited.
4. Arrange a schedule of business appointments with key distributor or agent candidates for the goods or services of participants
5. Provide information for distribution overseas describing the participants. their companies. goods or services and. where appropriate. their marketing objectives Where necessary. this material will be in the language of the country visited.

6. Provide a headquarters in each foreign location. as necessary. where individual business appointments can be scheduled and other delegation business transacted.
7. Host official receptions and or other hospitality events, where appropnate, at or in conjuction with. the Foreign Commercial Service posts to provide members with the opportunity to meet key local government officials and business leaders.
8. Provide transportation schedules for members to book appropriate flights.
9. Obtain confirmed hotel reservations for members in advance of each stop.
10. Provide clerical staff and interpreters as needed to assist members. Each post's commercial and logistical support as needed or arrange for outside logistical support.
11. Provide a U.S Government official or appropriate pnvate sector representative having extensive knowledge of the Delegation theme to serve as Director of the Trade Delegation.
12. Provide a qualified Department of Commerce Officer to coordinate logistics and administration

D. The Participant Agrees to:
1. Make a financial contribution to the U.S. Department of Commerce in an amount to be established for the event for use in funding all services provided to the participant, including market development, operating and hospitality costs of the Delegation. and other international trade promotional activities. A signed Participation Agreement (Form ITA-4008) is to be submitted with the contribution.
2. Furnish detailed descriptive company and product/service information sufficiently in advance of the visit to allow for compilation and/or printing and advance distribution.
3. Obtain information from the Department s Office of Export Administration. and/or from other licensing agencies. e g Nuclear Regulatory Commission. Department of Energy. and Office of Munitions Controls. U S. Department of State. as to whether existing laws or regulations might impede or prevent the participant from marketing its products or services or releasing U.S. origin technical data in any of the countnes to be visited by the Del egation. If problems arise in obtaining this information. the Department will provide such assistance or facilitation as may be necessary and appropriate.
4. Promote its individual business interests. e g. licensing agreements. or agent distributor anangements and other sales arrangements as may be appropriate.
5. Participate in scheduled briefings by the Department of Commerce and other agencies including the Foreign Service

posts.
6. Keep all business appointments which have been arranged and adhere to the program and its complete itinerary.
7. Contribute information for the delegation report and provide the results achieved on the Exhibitor and Mission Member Report Form (ITA-4075P) or successor document If the participant requests particular information to be treated confidentially. the Department of Commerce will honor the request to the extent possible under applicable law
8. Travel between the United States and abroad on U.S. flag carriers whenever practicable
9. Pay representative s travel. hotel and daily living expenses.
10. Obtain entry permit visas and/or other travel documentation where necessary prior to departure from the United States.
11. Participants representatives travel at their own risk It is recommended that they be covered by adequate insurance The company. on behalf of itself and any of its officers. employees or agents. agrees to save the U.S. Government harmless from liability for any illness injury loss of life. or damage or loss of property occasioned by or connected with participation in the Delegation.
12. The participant agrees to provide at his/her expense a qualified company executive who will participate in all delegation activities This person shall be authorized to discuss ,product lines or services. to give price quotations on various bases. as appropriate and to negotiate sales and related arrangements The representative should be designated at the earliest possible date and his/her name furnished to the Department of Commerce The representative must carry a valid passport and be a director or senior officer of the participating U S. company (the participant).

E. Other conditions
1. If, for any reason the participating company cancels its participation, its financial contribution will not be refunded unless written notice of cancellation is received by the Department of Commerce at least 45 days before the departure of the delegation, unless a replacement is found.
2. The Department may cancel a matchmaker delegation or the participation of any company for the convenience of the Government. In the event of such cancellation. any contribution made will be refunded.
3. It is understood that all applications for participation in the delegation are subject to approval by the Department of Commerce, and acceptance will be based on a

first come, first served basis.

Reprinted by permission

Commerce Department Export Services
The WTDR: A Good Way to Screen Trading Partners

In every issue, Business America *mentions some of the export services available to U.S. companies from the U.S. Department of Commerce's International Trade Administration. We thought it would be useful — from time to time — to take a single major service and explain it in detail. We start now, with this article on the World Traders Data Report (WTDR).*

Suppose a U.S. exporter receives a significant order from a Japanese importer he knows nothing about. Suppose a firm needs background on a potential overseas sales agent. Or suppose an American manufacturer needs to know the various product lines handled by a prospective foreign distributor.

In international trade, long distances and unfamiliar business practices make it particularly important to get an accurate reading on a trading partner's reliability. Good information is the best way to reduce risks and avoid potential problems.

How can a U.S. firm get solid information about overseas business partners at very little cost?

An excellent way is to order a World Traders Data Report (WTDR) from the U.S. Department of Commerce through its U.S. and Foreign Commercial Service in the International Trade Administration. The WTDR program is a special service for exporters that provides thorough, confid ntial background reports on potential foreign trading partners, including buyers, distributors, agents, and retailers.

A WTDR will assess a potential trading partner's reputation and recommend whether to conduct business with the firm and on what basis. In a convenient one-tothree page format, a WTDR provides background on:

- Reputation and payment history
- Trade and credit references
- Product lines
- Number of employees
- Capitalization
- Sales volume
- Key officers or managers.

The report also may include subsidiary/parent relationships, the firm's U.S. customers, activities or prominent owners, recent news items about the firm, operational problems, and branch locations.

All information is current — 12 months old or less. Each report is developed from on-the-spot research by private firms or U.S. embassy staff and local contacts, who can get accurate background data from firms that might hesitate to respond to commercial credit agencies. The identity of the firm ordering a WTDR is held in confidence — the foreign firm does not know who requested the report. The service is especially useful in examining firms in less developed countries, where even routine commercial information can be hard to get, and in countries where business information is closely guarded.

A WTDR also is helpful to a firm applying for Foreign Credit Insurance Association coverage.

Many exporters have used the WTDR service to good advantage. Jeffrey Else, International Sales Director of MID-A-MAR Corp., Ltd., of Cedar Rapids, Iowa, said. "We have used the WTDR program for many years and will continue to use it as our main source of information in the final process of qualifying new, potential foreign clients. This information has been invaluable to us as a small business." Ronald A. Kissinger, Manager of International Business Development for E-Systems, Inc., of Greenville, Texas, said the program is "very beneficial in researching the creditworthiness of companies in the international marketplace, from marketing representatives to co-partners."

The WTDR program grew out of the War Trade Board Card used during World War I which involved the collection of information about the business activities of foreign individuals. In 1918-19, the card was developed into a formal report that became the basis for the modern World Traders Data Report. At first, WTDRs were free. In July 1932, a fee system was instituted — the first charge was $1 per report.

To order a WTDR, business people should contact the closest district office of the Commerce Department's International Trade Administration. All they need to do is supply the name, address, and other identifying information about the prospective trading partner. They may ask specific questions about the foreign firm. The Commerce Department will then check its international computerized Commercial Information Management System (CIMS) to see if current WTDR information relating to the request is already on file. If it is available, the information is provided in a printed report. If not, a request is sent to the U.S. embassy or consulate in the country where the firm is located. Turnaround time is 45 to 90 days for most countries. See inside back cover for a list of Commerce Department district offices.

Orders must include a firm's name, address, telephone number, and contact person. WTDRs are generally available worldwide. Exceptions include Soviet Bloc nations and some countries where commercial information is readily available from local mercantile credit-reporting agencies.

Reprinted by permission

Business America, September 11, 1989

Herman J. Maggiori

Comparison Shopping Service
TO FIND & ASSESS YOUR MARKETS

Will your product sell in Germany? Kenya? Brazil? Find out with our Comparison Shopping Service.

Our Comparison Shopping Service (CSS) offers you a quick, accurate assessment of how your product will sell in a given market. For a very reasonable fee, you get a concise report answering these critical questions:

- ❑ Does your product have sales potential in the market?
- ❑ Who is supplying a comparable product locally?
- ❑ What is the usual sales channel for getting this product into the market?
- ❑ What is the going price for a comparable product?
- ❑ Are purchasers of such products primarily influenced by price, or by other competitive factors, such as credit, quality, delivery, service, promotion, or brand?
- ❑ What is the best way to get sales exposure in the market?
- ❑ Are there any impediments to selling the product, such as quotas, duties, or local regulations?
- ❑ Who might be interested and qualified to represent or purchase your product in this market?
- ❑ Who might be an interested, qualified licensing or joint venture partner for your company?

To provide you with answers, one of our research specialists in your target country interviews importers, distributors, retailers, wholesalers, end-users, and local producers of comparable products and inspects similar products on the market. Your customized report usually is completed and in your hands within 45 days.

Especially valuable for small and first-time exporters with few foreign contacts and limited overseas sales expertise, CSS provides you with on-the-spot, current data you need to make marketing decisions — without the large travel, investigative, and other expenses associated with overseas product research.

Contact your nearest U.S. Department of Commerce district office to find out whether a survey of your product's marketability can be conducted in the country you've targeted for export sales. Please note that products manufactured outside the United States must be marketed using the name of the U.S. firm, and the content must represent 51 percent of the value of the finished goods.

Our Comparison Shopping Service puts your product on target!

U. S. DEPARTMENT OF COMMERCE • INTERNATIONAL TRADE ADMINISTRATION • U.S. AND FOREIGN COMMERCIAL SERVICE

Reprinted by permission

Catalog & Video/Catalog Exhibitions
TO PROMOTE YOUR PRODUCTS

Catalog and Video/Catalog Exhibitions showcase your products abroad in markets you don't have time to visit!

U.S. Department of Commerce Catalog and Video/Catalog Exhibitions offer a low-cost, low-risk way to generate leads, whether you're looking for sales or representation for your products or services. Using the resources of U.S. embassies worldwide, we show your catalogs or videos to potential agents, distributors, and other buyers in selected world markets. Our officers overseas:

√ promote the event to a targeted business audience
√ attractively display your catalog or video
√ provide staff fluent in the local language to answer questions
√ send you all trade leads and a list of all visitors

That's not all! We'll keep your catalogs active after the show, using them in subsequent promotional events or featuring them in embassy commercial libraries.

Custom tailored to meet the needs of small and medium-sized, new-to-export or new-to-market firms, Catalog and Video/Catalog Exhibitions have benefited thousands of U.S. firms since 1972. It's a great way to stimulate sales, with participants receiving an average of up to 50 leads.

Every year we organize several Catalog and Video/Catalog Exhibitions highlighting certain industries in selected markets. Chances are good we can help you meet your marketing goals. You can participate by following a few easy steps:

√ pay a small participation fee
√ send your catalogs or videos to the overseas exhibition sites
√ indicate your objective in each market
√ respond promptly to each trade inquiry you receive

Contact your nearest U.S. Department of Commerce district omce for t'ee information and a current schedule of our Catalog and Video/Catalog Exhibitions.

Our Catalog and Video/Catalog Exhibitions — your showcase abroad!

U. S. DEPARTMENT OF COMMERCE • INTERNATIONAL TRADE ADMINISTRATION • U.S. AND FOREIGN COMMERCIAL SERVICE

Reprinted by permission

Herman J. Maggiori

Commerce Department Export Services
Catalog and Video/Catalog Shows Generate Trade Leads

Catalog and Video/Catalog Exhibitions are an effective, low-cost vehicle for small and medium-sized U.S. firms to introduce their products and services in many overseas markets. The exhibitions provide firms with an opportunity to find customers and to solicit agents and representatives from qualified prospects. We describe the Catalog and the Video/Catalog shows in this second article in Business America's *series on Commerce Department export Services.*

The cost and time required for small- and medium-sized companies to travel to foreign countries to develop markets is often prohibitive. For many smaller markets, so little statistical and marketing information is available that it's hard for a company to know whether it has a reasonable prospect for sales there. Even developed markets represent largely unknown potential for small or novice exporters.

How can a firm test the waters without incurring steep travel and exhibition expenses?

Over the past 20 years, the Commerce Department has developed two low-cost trade promotion techniques to help such companies generate leads, whether they are looking for sales or representation for their products or services: Catalog and Video/Catalog Exhibitions. To participate, U.S. firms send their product catalogs, sales literature, and video presentations to the Commerce Department. In advance of the exhibition, overseas commercial officers in the Department's U.S. and Foreign Commercial Service work with local chambers of commerce, trade associations, and other business organizations to sponsor events at which local prospective agents, distributors, and buyers are invited to review the material presented by American companies and to evaluate whether business connections with them would be to their advantage. Each local firm visiting the event is interviewed about its qualifications and interests and is' directed at specific U.S. participant catalogs and videos.

A Catalog Exhibition costs a U.S. firm $100 to $300 to display its product catalogs and sales literature in 10 to 25 overseas markets. Fifty to 500 firms participate. A Video/Catalog Exhibition costs a firm $1,000 to $1,500 for the development of a video presentation that will he shown in 10 to 50 overseas markets. Participation is limited to 20 firms. The Commerce Department arranges for a private contractor to produce a master video show from audio-visual materials furnished by the participants. The show will usually be an hour long, with a three-to-four minute presentation for each participant. The video show will be made in the language of the countries where exhibitions are scheduled and will be converted into the video process used in each country.

Commerce Department overseas commercial officers provide a staff at the shows that is fluent in the local language. The commercial officers observe the reaction of visitors to the shows and prepare a report for each U.S. participant listing the names and addresses of visitors and a concise report on their particular interests. After a show, they keep the catalogs active, using them in later promotional events or featuring them in embassy libraries.

A typical participant receives 50 detailed, qualified leads for each Catalog or Video/Catalog show it enters. For example, BIRD-X, a Chicago firm representing bird and rodent control products and dental laboratory supplies, has received 120 trade leads as a result of participating in U.S. catalog exhibitions since last October. Mary Kisinger, the company's International Sales Manager, said, "We consider catalog exhibitions to be a very cost-effective means of showing our products overseas."

A Video/Catalog show featuring auto parts and accessories now making the rounds will eventually be seen in 20 countries in Latin America. In Monterey, Mexico, the two-day event drew 150 visitors, of whom 100 were considered "solid" business contacts. Results included four specific trade opportunities and 436 trade leads. In Honduras, the video was shown in Tegucigalpa and San Pedro Sula, with good attendance. Catalog shows now under recruitment or being planned include "Marketing USA" in the Asia/Pacific area and the Middle East; Tourism Equipment and Supplies in the Asia/Pacific area and the Caribbean; "Transportation Systems USA" in Europe, the Middle East, and Africa; Oil and Gas Field Equipment in Latin America, the Middle East, and Asia; Medical & Analytical Instruments, worldwide. Video events being developed include Plastics Production Technology in Latin America; Food Production Technology, worldwide; and Air-conditioning & Refrigeration, worldwide. A firm can obtain complete calendars of all Catalog and Video/Catalog shows from any district office of the Commerce Department's International Trade Administration.

Firms interested in learning more about such events, or how to participate, should telephone James Boney or Louis Quay on (202)377-3973. or write to Catalog Exhibitions Program, US&FCS/EPS, Room H2119, U.S. Department of Commerce, Wash., D.C. 20230.

Business America, September 25, 1989

Reprinted by permission

INTRODUCING
The 1990 Air-Conditioning and Refrigeration Video/ Catalog Exhibition

The Program

Join us in our high tech promotion of air-conditioning and re-frigeration products around the world. You and your team can now compete in the global marketplace economically and effectively, making overseas contacts without leaving home.

Here's how we can help! Up to 20 U.S. companies in the air-conditioning and refrigeration equipment industry will be selected to participate in this exciting video/catalog exhibition. Partici-pants supply a two to three minute video presentation or slides that can be used to produce a video show. After all video presentations are compiled into one tape, copies are distributed to U.S. embassies and consulates hosting the exhibitions.

Intense multi-media promotions, including press releases and personal invitations from the U.S. embassies or consulates, are directed to key local industry and government executives, inviting them to attend this exciting show.

The entire video presentation will be shown several times daily. Each company's full line of catalogs will be displayed adjacent to the presentation so that visitors may get more specific information on featured products and product lines.

The contacts you establish from this exhibition will help you to launch a profitable export program or expand your current one!

The Markets

(Based on 1989 U.S. Industrial Outlook)

Exports of air-conditioning, refrigeration, and heating equip-ment reached a record high of $2.0 billion in 1988, an increase of 29 percent from 1987. Exports accounted for 13 percent of all factory shipments. Almost every product category had increased sales internationally in 1988, with general air-conditioning ma-chinery and parts, room air-conditioners, and 1-3 hp compressors having the most significant market share.

The trend for increased international sales should continue throughout the next several years. In 1989 exports should grow 10 percent or more to $2.2 billion. Higher temperatures over most of the world have motivated consumers to buy air-condi-tioning units for the first time or replace outdated units. Higher temperatures combined with expanding foreign markets, new marketing initiatives, technological advancement of developing countries, improved U.S. products, and the competitive U.S. dollar should enable U.S. companies to continue to be successful in the export market.

The Benefits

Video/Catalog Exhibitions **save** you time and money.

Video/Catalog Exhibitions **promote** your products worldwide.

Video/Catalog Exhibitions **provide** priceless publicity and ex-posure for your firm.

Video/Catalog Exhibitions **give** you an opportunity to travel the world with your products in nine short months.

Video/Catalog Exhibitions **deliver** potential business leads to expand your markets.

The Itinerary

MIDDLE EAST and AFRICA	ASIA/PACIFIC
	China (PRC)
Algeria	India
Bahrain	New Zealand
Egypt	Philippines
Ivory Coast	
Ghana	EUROPE
Kenya	
Kuwait	Greece
Liberia	Portugal
Morocco	Turkey
Nigeria	
Oman	AMERICAS
Saudi Arabia	
Sudan	Bahamas
United Arab Emirates	Dominican Rep
Yemen Arab Republic	Chile
Zaire	Ecuador
	Guyana
	Honduras
	Mexico
	Uruguay

Highlights on one or two products that have the most potential for export and are the best examples of your full product line make the most effective presentations. A 3/4 inch U-Matic two to three minute video presentation with English narration and script, or slides with script, should be submitted along with a participation fee of $1,500. The fee covers the cost of editing, translating and narrating the video into Spanish or French, and overseas promotion expenses.

The Deadlines

Immediately—Return the reply card as soon as possible to receive detailed information.

Upon receiving information kit—Since only 20 firms will be able to participate, you will need to forward the enclosed participation agreement and $1,500 to secure a place in the video/catalog exhibition .

October 31, 1989—Forward video or video materials and English script for translation.

November 6, 1989—Forward catalogs overseas and to Wash-ington.

January 1990—Video/catalog exhibition begins.

Example of a Video/Catalog Exhibition (Reprinted by permission)

Trade Shows
TO PROMOTE YOUR PRODUCTS

Our high-profile trade shows launch your products abroad.

Trade Fairs, Solo Exhibitions~ and Trade Center Shows

To showcase your exports, we organize a wide variety of special exhibitions every year all around the world. Designed to promote U.S. products with high export potential, these events range from solo exhibitions representing U.S. firms exclusively at trade centers overseas to U.S. pavilions in the largest international exhibitions. We provide:

√ extensive local promotion
√exhibit transportation support
√ a turnkey exhibit booth
√ marketing support
√ "REPFIND" campaign

If you're interested in expanding your firm's export activities, our trade shows can provide the high-visibility promotion you need to line up your leads.

"There is a need for more exhibitions like this one at international trade shows. We are pleased the U.S. Government provides this kind orpromotional support and backing for U.S. industry."

Steve Feinman
International Sales
RMS Technologies
Marlton, New Jersey

Certified Trade Fairs

We also work with private show organizers, officially recognizing and supporting events that offer the best opportunities to exhibit U.S. products abroad. Exhibitors in these selected overseas events profit from the combined expertise of private show organizers and our trade specialists.

For more information about our trade exhibitions and certified shows, contact your nearest U.S. Department of Commerce district office.

We'll show the world your products!

U. S. DEPARTMENT OF COMMERCE * INTERNATIONAL TRADE ADMINISTRATION * U.S. AND FOREIGN COMMERCIAL SERVICE

Reprinted by permission

70

Trade Missions
TO PROMOTE YOUR PRODUCTS

Our trade missions open doors wide — worldwide.

Once you've identified your best export market, consider participating in our high-profile overseas trade missions. Scheduled in selected countries throughout the world, our customtailored trade missions help you find local agents, representatives, distributors, or direct sales. Some missions include technical seminars specially designed to promote sales of sophisticated products and technology in specific markets. Our trade missions open doors to host-country govemment and business leaders who otherwise would be difficult to contact. We provide:

√ advance planning
√ local publicity
√ appointments with qualified contacts
√ access to senior government omcials
√ logistical support
√ interpreter service
√ in-depth market briefings
√ background information on contacts

Designed to make the best use of your time, our 20 to 30 trade missions each year help about 175 U.S. businesses establish valuable overseas contacts in selected international markets.

" Country and government agency briefings were excellent. Meetings and appointments were well organized and on target."

Jon R. Lange
President
Lanmar International
Chicago, Illinois

In addition to planning customized trade missions, we support selected trade events organized by state and local govemments, chambers of commerce, trade associations, and other export oriented groups. We offer event organizers guidance and assistance, from planning through implementation, with our overseas staff helping to make appointments tailored to each mission member's products and objectives. These collaborative events provide a convenient way for you to meet essential business contacts right in the country you've targeted for your export sales.

For more information about our overseas trade missions, contact your nearest U.S. Department of Commerce district office.

Open the door to exporting!

U. S. DEPARTMENT OF COMMERCE • INTERNATIONAL TRADE ADMINISTRATION • U.S. AND FOREIGN COMMERCIAL SERVICE

Reprinted by permission

Herman J. Maggiori

U.S. Telecommumcations Mission
Finds Opportunites in India

by Ivan H. Shefrin
Office of Telecommunications
International Trade Administration

Business America, August 1, 1988

A U.S. Executive Level Trade Mission to India reports that the country's telecommunications market is much bigger than expected and that India welcomes collaboration with U.S. firms.

The mission, which visited India during the spring, included eight leading American telecommunications firms that explored commercial opportunities for direct sales. joint ventures, and licensing agreements. Led by Assistant Secretary of Trade Development Charles E. Cobb Jr. (now Acting Under Secretary for Travel and Tourism), the mission was also joined by William F. Ryan, First Vice President and Vice Chairman of the U.S. Export-Import Bank, and by Lew W. Cramer, Commerce Deputy Assistant Secretary for Science and Electronics.

Industry participants included senior executives from AT&T, BellSouth International, Digital Photonics, Motorola, Multitech Systems, Om Electronics Systems, Omnitel and Tellabs International. Also on the delegation were the Regional Director of the U.S. Trade and Development Program, the Commerce Department India Desk Officer, and an industry specialist from the Department's Office of Telecommunications.

The goal of the mission was to identify gaps in India's domestic production of telecommunications equipment and services. market segments where U. S. technology could be most competitive while not challenging India's goal of indigenous development.

Officials from the Indian Government and private sector also expressed interest in American telecommunications products beyond those offered by the eight companies participating in the mission. The participants were overwhelmed by business proposals from Indian manufacturers and end-users. Delegation members held more than 300 meetings. The group met with the key personnel responsible for India's massive telecommunications development program in New Delhi, Bangalore, and Bombay.

The size of the Indian telecommunications market exceeded their expectations. India plans to allocate about $40 billion to telecommunications infrastructure development over the next 12 years: $2-3 billion for 1988-90; $12-15 billion between 1990-1995; and $24 billion during 1995-2000. Since the telecommunications sector is generally profitable and self-financing, the delegation was told that

almost 80 percent will be funded from within India, eliminating much of the need for concessionary financing after the next 12 years; 40 percent of this $40 billion requirement may be met through direct imports.

For the next seven years, however, India requires about $3.9 billion in loans. The U.S. Export-Import Bank emphasized that the United States would be highly competitive on loans for telecommunications exports, especially offers made by export credit agencies of other governments.

During the mission, Eximbank worked to finalize two $10 million credit facilities with the Export-Import Bank of India and the State Bank of India to finance U.S. contracts under $5 million. Vice Chairman Ryan also expressed keen interest in cooperating with the Government of India in providing Eximbank cofinancing with loans from the World Bank and the Asian Development Bank, which recently finalized a $135 million loan for telecommunications in India.

Assistant Secretary Cobb signed a Trade and Development Program (TDP, administered by the State Department) agreement with the Indian Department of Electronics. The agreement will fund a $265,000 software feasibility study for automating a water treatment plant, to be conducted by Texas Instruments. The mission also reached an agreement in principle with the Indian Department of Telecommunications to provide TDP funding for a telecommunications training project to be administered by the Telecommunications Training Institute.

Indian Government and private-sector officials listed several areas in which they desire collaboration with U.S. firms: transmission equipment in a variety of categories; digital multiplexers; network maintenance and operations support packages; line testing and maintenance equipment; jelly-filled coaxial cable; fiber optic transmission equipment and componentry; digital microwave systems; VF and multi-access radio communications with an emphasis on rural applications; payphones; and a range of data communications products such as modems and local area networks. India needs about 500,000 public payphones.

Assistant Secretary Cobb delivered a personal letter to the Indian Minister of State for Communications from Secretary of Commerce C. William Verity calling for increased trade and investment in the telecommunications

sector. Despite the Indian Government's widespread calls for indigenous development, the Minister said that India welcomes foreign investment in the sector; he enthusiastically endorsed greater privatization of Indian's telecommunications production. Since the sector provides the Indian Government with a large positive revenue stream, he said the sector's development could be self-financing, eliminating the need for significant concessionary financing over the long run.

The group met with the leadership of the Department of Telecommunications and the Department of Electronics. Through working luncheons with the Confederation of Engineering Industry and the Indo-American Chamber of Commerce, participants had an opportunity to meet with more than 400 Indian private sector representatives interested in telecommunications.

The mission visited the facilities of three Indian telecommunications R&D organizations. They also met with Mahanagar Telephone Nigam Ltd. (MTNL), the recently formed telephone operating company for New Delhi and Bombay. and the Indian Railways Board. which in the next few months will issue a global tender for a $1 billion upgrade of its telephone and data communications network. The mission completed its tour with a stop in Bombay, where meetings were held with MTNL, Videsh Sanchar Nigam Ltd. (VSNL — providing international telecommunications services), and other state and private telecommunications organizations. VSNL provided the delegation with a procurement list of equipment needed over the next two years. including earth station antennas; echo cancelers; video conferencing units; high power amplifiers; wave guides; modulators; multiplexers; filters; companders; test instruments; line conditioners; and power supplies.

Asked for advice on how U.S. companies can best enter the Indian telecom market. an adviser to Prime Minister Gandhi said: ~Bring in one or two products at no cost, try it out and take the model with you so that everyone knows it works. Talking to the top people can sometimes restrict the information flow, to prove your point to the public and mid-level technicians. Do performance studies yourself, rather than relying on us to do them for you. This will convince the public of what you have to offer. But first make sure nobody else

Example of a Trade Mission (Reprinted by permission)

72

is doing it indigenously within India. Don't use agents, your embassy people will do a better job for free. The system is already open and you don't need an agent to open doors. And work with either a government-owned company or LI joint-sector (public-private owned) corporation."

In Bangalore, the trade mission toured the facilities of Texas Instruments, which maintains a 100 percent export-only software development center linked directly via satellite to London and Texas. Software can be written and tested in real time at a fraction of the cost in the United States. The delegation learned that Indian-produced software can provide a cost-effective alternative to U.S. designs. One of the many software projects discussed was converting telecommunications equipment from North Americ;In to European standards, readying U.S. exports for the Indian market. The group also visited the manufacturing facilities of Indian Telephone Industries, the largest telecommunications producer on the subcontinent, and Bharat Electronics Ltd., India's largest electronics defense contractor. Both these companies are located in Bangalore, India's center of high-technology manufacturing. The city presently hosts an estimated 75 percent of the country's manufacturing capacity in communications, computers, peripheral and electronic components, as well as other high-tech products.

The trade mission saw firsthand evidence in Bangalore that U.S. investment and collaboration in India's high-technology marketplace is both feasible and profitable. The United States is now India's largest trading partner, and in 1987 led all other countries in approved collaborations — joint ventures and technology transfer agreements. With 212 projects approved, the United States pushed ahead of Great Britain for the first time since 1957.

U.S.-Indian commercial relations are clearly broadening. To strengthen the climate for commercial ties, Prime Minister Gandhi and President Reagan signed a historic Trade Expansion Initiative agreement in September 1987 calling for increased Indo-U.S. trade and investment. The trade mission in the spring and an earlier mission last fall were followups to the initiative. The next major initiative is the Commerce Department's 1989 trade fair with the Confederation of Engineering Industry. Recruitment has begun for the "USA Partner Country Exhibition" at the 8th Indian International Engineering Trade Fair Feb. 19-26 — the most ambitious export promotion activity ever taken by the United States in India. The Commerce Department already has contacted more than 25,000 U.S. firms about the fair, at which telecommunications is one of six highlighted industrial sectors. Interested firms should contact Jerry Morse at (202) 377-5907 or Terry Rettig at (202) 377-4466 .

Despite the opportunities and growth in its telecommunications market, India is still a tough place to do business and U.S. firms face many challenges. By and large, India still takes a piecemeal approach to telecommunications development — bids are issued on a project-by-project basis. The decision-making process is bureaucratic and cumbersome, and problems remain with India's treatment of investment and intellectual property issues. Strict licensing rules control which companies will manufacture what products, at precise output levels and locations. Market entry and exit are strictly controlled with government protection for Indian companies that would otherwise fail. There are local content requirements for manufacturing, and a policy of discouraging technology imports in those areas where India is or hopes to become — self-sufficient, such as small digital switches and PBXs.

On the bright side, while U.S. export controls are frequently cited as a barrier to increased trade, the Commerce Department in fact approved 94 percent of all license applications in 1987 or a total of 3,916 valued at $536 million. Only 50 export licenses were denied. As a result of a Memorandum of Understanding between India and the United States, the number of license applications and approvals increased 500 percent between 1983 and 1984. Now that the new Indian Import Certificate procedure has been agreed to, the number of approvals should continue to increase.

U.S. firms also have several advantages over their foreign competitors when doing business in India: many Indian officials and technicians prefer U.S. equipment and technology, having worked and studied in the United States ... there is no language barrier, making technical assistance and contract negotiation easier than with Japanese firms ... U.S. technology has a reputation in India as the world's best ... and the low value of the U.S. dollar relative to other foreign currencies makes U.S. companies more competitive on a price basis.

One participant made a sale during the trade mission and began the application procedure to manufacture its products near Bombay. Another received a letter of intent, a second finalized an ongoing collaboration agreement, while a third made arrangements for a group of Indian engineers to visit its U.S. plant for six weeks and collaborate on a software project. One other company already has begun producing modems in India, while a fifth was confident of establishing a permanent presence soon.

During the mission, AT&T announced it would be opening a permanent liaison office in New Delhi by September. All the participating companies promised to follow up immediately on leads.

Liberalized economic policy trends have encouraged firms to take an unprecedented interest in India, and U.S. companies have begun to make progress in the Indian telecommunications market in recent years. While India is not a place to go for quick sales or short-term profits, the trade mission found it to be a market that rewards diligence, persistence and constant follow-up.

Reprinted by permission

Commercial News USA
TO PROMOTE YOUR PRODUCTS

Exporters! Send your message around the world via *Commercial News USA* !

You know your product has export potential. Now you can prove it! *Commercial News USA,* our high-profile export catalog-magazine, can launch or expand your company's export sales — *at a fraction of the cost of commercial advertising.* With a single listing in Commercial *News USA,* you'll reach more business representatives and potential customers than you could in years of sales calls — *without ever leaving home!*

Distributed worldwide, *Commercial News USA* reaches more than 100,000 screened business readers eager to know about your new products. Especially beneficial to small and mediumsized firms, this convenient program can help you generate sales leads, identify profitable markets for your new products, and locate agents, distributors, licensing partners, and buyers. See what past participants say about *Commercial News USA.*

"It's an inexpensive way to tell the world 'Hey, here we are!'"

> L.S. Fox
> Sales Manager
> Service International
> Colorado Springs, Colorado

" There was more response from that one ad than any other single ad in our ten years of business. "

> Elizabeth N. Kuzia
> Vice President
> Stanley Solar and Stove Inc.
> Manchester, New Hampshire

"Without this program, we would never have been able to do any exporting. That's what got us started. "

> Fred Schweser
> Chairman
> Bird Corporation
> Elkhorn, Nebraska

U. S. DEPARTMENT OF COMMERCE * INTERNATIONAL TRADE ADMINISTRATION * U.S. AND FOREIGN COMMERCIAL SERVICE

Reprinted by permission

The benefits of a single listing in *Commercial News USA* can add up to a significant return on your investment:

❏ **Low-cost options:** A nominal fee gives you a standard listing and a photo of your product in this attractive publication. Larger listings are available for higher visibility.

❏**High Profile:** Ten issues each year get the news out quickly. And you can repeat your message during the year for multiple impact.

❏**Broad Distribution:** We offer worldwide distribution through U.S. embassies and consulates to more than 100,000 screened business addresses in 140 countries.

❏**Multiplier Benefits:** Our commercial officers overseas select product listings for reprint in newspapers, trade journals, and other publications — often in the local language — greatly increasing promotional impact *at no additional cost.*

❏**Direct Response:** Potential business representatives or customers contact you directly, using an address code so you can easily evaluate your *Commecial News USA* promotion results.

Commercial News USA **regularly promotes new U.S. products — those on the market less** than three years — in a range of industry categories. Also eligible for promotion are services, trade and technical literature, and both new and established products in selected industries. All products in *Commercial News USA* are at least 51 percent U.S. parts and 51 percent U.S. labor.

It's easy to participate: Contact your nearest U.S. Department of Commerce district office for a short application. which your trade specialist will help you complete, and send it to *Commercial News USA* along with a photo of your product. We'll publi.sh your information in the next available issue and send you a courtesy copy along with a checklist to help you respond to overseas inquiries. Your trade specialist will also help.you plan a strategy to handle responses effectively.

Commercial News USA promotes your products all over the map!

Reprinted by permission

Herman J. Maggiori

Foreign Buyer Program
TO PROMOTE YOUR PRODUCTS

Show your products to foreign buyers here in the United States!

When you exhibit at our Foreign Buyer shows, you meet potential customers from all over the world — *without leaving the country!* Every year our Foreign Buyer Program supports a number of major domestic trade shows featuring products and services in specific U.S. industries with high export potential. Show organizers cooperate with our staff to encourage foreign attendance, to serve visitors from overseas, and to offer an effective showplace for the latest U.S. technology.

Our officers at U.S. embassies and consulates worldwide recruit qualified foreign buyers to attend the show, as individuals or as members of our organized delegations. Foreign Buyer shows are extensively publicized through embassy and regional commercial newsletters, in *Commercial News USA* catalog-magazine (more than 100,000 overseas distribution). and by foreign trade associations, chambers of commerce, travel agents, government agencies, corporations, import agents, and equipment distributors in targeted markets.

At every Foreign Buyer show, we sponsor an International Business Center where we provide introductions, interpreters, multilingual brochures, counseling, and private meeting rooms for your convenience. As an exhibitor, you enjoy these special benefits:

√ face-to-face meetings with foreign buyers and representatives
√ your products displayed to an international audience
√ fresh international sales leads
√ a chance to create or expand markets overseas
√ on-the-spot export counseling

Foreign Buyer shows present a broad range of products and services, primarily of U.S. origin, with good prospects for increased international sales. Leading industry events in the United States, these shows offer exhibitors the combined support of private show organizers and our professional staff.

Show organizers in your industry will be interested in the special advantages offered by our Foreign Buyer Program. Contact your nearest U.S. Department of Commerce district office for more information, including a list of selected shows.

Our Foreign Buyer Program brings the buyers to you!

U. S. DEPARTMENT OF COMMERCE • INTERNATIONAL TRADE ADMINISTRATION • U.S. AND FOREIGN COMMERCIAL SERVICE

Reprinted by permission

International Trade Administration/US&FCS District Offices

*DENOTES REGIONAL OFFICE WITH SUPERVISORY REGIONAL RESPONSIBILITIES
•DENOTES TRADE SPECIALIST AT A BRANCH OFFICE

ALABAMA
Birmingham — Rm. 302. 2015 2nd Ave. North, Berry Bldg., 35203, (205) 731-1331
ALASKA
Anchorage — 222 West 7th Ave., P.O. Box 32, 99513, (907) 271-5041
ARIZONA
Phoenix — Federal Bldg. & U.S. Courthouse, 230 North 1st Ave., Rm. 3412, 85025, (602) 379-3285
ARKANSAS
Little Rock — Suite 811, Savers Fed. Bldg., 320 W. Capitol Ave., 72201, (501) 378-5794
CALIFORNIA
Los Angeles — Rm. 9200, 11000 Wilshire Blvd., 90024, (213) 209-7104
Santa Ana — 116-A W. 4th St., Suite #1. 92701, (714) 836-2461
San Diego 6363 Greenwich Dr., Suite 145,. (619) 557-5395
San Francisco Fed. Bldg., Box 36013, 450 Golden Gate Ave., 94102, (415) 556-5860
COLORADO
Denver — 680 World Trade Center, 1625 Broadway, 80202, (303) 844-3246
CONNECTICUT
***Hartford** — Rm. 610-B, Fed. Office Bldg. 450 Main St., 06103, (203) 240-3530
DELAWARE
Serviced by Philadelphia District Office
DISTRICT OF COLUMBIA
•**Washington, D.C.** — (Baltimore, Md. District) Rm. 1066 HCHB. Department of Commerce. 14th St. & Constitution Ave.. N.W. 20230, (202) 377-3181

FLORIDA
Miami — Suite 224. Fed. Bldg., 51 S.W. First Ave., 33130, (305) 536-5267
•**Clearwater** 128 North Osceola Ave. 34615, (813) 461-0011
•**Jacksonville** — 3100 University Blvd. South, Suite 200A, 32216, (904) 791-2796
*Orlando College of Business Administration, CEBA 11, Rm. 346, University of Central Florida, 32802, (407) 648-1608
•**Tallahassee** — Collins Bldg., Rm. 401. 107 W. Gaines St., 32304, (904) 488-6469
GEORGIA
Atlanta — Suite 310. 4360 Chamblee Dunwoody Rd., 30341, (404) 452-9101
Savannah 120 Barnard St., A-107, 31401, (912) 944-4204
HAWAII
Honolulu 4106 Fed. Bldg., P.O. Box 50026, 300 Ala Moana Blvd., 96850, (808) 541-1782
IDAHO
•**Boise** (Portland, Ore. District) — Hall of Mirrors Bldg., 700 W. State St., 2nd fl, Boise, Idaho 83720, (208) 334-3857
ILLINOIS
Chicago — Rm. 1406 Mid Continental Plaza Bldg., 55 East Monroe St., 60603, (312) 353-4450
•**Palatine** W.R. Harper College, Algonquin & Roselle Rd., 60067, (312) 397-3000, x2532
•**Rockford** — 515 North Court St., P.O. Box1747, 61110-0247, (815) 987-8123

INDIANA
Indianapolis — One North Capitol Ave., Suite 520, 46204, (317) 226-6214
IOWA
Des Moines 817 Fed. Bldg., 210 Walnut St., 50309, (515) 284-4222
KANSAS
•**Wichita** — (Kansas City, Missouri District) 7591 River Park Pl., Suite 580, 727 North Waco, 67203, (316) 269-6160
KENTUCKY
Louisville — Rm. 636B, Gene Snyder Courthouse and Customhouse Bldg., 601 W. Broadway, 40202, (502) 582-5066
LOUISIANA
New Orleans 432 World Trade Center, No. 2 Canal St., 70130, (504) 589-6546
MAINE
•**Augusta** — (Boston, Massachusetts District) 77 Sewall St., 04330, (207) 622-8249
MARYLAND
Baltimore 413 U.S. Customhouse, 40 South Gay and Lombard Sts., 21202, (301) 962-3560
MASSACHUSETTS
Boston — World Trade Center, Suite 307 Commonwealth Pier Area, 02210, (617) 565-8563
MICHIGAN
Detroit — 1140 McNamara Bldg., 477 Michigan Ave., 48226. (313) 226-3650
•**Grand Rapids** 300 Monroe N.W., Rm. 409, 49503, (616) 456-2411
MINNESOTA
Minneapolis 108 Fed. Bldg., 110 S. 4th St., 55401, (612) 348-1638

Reprinted by permission

MISSISSIPPI
Jackson — 328 Jackson Mall
Office Center, 300 Woodrow
Wilson Blvd., 39213, (601)
965-4388
MISSOURI
***St. Louis** — 7911 Forsyth
Blvd., Suite 610, 63105, (314)
425-3302
Kansas City — Rm. 635. 601
East 12th St., 64106, (816)
426-3141
MONTANA
Serviced by Boise, Idaho
District Office
NEBRASKA
Omaha — 11133 "0" St.,
68137, (402) 221-3664
NEVADA
Reno — 1755 E. Plumb Ln.,
#152, 89502, (702) 785-5203
NEW HAMPSHIRE
**Serviced by Boston District
Office**
NEW JERSEY
Trenton — 3131 Princeton
Pike Bldg., #6, Suite 100,
08648, (609) 989-2100
NEW MEXICO
**Albuquerque (Dallas, Tex
District)** — 625 Silver SW.,
3rd Fl., 87102, (214) 767-
0542
**Santa Fe (Dallas, Tex
District)** — c/o Economic
Develop. and Tourism
Dept.,1100 St. Francis Drive,
87503, (505) 827-0264
NEW YORK
Buffalo 1312 Fed. Bldg., 111
West Huron St., 14202, (716)
846-4191
•Rochester — 111 East Ave.,
Suite 220, 14604, (716) 263-
6480
New York — Fed. Office
Bldg., 26 Fed. Plaza, Rm.
3718, Foley Sq., 10278, (212)
264-0634
NORTH CAROLINA
***Greensboro** 324 W. Market
St.. P.O. Box 1950, 27402,
(919) 333-5345
Serviced by Omaha District
Office

OHIO
***Cincinnati** — 9504 Fed.
Office Bldg., 550 Main St.,
45202, (513) 684-2944
Cleveland — Rm. 600, 668
Euclid Ave., 44114 (216)
522-4750
OKLAHOMA
Oklahoma City — 5
Broadway Executive Park,
Suite 200, 6601 Broadway
Extension, 73116, (405) 231-
5302
•Tulsa — 440 S. Houston St.,
74127, (918) 581-7650
OREGON
Portland — SuitE 242, One
World Trade Center, 121
S.W. Salmon St., 97204,
(503) 326-3001
PENNSYLVANIA
Philadelphia 475 Allendale
Road, Suite 202. King of
Prussia, Pa., 19406, (215)
962-4980
Pittsburgh — 2002 Fed.
Bldg., 1000 Liberty Ave.,
15222, (412) 644-2850
PUERTO RICO
San Juan (Hato Rey) — Rm.
G-SS Fed. Bldg., 00918,
(809) 766-5555
RHODE ISLAND
•Providence (Boston,
Massachusetts District 7
Jackson Walkway, 02903,
(401) 528-5104. ext. 22
SOUTH CAROLINA
Columbia — Strom
Thurmond Fed. Bldg., Suite
172, 1835 Assembly St.,
29201 (803) 765-5345
•Charleston — JC Long
Bldg., Rm. 128, 9 Liberty St.,
29424, (803) 724-4361
SOUTH DAKOTA
Serviced by Omaha District
Office
TENNESSEE
Nashville Suite 1114,
Parkway Towers, 404 James
Robertson Parkway 37219-
1505, (615) 736-5161

•Knoxville — 301 E. Church
Ave., 37915, (615) 549-9268
•Memphis The Falls
Building, Suite 200, 22 North
Front St., 38103, (901) 544-
4137
TEXAS
***Dallas** — Rm. 7AS, 1100
Commerce St., 75242-0787,
(214) 767-0542
•Austin — P.O. Box 12728,
816 Congress Ave., Suite
1200, 78711, (512) 482-5939
Houston — 2625 Fed.
Courthouse, 515 Rusk St.,
77002, (713) 229-2578
UTAH
Salt Lake City — Suite 105,
324 South State St., 84111,
(801) 524-5116
VERMONT
Serviced by Boston District
Office
VIRGINIA
Richmond — 8010 Fed.
Bldg., 400 North 8th St.,
23240, (804) 771-2246
WASHINGTON
Seattle 3131 Elliott Ave.,
Suite 290, 98121, (206) 442-
5616
•Spokane — West 808
Spokane Falls Blvd., Suite
625, 99201, (509) 353-2922
WEST VIRGINIA
Charleston — 3402 Fed.
Bldg., 500 Quarrier St.,
25301, (304) 347-5123
WISCONSIN
Milwaukee — Fed. Bldg.,
U.S. Courthouse, Rm. 606,
517 E. Wisc. Ave., 53202,
(414) 291-3473
WYOMING
Serviced by Denver District
Office

Reprinted by permission

Other Market Research Sources

Depending upon the type of product to be exported, (consumer, industrial, electronic, automotive, etc.), there are numerous additional sources of market information available, many of them at public libraries.

Consulates or Foreign Trade Offices

Much information on general business conditions can be obtained by contacting the consulates, of foreign trade offices or tourist offices of foreign countries located in major U. S. cities. Booklets and studies are published by many foreign governments, their chambers of commerce and banks which contain a great deal of useful information about their countries. Most foreign consulates and banks in the United States have resident commercial or economic officers on their staffs.

Retail Directories

Manufacturers of consumer goods and packaged food products can find a wealth of information regarding distribution in retail stores, department stores, or supermarkets by consulting directories such as *Stores of the World*, published in London by Newman Books Ltd. Many large foreign department stores have resident buying offices in the United States and are always looking for new products. The business and classified sections of many large-city newspapers, such as the *New York Times*, regularly list foreign buyers visiting their cities.

General Directories

There are many general types of directories covering a wide range of products and industries which will give important information about local manufacturers, distributors and retailers. There are also "directories of trade directories," e.g. *Trade Directories of the World*, publishes by Croner Publications of Queens Village, New York, which contains listings of business directories published throughout the world. Some other useful directories include:

Kelly's Business Directory

This contains listings of over 84,000 organizations doing business in the United Kingdom, classified under 10,000 trade and professional headings. Data includes information about each company in a separate section and lists brands and trade-names and the companies who produce the products. A copy of this directory may be obtained through Windsor Court, East Grinstead House, East Grinstead, West Sussex, RH19-1 KB, England.

International Directory of Importers

A seven-volume reference set consisting of two volumes for Europe, and one each for South and Central America, Asia, the Pacific region, the Middle-East and Africa. There are over 100,000 entries in the alphabetical listings under numerous commodity headings. Also included are comprehensive sections with detailed company information. This may be obtained by writing to 195 Dry Creek Road, Healdsburg, California 95448.

The International Trade Statistics Yearbook

Published by the United Nations, Department of International and Social Affairs in New York, this is a two-volume book which gives trade statistics by commodity for 153 countries. The latest edition covers the years 1975-1987, so you would be able to study country and regional trends in both import and export activities. There is detailed data for individual countries and it analyzes the flow of trade between countries. Imports are detailed by commodity classes and are tabulated according to Standard International Trade numbers, giving you data which is in internationally comparable product categories.

Australian Register of Manufacturers and Importers

This lists all Australian importers by product category. Address: Who's Where Publishers Pty. Ltd., 9 Napier Street, North Sydney, N.S.W., Australia.

The Official Export Guide

This guide, published annually, is one of the most comprehensive and useful directories and ought to be in every exporter's library for frequent reference. The contents include practically all the data you need to know about a country's trade, investment data, required documentation and fees to be paid on shipments, import controls, trade restrictions, products which are best prospects for import into the country, and literally dozens of other facts which an international marketer needs to know about the countries with which he is working or intends to visit.

The Oxford Economic Atlas of the World

This Atlas shows in graphic and map form many aspects of the world's manufacturing industries, transportation facilities (air, rail and water), agricultural, mining and metals industries, demographics and societal and political systems. Address: The Oxford Press, Ely House, London, England.

Port Import and Export Reporting Service (PIERS)

PIERS is a service available on a subscription basis from the Journal of Commerce, 110 Wall Street, New York, New York 10005. PIERS tabulates all imports and exports arriving at or departing from 47 major U.S. ports. Data is tabulated weekly, monthly or on-line (according to your needs) and shows the name and location of the U. S. consignee for imports or the U.S. exporter and includes the country of origin or destination and quantities and weights shipped. Utilizing these reports, you can keep track of what your U.S. competition is exporting, and also find out if there are competitors overseas shipping comparable products to the United States.

Trade Associations

Trade Assoications can also be very helpful in supplying market data and memberships lists which can be a source for locating and becoming familiar with competitors in the markets. Check with your industry group's international division for lists of foreign members and other international data available.

Credit Rating Organizations

Organizations such as Dun and Bradstreet as well as large commercial U.S. banks with active foreign divisions, can be excellent sources of information. Both types of organizations have branches or foreign correspondents who provide important commercial credit and payment information which can be most valuable in making selections of distributors or customers with whom you may want to work.

As you can see, there is a wealth of material available to the international marketer which can be useful even before he sets out on a personal exploration of his targeted markets. There is no doubt that personal visits to these markets will provide the best information and data. This will be covered in detail in a later chapter. Doing some thorough homework before you even consider a personal trip will aid you in utilizing your time abroad to the maximum degree possible and help to determine what additional data you need and where and how to find it.

Chapter 4

INITIATING EXPORT OPERATIONS

After completing preliminary target market research, you've made the decision to export! You've decided that exporting your product is the way to go, and you've made a firm commitment to join the growing list of American companies who are successfully marketing their products abroad.

Good! If so many others can do it, why not you? You've already taken the first giant step. There are more ahead. But first things first. Let's now look at everything you want and need to know to get the show on the road. Let's get you and your company organized to enter into the global marketplace.

Assuming you have completed an aggressive, in-depth, and realistic preliminary market survey and selected some prime target markets, and you are convinced that your products will be successfully absorbed by a burgeoning overseas market hungry for quality items, the next step is to decide how you will go about organizing your company to launch your products in the foreign markets you have targeted.

In recent years some companies have established some overseas operations in the form of foreign manufacturing subsidiaries, partners or branch offices. They probably used this approach because of import restrictions which prevented them from exporting U.S. made products. These foreign entities are currently selling only the parent companies' locally manufactured or assembled products, and not importing either the higher quality or high-tech products made in the U.S.A. If the markets in which these foreign operations are being carried out are now ready to accept the U.S. made products, the parent company will have a ready-made sales and distribution channel to import and sell them.

If this is not the case, and most companies do not have such operations, there are several methods of selling products overseas. The most common are to utilize the services of either independent distributors, manufacturer's agents direct sales to end-users and retailers, or a combination of all three of the above. There are also indirect methods which can be considered.

The ultimate decision must be based on the nature of the products involved (manufactured goods and equipment, consumer goods, food or agricultural products etc.), and on the normal or usual methods and channels of distribution used for your type of products in the targeted markets.

Most firms will choose independent stocking distributors in most markets, and agents in markets where it might not be possible to have a distributor because of local legislation and import restrictions prohibiting stocking of imported products for resale.

Another reason for choosing to use an agent is because a product does not lend itself to stocking, e.g. heavy machinery. We will examine all of these possibilities in the following pages.

Initiating Export Operations

There are several approaches to initiating export operations. A manufacturer might consider an indirect approach which could involve working with one or more outside intermediate companies. Sales, for example, could be made to United States buyers who will later export them. Another approach might involve sales to export commission representatives, export management or trading companies, or they might be "piggy-backed" through another non-competing manufacturer's export department. This type of indirect exporting can be accomplished by using the firm's domestic sales and customer service personnel. Many companies however, opt for direct exporting through their own in-house export departments.

Before selecting one of these methods to begin export operations, the manufacturer must review its overall export plan and marketing strategies to decide which method it will adopt and the extent to which it wants to become involved in the export process, and how that choice will coincide with the fulfillment of the overall plan.

The Indirect Approach

The company can consider a minimal involvement by seeking domestic firms who are familiar with exporting and who are actually buyers for overseas end-users or distributors of the company's products. The buyer will pay for and ship the products to the overseas contact thus assuming all the risks of shipment and payment. The manufacturer may not even know the name or location of the ultimate consignee.

A similar type of transaction can be handled by Export Commission Representatives who, on behalf of overseas firms or governments whom they represent in the United States, "shop around" for products their principals require. Some foreign governments maintain official purchasing offices or missions in New York and other major U.S. cities. The representative, agent or official buying office sends out bids or requests for quotations to possible suppliers. You learn who they are and register your company with them so you will be on their bid-list.

On the other hand, a company can determine who these buyers are and have company salesmen call on them to determine if their principals or governments have a need for the company's products.

The representative or agent purchases the products from the manufacturer, pays for them directly, and handles all the details of exporting. For the manufacturing company, this method is akin to a domestic sale.

Another outlet for "domestic exports" for a company not wishing to become fully involved in exporting, is to work through Export Management Companies. The EMC will operate as the export department of several manufacturers which are usually companies who manufacture similar, but non-competing products. They will often work with a manufacturer on a long-term basis under a mutually-agreed-upon contract covering some or all of the manufacturer's products. EMC's usually have exclusivity in all territories to be covered, but others might be willing to work on a non-exclusive basis.

Contracts should initially be limited to one or two years to allow the EMC to establish the product line throughout the territories, set up proper distribution and sales outlets and develop a good customer base, and the manufacturer will have time to judge the success or failure of the EMC. Here too, the manufacturer does not assume all the risks involved in exporting, but if a suitable contract is worked out, it can maintain some control of the overall operation, even to knowing the ultimate destination of products.

In order to gauge the effectiveness of these indirect exporting approaches, the manufacturer should keep track of all sales made to the outside companies. When these indirect export sales reach a significant volume in the number of foreign markets, it is probably time for the manufacturer to consider the benefits of establishing its own in-house export department. It should be remembered that in most cases the intermediate exporter either receives a commission from his principals, or marks up his selling prices to them to obtain his profit. These practices could make the manufacturer's products non-competitive against local products or those exported from other countries, which means the EMC is not getting as many sales as he could in a given market; or perhaps because of his higher pricing, he has not been able to enter the market at all.

Direct Exporting

Exporting on a direct basis with an in-house export department or international division is therefore the approach used by the majority of companies who wish to be fully involved in their operations, in complete control of pricing, shipping and financing, and obtaining a more intimate knowledge of their markets.

An effective international operation will usually employ a combination of the four basic approaches discussed. Based on the ability of the company to provide resources to the export effort, the basic structure for such an organization could be either one person and an assistant, or a department based on separate management from domestic sales, headed by an experienced international sales and marketing executive, preferably reporting to the chief executive officer, or to a senior operating executive of the company such as the executive vice-president.

Organizing for Export

While some companies, especially smaller ones, may feel the chief sales executive or sales manager should be responsible for export sales, this may not necessarily be the most effective structure. The domestic sales executive may not have adequate training, experience or patience to deal with dozens of diverse foreign markets to allow him to make correct decisions regarding quotations, shipments, collections or contractual disputes. Thus sales and opportunities for sales could be lost by misunderstandings or lack of knowledge about how a given market operates.

In order to take advantage of all opportunities for sales and sales expansion, there should be one person solely responsible for conducting export sales operations with direct line responsibility to senior management. Later in this chapter we will discuss in detail the objectives, functions and background of the international executive.

The start-up export unit can be initially staffed with the international executive, a secretary and one or more clerical persons. As indicated earlier, the new-to-export company can utilize not only its own in-house export unit to obtain sales, but also one or more of the indirect outlets.

While the head of the department formulates and carries out the broad market planning and marketing effort in accordance with the overall company export strategy, initial sales can be made through the indirect outlets. It need not be necessary to include in the start-up unit the many support functions which a full-fledged sales department requires, such as an order entry, invoicing, packing, or shipping group. As long as each support operation is made aware of any special differences in their normal procedures required by the export unit, full use of these operations can usually be made by the export department.

Often the differences can be handled by the respective supporting departments with little or no deviation from their standard practices. In those situations where this might not be so, export personnel can modify certain elements of a transaction in order to conform to export requirements. For example, some export shipments require more hard copies of invoices than the computer is programmed to produce, or the invoice will require certain declarations or statements on them. The export department simply accepts the number of invoices available, types the required material on them, and with the excellent copier machines available today, makes the required set of export invoices. The sale is then entered on the company books and credited to the export department in the normal manner.

When the company has attained a substantial volume of sales, a full staff may then be put in place. This staff, under the direction of the international executive, could consist of sales managers for different world regions, e.g. Europe, Asia, Africa etc., sales correspondents handling administrative details and customer service for each of the sales managers, clerical or secretarial personnel for each region, separate customer service and/or technical or field service personnel, and invoicing, documentation, packing and shipping departments.

No less a part of the export operating unit than company employees are the overseas distributors and agents which the company appoints in every market. Separate chapters following are devoted to establishing and maintaining a worldwide distribution distributor/agent network.

There are other international organizational structures possible depending upon the size of the company, its product line or lines and company organization of those products, such as specialized product divisions.

Large international corporations often have separate autonomous subsidiary companies responsible to the parent company chairman, chief executive officer or a corporate international operations chief. The subsidiary, headed by a president and a full corporate staff, may be structured regionally; regionally by different product lines; and with each region or product having its own staff of sales, marketing, service and support managers and operating personnel. Often such a subsidiary company will also handle the export of other non-related manufacturers' products as a so-called cooperative exporter.

Additionally, some companies become large enough in their international operations to warrant establishing sales or manufacturing facilities in one or more overseas locations.

In addition to, or instead of, establishing company-owned manufacturing, sales and marketing operations overseas, companies can expand their international operations into licensing or joint-venture arrangements with one or more partners.

Moreover, organizational structure can be so planned that the United States international unit can coordinate the export of the company's overseas manufacturing subsidiaries, although it is more common that the foreign-producing unit will handle export orders directly from its base of operations.

In any company, regardless of size, the responsibility of the export unit must be clearly described so that all other company units understand the function of the export department. In most companies the export unit is responsible for all facets of sales and marketing throughout the world except for the 50 United States.

Many companies also exclude sales to Canada because of the special economic and political relationships existing between the two countries. Some would also exclude Puerto Rico as an export territory because of its commonwealth status, but experienced exporters know this is an incorrect policy because, by its very nature, language and culture, Puerto Rico is decidedly a major part of the Latin American region and merits the same research, study and attention as any other foreign market.

The International Executive and Staff

As discussed earlier, the in-house export or international operations unit should be headed by a full-time executive responsible for all phases of the company's international activities. Since this person will, in effect, represent your company in many parts of the world to users, distributors, bankers and government officials, and will have to project to all of these a favorable image of your company, your products, and yes, even of the United States, the selection of this executive should be undertaken very carefully. Much thought and consideration should be given to basic personal characteristics.

Ideally, he or she should be a person of high business and personal integrity, able to perform as an entrepreneur with limited direction by senior management as a poised and confident professional. Since the executive may eventually be responsible for a large export activity including considerable staff and foreign distributors, he or she must also have strong administrative and personnel handling skills. Some experience in international trade, fluency in foreign languages as well as knowledge and awareness of cultural differences in the many countries with which the company will work, are all pluses to look for in a candidate for this important position.

In addition, prior travel in overseas markets, a capacity for hard work (overseas travel sounds exciting, but it can be very arduous often involving long workdays in sometimes primitive, hot and dirty locations, strange customs, language and food), and familiarity with your product line, are all additional things to look for when interviewing.

Women As International Executives

In the above paragraph we used the words, "he or she" in talking about the international executive. We did so because the high qualifications required for the position are not the exclusive characteristics of men. Many women have the same or better abilities for the job. In some cases, they even have an advantage. For example, Jolie Soloman, writing in the *Wall Street Journal,* noted in a June 2, 1989 article, "...many women feel they have an advantage in business overseas for the same reason they have trouble in business at home: their different upbringing. Consultants say women are generally more patient than men and more interested in creating harmony and consensus." These qualities are most important to successful negotiations with overseas colleagues. We have personally known many outstanding women international executives.

While a sensitivity to local cultures is important in respect to sending a woman executive to countries such as Saudi Arabia, Pakistan or Japan, such concerns should not dissuade a company from having a woman manager work in most countries. Although in some cultures the local women have many restraints on their activities, foreign women are usually treated differently. The very fact that they are foreigners provides acceptance allowing them to work comfortably and capably with any overseas business person.

The important thing is to hire the person who best fits the personal and business qualifications you have established for the position.

It is of the utmost importance also that the international executive have a full voice in the company's planning, marketing and budgetary activities in order that the international unit's needs, programs and problems are given consideration at the highest levels of management. This means putting the company's commitment to exporting into action to enable the international executive to work effectively with other company executives and inter-departmental support services.

Another point to keep in mind regarding the position of international sales and marketing director is that there will be strong competition from the company's foreign competitors, many of whom are more geared to overseas sales than many American companies. A higher priority is placed on overseas sales by many European and Asian companies than by American firms and their international executives are usually highly-trained, experienced and multi-lingual. Give yourself a fighting chance in the world markets in which your man or woman will be facing this formidable competition, and hire the best you can find.

There are many titles currently in vogue which can be given to the head of the international unit. Some of these are: export sales and marketing manager, international sales manager, director international sales and marketing, vice president international sales, vice president international operations. When deciding on the title to use, keep in mind that to foreigners, the position of the international manager in his company's hierarchy is very important. They need to know that the person with whom they are dealing occupies an important position is the company, that he has authority to deal with them, and that his decisions and negotiations will be honored by the company. Very often these points are made clear by the American executive's title.

Be aware that in many international departments, the title export manager is given to the person who supervises the processes of order entry, invoicing, export licensing, packing, shipping and financing, i.e. all the administrative export functions except those relating to sales, marketing and policy administration.

Typical job descriptions for the head of an international department and other staff positions could be as follows:

Position Descriptions
Director International Sales and Marketing
Reports to: The President

Objective: To establish a corporate, long-term global international sales and marketing unit with responsibility for market research and planning, formulating policy, and developing and implementing sales, distribution and marketing programs to obtain and maintain maximum sales and profits.

Basic Responsibilities
- Establish operating policies
- Select, train and supervise personnel; establish duties and procedures for the department.
- Develop and operate within annual sales and expense budgets.
- Establish export selling prices, discounts and payments terms.
- Establish and maintain distribution and representation channels and seek their cooperation in preparing long-range programs for initiating and increasing sales and profits.
- Travel to overseas markets to perform personal market studies, evaluate and direct distributors' efforts, and establish personal contact with end-users and other contacts within the market.
- Recommend sales and product training programs for distributors and other programs to improve market share.
- Identify new products which could be brought into overseas markets.
- Establish and maintain strong liaison with all company support groups—planning, manufacturing, engineering, accounting, new product development.
- Establish connections with freight forwarders, banks, and insurance companies to move, finance and protect export shipments.
- Expand international operations by developing prospects for joint-ventures, licensing, acquisitions and overseas subsidiary and sales companies.

Export Manager (or Manager—Export Administration)

Reports to: Director International Sales and Marketing
Objectives: To supervise, train, direct and coordinate export administration personnel.
To maintain a steady flow of export orders, shipments and documentation to provide staffing for all customer service activities.
Basic Responsibilities
- Supervise export department personnel
- Establish and maintain export department systems:
Order Entry

Export Invoicing

Order follow-up with manufacturing

• Establish export packing specifications and supervise packing personnel.

• Maintain control of incoming Letters of Credit.

Establish system to keep track of expiration dates.

Examine terms and conditions of all Letters of Credit.

Establish liaison with banks.

• Establish relationships with freight forwarders (air and sea), shipping companies

• Establish and implement company export statistics reporting system.

• Establish systems and procedure to implement U. S. export licensing regulations.

• Train and supervise in-house sales correspondents.

• Maintain close working relationship with all company support groups.

• Assist the Director of International Sales and Marketing as requested.

• If all of a company's products are subject to U. S. export licensing, it may be necessary when some volume of sales is reached, to include on staff an experienced person to interpret and implement the Export Control Regulations, and perform all the tasks required, such as filing applications for licenses, keeping track of shipments and values made against each of them, making sure foreign distributors comply with controls, etc. (See further discussion of U. S. Export Licensing in Chapter 3).

Export Sales Correspondent (Customer Service Representative)

Reports to: The Export Manager

Objectives: To maintain a prompt flow of correspondence between the home office and the world-wide distributor/agent network.

Basic Responsibilities

• Maintain close liaison with overseas distributors/agents, OEM customers in assigned countries.

- Respond to all distributor/agent and customer inquiries regarding products, orders, shipping, payment problems etc.
- Interpret order and pricing details, financing, import license, Letter of Credit requirements and conditions.
- Check compliance with required special invoicing, declarations, packing and shipping details.
- Maintain close liaison with freight forwarders, banks and other entities dealing with companys overseas representatives and customers.

Note: In some companies, after sufficient volume of sales has been built up and there is a widespread distributor network, or, if a company has many distributors plus customers (OEMs) to whom it sells directly, several sales correspondents may be needed to handle the large volume of correspondence, orders and problems.

In such cases, each correspondent is assigned a group of countries within a specific world region or parts thereof, e.g. Latin America, Europe, Asia, Pacific etc. Each correspondent should have or acquire intimate knowledge of his or her assigned countries including its language, economics, cultures and business practices.

Clerical Staff

- Shipping and Documentation
- Order entry and pricing
- Secretarial

Technical Service and Repair Functions

If products are of a nature that require in-house service, repair or replacement, it may be necessary to have one or more persons dedicated to performing these functions for the export division. They may be part of the export operation, or be assigned to service products for the export customers.

In many cases companies train their foreign distributors to perform at least some, if not most, service and repair jobs in the foreign territories; however, some reserve the right to perform major service activities (such as repair of a printed circuit board) in-house by having products or components returned. (See Product Service Agreement at the end of Chapter 9).

In some cases, if the product is of a high-technology, or very complicated or exceptionally large, e.g. turbines, steel mill equipment and the like, companies will have highly-trained staffs of technical experts or sales engineers who travel world-wide, or who may even be resident in several regions around the world ready to provide trouble-shooting, make repairs, advise distributors and customers on technical matters or give technical seminars.

The Export Department

The charts on the following pages illustrate some possible ways companies can set up their export departments from the start-up stage to a full-fledged international division with overseas operating units.

Chart I can be used in sections starting the export program with a sales and marketing director, responsible to the company CEO or executive vice president. He will be doing the market research and planning, formulating sales and financing, policies and strategies for market entry and distribution, and obtaining some sales.

The manager of export, (export manager) administration, or an assistant to the director, will handle order entry, pricing, processing and the documentation for shipping and financing.

The secretary will handle incoming and outgoing correspondence for both people and probably learn to take care of some routine matters on her/his own to speed the flow of responses.

As the company moves ahead in its export operation and markets are added, orders increase and there is a steady flow of sales, additional personnel as shown on the chart can be added to handle the increased volume and special needs such as export licensing and technical service and support.

Chart II shows how a fully integrated manufacturing company has organized its in-house export department for exporting its U.S. made products as well as for the administration of its overseas manufacturing subsidiaries in the United Kingdom and its warehouses and sales offices in Canada, Mexico, France and Germany.

This chart does not include an additional eleven people making up the full international division. This group was the responsibility of the manager of export administration and included the positions shown on Chart I among others. In some cases two or three people performed similar functions for the several overseas units.

However you organize, whether small or large, do all you can to utilize company support functions and services. This will help you to keep your export organization "lean" in terms of personnel and other expenses, and you won't have to "re-invent the wheel" to accomplish what needs to be done to have a smooth-running, competent, international operation. Every company has its specialized units such as advertising, accounting, legal, finance, manufacturing etc. Use them to your best advantage.

ORGANIZATION CHART I

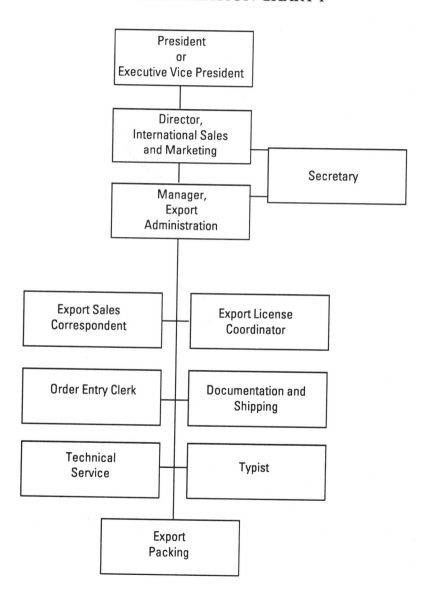

ORGANIZATION CHART II

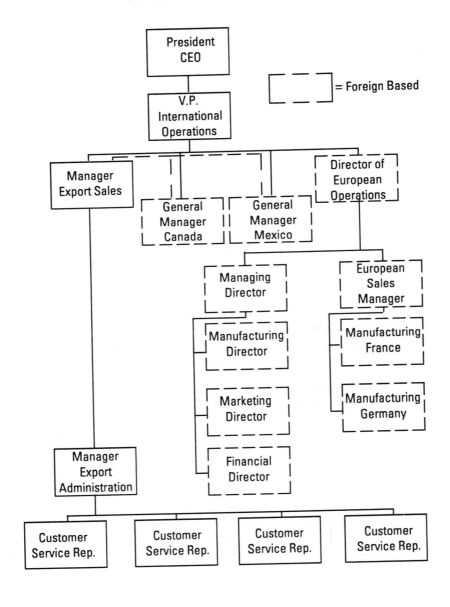

Chapter 5

DO I CHOOSE A DISTRIBUTOR OR AN AGENT?

This decision is a "biggie", and vital to your financial and business success in overseas markets. Do you need a distributor to stock your products, sell them, and be your presence in a foreign market, or should you choose an agent acting as your salesman to sell your products and send you orders? Not an easy choice to make unless you know the advantages adherent to each. Go slowly! Think carefully! The future success of your company's export program will ride on the type and quality of overseas representation you select at the outset. Time and consideration spent here will pay off in the future through sales and peace of mind. Remember, the people you choose to work with will, in effect, become members of your corporate team.

Establishing a worldwide distributor/agent network is by far one of the most important and rewarding functions an international executive is called upon to perform. The foreign distributors and agents selected by you will be your eyes and ears in foreign territories, stocking and selling your products and representing your company in world markets. You will learn a great deal from them. They will project your company image and promote its products throughout the territories in which they work. They can make your company's name well known in the countries in which they represent you and throughout the world. It is vital, therefore, that the choice of distributors or agents be made with the utmost care because they will be people with whom you will need to establish close and long-term relationships which could prove to be most valuable assets to your company. In addition, they will often become good, personal friends.

Do you know the differences between distributors and agents and the advantages and disadvantages of one over the other? Let's take a comprehensive look.

The Distributor

A distributor is an independent businessman or firm who imports for his own account. He purchases products at the best discount available for stocking and re-selling them to end-users at a mark-up which provides him profit. A distributor enables a manufacturer to deal with only one customer in a foreign market—the distributor himself. Some of the many other basic benefits accruing to the manufacturer who uses an independent stocking distributor are:

1. A strong incentive to promote and sell the products. Since a distributor has a significant personal investment in the company by virtue of the products he has purchased for his stock, you can be sure he will promote and sell that stock.

2. The manufacturer need not make a large capital investment in the market.

3. A distributor's orders will be for larger quantities than a manufacturer would receive from individual customers in the territory, thereby providing savings to the company in manufacturing, invoicing, packing, shipping and financing the products.

4. The credit risk entailed in shipping to many customers is eliminated for the manufacturer and is assumed by the distributor.

5. The distributor has a sales force which can be trained in the use, sale and service of your products.

6. The distributor's sales force provides a local sales organization to cover the territory regularly and pay repeat calls to check on customer satisfaction. Often the distributor will be selling your products to some of his regular customers for other items he represents.

Types of Distributors

Distributors come in many different shapes and sizes, and perform various and diverse functions. The nature of your products will dictate the type of distributor for which you will search. You must determine if, in your target markets, your products are sold through "normal" distribution channels, or if they are such that you would require a highly specialized distributor. Some distributors handle various types of products and sometimes hundreds of different items in many different trades such as hardware, industrial, textile or consumer goods.

Others carry only a few specialized items in these categories, but from many different manufacturers. Still others have become so specialized, they will stock products of only one or two manufacturers. As an example, a manufacturer who wants to export small machine tools must determine from prior research of foreign markets if his machine tools require a specialist to sell, install, service and train customers in using them. He must know if a "general" type industrial distributor can give him adequate coverage and service in the market. Even before he begins the actual search, evaluation and selection process, it behooves the manufacturer to make this decision carefully.

A clue to the type of distributor you will require in your foreign markets can be found by studying the types of distribution used by your company's domestic sales group in the U.S. market. Then adapt your thinking and searching for someone similar overseas. A word of caution in this respect however, because as you have seen in our earlier discussions, there are many factors present in foreign markets which are not true of the U. S. market. So you will not necessarily be looking for exact duplicates of your domestic distributors.

The Manufacturer's Agent

There are sometimes good reasons for working with agents as opposed to independent stocking distributors. While the two differ legally and in the way they will work for you, many of their basic operating practices are quiet similar. Agents, like distributors, make a commitment to sell and promote your product line in a given territory. The prime difference between them is that agents do not stock your product. In their sales capacity they will call on customers, obtain orders from them, and send them to you. You must ship them directly to the customers, and when they pay you, you pay the agents a commission on the sale. Agents should do all the other things a distributor does to promote, advertise, exhibit and service your products.

When To Use An Agent

While working with agents may, in some countries, be either the best or only way to enter a market, a company should also be aware that this method of selling in foreign markets means that it must deal directly with many end-users, sometimes several hundred. The company must then be prepared to deal with the problems associated with carrying a large overseas customer load and to assume the credit and commercial risks this would entail.

The credit risk can be somewhat mitigated if, as indicated earlier, you clearly specify to the agent that his commission is not due and payable until after the company has received payment for the goods shipped. Then, if a payment problem arises, the agent can be called upon to visit the customer and press for payment. Otherwise, he will not receive his commission. Knowing that his commission will be delayed, or possibly not paid at all, if a customer defaults on his obligation, the agent should, in the beginning, make every effort to check on a customer's credit-worthiness before sending an order to you.

Companies who have manufacturing or sales subsidiaries abroad often use agents as their local sales force rather than hiring salesmen as full time employees. Since agents are paid commission only on orders shipped or paid for, the company is not burdened with on-going payroll expenses. Most frequently however, agents are utilized in markets where local laws or restrictions preclude using an independent distributor who will stock the products for re-sale, or in small, less-developed countries where distribution is not yet a fully developed art.

Agents can also be used successfully by companies who manufacture heavy equipment, machinery, aircraft, specialized vehicles or military equipment, or other big-ticket items which cannot be easily stocked.

Another case when a company might decide to use an agent instead of a stocking distributor is if the market is too small to warrant the carrying of large stocks of products by a distributor, yet the company knows it could sell some quantity there. In such cases an agent would be the ideal sales channel to use. An example of such a market would be Cyprus. There is good potential in this market for many products, however, since it is a small country with a small industrial and consumer base, the market for many products would be saturated.

Agents' Sales Commissions

As noted above, it is usually agreed upon that the agents' sales commission in a pre-arranged amount, will be due and payable after the principal has been paid by the customer. There could be problems, however, in the method you use in paying an agent.

Some countries have stringent regulations prohibiting the payment of sales commissions in foreign currency. Several countries, for example India, require that the commission due to be paid, be indicated on proforma invoices or sales contracts which are sent to the agent at the outset of the negotiations and commission payments are not included in the foreign exchange cost of that transaction. These proformas and/or sales contracts must be registered with and approved by the import authorities prior to the issuance of an import license. In such cases, commissions are paid by the importer (end-user) in local currency.

While most agents in countries with such requirements accept these practices, some will try to circumvent them because they want to obtain hard currency in payment of their commission. They will therefore request a principal to "play games" with commissions and to state on the proforma invoice or the sales contract an amount less than the full percentage to be paid locally. The agent then requests the principal to send a check in dollars for the difference to his U.S.A. bank account. Be alert! This is a dangerous practice and can lead to severe penalties for both parties. The laws and regulations regarding payment of commission must be carefully checked for each country, and corporate legal advice should be sought regarding U. S. law on the subject before agreeing to any such scheme.

Choosing An Agent

Choosing an agent should be done even more carefully than choosing a distributor, using basically the same checklist to evaluate potential. Ideally an agent will be one who is already representing similar, but non-competitive, products, and be familiar with your industry. In your selection, be cognizant that there are so-called "order-takers", or "collectors", who have caused a lot of grief to many companies. There are, unfortunately, a lot of them out there!

"Order takers" sit back and wait for customers to come to them, rather than go out in the field and actively promote and sell products. They take on too many lines making it impossible to do justice to more than a few of them, and these will only be the ones they consider easy to sell or pay high commissions.

"Collectors" are much the same. They write to dozens of companies soliciting catalogs but with no real interest in actively representing most of them.

You must be sure the agent you select will devote adequate time and effort to learning your products and promoting them diligently. He should have a good reputation in his country as an honest, hard-working representative and be respected by his principals.

A lot of money, time and effort can be lost, as well as many good sales opportunities, because of lazy, incompetent agents. The good reputation of your company can also be damaged by such poor representation.

Plan your checklist carefully and make your choice only after you have thoroughly checked all sources of information about your prospect.

Advantages of Working With An Agent

1. Selling prices in the market can be closely controlled by the manufacturer because the agent sells to customers from the manufacturer's price list.
2. The manufacturer can exercise more direct control over credit terms and policies extended to customers in the agent's territory.
3. The manufacturer will know the names of all the customers who purchase his products, a fact which will help him to get to know the market more intimately.
4. In many markets it would probably be easier, or at the very least, less costly to terminate an agent or to change some terms of the contract, than it would be with a distributor.
5. The manufacturer can exercise considerably more control over the activities of an agent than he can over those of a distributor.

Keep in mind however, that although the manufacturer will have somewhat more control over an agent, this must be measured against the major disadvantages of the manufacturer having to accept many orders, usually small ones, as opposed to the normally large orders from distributors. He will also have to bear the credit risks for every customer from whom the agent takes an order.

Having digested the foregoing information and studied your markets, you should now be ready to make the important decision on who will sell your products overseas—a distributor or an agent. In some cases you may even have to choose both!

Your decision on whom you will work with in a given market will depend heavily upon the type of products you are selling, the customary channels of distribution employed in your target markets, and whether or not regulations in a particular market mandates the use of agents.

In the absence of prohibiting legislation, most companies have found working with independent stocking distributors to be more economical, advantageous and profitable. Since most exporters choose to use distributors in most markets, our discussion in the following chapters will focus principally on the methods for locating distributors and the criteria to be used for selecting them. Keep in mind however, that many of the same methods and criteria used for locating and selecting distributors can also be applied to locating and selecting agents with the obvious exception of the physical warehouse criterion required of a stocking distributor.

It is relatively easy to find an agent who will offer to sell your products on a commission basis. There is no investment on his part except a little time to learn something about your product and to put out a few "feelers" in the marketplace.

Before you expend to much of your time and money setting up an agent who makes such an offer to you, be sure he will expend his time and money to put effort and time in promoting and selling your line. Check carefully other lines an agent is representing. He may be carrying a competitive line and may be hoping to "lock-up" the market by taking on yours so no one else can get in and compete with him.

Giant steps are great to take, but look before you leap!

Chapter 6

LOCATING DISTRIBUTOR CANDIDATES

You've already come a long way. You have decided to work with distributors in most of your target markets. Great! Now, how do you go about finding the ones who will represent your company in foreign markets where your trade names and company reputation do not yet ring a bell with prospective customers.

Searching out and selecting the right distributor can be time consuming and tedious, but careful selection is important if you want lucrative sales and a financially successful venture into the world of overseas selling.

Usually your overall international plan will determine how to go about locating overseas distributors. A basic consideration is the cost involved in the search because building a successful distributor network does require time and expense, notably in the amount of foreign travel required in visiting prospects and in the final selection process. This should be part of the corporate commitment since having a good network of distributors will enable you to obtain good market share around the world resulting in substantial and profitable sales. You may have to go through a series of distributors in given markets before you find one with whom you are completely satisfied. Therefore, the selection process must be undertaken with great care. It is a good idea to have a list of several candidates in each target market, investigate each one of them, and choose the best two or three as determined from preliminary investigation. You can then use this list to make your final choice.

An easy way to start the initial search is to review all the letters of inquiry you might have received from foreign distributors in various countries who are interested in carrying your line of products. They may know your company by reputation from having seen your products in a U.S. trade show, or from advertisements in U.S. publications, many of which are circulated overseas. Some of these should prove to be excellent candidates for consideration since they already have an apparent interest in your company.

Be aware though that many overseas distributors are "collectors." They often write to U. S. companies requesting literature, not out of any real interest in handling their product lines, but out of curiosity to see what new products may be available. Agents, perhaps, are more prone to do this, collecting hundreds of catalogs and displaying them in their offices so anyone (especially U.S. international executives) visiting them will believe they are actually representing all the companies whose catalogs and brochures are strung out on racks or tables in the agent's office.

There is probably no way you can screen out the collector from one who has real interest in your company and your products, so it is a good idea to respond to such inquiries with a small amount of product literature, perhaps a couple of single-page brochures and a cover letter designed to elicit a response which will indicate the extent, if any, of the inquirer's interest.

Sources

Don't lose heart! There are still many other ways you can find out who's out there who might be interested in working with you.

Do you know some business colleagues who export non-competitive products in the same or similar industry or business? Ask them about their overseas distributors. Most people involved in international sales are more than willing to help someone who is just getting started. Passing on information such as names of distributors is one way of being of real assistance. They probably can supply the names of people who would be interested in taking on your line. If they are actually working in the same basic industry or trade, they could be strong candidates who will sell your products to customers to whom they are already selling other similar products. This will give you a quick start in those markets. A sample letter to a potential distributor follows:

Herman J. Maggiori

Sample letter to a prospective distributor

A. B. C. Company, Inc.
4 Porter Road
Pinewood, Ct. 06051

April 11, 1991

Mr. Kian Ho Yung
X.Y.Z. Distribution Company
5 Woochow Road
Hong Kong, B.C.C.

Dear Mr. Kian,

We have received your name from Mr. Allan Stevens, the international sales director of Kellingwood Manufacturing Company, Philadelphia, Pa. Mr. Stevens told us you have done an excellent job of selling his products as Kellingwood's authorized distributor in Hong Kong. He mentioned that you might be interested in our line.

Our company manufactures a similar, but non-competing product - a computerized graphic arts machine designed to automate production of letters and graphic symbols. Since you have worked so well for Kellingwood Manufacturing Company serving the same basic industries and customers for which our products are designed, we think you might be interested in adding our line to those which you are already selling.

We are enclosing several brochures describing all of the equipment we manufacture. We will appreciate your reading this literature and letting us know if you might be interested in distributing our products. We are also inclosing a copy of our most recent annual report so you will know something about our company.

Our initial market research has shown that our equipment would have good acceptance in your market, and would provide you with a good volume of sales at what we believe would be a good mark-up.

If you are interested, we would like to hear from you and in your response we would appreciate your commenting on the following:

* The size of your facilities (warehouse etc.)
* Your annual dollar volume of sales.
* Facilities for demonstrating equipment
* The size of your inside and outside sales force.
* The extent of your territory and how frequently it is covered by your sales force.
* The average number of sales calls made per week.
* How you would propose to market our products in your territory, (advertising, trade shows, seminars etc.)
* Any other comments to help us know you and your operation better.

If you would be interested in handling our line, and your comments to the above are favorable, I will plan to visit you in the near future to give you full details about representation.

I look forward to hearing from you.

Sincerely,

Matthew Griffen,
Director, International Sales

Note: The above letter, with appropriate variations in wording, can be used to follow up on inquiries you receive directly from distributors abroad, or to determine if there is real interest on the part of distributors or agents whose names you have found in directories or other sources.

The U. S. Department of Commerce

One of the prime sources for leads to distributors is the U.S. Department of Commerce International Trade Administration district offices. Don't fail to contact your local district office at the very outset of your search for overseas distributors. There is a wealth of information available to you, much of it at no cost or at a nominal fee.

These offices, for example, can provide a variety of services such as a *Trade Opportunities Program* which will identify possible overseas distributors.

Another ITA service is called *Matchmakers*, designed to locate potential distributors and then set up meetings for you in their respective countries. This is an excellent program because the prospects have been pre-screened and evaluated for you by U. S. Embassy personnel.

Additional ITA services to help you find distributors include *Catalog and Video/Catalog* exhibitions which allow you to use U.S. Embassy resources to show your catalogs or videos to potential distributors or agents around the world. *Foreign Buyer Program* allows you to meet potential representatives in the United States when your company exhibits at ITA's *Foreign Buyer Shows;* or you can participate in one of ITA's 20 or 30 annual *Overseas Trade Missions* scheduled for selected countries. The article on pages 72 and 73, reprinted from the August 1988 issue of *Business America*, the Department of Commerce's magazine of international trade, describes a successful trade mission to India and will give you an idea of the types of market information which can be obtained from these missions.

All of these and other super-services which can lead to locating distributors in far-flung parts of the world were described in the exhibits in Chapter 3.

There is literally no end to the valuable help you, as a taxpayer, can request and receive from the U. S. Government to help you establish a global distributor network.

In addition to services and programs available through the International Trade Administration, the U. S. & Foreign Commercial Service (US&FCS) provides access to distributor-finding programs through its on-site staffs working in over 60 countries around the world. These staff members have intimate knowledge of the countries in which they are stationed. Many of them are nationals of the countries. They are well-acquainted with the industrial, commercial and financial communities and can supply qualified leads and information about prospective distributors.

In many countries, the US&FCS operates *U. S. Trade Centers* and, among other activities, sponsors trade shows. For example, the U.S. Trade Center in Mexico City has, for eight consecutive years, staged highly successful all-American exhibitions which have helped many U.S. firms locate good, reliable distributors or agents. These REP-COM exhibitions provide a very inexpensive ($900 for an initial booth, $700 for each additional booth) means for U.S. companies to exhibit their products, usually over a three-day period.

The Trade Center provides everything needed to mount a company's display including booth construction, graphics, carpeting, furniture, customs clearance assistance, unpacking, installation, repacking equipment, reception and hospitality services, utilities and housekeeping. Most important, it also guarantees a large, qualified attendance at the exhibition, and if you have told the project manager you are looking for a distributor or agent, he or she will be sure some qualified prospects are invited for you to interview so you can give an on-the-spot demonstration of all of your products and answer questions as well. U.S. embassies and consulates abroad also have commercial attaches who can be very helpful in locating distributor candidates. You should send your product literature to the foreign post and explain any special qualifications you would like the distributor to possess. Most embassies employ foreign nationals in their commercial sections who have a wide range of expertise in the commerce and industry of their countries and are qualified to provide expert services.

Directories

There are many business directories published in the U. S. and overseas which can provide excellent leads not only for possible distributors, but also for customers. Consult *Trade Directories of the World* for a listing of all such directories. Your district office of the Commerce Department, your State Office of International Trade, the Regional International Trade Office of the Small Business Association, and your public library may all have world directories available. Also, go back to Chapter 3 under the section "Other

Market Research Sources." Many of the directories suggested will be good sources for locating distributors.

In addition, U.S. and foreign organizations can make available lists of potential distributors. Among these are various industry and trade associations in which some of the best foreign distributors have membership, and foreign chambers of commerce, some of which have offices in major U.S. cities as well as in their home countries.

Other excellent sources of information for locating possible distributors include the many U. S. banks which have active international departments and overseas correspondent banks, ocean and air freight carriers and courier services, and export magazine publishers.

Probably the best method of locating distributors is your own personal trip abroad. This will normally be reserved for the final screening and selection of your previously selected candidates.

EVALUATING AND SELECTING POTENTIAL DISTRIBUTORS

In the search for distributors, you will no doubt have developed a large file of potential names, data and information about possible distributors in many markets. At this point, the next step is to develop a checklist of all the elements you feel a good distributor should have to be successful in selling your products in specific markets. This checklist will help you to separate the chaff from the potential wheat, and to come up with a list of candidates with whom you will want to have further discussion.

In creating this checklist, keep in mind that you cannot have uniform standards for distribution in all countries. Much depends upon the many differences among world markets and the people who work in them as well as differences in selling and in business and commercial practices. There are also differences in cultures which have a bearing on how distributors in different countries conduct their businesses, not only with local customers, but also with the principals whom they represent.

Your evaluation checklist should include a number of factors to be applied to all of the candidates you will consider. There will undoubtedly be other factors which you will either add or subtract from your checklist depending on the market with which you are dealing.

The criteria you establish for selection of a distributor are not the lone factors that will enable you to come up with the best distributor. Even though a firm may meet all the major standards which you have decided make a good distributor, it does not necessarily follow that you should choose it to be your distribution outlet. Meeting the standards allows you to pare down your list to "possibles," but the most important factor is personal contact when the final determination is made.

A great deal of personal judgement must also be applied. There are many times when an executive's experience in dealing with people will prompt him to "just know" when a person is the right choice, even though he may not have scored 100% on the checklist of desired qualities.

The Evaluation Checklist

The list itself can be a very simple one with just a few elements required, or it can be a long list incorporating 20 or 30 factors. Most companies feel there are probably between 10 and 15 areas which must be included in evaluating a distributor's suitability to handle its products. Some specific elements to which most companies want answers are:

1. Interest in your products and your company

This is sometimes difficult to determine from initial research unless you have had a letter indicating real interest or have spoken to a candidate on the telephone (Keep your eye out for "collectors!").

2. Experience With A Similar Product Or Industry

If the distributor is already selling similar or allied, but non-competing products, it will indicate he is already aware of the salability of your products and probably knows who the customers are who will be interested in them. This is a strong factor in his ability to obtain sales for you without too much time lost having to research the market for customers.

3. Types of Customers Distributor is Now Selling

Find out if the prospect is working with the customer categories who purchase and use your products. Find out if he sells to end-users, retail customers, original equipment manufacturers (OEMs). If he sells to local or national government agencies, find out if he has good relationships with the buying authorities.

4. Reputation

The candidate should have a good commercial reputation with:

a. Customers

b. Banks

c. Customs services

d. Government agencies

e. His colleagues

f. Foreign principals

You will want to work with someone who is well-thought of in terms of his ethics, business acumen, honesty, and personal integrity.

5. Credit Standing

This is one of the most important criteria you will need to judge. The distributor you will want to work with should have adequate and sound financing and working capital. He will need financial strength if he is to purchase your products for stock and pay you promptly. Also, he will need to be in a good cash-flow position to extend credit to his customers. If a distributor is not in a financial position to extend credit to his customers, you may lose sales! Ask the prospect to supply you with credit references whom you can check—including other U.S. and foreign companies with whom he works. International Dun and Bradstreet can give you a comprehensive report, and the International Trade Administration can obtain World Traders Data Reports for you which includes the prospect's financial history. You can also check with his local bank to determine his financial and payment history for the past two or three years. Don't be timid about asking the prospect questions about his credit and financial standing. He expects you to do so. If you don't, you could be left holding a large (empty) bag and looking at a lot of lost sales in the territory. Companies who do their credit-checking homework thoroughly, rarely have real payment problems with their distributors.

6. Installation and After-Sales Service

In today's high-tech world, many products require installation and start-up by well-trained company technicians or engineers. In addition, these products will usually require on-going maintenance and sometimes will need to be repaired or have parts or components replaced. If your products are in this category, be sure your distributor candidate has the technical ability required to carry out these tasks. If you are fortunate to find someone with a high degree of technical training and experience in the type of products you are manufacturing, all you will need to do is train him in how to perform the necessary functions on your products. At the very least, he should have some technical knowledge so you can train him sufficiently to work well with his customers in satisfying their installation and repair needs.

7. Sales Organization—Strength and Ability

Be sure that your prospective distributor is, first and foremost, a good salesman who will aggressively sell your products in his assigned territory. Some distributorships you will encounter will be one-man operations with the owner handling all phases of the business. Others will consist of a few to many people, including a sizeable staff of outside and inside sales people. The manufacturer must also analyze the distributor's organization to be certain it can cover the market adequately and not lose sales or fail to be responsive to customer's needs. You should find out how many salespeople will cover the territory, and how frequently they will make sales calls on both established and prospective customers.

In respect to market coverage, some territories are quite large in area, so you must make sure a distributor has enough salespeople to cover all of the major trading areas. For example: You are considering a distributor in Colombia, a very large country with at least five major cities. The distributor is based in Bogotá, the capital. The other four major cities of Medellín, Cali, Barranquilla and Bucaramanga are located at considerable distances from Bogotá. Because of the distances, the poor network of highways and the rugged geography of the country, most people have to use air travel to reach them.

In order for a manufacturer to obtain complete coverage of the Colombian markets, he would have to be certain the Bogotá-based distributor he is considering has branch offices in each of the cities noted, and that each branch is staffed with the necessary sales and support personnel to cover the city and surrounding towns. If this is not the case, separate distributors will have to be appointed for each market area (city) because customers in those cities will not buy from distributors in Bogotá.

There are many other world markets which are so large, and the major trading areas so dispersed, that the only way to cover then adequately is with distributors who have branches around the country. This is true of countries like India, Australia, South Africa and even some of the European markets like France, Germany, and yes, the Soviet Union, which, one day will open its doors to increased trade with the United States.

Don't wait to determine this important factor until after you have appointed a distributor and find that he cannot give you total market coverage because his home-based salespeople cannot make frequent enough trips to distant cities. You'll be out of luck if you have signed an exclusive contract with him to cover the entire market. At a later date you will not be able to appoint additional distributors to cover the other areas.

8. Physical Facilities

One of the great advantages of a manufacturer working with distributors is the fact that they will place sizeable quantity orders. You will therefore, obviously look for a distributor who has adequate warehouse facilities to stock an in-depth quantity or assortment of your products.

Very often the distributor's level of stock makes the difference between making or losing sale. It is very disconcerting for a manufacturer to get a telephone call from a distributor who needs a product "yesterday," because he's out of stock, and a customer wants it now and won't wait for the next scheduled shipment. An "out-of-stock" situation may mean the distributor is really great and has sold his stock very quickly. Often however, he may not have forecast properly or failed to place large enough orders to take care of his market. Perhaps he is not keeping tight control of his inventory position and not sending timely orders to the factory. Check with other suppliers on how your prospect has handled these situations with their products.

Other physical facilities you will want to check out with prospects include:

a. The location of their business. They should be centrally located so customers can visit their showrooms and service facilities easily. There should be ample parking facilities.

b. Communication with overseas distributors should be easily accessible. Considering the distances, different time zones and language problems, the distributor should have telephone, telex and FAX equipment so no time is lost in discussing urgent business matters. Many times a telephone call followed up with a FAX showing diagrams or drawings can solve an urgent technical or break-down problem.

c. If installation, maintenance and repair of your products are critical aspects of customer service, the distributor should have trained personnel, ample space, tools, equipment and spare parts on hand to take care of the customer's requirements in these areas without delay or down-time on the customer's equipment.

d. If your products require special handling or storage facilities, make sure the distributor's warehouse is completely suitable to protect his stock.

9. Marketing and Promotion Capabilities

You will want to know if your prospective distributor is truly marketing-oriented and how he would go about marketing and promoting your products. This is especially important if your products are new to the local market or industries, or if there is significant competition from locally-made or other imported products. For such products, the initial marketing and promotion tactics can spell the success or failure of your market penetration. Ask your prospect to send you a proposed marketing plan outlining how he expects to get your products introduced and sold in his territory. Among the items he should include in his plan are the extent of local advertising he would do, local-language catalogs or brochures he would produce, trade-shows in which he would exhibit, and seminar or open-house shows he would hold for prospective customers. Assure him of your company's support in these promotions.

10. Familiarity with U.S. Business Practices

Just as you should know how business is done in your prospect's countries, they should know what is expected of them in dealing with a U.S. company. Your candidates should have at least some knowledge of English (even if you speak their languages). It would be difficult, to say the least, to impart to a non-English speaking distributor all the knowledge and information he should have about your company and products.

A foreign distributor should also be aware of the ethical and legal practices followed by U.S. manufacturers so he does not ask you to do things to contravene them.

He should also be familiar with U.S. product standards and measurements so he can effectively sell those which have different specifications from local items.

11. Distributor's Past Performance

Try to ascertain the degree of success (of failure) the distributor has had with lines similar to yours. Determine if there has been a good growth pattern of sales and profit, and if he does as good a job, or better, than his competitors.

12. General Characteristics

The people you will want to work with should be "good people." Hopefully, you will be working with them for a long time and they will be crucial to your success throughout the world. You therefore want to know that you are dealing with basically honest men and women of good character, high integrity and high moral values.

These same characteristics should carry through to the whole distributor organization, especially so, to the sales people who have frequent and direct customer contact. They, in effect, represent your company. Your image is at stake every time they come in contact with the customers they call upon.

You will expect distributors and their salesmen to demonstrate interest and enthusiasm for your product line. They should also display an aggressiveness in selling your products and a willingness to study and be trained and pass their knowledge on to customers so they, in turn, will be happy with your product and with your company.

These are some of the basic elements you will want to discuss in your first contact with prospective distributors. Based on the type or types of products or services you are hoping to export, there will be other criteria and questions you may need or want to add to the above to obtain good profiles of the potential distributors on your list.

Paring Down The Selection

You will probably have developed a relatively long list of prospects from your research, so it will have to be pared down to a manageable number. After you have selected those who appear most qualified, the next step is to write a letter to everyone on your list to determine if there is serious interest in taking on your line. With this first letter, tell the prospect where you got his name, and ask if he is interested in working with you. Include, or send under separate cover, complete product information and explain why you feel your products can be successfully sold in his market. Also, include information about your company, perhaps an annual report or a corporate capability brochure, so your prospect can learn something about your company.

Ask the prospect if he is interested in pursuing the matter further and request a prompt reply. A few preliminary questions from your distributor evaluation checklist may also be asked in this first letter. You will probably want to wait, however, until you have an expression of interest before requesting the bulk of information needed to complete your profiles. If possible, the letter and product literature should be in the prospect's language in order to establish an immediate good rapport and indicate to him there will be no problems in future communications.

When replies are received, separate the positive ones, and based on your careful analysis of the responses and further information the letters will have given you, write a follow-up letter tailored along the lines of your checklist requesting the additional information you need to complete your profile. Most distributor companies who are really interested in working with you will have no problem in responding to your questions. In this letter you should also tell the prospect you are interested in him and that, based on his further response, you will visit with him and other prospects to conduct an on-the-spot survey prior to making a final decision.

The Selection

Very few companies ever make the final selection and appoint a distributor without having first visited him personally. Such a visit gives a much better idea of the person and the company you have chosen to represent you. You can see his facilities, meet his salesmen and get to know the market personally. It is also a good idea to visit some important potential customers to whom you can introduce your products personally, and if you have made the decision, your new distributor!

At this time, you can note the type of relationship between the customer and your distributor. Such a visit will also give you the opportunity to discuss your own marketing plan for the territory and you can get the distributor's further ideas about how he plans to sell your products now that he has been given your personal input.

The personal visit and interview will also give you a chance to judge your candidate on several personal characteristics such as:

Neatness of appearance—will he make a good impression on your customers and your company management when they meet him?

Comprehension of what is expected of him in representing your company.

Realism in conveying to you what he can do for your company. Make sure he's not a "pie-in-the-sky" type, or a braggart.

Humility—willingness to learn from you and to share his thoughts with you on how to attain mutual goals. You don't want an "I know it all" type.

Honesty—no shady deals to accomplish goals.

Personality—a people-oriented person who expresses himself well; a looks-you-in-the-eye type when talking to you. This will be a good time to re-check how the distributor is handling and selling other lines, and a good indication of how he will probably work with yours. You want to be certain he will put the required time and effort into selling your products. Check to see if there have been only negligible sales of some of the lines and the reasons for them. Find out if it has been due to poor emphasis on the distributor's part, if it was due to competition, or if the principal failed to support him in some way. Clarify personally, any questions this may raise in your mind.

Summary

Selecting distributors is hard work, but it's fun too. Making the right choices can be nerve-wracking, but if you've done your homework carefully, met with your prospects and carried out an objective evaluation, your should be very gratified that you are at last on the international road to success and profits.

Remember, you don't have to get 20, 30 or 50 overseas distributors all at once, or in a short space of time. Just as the old cliche says, "Rome wasn't built in a day", so it is true that building a worldwide distributor network takes time, effort, and lots of patience.

Work with a few distributors first to see how it goes; how you feel about them, and how they feel about you, your company and your products. Learn their good and bad points. See how they operate for you and sell your products. Remain flexible. Make adjustments with them. Give more training and help if needed.

You will learn a lot from your experience with the first few distributors you appoint. Use this new knowledge when you continue your distributor search in additional target markets.

Chapter 8

WHAT A DISTRIBUTOR WANTS FROM A PRINCIPAL

Every coin has two different sides. No fair flipping with a two-headed coin. To be fair in your deliberations in searching for, selecting and evaluating a distributor, look at the other side of the "coin".

Distributors also search for, select and evaluate companies they want to represent. They too, have a "principal" profile consisting of elements they look for in principals whom they might approach or who come to them seeking their services. Good distributors are besieged by manufacturers who want them to sell their products.

First, and probably foremost, among a distributor's "wants" is a good quality product line manufactured by a prestigious manufacturer...a line which is well-known, will be easy to sell, and with little or no competition. Of course, not every product or manufacturer will meet these ideal criteria, but it will be your job to convince a potential distributor that even though you might not be a Fortune 100 or 500 company, and that your product may have some competition, yours is a serious company manufacturing a quality product which has good sales prospects in his marketplace.

Be prepared to show potential candidates how your company can benefit him if he agrees to carry your line. Show him how you meet competition, not merely by lower pricing, but with a product designed to do what it's meant to do better than anyone else's with specific marketing ideas, better service capabilities and warranties, and strong commitment to better research and development.

Among other important things, a potential distributor will want from a manufacturer are:

1. Commitment to him and to the market

A distributor wants to know that a company is not going to use him just to enter a market and "make a quick buck." He wants a company who will make a strong investment in time and effort in the market to support him in developing a demand for the products he will represent. Convince the distributor you are in the game for the long run, and that your commitment to your management to be successful in overseas markets includes an equal commitment to him as well.

2. Protection in his territory from third party sales, including direct sales by your company to customers in the distributor's defined territory

Usually third party sales occur without the company's knowledge, or they may be something over which the company has no control. Whenever the company does find out about them, or the distributor tells someone it is happening, the manufacturer should take steps to stop such sales to protect the distributor. Products can sometimes be shipped into a foreign territory by a U. S. company who has bought products from the principal as a domestic (U.S.A.) buyer, and who may have a contact overseas who needs the product

Occasionally a principal's distributor in another adjacent territory may ship to another distributor's territory. It is also possible for the company to make an arrangement with an authorized distributor so the company can sell directly to certain classes of customers in his territory; for example, to large OEM accounts, government agencies, or perhaps to U.S.Armed Forces installations in the country. This is often done when such sales are for larger quantities or products than a distributor would normally carry in his inventory. However, in almost all such cases, a manufacturer will, in fairness, have covered this possibility in the contract with the distributor and will pay him a commission on these sales.

In addition, there is often a clause in the contract obligating the distributor, as a quid-pro-quo, to service products shipped to these types of accounts.

Occasionally, in order to demonstrate loyalty to the distributor, companies will pay the distributor a small commission on any third party sales made in the territory ever though the company had no control over the shipment.

The important thing is to demonstrate to the distributor that you will protect him from anyone making unauthorized sales in his market. There can also be some strange and unauthorized ways in which a company's products can show up in a territory. While unusual, they are worth noting here as something that could happen in any marketplace. A manufacturer should be prepared for the unusual and be able to protect his overseas distributors.

One manufacturer of computerized graphics systems received frantic telephone calls from two of its overseas distributors in contiguous territories complaining they had discovered that several of their prospective customers had purchased systems locally at unusually low prices they could not possibly meet. The distributors, at first glance, felt the manufacturer had sold the systems directly to the customers by-passing the distributors. This, of course, was not true. After some fast and in-depth investigating, they found that a former employee of one of the companies had sold them. The ex-employee had apparently found a source for the systems in the U.S.A., imported them in quantity at very low prices, and resold them to customers on the prospect list which he had acquired as an employee.

The authorized distributors also found the former salesman was representing himself as an authorized distributor of the manufacturer and claimed he could obtain any model system in the line, as well as authentic spare parts for repairs or updates to the systems. In addition the "pirate" distributor was also copying the company's copyrighted software and selling it at a fraction of the official selling price!

How do you protect your authorized distributors from these "pirates?" In this case, the company also needed protection against the "pirates" infringement of its copyrighted products.

Fortunately, the distributors were able to obtain, at the company's request, serial numbers of several systems in each territory. These numbers were logged when the systems were shipped and the company records showed that the systems were shipped to one of the company's U.S. Distributors. The invoice numbers and the dates were also logged, giving the manufacturer incontrovertible proof of the source of the "pirate" systems.

The authorized U.S.A. distributor who, feeling he could "make a fast buck," since he wouldn't have to install the systems, train the users, or service them, had agreed to sell them when the ex-employee proposed the scheme to him. Because the company had protected itself by including a clause in its contract with the U. S. distributor stating in effect, that the U.S. distributor was authorized to sell only in the U.S.A. in any area where he could provide installation, training and service, it was able to terminate the distributor immediately.

The manufacturer then arranged for a nearby distributor to acquire the terminated distributor's stocks, preventing him from unloading additional systems to the foreign "pirate" or the U.S. market at distributor prices.

Meanwhile, based on the existing commercial and copyright laws of the two foreign markets involved, the company was able to obtain an indictment against the ex-employee who was then brought to trial and convicted of infringement and falsely representing himself as an authorized representative of a foreign company.

The remuneration obtained as a result of the trial decision was shared by the company and the distributors. This was a super example of a company's efforts to protect its distributors and served to strengthen the good relations between the parties.

A similar situation could arise when a prospective over-seas customer travels to the U.S. and seeks out a company's domestic distributor believing he can buy the product cheaper than from his local distributor in his home market. Every effort should be made by the company to prevent its domestic distributors from being party to these sales.

In the first case cited above, the U.S. distributor was also guilty of shipping the computerized systems overseas without the required validated U. S. export license, so the "fast buck" he made turned out to be a costly one!

In the case of an overseas customer buying in the United States, the U.S. distributor would also be liable to criminal and civil penalties if the product he sells is on the Export Commodity Control List and he does not provide export license data for the items being taken out of the United States by the customer.

These facts should be brought to the attention of your domestic sales executives so they may caution their U.S. distributors not to get involved in unauthorized shipping of the company's products overseas or selling to visiting foreigners looking for a bargain.

3. Freedom to "do his thing" in his territory as an independent businessman

To a large degree, a principal should give the distributor a fairly free-hand to work his market as he sees fit. Let's face it...you can't tell an independent businessman how to run his business!

But the company should retain some measure of control over the distributor's actions in respect to adherence of company policies, and certainly in regard to the contract you both signed. You don't want him doing things which can put your company in a bad light, cause serious legal problems or alienate customers.

Some distributors will look at too frequent visits by an international sales executive or a regional sales manager as an intrusion or excessive control. While visits are important to maintain good communications and support, they should be well-spaced and meaningful.

Most distributors don't want to be bogged down by having to send frequent reports to the home office, but companies should insist on receiving at least quarterly sales reports and regular sales forecasts to enable them to keep track of market results and to plan their future production needs.

4. Support

There are several aspects to the "support" a distributor wants from a principal.

a. Prompt shipment of scheduled stock orders.

The distributor cannot afford to be short of stock which could cause loss of sales, especially if there is a competitor in the marketplace who does have the required product readily available. This can also be applied to replacement parts needed for service or repair. Delays in providing prompt service could cause a customer expensive down-time on production equipment and jeopardize future sales to him by the distributor.

b. Advertising and Promotion

Advertising and Promotion Support is a major "want". In most overseas markets, companies will leave the advertising and promotion details to the distributor, but most of them look to their principals to provide tangible support in the form of an allowance to defray some of the costs of placing advertising in local media, or for participating in local trade shows.

Often this allowance takes the form of credits to the distributor's account for one-half of the space costs for advertising and/or booth space at a trade show. Another form of help would be to send company personnel to the market to assist at the distributor's booth during important promotions.

Many companies also provide distributors free art work (transparencies, slides etc.) to be used by a distributor to produce local-language brochures, catalogs or promotional pieces.

c. Product Training

Product Training, while an obvious requirement for a distributor, must be thorough and in-depth. He should be taught by your best technical and marketing people how to use, service, maintain, repair, promote and sell your products. Depending upon the complexity and sophistication of the line, this training is often best accomplished by having the distributor spend some days at the home office and factory.

d. Credit terms

Credit Terms, especially in the beginning of the relationship, are important to the distributor. Most likely he will place a good-sized order for his initial stock, representing a significant investment. In the distributor evaluation process, the company will have checked the credit and financial position of the distributor. Assuming it was satisfactory, the company may want to comply with the distributor's request for more-extended-than-usual terms, at least for the initial stock order. Wearing the hat of credit manager, the international executive will have to make a judgement as a risk-taker, but not a gambler, at this point. His recommendation to management regarding acceptance of favorable terms should be based on the facts discovered during his credit investigation.

5. Communication

Communication should be regular between the two parties so the distributor does not get to wonder, "Does anybody know I'm out here? Does anybody care?"

Too often manufacturers start up a distribution outlet, load it with product and then leave the poor distributor out in the field on his own. There should be one person at the home office with whom the distributor can be in contact at all times to handle any problem which arises in the market. It is an upsetting feeling to be thousands of miles way, have an irate customer hounding you for an answer or solution to a problem he is having, and not be able to reach anyone at "home" for help. Communications on any subject should always be helpful and constructive.

6. Home Office Visits

Visits To The Home Office rank high on a distributor's want list, and along with good communication, should be high on the manufacturer's list of conditions to grant "his man in the field." It is very important to make a distributor feel he is part of your corporate team. What better way to accomplish this than to have him visit your place once in a while instead of you always going to his.

There are so many benefits to this type of visit that some companies even pay the distributor's travel and subsistence expenses—at least occasionally if not for every trip. During the visits the distributor should meet with all international department personnel, service technicians, production staff, accounting and credit department staffs, and above all, get to know all members of senior management from the president on down.

The distributor is an important team member who is working hard to introduce and sell your products, and he deserves to be recognized as a vital element in the continued growth of your company.

Many companies have annual or bi-annual distributor meetings at the home office to which all overseas distributors (and agents) are invited. These meetings serve to review the previous year's successes (and failures, if any), to introduce new products and concepts in presentations by senior company executives, and discuss ways in which each party can help the other. It is always exciting for the distributors to meet their foreign colleagues, exchange ideas with them, and to sense the worldwide scope of the company they are representing.

The Bottom Line

It is evident that selection of distributors involves both the company and the candidate in the process. It does little good for the company to be hard-nosed in its selection of a distributor and insist on having everything its own way.

The distributor prospect has as much right to state and discuss what he'd like from the company, as the company has to make certain demands of the distributor. You will often have several candidates who are rated by everyone as "tops" in their field, and who can pick and choose principals almost at will because of their good reputation. With these types you will be in stiff competition with many other companies for their services—perhaps even with some of your competitors! You must be able to offer your prospect not only superior products and assistance, but also concede to as many of his wants as possible and practical. Remember, a prospect can turn you down too!

In many cases, you will have to prove to the prospect that your line will offer good sales and profit potential; that your products will have wide acceptance in his market; that yours is a reputable company committed to working overseas; that you can offer him much valuable assistance in achieving success in the sale and marketing of your products.

The end-result of the mutual selection process should then turn into an enduring partnership in which both partners are happy and successful in having chosen each other.

Chapter 9

NEGOTIATING THE DISTRIBUTOR CONTRACT

By now you have made a careful selection of a distributor as discussed in Chapter 7 (EVALUATING AND SELECTING POTENTIAL DISTRIBUTORS). Now you are ready to start negotiating a contract and discuss its terms. This means spelling out in detail the specific actions, rights, responsibilities and functions of each of the parties which will determine your future as business partners. The best time to do this is at the time of the personal visit during which you actually agreed to work together.

Business and commercial empires in past decades were founded, and fortunes made, by two parties entering into a business relationship with no more than a handshake. In today's hi-tech, computerized world however, business relationships have become infinitely more complex. Many of the intimate, ethical "your hand-shake-is good-enough-for-me" types of relationships of the past, have been replaced by impersonal, litigation-conscious, "fast-buck" operators with whom it would be disastrous to make such a deal.

A multitude of things can happen in the course of a business partnership which, without a solidly written, binding contract, may cause irreparable losses to one or both parties. Imagine an international sales and marketing executive making a handshake agreement today with a foreign distributor. A short time later the executive leaves the company or he dies. No one can know the exact deal he made with the distributor who in turn could make all kinds of spurious and unfounded claims on the company

As noted earlier, it is best to negotiate a contract during a personal visit with the distributor you have selected. It is a good idea to have with you on your visit a copy of a standard distributor contract to use as a working and discussion copy. Before leaving your office to visit potential distributors, do some research on the laws relating to distributor contracts in each country you will be visiting, especially laws relating to termination or cancellation of the agreement.

As we learned in a previous chapter, in some countries the distributor is protected by laws governing the termination or cancellation of an agreement, and trying to terminate or cancel it could cost you a great deal of money in compensation or damages. Discussions during the negotiating process should therefore take into consideration any local laws which could be burdensome at some future stage in the relationship. In addition, the contract must also be in compliance with U.S. trade and anti-trust laws.

Important Clauses to Include

Any agreement between principal and distributor should include all of the things a principal expects the distributor to do. It should also include all of the things the principal will do for the distributor. Most contracts have several other elements or working clauses which must be included to satisfy the wishes and needs of the two parties. Many of these clauses will require discussion and negotiation before they become part of the final agreement.

During this discussion, keep in mind the check lists you prepared in your evaluation processes of what you want of a distributor and what he wants of a principal (review Chapters 7, (EVALUATING AND SELECTING POTENTIAL DISTRIBUTORS), and 5, (DO I CHOOSE A DISTRIBUTOR OR AN AGENT?). This will be the time to decide if you can obtain all the points you want in the contract as well as points on which you may have to yield. You will also decide which of the distributor's wants you will, or will not, grant. If you feel you have selected a truly excellent distributor, you will probably agree to some conditions proposed by him which you might not ordinarily grant. Similarly, if a distributor really wants the line and knows he can sell it easily and at a good profit, he will yield to you on some conditions which he might not agree to with other product lines. Negotiating a contract is a fine art with much give and take by both parties. Conducted in the right spirit, with neither party attempting to dominate the other, and with each wanting to achieve success in the market, it can be fun to work toward a fair agreement with which you will both be happy.

Among the many important clauses which should be included in the agreement are:

1. Exclusive or Non-Exclusive Contract

This clause and the clause regarding cancellation or termination of the contract are probably the two which will cause most concern to both parties in the negotiation process. An Exclusive contract means that the distributor you appoint will have sole selling rights in the territory stipulated in the contract. The manufacturer cannot appoint another distributor to sell his products in the same territory, nor can the manufacturer sell directly to customers unless certain customers or classes of customers are specifically excluded from the distributor's selling rights. Exclusive also means that the manufacturer has the duty to protect the distributor from third parties selling into the territory. (More on that later.)

A Non-Exclusive Distributor Contract means that the appointed distributor does not have exclusive selling rights in the territory. The manufacturer has the option at any time of appointing one or more other distributors to sell his product in the market.

Almost universally, the distributor will want to have an exclusive contract and be the only authorized distributor in his territory. He doesn't want to have another distributor "cashing in" on his advertising, promotion, and the expensive sales calls made by his sales force. He wants to be the only source of the manufacturer's products. The primary basis for granting a distributor exclusivity in any market is that the international executive be certain that the chosen distributor is capable of covering his territory adequately.

The distributor must be able to cover with regularity, all customers in all classes of trade who are potential users of the products he is representing. In the absence of this certainty,especially in large markets, it may be better to make the agreement non-exclusive so that the company can have two or more authorized distributors to ensure adequate and full market coverage. In any case, the company must be certain that granting an exclusive contract does not violate any U. S. or foreign laws regarding exclusive territory agreements. The Sherman, Clayton and Robinson-Patman Acts in the U.S.A., and certain parts of the Treaty of Rome, might be examined on this point.

Sometimes a company may decide on having a non-exclusive contract for at least a trial period of a year to determine how the distributor will handle the market, after which the contract would either be amended to an exclusive distributorship or remain non-exclusive with the company making appropriate changes in market representation. In a way, this constitutes a threat to the distributor indicating that if he doesn't do a good job in the market, he will face competition from additional distributors working the same line.

The decision on whether to go exclusive or non-exclusive requires a great deal of judgement and a good knowledge of the man and marketplace with which you are dealing. Tread carefully!

2. Cancellation or Termination of the Agreement

Even as once-happy marriages sometimes end in separation, so too, can once-flourishing business relationships come to an end for a variety of reasons. Because one or both parties may someday want to terminate or cancel their agreement if all does not turn out well, the contract should be very clear as to the basis under which cancellation or termination may take place. Many contracts state that either party may terminate the agreement without cause by giving advance notice (usually six months). This can happen when one of the parties simply does not want to continue working with the other. Alternatively, either party may want to terminate the contract because of some material failure of the other to do something agreed to in the contract. In such cases the party wishing to terminate writes to the other party giving notice that if the "failure" continues for a specified number of days after receipt of the notice, the contract is terminated.

To provide for such termination or cancellation, it is a good idea to specify a specific term to the contract rather than leaving it open. For example, it could be stated that the term of the contract is for two years, renewable, unless one of the parties gives written notice 60 or 90 days prior to the expiration date of the contract.

Having given such written notice, and unless there is overriding local legislation, there should be no legal penalties against the party not wanting to renew or extend the agreement.

While it is a good idea to include such clauses in a contract, care and thought should be given to the fact that cancellation clauses may trigger uncertainty in the minds of both parties as to how long they will work together. On the other hand, if each is aware from the beginning that if he does not perform or live up to the expectations of the other, he may lose a distributor or a principal...usually a significant loss to both. This makes the cancellation clause an incentive for each one to do a good job.

From the manufacturer's point of view, losing a distributor means starting all over again with a new one (finding, evaluating, selecting, etc.), and suffering lost sales and profits in the meantime.

The question of termination will be discussed further in Chapter XI, EVALUATING A DISTRIBUTOR'S PERFORMANCE.

3. Territory

The Territory in which the distributor will have selling rights should be clearly defined. It should also be stated if the distributorship extends to selling all markets (customers) within the limits of the territory, or if it excludes certain industries, trades or types of customers.

4. Product Definition

Definition of Products for which the distributor is granted selling rights in the territory should be stated. Some companies have more than one type of product in their range and the distributor chosen to sell a particular part of the line may not be qualified or suitable to sell all of the company's products. This clause should be so written that the company reserves the right to appoint one or more additional (exclusive or non-exclusive) distributors to sell these other products. The company should also reserve the right to add or delete products from the list of those the distributor is given the right to sell, by giving adequate written notice to the distributor.

5. Evaluating Sales or Purchase Quotas

This can sometimes cause some heated discussion between principals and the distributors, especially if the products to be sold are new to the market. The main purpose of setting a quota is to give both parties specific goals at which to aim. The distributor will usually work harder if there is an incentive to reach a specified level of sales; the principal wants some assurance that its costly efforts in setting up the distributor to penetrate the market will be paid back by reaching or surpassing the quota. In addition, the company can use these numbers in its sales and production forecasts.

Since both parties will have done their market studies, and at this point know to a large degree what the demand for and marketability of the products is likely to be, agreement should be easily reached on a realistic quota in dollars or units. The quota should be set as a realistic number so a distributor will not lose heart by having to aim at an impossibly high number.

As a further incentive for the distributor to work hard toward meeting the quota which has been set, some companies insert a sales requirement clause in the contract. This would be a statement which gives them the right or option to revoke the distributor's exclusive rights, or in the case of a non-exclusive distributor, revoke his selling rights in the territory if the distributor fails to meet his quota. Often this option is not exercised unless the distributor does not meet the quota by 50 or 75 percent. There may be very valid reasons why a distributor could not attain the sales goal, so this revocation of rights must be judiciously applied.

After the first year, quotas for future years can be more realistically established by basing them on past performance and current market conditions.

6. Customer Development

This is an essential function into which the distributor must put substantial efforts. Several clauses specifying what the distributor is expected to do in developing a strong customer base for the company's products should be included in the contract. It would be helpful to specify the industries and customer groups which the distributor should contact in his sales efforts. To be certain that the distributor will cover all possible customers, it would be a good idea to include a clause stating that if an industry or customer group has not been serviced by the distributor, the company has the right to notify the distributor in writing that he must start servicing them within a specified time, usually 30 days. If the distributor does not comply, the clause would allow the company to exercise the option of revoking the distributor's selling rights with respect to those industries or groups and appoint another distributor to cover those market segments. Sometimes the company can choose to sell to those customers directly with no commission paid to the distributor.

7. Pricing Basis

The Pricing Basis to the Distributor should be stated and a current distributor price list should be part of the contract as a separate attachment. Any discounts available to the distributor should also be noted.

In this article or clause, the manufacturer should also reserve the right to revise prices by giving prior notice to the distributor of the effective date of the new prices. The clause should also note to which pending orders the revised prices will apply.

8. Suggested List Prices

Suggested List Prices to customers should also be attached to the contract and the relative clause should state that the manufacturer must be advised of any increase or decrease in the suggested list price. The key word here is "suggested", since price cannot be legally fixed. There should be some compliance made however, by the distributor, since selling at higher than suggested list prices can mean loss of sales because potential buyers often know what normal selling prices are in the U.S.A. or other foreign markets. If a distributor is perceived as a price-gouger and people refuse to buy from him, the company loses the sale to competitors.

9. Payment and Shipping Terms

Terms are normally spelled out in a separate article, although some companies include these points in the article on pricing. Terms will be negotiated with the distributor, and the company's decision of what terms to give the distributor will depend upon the outcome of its research into the credit standing and financial position of the distributor. This matter was discussed in an earlier chapter, but it bears repeating here. Payment terms must be carefully considered. It would be safer to work with either a Letter of Credit or Sight Draft terms until some current and personal credit history has been established, at which time more lenient terms can be given.

10. Maintaining Adequate Stock

A clause relating to Ordering of products by the distributor ties in with another item usually included in a contract, namely, the Requirement To Maintain Adequate Stock of the company's products to enable the distributor to properly serve the market. Depending upon the product, this is best accomplished by suggesting that the distributor place regular, scheduled orders so there will be a constant flow of goods on its way to the distributor's warehouse. A condition of the distributor's continued right to sell is that he maintain adequate stock, and this fact should be spelled out in the contract.

11. Installation, Training, and After-Sales Service

These are each items which merit substantial statements by way of descriptive clauses in a contract stating the distributor's responsibility in these areas.

If the products require installation, assembly, or start up, the contract should note the distributor's agreement to perform any of these functions. The Company's responsibility in this respect is to provide the distributor and his personnel with training in how to perform these jobs as well as how to service, maintain, and repair products. A clause in this type of article could offer the distributor the alternative of entering into a contract with an an outside service organization to provide repair and maintenance on the products. To protect itself, the manufacturer should stipulate that personnel of that service company be trained at the manufacturer's plant.

12. Warranties

Warranties should be given that the products are free of defects in material and workmanship for a given period of time. It should also be very clear what the company "warrantees" it will do regarding any defective products; what the distributor's responsibilities are in providing in-warranty service; and how he is to handle out-of-warranty problems.

13. Advertising and Promotion

Advertising and Promotional Support is given to many distributors by their principals. The extent of this support and what the distributor must do the receive such support can be the subject of an article in the contract. The principal should clearly define that (for example) he will reimburse the distributor for 50% of his advertising space cost (excluding art work, production etc.) and 50% of his booth space costs for exhibiting the products at a trade show. The article should require submission of documentation of these costs by the distributor as a requisite for reimbursement. It must also be included in this article if the company will reimburse the distributor for product seminars he organizes, brochures or catalogs in local language which he produces, or, if it will supply him slides or transparencies for use in producing product literature locally. Some companies also provide home office sales, marketing or engineering personnel to attend trade shows in which the distributor participates.

14. Reports Required from the Distributor

Reports required from the distributor are the subject of another important clause. Remember, the distributor is not a company employee, and therefore it can be "sticky" to require him to feed you with a constant stream of reports. However, you should make it clear to the distributor that he must inform you on a regular basis:

    a. How many units he proposes to sell in the next quarter.
    b. How many units he sold last month.
    c. In what shows he plans to exhibit.
    d. In which media he will advertise in the next six months.
    e. What his marketing plan is for the next six months.
    f. What new local laws are contemplated or have been put into effect which have a bearing on your mutual business.
    g. What the competition is doing.

h. Anything that is happening in the market that helps or hinders your mutual goals to sell products.

This information will help you do a better job in production-planning, budgeting, anticipating problems, meeting or beating competitive actions, and giving your distributor the kind of support he needs.

15. Competitive Products

Competitive Products are often carried by many top distributors, and it is possible that the one you chose in your prospect evaluation process also does. The question you must answer in your own mind when you chose a distributor is whether you will accept his carrying a competitive line, or if you will insist on a clause in your contract prohibiting his doing so.

In some industries, it is a common practice for distributors to carry more than one brand of products in order to be able to supply his customers with whichever type or brand he might need for replacement or for O.E.A. requirements. This is especially true of specialized distributors handling industrial products such as bearings, power transmission and material handling equipment, power tools, lubricating products and many others. You must be aware of what marketing methods are employed by various industries and distributors in your chosen markets and act accordingly in respect to this clause.

It is always more advantageous to you if your distributors stock and sell only compatible lines of products which are not in direct competition with yours.

16. Third Party Sales

This is an item which should be covered in the contract by a clause defining such sales and the rules for handling them. If the distributor has exclusivity in the territory, it is the principal's obligation to protect him from someone (including the principal) encroaching on his market by making unauthorized sales. Third party sales are often made into foreign markets by U.S. export houses who manage to obtain products from manufacturers or the manufacturer's distributors, neither of whom is aware the "customer" is buying for export. Many times also, U.S. distributors may knowingly sell products to such exporters or to foreigners visiting the U.S. hoping to get a better price than they can get from their local distributor. Lastly, a manufacturer may define certain accounts or types of customers as "house accounts" to whom sales will be made directly. In this, and in some of the other cases, the company will specify a commission to be paid to the distributor.

For some situations the manufacturer should have, as part of this clause, a disclaimer stating that if its products are shipped into the territory without its knowledge, no commission will be paid to the distributor. Since the company wants to protect itself as well as the distributor (and also keep him happy) from unauthorized sales, a lot of judgement and discretion must be used in the application of this clause.

17.General Clauses

General Clauses are necessary to define such matters as:

    a. The Governing Law of the agreement (usually cited as the law of the manufacturer's home state and the United States of America.

    b. Selection of Forum for the settlement of disputes relating to validity, interpretation or performance of the agreement.

    c. Consent to Jurisdiction of (U.S.A.) courts or of the International Chamber of Commerce for the adjudication of any disputes.

    d. Force Majeure absolving both parties of liability in case of non-performance of certain responsibilities by reason of occurrence of acts of God , war, etc.

    e. How Notice shall be given regarding various changes, requests, demands or other communication required or permitted by the agreement.

SUMMARY

Many of the elements discussed constitute "boiler-plate" sections of most contracts and usually do not cause any problems in the negotiating stage. Others are clearly factors which the company, the distributor, or both consider optional, and which can be granted by one or the other to enhance, or even clinch, the relationship between the two parties.

On the following pages are samples of two distributor contracts and a product service agreement. The first sample is a fairly complete one in the sense that it incorporates most of the various elements discussed in this chapter. It should not be considered a standard contract applicable to any and all companies selling many different type of products. It worked well as the contract for one specific company and the products it manufactured.

It was also in line with that company's particular business philosophy and its international action plans and goals.

The shorter version is an illustration of a very simple contract between a principal and a distributor which many companies have used successfully. Note, however, that it does not include many of the elements describing each party's rights and responsibilities, and what each party covenants it will do.

The sample Product Service Agreement elaborates on the section in many contracts stating that the distributor will provide product service. This type of agreement states specifically what the manufacturer expects the distributor to do in terms of servicing the products, what it will, or will not, pay for and how the distributor is to report the service problems to the manufacturer in order to obtain reimbursement for expenses for in-warranty or out-of-warranty service.

The sample agreements in this chapter and in Chapter VII, are included for the purpose of illustrating how some companies have negotiated contracts with their representatives in overseas markets. The samples are not intended to give legal advice and, as noted on several occasions throughout the text, competent legal investigation and advice on these matters should be thoroughly sought in each country in which a company plans to conclude such agreements. In addition, every principal should also be aware of United States legislation regarding a variety of marketing practices before presenting or signing any distributor agreements.

By following good business practices, being aware of legal constraints, conducting personal on-site negotiations, exercising ethical conduct throughout, and using good judgement and consideration for the other party's position, a fair and mutually agreeable contract can be quickly and amicably concluded with your foreign distributors. Then you can both get down to the business of manufacturing and selling products.

INTERNATIONAL DISTRIBUTOR AGREEMENT

This Agreement is made and entered into this _____ day of
_____ 19____, by and between __ABC COMPANY__ a (name
of state) _____Corporation with principal offices in
_____, (hereinafter referred to as "ABC"), and
XYZ DISTRIBUTION COMPANY located at __(address)__ , (hereinafter
"XYZ").

WITNESSETH

WHEREAS ABC is the manufacturer of Systems for _____
_____(list purpose)_____, and as used in this Agree-
ment such systems shall mean ____(description/names of products)_____
WHEREAS ABC desires to establilsh and develop markets outside the
United States for the Systems, and,
WHEREAS XYZ desires to purchase the Systems for resale and is willing
to commit substantial efforts and resources to the establishment and development of markets in the Territory for the Systems, NOW, THEREFORE
in consideration of their promises below, the parties have agreed as follows:

ARTICLE I

APPOINTMENT OF XYZ

ABC hereby appoints and XYZ accepts appointment as ABC's exclusive
distributor in the Territory of the Systems, subject to the limitations and
restrictions hereinafter set forth.

XYZ's distribution rights to the Systems are conditioned upon XYZ's
discharge of its obligations under the terms of this Agreement. XYZ is not
an agent or legal representative of ABC for any purpose whatsoever and shall
have no authority to assume or create any obligation, express or implied, on
behalf of ABC.

ARTICLE II

MARKETS AND TERRITORY

XYZ's distributorship under this Agreement includes all markets in the country of _____ (hereinafter "the Territory.")

ARTICLE II-A

THE PRODUCTS

During the Term, as hereinafter defined, XYZ may purchase from ABC under the terms and conditions hereof, the Products including accessories and supplies therefore, listed on Attachments___ through __ hereto. ABC reserves the right to add or delete Products from Attachments__ through__ on ninety (90) days prior written notice to XYZ.

ARTICLE III

PURCHASE AND SALES REQUIREMENTS

A. XYZ agrees it shall purchase at least fifty (50) Systems from ABC for delivery over the term of this Agreement. For each renewal period, ABC will establish new purchase quantities based upon current market conditions and the sales history for the prior periods. Should XYZ not meet the required purchase volume in any period, ABC may immediately revoke XYZ's exclusive rights. Because of the complexity of the systems, and in order to ensure proper functioning, and further to ensure the successful implementation of the warranty program, XYZ shall purchase the components for the systems and all tools and spare parts therefore, only from ABC

B. Because of the significant commitment ABC is making to XYZ in the granting of an exclusive distributorship in the Territory, XYZ agrees it shall not develop, manufacture, or sell products identical to or similar to, or competitive with the Systems during the term of this Agreement and for a period of one (1) year after the termination of this Agreement for any reason.

ARTICLE IV

CUSTOMER DEVELOPMENT

XYZ acknowledges that an essential consideration for the granting of an exclusive distributorship is the use of its best efforts to promote the Systems and develop customers for those systems.

Accordingly:

A. XYZ will diligently pursue all existing and potential industry or customer groups for the Systems including, but not limited to: (List all classes of trade and customer groups to be contacted.)

B. XYZ will exhibit the Systems at appropriate tradeshows, advertise them in appropriate trade publications, and aggressively promote them through seminar demonstrations and direct sales contacts. ABC agrees to reimburse XYZ for____ percentage of all advertising space costs to XYZ for advertisements for the Systems in trade publications, magazines, and newspapers. Selection of publications and advertisement frequency are subject to ABC's prior approval which shall not be unreasonably withheld. ABC further agrees to reimburse XYZ for____ percentage of the costs to XYZ of all booth space XYZ may use for the showing of the Systems. If ABC's equipment is included as part of a larger exhibit, then ABC will reimburse XYZ for____ percentage of the cost of the space XYZ actually uses for the Systems. Selection of shows is subject to ABC's prior approval which shall not be unreasonably withheld.

C. In the event an industry or customer group in the Territory is or has been outside XYZ's normal business coverage or within XYZ's normal business coverage but has not been serviced, ABC shall have the right to give written notice to XYZ identifying that industry or customer group, and XYZ shall be obligated to commence to service that industry or customer group within ninety (90) days following the written notice. Satisfactory means for providing said service includes, but is not limited to, establishment of sub-distributors that service the potential market and/or hiring direct salespersons experienced in selling to the potential market. Failure of XYZ to service that industry or customer group within the ninety (90) day period to the satisfaction of ABC shall give ABC the right upon thirty (30) days' advance written notice to declare XYZ's distribution rights revoked with respect to that industry or customer group.

D. Material failure of XYZ to develop industries or customer groups as described in Paragraphs A, B and C hereinabove to ABC's satisfaction shall entitle ABC to declare XYZ's distribution rights revoked if the material failure continues for thirty (30) days or more after written notice to XYZ listing the specific acts or inactions constituting said material failure.

ARTICLE V

ORDERS: SHIPMENT SCHEDULES

A. All orders of Systems, spare parts, tools, materials, and other items listed under this Agreement shall be initiated by XYZ's order document. The order document shall refer to this Agreement, specify the items desired by appropriate identifying description and number per ABC's price lists and by quantity, and propose a delivery schedule. ABC will within fourteen (14) days notify XYZ of its acceptance of the order and of ABC's shipment schedule, which shall be shipment schedule for that order. ABC shall use its best efforts to comply with the proposed delivery schedule whenever possible. The terms of this Agreement shall supersede any inconsistent terms of XYZ's order or ABC's acceptance.

B. XYZ may, by written notice reschedule delivery dates of up to (percentage)___ of any systems order previously accepted by ABC and scheduled for delivery, as follows:

1. ABC must receive the notice at least three (3) months prior to the previously scheduled delivery dates.
2. If the Systems were previously scheduled for delivery during a period between three (3) and six (6) months following ABC's receipt of notice, ABC can grant a one-time delay of up to ___ months.
3. If the Systems were previously scheduled for delivery during a period between___ and___ months following ABC's receipt of notice, ABC can grant a one-time delay of up to___ months.
4. XYZ may request delivery in advance of its previously scheduled delivery, and ABC agrees it will use its best efforts to meet the revised delivery schedule.

5. ABC may treat a request for a longer delay than those described above for any one (1) shipment as a cancellation of the order for those Systems.

6. A ____% cancellation charge shall apply to all Systems ordered and subsequently cancelled.

C. With the exception of spare parts orders, the minimum order quantity for any item is ____ units.

D. For purposes of aiding ABC's future production planning, every ninety (90) days after signing this Agreement, XYZ will provide ABC with an updated projection of its monthly Systems needs for the following twelve (12) month period.

ARTICLE VI

PRICES TO XYZ

A. Current ABC export prices for the Systems are contained on Attachment A hereto. These prices are subject to change by ABC upon ____( ) days advance written notice. Revised prices will apply to equipment on order at the time of price change which is scheduled for delivery more than ____( ) days from date of price change notice. Revised prices will also apply to equipment ordered after notice of forthcoming price changes if such equipment is scheduled by ABC for delivery beyond the ninety (90) days notice period. The prices specified are in U.S. dollars, exclusive of taxes and other governmental charges, freight, insurance, and other transportation charges. XYZ shall pay all these charges. If ABC prepays any of these charges for XYZ's account, such charges shall be invoiced with the purchase price by ABC on or about the shipment date. Invoices shall be issued in the name of XYZ. Payment of all invoices shall be net ____ days from date of invoice

B. ABC will ship all products _(Specify FOB or CIF etc.)_ to XYZ's address in_ (Territory)_

ARTICLE VII

SUGGESTED LIST PRICES FOR XYZ'S CUSTOMERS

Suggested list prices to XYZ's customers for the Systems are attached hereto as Attachment B. XYZ shall notify ABC of any increase or decrease in the suggested list price for Systems.

ARTICLE VIII

REPORTS

A. XYZ shall promptly report to ABC anything that could adversely affect sales of the Systems, such as devaluation of local currency, introduction of a competitive system, and potential changes in industry or customer group requirement.

B. XYZ shall be subject to annual audits by ABC at ABC's cost for the purpose of determining or verifying XYZ's sales figures. XYZ shall maintain records of these sales, inventory, and any other item relevant to this Agreement in accordance with generally accepted accounting principals. ABC shall have the right to determine the dates of these audits, upon thirty (30) days' advance written notice to XYZ and without unreasonably interfering with XYZ's normal operations.

C. XYZ shall report and certify to ABC within thirty (30) days after the end of each month., during the term of this Agreement, its sales figures for Systems for that month. Sales figures shall include the number of systems sold and the prices at which they were sold to end users.

ARTICLE IX

TRADEMARKS, TRADENAMES, LOGO

A. ABC will supply Systems hardware in ABC's standard color and with ABC's logo affixed. XYZ may, with ABC's permission, place its own logo on the equipment along with the ABC logo for purposes of local identification where, in XYZ's opinion, XYZ's name may be more widely recognized than ABC's name.

B. Neither XYZ nor ABC shall use the other's name or any trademark owned or used by the other party, whether or not such trademark is registered, as part of its firm or business name or in any other way except to designate the products to which the trademark attaches. XYZ and ABC agree to take no action which could infringe upon, harm, or contest rights of the other in and to its trademarks and to be responsible for ensuring the integrity of the promotion and sale of the Systems.

C. Upon termination of this Agreement for any reason, XYZ and ABC shall immediately discontinue using and dispose of all signs, stationery, advertising material, and other printed matter in their possession or control containing the other party's name or any other trademarks owned or used by the other.

D. XYZ and ABC shall also immediately take all appropriate steps to cancel any listing in telephone books, directories, or other public records containing the other's name or any of the other's trademarks.

E. XYZ can refer to itself as an authorized distributor for ABC Systems within the Territory; provided if ABC shall revoke XYZ's distribution rights, XYZ shall immediately cease from advertising stating in express or implied terms that it is an authorized ABC distributor.

ARTICLE X

DOCUMENTATION AND CONFIDENTIALITY

From time to time during the term of this Agreement, ABC shall provide XYZ with documentation and technical information so that XYZ and its employees, or those working under its control, may provide installation and training and some routine service for Systems to its customers. XYZ shall use all reasonable care to limit the use of this documentation and information to these purposes and shall prevent disclosure to all parties except those with a need to know. "Reasonable care" shall mean at least the care which XYZ exercises with respect to its own confidential material. XYZ shall not use or allow use of this documentation and information for the purpose of manufacturing the Systems or similar systems or related products.

ARTICLE XI

INSTALLATION, TRAINING

A. XYZ agrees that the installation of the Systems and training of its customers in their use shall be the responsibility of XYZ.

B. Throughout the term of this Agreement, ABC agrees to provide training in servicing and maintaining the Systems at ABC's facility at no charge to XYZ. XYZ will pay the travel and living expenses of XYZ's personnel while receiving this training.

C. XYZ shall at all times during the term of this Agreement have and keep in its employ a sufficient number of service personnel adequately trained in the maintenance of the Systems.

Alternatively, XYZ may contract with a service organization to provide repair service and maintenance on the Systems. In such a case, the service organization selected shall be subject to ABC's approval. The personnel from the servicing organization must be adequately trained in the maintenance of the Systems, said training to be acquired by attending a training program at ABC's facility.

ARTICLE XII

WARRANTY, SERVICING

A. ABC warrants its Systems to produce_____ of a quality which is commercially satisfactory for their intended use and warrants that its Systems shall be free of defects in material and workmanship for a period of ninety (90) days from the date of first use at a customer's facility. At ABC's option, this warranty is limited to repair or replacement at ABC's facility, shipping costs to and from ABC to be borne by XYZ's customers. Accidental or malicious damage or damage caused by unauthorized attempted repair shall not be covered by this warranty.

THERE ARE NO OTHER WARRANTIES, EXPRESSED OR

IMPLIED, INCLUDING THE WARRANTY OF MERCHANTABIL-ITY, OTHER THAN THOSE SPECIFIED IN THIS AGREEMENT.

B. During the initial ____ ( ) day or any extended warranty period, XYZ agrees to provide warranty service to its customers in the form of printed circuit board swapping and mechanical repairs and adjustments. XYZ will return, freight prepaid, faulty circuit boards and components under ABC's warranty to ABC for repair free of charge by ABC or, at ABC's option, replacement. Once the faulty circuit boards and components are repaired, ABC will return them to XYZ to replinish XYZ's Spare Parts Kit(s).

C. XYZ agrees to provide on-going out-of-warranty service to its customers in the form of printed circuit board swapping and mechanical repairs and adjustments. XYZ will return faulty circuit boards and components to ABC for repair or replacement. Repairs to the electronic circuitry and major mechanical repairs for systems out of warranty will be charged to XYZ on a time-and-materials basis when the circuit board or major system component is returned to ABC's facility.

D. Upon the signing of this Agreement, XYZ agrees to purchase from ABC, Spare Parts Kits for the (products) . For every ____ ( ) of each type of system which XYZ purchases, XYZ shall purchase one (1) additional Spare Parts Kit. Beyond this, XYZ agrees to maintain an adequate supply of spare parts to provide reasonable service. A list of items included in the Spare Parts Kits is found in Attachments __ & __ . In addition to the Spare Parts Kit, individual spares may be purchased. The price lists for the spare parts kits and for individual spare parts are presented in attachments __ & __ .

E. Under no circumstances shall XYZ make any warranties or representation to its customers on behalf of ABC beyond those ABC makes to XYZ in this ARTICLE XII. XYZ shall indemnify and hold harmless ABC against any costs and damages resulting from any such warranties or representations.

ARTICLE XIII

PATENT INDEMNITY

ABC shall hold harmless, indemnify and defend XYZ from and against any claims, actions, liabilities, or damages arising out of or based on alleged patent or trademark infringement because of XYZ's sale of Systems provided that:

A. XYZ permits ABC to represent XYZ in the defense or settlement of any claim, or action based thereon, and ABC shall have complete and absolute control of such defense or settlement.

B. XYZ notifies ABC in writing of any claimed infringement within fifteen (15) days of knowledge thereof and provides ABC with all information ints possession concerning such claim, and,

C. XYZ cooperates with ABC in the defense of any claim or action and makes available to ABC information, data, and evidence in its possession or under its control that may be requested by ABC in connection with any such defense.

ARTICLE XIV

MISCELLANEOUS

A. Limitation of Liability. ABC shall in no event have obligation or liability to XYZ or any other person for loss of profits, loss of use, or incidental, special or consequential damages, even if ABC has been advised of the possibility thereof, arising out of or in connection with the sale, delivery, use, repair, or performance of any of ABC's products falling within the scope of this Agreement for any reason.

B. Term. The term of this Agreement shall be for one (1) year and thereafter may be extended by written agreement of both parties for successive one (1) year periods.

C. Termination. Either party may terminate this Agreement without cause after six (6) months' advance written notice. Further, either party may terminate this Agreement upon material failure of the other party to observe, keep, or perform any of the covenants, terms, or conditions of this Agreement if the material failure continues for thirty (30) days or more after written notice to the other party listing the specific acts or inactions constituting said material failure.

D. Representations. XYZ and ABC represent that they have not and agree that they will not, in connection with transactions made pursuant to this

Agreement, make any payment or transfer anything of value directly or indirectly to any government official or employee or to any other person or entity if such payments or transfers would violate the laws of the country in which made or the laws of the United States of America. It is the intent of the parties that no payments or transfers of value shall be made which have the purpose or effect of public or commercial bribery, acceptance or acquiescence of extortion, kickbacks or other unlawful or improper means of obtaining business.

GENERAL

1. Any assignment or attempted assignment by either party, in whole or in part, of its rights or obligations under this Agreement (other than the right to receive payments) or any other interest in this Agreement without the other party's prior written consent shall be void.

2. (a) Governing Law. This Agreement shall be governed and construed in accordance with the laws of the State of _____ , United States of America.

(b) Selection of Forum ABC and XYZ agree that the United States District Court for the District of ___ or the Superior Court for the Judicial District of _____ / _____ at _____ , shall be the sole and exclusive forum for the adjudication of any dispute relating to the validity, interpretation, or performance of this Agreement.

(c) Consent to Jurisdiction. XYZ submits to the personal jurisdiction of both the United States District Court for the District of_____ and the Superior Court for the Judicial District of_____/ _____ for the adjudication of any dispute relating to the validity, interpretation, or performance of this Agreement.

3. Entire Agreement. This Agreement constitutes the entire agreement and understanding between the parties concerning the subject matter hereof and supersedes all prior agreements, negotiations, and understanding of the parties with respect hereto. No representation, promise, modification, or amendment shall be binding upon either party as a warranty or otherwise unless it is in writing and signed on behalf of each party by a duly authorized representative.

4. Legality. In the event that any provision or provisions of this Agreement shall be construed to be invalid or unenforceable for any reason, such invalidity or unenforceability shall not be deemed to affect the remaining provisions hereof, and the Agreement shall be construed and enforced as if such invalid or unenforceable provision or providions had never been inserted herein.

5. Force Majeure. ABC shall not be liable for delays in delivery or nondelivery of products under this Agreement caused by acts of God, acts of civil or military authority, fire, flood, strikes, war, epidemics, shortage of gas, power or other causes beyond ABC's reasonable control. XYZ shall not be liable for breach of contract if it does not purchase any minimum quantity of Systems by reason of the occurrence of acts of God, acts of civil or military authority, fire, flood, strikes war, riots, epidemics, or other causes beyond XYZ's control.

6. Notice. Any notice, request, demand, or other communication required or permitted hereunder shall be deemed to have been properly given and received upon the passage of ten (10) days after air mail deposit by either party in the United States mail, or   (country)   mail, first class registered, with postage prepaid. For the purposes of this subparagraph the addresses of the parties (until written notice or change shall have been given) shall be as follows:

ABC COMPANY

Attn.
Telephone:
Telex:
Fax:

XYZ COMPANY

Attn:
Telephone:
Telex:
Fax.

IN WITNESS WHEREOF, the parties have executed this Agreement as of the day and year first above written.

ABC COMPANY

BY _____

DATE _____

XYZ DISTRIBUTION

BY _____

DATE _____

INTERNATIONAL DISTRIBUTOR CONTRACT

AGREEMENT made at _____ , _____ , United States of America, this ____ day of _____ 19_ , between____ ABC COMPANY, a corporation of the State of _____ , having its principal offices at _____ , United States of America, (hereinafter called "ABC" and _____ XYZ DISTRIBUTION ____ located at _____ , (hereinafter called "XYZ"). THIS CONTRACT SUPERSEDES ALL PREVIOUS AGREEMENTS BETWEEN ABC AND XYZ.

IT IS AGREED:

1. Except as provided in Paragraph 7 hereof, ABC grants to XYZ the exclusive right to purchase and to re-sell, in___ (The Territory) ___ the products manufactured by ABC identified as____ (describe products) ___ , subject to the terms and conditions set forth herein.

2. XYZ will use its best efforts to increase the sale of ABC's products as specified in Paragraph 1 in____ (Territory) .

3. XYZ will not purchase, handle, or sell any other make or makes of equipment like or similar to that of ABC specified in Paragraph 1 hereof which can, in any way or manner, be considered competitive thereto. For the purposes of this agreement, it shall be understood that any equipment performing the same use or function of that made by ABC will be considered competitive thereto regardless of specification or design.

4. XYZ agrees to keep a representative stock on hand at all times to facilitate prompt distribution and shipment to customers and to give adequate and prompt service of ABC's products included in this agreement.

5. All payments made under this contract shall be in U.S. currency, and shall be made in accordance with terms mutually agreed upon by both parties of this contract.

6. In the event there is any difference between the law of the State of _____ ,in the United States of America, and the law of_____ , touching any dispute which may arise between ABC and XYZ, this contract shall be interpreted in accordance with the law upon the subject of the State of _____ , in the United States of America.

7. Sales to governments, United States of America or other, purchasing commissions, government agencies or purchasing agencies, located in the United States of America serving industrial organizations, as for example petroleum producing and marketing companies, mining, construction and supplies companies, and direct sales by ABC of its products to other manufacturers, wheresoever located, for use as original equipment on any vehicle, machine or machine elements, wholly or partially assembled, or parts thereof, do not fall within the terms of this agreement, and commission will be paid on any such sales at the sole discretion of ABC.

8. This agreement, unless sooner terminated by agreement of the parties, shall be in effect for a period of one (1) year from effective date and thereafter may be extended by written agreement of both parties for successive one (1) year periods.

This Agreement may be terminated by either party for breach by the other, by either party giving sixty (60) days written notice.

IN WITNESS THEREOF, the parties hereto have caused this instrument to be executed the day and year first above written:

THE ABC COMPANY

BY _____

Date _____

XYZ DISTRIBUTION

BY _____

Date _____

PRODUCT SERVICE AGREEMENT

This is an agreement between ABC Company of_____and XYZ Distribution of_____.

The purpose of this agreement is to outline and confirm an understanding between ABC and XYZ for service and repair of equipment manufactured by ABC.

PROCEDURE FOR INITIATING SERVICE

In warranty and out of warranty service will originate from the customer contacing either XYZ or ABC.

Authorization by ABC must be obtained in writing, letter, telex or facsimilie, prior to performing any service or repairs for which ABC will be obligated to pay expenses.

INVOICES FOR SERVICE AND PARTS:

Invoices for in-warranty service will be sent to ABC. Costs of service and parts shall not exceed the rates outlined under schedule of service and parts.

Invoices for out of warranty service will be billed directly to the customer by XYZ. ABC will not be obligated for any out of warranty expenses except as might be agreed to by authorized* personnel at ABC and XYZ.

All invoices to ABC will list the following:
1. service hours and charges
2. transportation —time and charges
3. parts cost (description of items)
4. serial numbers of units upon which service was performed
* See Schedule A attached.

SCHEDULE OF SERVICE AND PARTS RATES:

LABOR: Invoice for actual hours of work plus actual transmit time to and from site of service, however the hourly rate for transit time must not exceed the labor rates noted below:
1. Weekdays—$ /hour
2. Saturdays, Sundays, Holidays,—$ /hour

It is further agreed the labor rates will be reviewed at least on a yearly basis for possible adjustment against higher costs and/or currency exchange fluctuations.

TRAVEL

1. $ /mile, auto only
2. Public transportation—at cost

LIVING

1. At cost when overnight is required only
2. Telelphone, and Telex or FAX to ABC at cost.

PARTS

1. Purchased parts are to be invoiced at no more than their puchased value plus 20%.
2. Manufactured parts will be invoiced at standard selling prices in effect at time of shipment.

SERVICE REPORTS

A brief descriptive report is required to be submitted with each invoice describing the details of the service performed and any suggestions regarding product changes or modifications which may seem applicable. The customer's name, location, model number of equipment and serial numbers are required as part of all reports.

This agreement is effective on the date shown below and shall remain effective until terminated by either party.

Termination of this agreement may be made by either party in writing by authorized personnel of the party desiring termination.

ABC COMPANY
BY
DATE

XYZ DISTRIBUTION
BY
DATE

SCHEDULE A

The following ABC Company personnel are authorized to give approval for service.

Name	Title
	President
	Executive Vice President
	International Sales Manager
	Vice President Marketing
	Vice President Engineering
	Director Quality Control

Chapter 10

NEGOTIATING AN AGENT CONTRACT

The basic contract to be concluded with an agent should be much the same as the distributor contract, and should include many of the same clauses. You have learned from Chapter 5, (DO I CHOOSE A DISTRIBUTOR OR AN AGENT?), the differences between an agent and a distributor. These differences will dictate the manner in which you will phrase the clauses you include in the agent's contract.

The Legal Definition of an Agent

Keep in mind that the title "agent" can legally be interpreted in many different ways, both in the United States and in many different countries abroad. In most instances the agent you appoint will function only as your sales supervisor or sales person in a strictly defined overseas market, and you should state this in the contract.

In addition, as a disclaimer, you should also make clear in the agreement that the agent is not, in legal terms, an agent or legal representative of your company for any purpose other than that stated in the agreement. Also, be sure to state that he is not granted any right or authority to assume or create any obligation or responsibility, express or implied, in behalf of, or in the name of, your company or to legally bind your company in any manner whatsoever.

Legal Standing of Agents in Some Foreign Countries

Contracts between agents and principals are normally entered into in accordance with the so-called free will of the parties, and the agreements contain expressions of the manner in which each agree to do business. Most countries recognize the principal and allow the parties to establish mutually agreed upon terms and conditions.

In many countries however, there can be exceptions in the form of laws which can override at least some of the clauses of the principal-agent agreement. These laws are principally aimed at offering some protection to the agent in the event the principal wishes to terminate the contract. At times there have been serious abuses of agents' rights when a principal has unfairly terminated an agent, and some agents have thereby suffered financial and commercial losses. Some foreign governments have, therefore, enacted protective legislation which establishes specific procedures and requirements, often including obligations to compensate the agent when his representation is terminated without just cause.

While these local laws do not usually preclude termination, they may, in fact, impose heavy penalties for doing so. It is important therefore, to investigate where such legislation does exist, and how the principal might be able to forestall any problems should the time come when developments may require the need to either change the agreement or compel the principal to terminate it.

Clauses relating to termination must be carefully worded. You don't want to be stuck with an ineffective, lazy or incapable agent to whom you would have to pay a heavy indemnity if it becomes necessary to cancel his contract. Consult with your legal counsel to be sure your agreement complies with local legislation regarding termination in each of the countries in which you will be working with agents. All clauses and provisions of the contract should be checked to be sure they are permissible under the laws of each country. The following are some examples of the protective laws established by some countries. You should be aware of these. Note that some of these can also apply to distributors.

- Laws that place agents on the same legal status as employees, thereby entitling them to the benefits given all employees under local labor laws government the termination of employees. Local courts may construe an agent to be an employee of the principal.

- Some laws require that agents be compensated for loss of future commissions. If local labor laws are written strongly in favor of the agent, compensation could take the form of a pension. Sometimes this law may even include severance pay for an agent's employees who are discharged because of termination of the agent.

- Laws requiring proper notice of termination to be served on the agent.

- Laws which allow the agent served with a termination notice to contest the termination by submitting it to arbitration to determine if there was just cause for the termination.

- Laws which prevent your restricting an agent's commercial activity in the same industry or products for more than a certain number of years after termination.

These and many other laws can affect your agency agreement if it is not prepared and written with the assistance of legal council familiar with the national and local laws of each country in which you are working with an agent.

The following pages include samples of two types of agent agreements as general guidelines.

MANUFACTURER'S AGENT AGREEMENT

THIS MANUFACTURER'S AGENT AGREEMENT is made effective as of _____, 19___, by and between ABC Corporation of the State of _____ having its principal office at _____, hereinafter referred to as ABC, and XYZ AGENCIES, hereinafter referred to as XYZ. hereby ABC appoints XYZ its Agent to sell its line of products identified as "Products" upon the following conditions.

1. APPOINTMENT AND TERRITORY

ABC hereby appoints and grants to XYZ the exclusive rights to promote, distribute and market Products in (country) hereinafter referred to as the "territory".

2. ACCEPTANCE

XYZ hereby accepts said appointment and grant and agrees to use its best efforts to promote, distribute and market said Products in the territory in accordance with the provisions of this Agreement and within ABC's terms and conditions of sale, annexed hereto as Appendix A, and as may be later amended.

3. INDEPENDENT CONTRACTORS

It is agreed that XYZ is an independent contractor. This agreement does not constitute XYZ the agent or legal representative of ABC for any purpose whatsoever. XYZ is not granted any right or authority to assume or to create any obligation or responsibility, express or implied, in behalf of or in the name of ABC, or to legally bind ABC in any manner.

4. SELLING EXPENSES AND ADVERTISING MATTERS

ABC shall not be responsible to XYZ for any expense of advertising or selling the products. Notwithstanding the above to the contrary, ABC may aid and assist XYZ in its work of promoting the sale of the Products, all at XYZ's expense. ABC shall supply XYZ from time to time with a reasonable amount of catalogs and all other advertising matter of ABC, which catalogs and such other advertising materials are printed in a language other than the English language. Catalogs and such other advertising materials printed in a language other than the English language shall not be the responsibility of ABC; however, all such catalogs and such other advertising materials must be consented to in writing by ABC before use, and such consent shall not be unreasonably withheld so long as such catalogs and such other advertising matter protect ABC trademarks, trade name, and price structures.

5. PRICES

All sales of Products by XYZ will be in accordance with the price list and discount structure as agreed upon by the parties in writing. Notwithstanding the above, ABC reserves the right to change prices at any time upon sixty (60) days' notice to XYZ. Orders taken by XYZ within said sixty (60) day period shall be at the ordered price, provided the confirmed order is received by ABC within said sixty (60) days of XYZ's receipt of notification of change of price.

6. FILLING OF ORDERS

ABC shall have the right to accept or reject any order, but once any such order is accepted, ABC shall use its best efforts to process and fill such order. ABC shall not be responsible to XYZ or its customers for the delay in or failure to deliver any ordered Products because of the lack of availability of raw materials, Acts of God, of labor shortage or dispute, or any other act or acts beyond the control of ABC.

7. COMMISSIONS

All commissions provided for hereunder shall not become due and payable until full settlement has been received by ABC for the Products sold with respect to which such commissions are computed.

On orders obtained by XYZ for direct shipment from ABC to customers in the territory at export prices, ABC will pay to XYZ a commission of ____percent (___%) on the F.O.B. factory price.

On orders obtained by XYZ for direct shipment from ABC to OEM customers in the territory, the prices to be quoted will be established by ABC. On all such orders, ABC will pay to XYZ a commission not to exceed ____ percent (___%) on the F.O.B. factory price to the OEM customer. The percentage of commission shall be agreed upon by ABC and XYZ.

ABC reserves the right, either by itself or through others designated by it, to handle business arising from OEM customers and governmental agencies in the territory directly, but in all such cases ABC shall pay to XYZ a commission not exceeding _____percent (___)% on the F.O.B. factory price. The percentage of commission shall be agreed upon by ABC and XYZ.

ABC shall accept orders from exporters and agents domiciled in the United States for export to the territory. In all such cases, ABC shall pay to XYZ a _____percent (___)% commission on the F.O.B. factory price.

In the event any product is shipped to the territory without the knowledge or consent or control of ABC by United States or other manufacturers, XYZ shall not be entitled to receive any commission.

8. PAYMENT

XYZ shall cause its customers to establish an irrevocable, confirmed letter of credit confirmed by a New York bank, issued in the name of ABC. Each such letter of credit is to be in the full amount of the corresponding order, and is to be payable upon presentation of a sight draft with documents attached to said bank or as the parties may otherwise agree.

In the event XYZ recommends direct shipment to the customer on payment terms other than by irrevocable letter of credit, XYZ will arrange to supply ABC with credit information and references of such customer. In the event of any delay in payment, XYZ will diligently pursue the matter until full payment is received.

Payment for all Products shall be made in the currency of the United States of America.

9. SUB-AGENTS

XYZ may seek the aid of others in the territory to help XYZ promote, market and distribute the products in the territory. XYZ shall obtain prior approval of ABC of all arrangements with sub-agents and others for the sale of the products in the territory.

10. TRADEMARKS, TRADE NAME, ETC.

XYZ recognizes ABC's ownership of its trademarks and trade name, and will not take any action which will prejudice or harm said marks or name, or ABC's ownership thereof, in any way.

The decision of ABC on all matters concerning its trademarks or trade name shall be final and conclusive and not subject to question by XYZ. ABC will protect and defend its trademarks, trade name, and patents at its sole cost and expense, but ABC shall not be liable to XYZ for any loss or damage suffered by XYZ by XYZ's use of trademarks, trade name or patents or as a result of any litigation or proceeding involving the same. XYZ will cooperate fully with ABC in the defense and protection of its trade marks, trade names or patents, and will promptly and fully advise ABC of any use in the territory of any mark, name or use infringing ABC's trademarks, names or patents. XYZ will at ABC's request and cost, join with ABC in making application to the appropriate official or officials within the territory for registration of XYZ as a representative user of ABC's trademarks, names or patents. Nothing herein contained shall be construed as conferring upon XYZ any right or interest in said trademarks, or in its registration, or in any designs, copyrights, patents, trade names, signs, emblems, insignia, symbols and slogans, or other marks, used in connection with the products.

11. XYZ COVENANTS

XYZ covenants that it will actively promote the Products of ABC in the territory and will not sell or offer to sell equipment of others competitive with ABC where ABC is willing and able to supply the required Products.

XYZ covenants that no ABC Product sold by XYZ in the territory will be re-exported from the territory without ABC's prior written approval except when incorporated in machines or equipment, or spares for the same, which is being exported.

XYZ covenants that it will not promote, sell or distribute ABC's Products outside of the territory without ABC's written approval.

XYZ covenants that it will maintain an adequately trained staff as well as a reasonable amount of representative spare parts inventory to provide after-sales service to customers in the territory.

XYZ covenants it will keep ABC informed of matters and developments within its territory which may affect the sales of ABC's Products.

12. DURATION AND REMOVAL

This Agreement shall commence on the effective date as set forth in the introductory paragraph of this Agreement and shall continue for one (1) year thereafter. This Agreement may be extended by written agreement of both parties for successive one (1) year periods. Each party agrees that, if it elects not to renew this Agreement, it will mail or otherwise provide to the other party written notice of its intention not to renew, at least sixty (60) days prior to any anniversary date of this Agreement. If neither party provides such notice, this Agreement will be deemed renewed for the next year by mutual agreement.

13. TERMINATION

The parties agree that this Agreement may be terminated at any time without liability of one party as against the other for any valid business reason upon sixty (60) days' written notice to the other party, except that the written period shall be fifteen (15) days if: (i) either party shall cease to function as a going concern, or a receiver for it is applied for, or a petition under any Bankruptcy or Reorganization is filed by or against a party, or a party makes an assignment for the benefit of credits; (ii) the situation among nations renders the performance of this Agreement impracticable; (iii) currency controls make trade between the United States and a country in the territory substantially impracticable; or (iv) XYZ assigns this Agreement.

14. OBLIGATIONS UPON EXPIRATION OR TERMINATION

In the event of expiration or termination of this Agreement, ABC agrees to fulfill all XYZ's orders in order to satisfy all contractual obligations provided that (i) such orders were entered into prior to the date of the written notice of intention not to renew the Agreement or a notice of termination, and (ii) XYZ or its customers make credit arrangements satisfactory to ABC.

XYZ shall return prepaid to ABC any models or samples, catalogs and other advertising materials upon the expiration or termination of this Agreement.

XYZ shall abandon all use of ABC's trademarks, trade names, and patents upon the expiration or termination of this Agreement.

15. NOTICES

Any written notice, consents, etc., required by this Agreement shall be sent either by facsimile, telex or first class airmail, postage prepaid, certified, to the following address:

(list address of ABC Company)

(list address of XYZ Company)

In the event that a party's name, address, or facsimile or telex number changes, notice of such change shall be given to the other party and all future notices, consents, etc., shall be addressed in accordance with such change.

16. ASSIGNMENT, SUCCESSORS

The rights conferred on XYZ herein are personal and may not be assigned, in whole or in part, without ABC's written consent. As used herein, the term "assigned" shall mean, in addition to any assignment by contract, any merger or consolidation of XYZ with any other corporation, any change in the ownership or control of XYZ. Except as set forth above, this Agreement shall be binding upon the parties and their respective successors and legal representatives.

17. CHANGES AND AMENDMENTS

No change, addition or erasure of any portion of this Agreement shall be valid or binding upon either party unless signed or initialed by a duly authorized representative of the parties hereto. Any amendment to this Agreement must be in writing and signed by the parties hereto.

18. NO WAIVER

The failure of either party to require the performance of any term of this Agreement, or the waiver by either party of any breach under this Agreement, shall not prevent a subsequent enforcement of such term nor be deemed a waiver of any subsequent breach.

19. GOVERNING LAW AND DIVISIBILITY

This Agreement is to be construed as having been executed under the laws of the State of _____ , United States, and is to be governed according to such laws.

It is understood, however, that the promotion, marketing and distribution of the Products will take place in the Territory, and therefore, any provision of this Agreement which in any way contravenes the laws of any government or other jurisdiction in connection with the performances of this Agreement shall be deemed not to be a part of this Agreement, although all other parts of this Agreement shall be deemed to be binding.

20. ARBITRATION

All disputes not settled or adjusted concerning this Agreement or its effects shall be settled by arbitration in accordance with the rules then pertaining of the Rules of Conciliation and Arbitration of the International Chamber of Commerce.

The party requesting arbitration shall send to the other party a notice requesting arbitration and appointing its arbitrator. Within sixty (60) days thereafter, the other party shall notify the party requesting arbitration of the name of its arbitrator. The two arbitrators so appointed shall thereafter meet to select the third arbitrator, and failing such appointment, the third arbitrator shall be appointed by the then president of the New York City, New York organization of the International Chamber of Commerce. The arbitrator's award shall be made by a majority of the arbitrators, which decision shall be final. The decision of the arbitrators shall not contravene the laws of the State of_____ , United States. The arbitration hearing shall be in New York City, New York, United States. Each party shall bear the cost of the arbitrator selected by it and all parties shall equally bear the costs of arbitration and of the third arbitrator.

21. HEADINGS AND NUMBER

The headings of this Agreement are inserted for convenience of reference only, and are not to be considered in the construction of the provisions hereof.

The singular number and pronouns shall include the plural number and pronouns unless the context requires otherwise. This Agreement is based on the assumption that XYZ's business is in the corporation or partnership form, and in the event that it is not, then the word "its" shall include the masculine and feminine pronoun, as the case may be, unless the context requires otherwise.

22. COUNTERPARTS

This Agreement may be executed simultaneously in two (2) or more counterparts, each of which shall be deemed an original, but all of which shall constitute one and the same Agreement.

IN WITNESS WHEREOF, the parties have executed this Agreement as of the date below their respective signatures. Each of the signatures hereto has been duly authorized in full compliance with all legal requirements.

ABC COMPANY

BY_____

DATED_____

XYZ COMPANY

BY _____

DATED _____

AGENT AGREEMENT

AGREEMENT made at _____ , _____United States of America, this__ day of_____ 199_ , between___ABC COMPANY___ , a corporation of the State of_____ , having its principal offices in _____ , (hereinafter called the "Principal"), and___ XYZ AGENCIES___ , of__ _____ (hereinafter called the "Agent"). THIS CONTRACT SUPER-SEDES ALL PREVIOUS AGREEMENTS BETWEEN ABC AND XYZ.

IT IS AGREED:

1. Except as provided in Paragraph #7 hereof, the Agent is hereby appointed by the Principal as its sales supervisor on its line of products describe products___ , for the country of _____for a period of one year from the date of execution of this contract, with the authority to supervise the Principal's sales in _____ subject to the conditions herein contained.

2. The Agent hereby accepts such appointment and agrees with the Principal that he will, during the term of this agreement, diligently apply himself and his efforts in the development of sales of said products for the principal within the territory hereby assigned to him, that he will periodically submit reports to the Principal of his activities and progress in such work, and will at all times keep the Principal informed of matters and developments within his territory tending to affect the interests of the Principal.

3. It is understood that nothing in the terms of this contract gives the Agent the right to make any commitments or sign any contracts on behalf of the Principal. Such rights are reserved exclusively for the Principal.

4. During the terms of this agreement, the Agent will not directly or indirectly represent any products competitive with those manufactured by the Principal and included within the meaning of this contract; that any product performing the same basis function as one made by the Principal shall be deemed to be competitive for the purposes of this agreement.

5. Except as provided in Paragraph #7 hereof, the Principal agrees to pay to the Agent a commission equal to 10%, unless otherwise agreed upon, of the net merchandise value of all the Principal's products sold and shipped by the Principal to the territory assigned to the Agent under the terms of this agreement; the "net merchandise value" shall be construed to mean that net amount received by the Principal for products sold after the deduction of all discounts, transportation, insurance and forwarding charges; that such commissions will become due and payable after the proceeds for shipments made shall have been received by the Principal.

6. This agreement shall operate and continue in force for a period of one year from and after the date hereof, and continuously thereafter until cancelled. It is agreed that either party may cancel after the initial period of one year by giving thirty days written notice to the other; that any letter, telex or facsimile expressing such intent, duly given thirty days in advance, shall be construed as sufficient and proper notice for the purpose of this paragraph.

7. Sales to governments, United States of America or others, purchasing commissions, government agencies or purchasing agencies located in the United States of America serving industrial organizations, as for example petroleum producing and marketing companies, mining construction and supplies companies, and direct sales by the Principal of its products to other manufacturers, wheresoever located, for use as original equipment on any vehicle, do not fall within the terms of this agreement, and commissions on any such sale will be paid at the sole discretion of the Principal.

8. In the event a legal determination of this document shall become required, such determination shall be made according to the laws of the State of _____ , United States of America.

IN WITNESS THEREOF, the parties hereto have caused the execution of this instrument at the said City of_____ ,State of _____ , United States of America, the day and year written above.

ABC COMPANY

BY_____

TITLE _____

XYZ AGENCIES

BY _____

TITLE_____

Chapter 11

EVALUATING FOREIGN DISTRIBUTOR'S PERFORMANCE

Now that you have distributors in foreign markets, you expect that they will give you their best efforts in providing sales and profits for your company. Since the distributor is an independent businessman, you will not be able to have the same controls over his activities that you would have over your own sales force. Therefore, you will have to organize a regular (usually annual) program for evaluating his performance and for ascertaining that he is complying with all the terms of the distributor contract.

Performance Evaluation Checklist

There are many different methods available for implementing an evaluation program, depending upon the nature of the market and the types of products and customers involved. Assuming a distributor has received good product training by your company—its use, how and where to sell and promote it, and how to service it—he should be making sales in a reasonable time after the contract has been signed. You should then start looking at his performance based on a list of points you will have established for evaluation. Every company will have certain factors in a checklist to aid in performing a distributor evaluation. The list will include some or all of the following:

• Check if the distributor is following the marketing plan you and he developed in the final stages of your selection and negotiating processes. This plan should have spelled out the basic requirements for penetrating the market and defined the mutual goals at which you were aiming, and how each would be accomplished. The major elements of the plan should, at the time evaluation takes place, be in the execution or accomplishment stages.

• Check all of the distributor's activities, both short and long-range, to determine the effectiveness of his effort against the marketing plan. You will want to be sure he is on track meeting the planned goals of selling your products and obtaining significant market penetration.

One of the major elements of the marketing plan, and a prime effort in obtaining desired market share, is the distributor's use of local advertising, promotion, and trade shows. High on your evaluation check list should be finding out if the distributor is following his portion of the plan with respect to the timing, layout and content of his advertisements; his use of correct media; his participation in the most meaningful trade shows available in his market; and the number and quality of product seminars and other promotions he conducts.

If you are offering the distributor reimbursement for any of the promotional activities noted above, make certain he is submitting proper documentation to the company in a timely manner. You should ask him to make reimbursement submissions at least quarterly

• Keep track of distributor's purchases from you to be sure he is maintaining proper stock levels. Lack of stock can mean lost sales, especially if your competitor's distributor is keeping his stock levels up and able to satisfy even your customer's needs.

• Check if the distributor has met the current period's sales quota. Look at this in terms of his purchases from you versus his sales to end-users. He may have met his quota by purchasing products from you, but the merchandise may not have been sold to customers. Check the distributor's inventory turnover ratio.

• If this is not the first performance evaluation, compare the distributor's sales with prior periods' sales to obtain a picture of his growth, or lack thereof, in the market.

• Be sure the distributor's sales force is spending adequate time in the field calling on customers and selling your products. In this same area, find out:

a. If the salespeople are fully trained to sell the products, close the sale, install the products and train the customers in using them.

b. The average number of sales calls per sales person, the number of presentations made by each, and the total dollar and unit sales achieved.

c. The number of new accounts obtained in the prior year, and if any accounts were lost, find out why.

d. If the distributor seems to be carrying too many lines to give yours the attention it requires

• The level of competency of the inside/telephone counter sales people. They should be well-trained to handle written, verbal and personal inquiries from potential customers or product application queries (or complaints) from regular customers.

• You should check with a number of customers to find out:

1. If sales people visit them on a regular basis after sales have been made to:

a. Help them learn more about the product and its application.

b. Give products regular maintenance and check if they are working properly.

c. Supply them with information on new uses developed for the products or about modification and updates available.

d. Inform them about new products.

2. If the distributor's response to complaints, problems, requests for product service (repair, replacement parts) is quick and effective.

• Check that the distributor is providing you with effective market reports, not only sales and customer activity, but also information on competitor 's activities, products and market share. You should also be kept informed about any local situations such as new construction or development projects which could affect sales and new laws or regulations regarding imports or currency controls. The distributor should also give you, from time to time, customer feed-back and reactions about the products they are using as well as any ideas for modifications or new products they would like to see.

• Make sure the distributor sales force is calling on all possible users in all industry segments of the market and not missing out on sales to certain classes of trade.

• Check to see if the distributors and his retailers are displaying your products properly and in the best positions. It is especially important that many consumer-type products be displayed at or near check-out counters or in high-visibility floor displays.

• Find out how the distributor operates against his competitors. Determine if his approach is antagonistic and what his pricing policies are vis-a-vis those of your competitors.

• Be sure the showroom area is attractive and large enough. Also, determine that the people giving demonstrations are fully trained to do so properly so as not to risk losing a sale by giving a poor presentation to a potential customer.

• Find out if the distributor is losing orders to competition. If so, are the orders lost due to price, to better product quality or features, or to poor selling ability by the sales force.

• The attitude of the distributor and his entire staff is an important factor to evaluate, especially if sales are falling or if they simply have not been at acceptable levels for a period of time. Attitude includes a high level of interest and enthusiasm shown by the distributor's staff to promote, sell, service and train prospects and customers. This interest is contagious when displayed to customers and can only serve to increase sales. You can tell by the time and effort devoted to the line if the level of interest is acceptable.

Another attitude to consider is that of cooperation by the distributor in carrying out marketing plans and special promotions, having good floor space devoted to the company's products, either on shelves, showrooms or demonstration areas, and cooperating with the manufacturer in attending training schools or distributor meetings.

• Tie in your distributor's activities and sales results with the level of business and economic activity taking place in his territory. If the business, economic and industrial performance of the market is at a high level, find out if the distributor's activities and growth are also improving. In such a market the distributor's sales should be growing and his organization, sales people, inventory, working capital, service to more industries, etc., should also be keeping pace with the local growth.

Many additional factors can be used in the evaluation process including all of the criteria you used in selecting the distributor in the first place. Be sure he maintains all the "good things" he had going for him which prompted you to select him as your distributor.

One thing you must be aware of in performing distributor evaluations of your world-wide network is that all distributors cannot be evaluated and judged using the same set of criteria. Just as you have found differences in other aspects of sales, marketing, product adaptability, and many other factors in your work in overseas markets, so too, will you find differences in how distributors work and handle products in various parts of the world. This will be due to local economic and business conditions as well as to cultural differences, all of which must be taken into consideration as you proceed with your evaluation program.

It is a good idea to let the distributor know he will be evaluated by you on a regular basis, and that all aspects of his performance, organization and operations will be looked at closely; not so much in a prejudicial sense, but in order to be alerted to situations needing correction or to find areas in which improvement may be mutually beneficial. While the distributor should know this will be happening, it is not a good idea that he know the exact items in your checklist since he might take steps to make himself look good on those points only at the time you are checking him on them. He should also be aware that submitting to a periodic evaluation of his performance is a condition of his continuing to work with you and for you.

Self Evaluation is Important Too!

Companies should, before undertaking distributor evaluations, review their own level of compliance with their own responsibilities to their distributor family. A company may not be carrying out all of the contract terms or the verbal commitments made to distributors when signing them on. It may not have given them all the product training or other sales help promised. If you are lacking in some areas, you should take steps to correct the situation so as not to impede the distributor's performance in any way, or have the distributor so dissatisfied with you that he will not want to continue selling your products. It works both ways.

The End Result

At the completion of individual distributor evaluations, a careful analysis should be made of your findings. If you have done a good job in your evaluation, you will now be aware of any shortcomings or major faults in your distributor network and you should take immediate steps to correct them by advising each distributor of the problems you have encountered. Many times a distributor will not be aware that he is doing something wrong, or that his activities do not meet with your standards or criteria. In some cases your analysis will show that you have picked the wrong distributor, that he has misrepresented his ability, or some other serious, objectionable factor has come to light. Some of these factors could be grounds for termination.

Terminating a Distributor

Obviously, this is a serious step to take and should not be taken without thorough consideration of all factors involved. You have spent a lot of time, money and effort in finding, selecting, and training a distributor. It will cost you more time, money and effort to find a replacement. There should be very clear and strong grounds for termination after an evaluation has been done. A great deal of sensitivity should be exercised about the causes which are leading you to the conclusion that the distributor is not the best one for your company. You should do everything possible to correct whatever you feel is wrong by discussing the problem(s) personally, and seek corrections or improvements without having to take the ultimate step. Often, if the distributor knows you are displeased with his work for you, even to the point of considering terminating him, he may react favorably and do a real turn-around and become a good, successful distributor.

If, in the end, you feel he must be terminated, review your decision in the light of your contract and consult with your legal department for any possible legal (U.S. or foreign) entanglements. If your contract is well written and termination or cancellation clauses and procedures are properly spelled out, you should not have any problem in carrying out the process. Before you terminate a distributor, you should be sure to have a replacement available. It would be easiest if you could terminate the relationship by mutual agreement, however, this is not always possible. For example, on one occasion the author went to a Caribbean Island with the intention of terminating an agent who was not producing and was found to be spending most of his time in local hotel bars. During a meeting in my hotel room, he was informed that he would be terminated. He became quite belligerent and threatened that if he were replaced, he would do "bodily harm" to me. Obviously, he had already been at the bar prior to our meeting.

His ultimatum was that if I did not inform him later that day that he could retain the agency, he would "come after me." Since I had arrived the day before, and had already concluded arrangements with his replacement, (which the first agent did not know), I informed the new agent of what had happened. Together we made hasty arrangements to change my flight and hotel reservations for the next stop on my itinerary, and in a couple of hours, made a safe, retreat!

After completing the rest of my itinerary, I returned home by way of the same island and met with the new agent who informed me that "Old Jack" had quieted down and accepted his termination. I never found out what transpired between the two agents while I was away, but the end result was satisfactory.

In any event, before you terminate a distributor, you should be sure you have a replacement available.

Summary

Evaluation of a distributor and your relationship with him is a learning process for both parties. Basically, it is a process of measuring actual against planned performance. You establish the standards at which you want your distributors to work, and in the evaluation process you measure to what degree they have reached those standards. As a good principal, you should have laid a good foundation to enable your network of distributors to reach top performance and comply with your standards. By the same token, knowing what your distributors want and need in a good principal, you must, from time to time assess your own performance vis-a-vis the distributor's standards. You cannot expect great accomplishments from them if you or your company have not done what you said you would do for them in terms of training in product sales, use and service, advertising and promotional help, supplying sales leads and responding promptly and efficiently to queries and complaints. As with almost everything else in the foreign trade arena, evaluation is also a two-way street.

Chapter 12

KEEPING FOREIGN DISTRIBUTORS LOYAL AND HAPPY

Vital to the long-range success of an international sales operation is the establishment and maintenance of good rapport with overseas distributors. Most distributor/principal relationships work out well and both parties derive many benefits over a long period of time. But companies must continue to work diligently to maintain the mutual good feeling that is evident at the start of an association by continuing to build a high level of distributor loyalty and contentment. This is especially important during the break-in period so that the distributor does not feel you've left him out there all alone.

In Chapter 8, (WHAT DISTRIBUTORS WANT FROM A PRINCI-PAL), we discussed six subjects which most distributors bring up during the selection negotiations as conditions they would like to have incorporated in the agreement, or be assured that the principal will grant them. Those conditions can be the basis for constructing distributor policies which will strengthen the partnership you are entering with your distributor network.

In addition to these basic conditions, some of which can be enlarged upon, there are many other things a company can do to develop the loyalty and contentment of these new members of its working team.

Agenda for Keeping Distributors Happy

1. Communicate frequently, clearly, and promptly

Establish an open, direct line of communication between his office and yours. The distributor must know that he can contact you at any time at your home office or, in your absence, a designated member of your staff who can answer his questions, solve his problems, or listen to a complaint. Telex and fax lines should remain open and available around the clock. Remember, world time differences often means that your distributors are working while you are sleeping, and vice-versa. Leaving telex and fax lines open means they can communicate with you during their day, and you can respond during yours. In some cases you may even agree to exchange home telephone numbers to be able to handle emergencies more promptly.

Promptness is the operative word! Situations or questions which cannot be resolved or answered on-the-spot should be responded to within the shortest time possible...at least within 24 to 36 hours. A distributor located thousands of miles away should not be left with a problem unsolved or questions unanswered for days on end. This would definitely make him (and the customers involved) very unhappy...just the opposite of what you are trying to do.

2. Keep the distributor's interest at a high level during the first few months of the relationship

Feed him lots of leads. Help him with introductory product promotions and perhaps special announcements of his selection as your distributor in the territory. Supply him with special advertising reprints of your products to help launch them in the market. These and other personal, helpful gestures of your interest in him and his market will create a feeling of confidence in the distributor's mind that you really mean to cooperate with him and will accomplish much to maintain his interest at a high level.

3. Conduct regular, continuous training programs

In addition to regular product training, which should include plenty of engineering and technical assistance, you should, at the start as well as periodically thereafter, give your distributors "company" training programs. Include such subjects as:

- Instruction in product applications.
- The types of problems customers might encounter when using your products and how to solve them.
- Information about competitive products, their features, prices, selling strategies and how to sell against them.
- How the company obtains leads for the distributors and how leads can help develop a stronger customer base.

Leads come to the company from many sources such as advertising, trade shows, government sources, prospect's contacts with overseas embassies. Forward them promptly.

- Helping the distributor identify potential customers
- Informing distributors about advertising, promotions and trade show schedules, and products for promotion.
- Review of the company's history, its distributor policies, its business philosophy and future plans.

4. Home Office Visits

The company training sessions described above are obviously best conducted at the home office facilities of the Principal. Periodic visits to the home office are not only most important to maintain and improve distributor's morale, but are most sought for by the distributors themselves. Nothing creates a stronger sense of "belonging" than to invite or encourage a distributor to spend a day or two visiting the company. He will have the opportunity to meet your international staff with whom he will be working closely as well as other company management. Make a point of introducing him to your president, other key officers and management people. Let him see your products in the planning, manufacturing and packaging stages. Distributors like to know the companies they are representing are live, viable entities staffed by people to whom they can relate by phone, fax or telex when they go back home.

5. Hold meetings of all international distributors

Another good opportunity for distributor visits to the home office is extending an invitation to participate in a full meeting of all international distributors where they can get to know and exchange ideas with the rest of the international distributor family. In addition to such an annual or bi-ennial meeting, you can establish an international distributor advisory council to which you can appoint several of your top distributors on a rotating basis, to represent the interests of the full network. You can in this way, achieve two ends...find out what the distributor's problems are, and the distributors can be informed about the latest company trends and policies.

6. Keep them informed of future plans

Create close distributor association with your company by confiding your plans for future developments, and by asking for advice on new products, packaging, advertising, promotions, ways to improve sales, and the best way to foster the company's image and presence in the distributors' markets. Together with regular visits to the home office and your visits to them, these things will help create a solid distributor "family," cemented by a strong feeling of mutual confidence and cooperation.

Distributors should feel they can make recommendations and give you ideas about how to improve business, the products and how they are packaged, and the company's image in their territories. They will see things from a different perspective, and may come up with some ideas you hadn't thought about. This is all part of the effort needed to make them feel part of the company and key figures in its success.

7. Reward a distributor's achievements

Reward achievements in reaching or surpassing sales goals or other stated objectives by giving him a plaque or certificate, or by giving him an additional discount or a cash rebate on the period's sales. If possible, publicize his achievement in your company magazine. This will give him recognition among his peers and many also serve as incentive to other distributors to work harder to obtain similar rewards.

8. Keep them informed of changes in advance

Be sure to give distributors ample advance notice of, and reasons for, price changes, new product specifications, or other policy changers. When making such changes, take into consideration how they might affect your distributors, positively or adversely, and provide adequate justification for changes so the distributor can explain them to their salespeople and customers. Don't put the responsibility entirely on your distributors to "take care of things" in their territories.

9. Provide allowances for advertising and promotion

If you haven't already done so in your distributor's contract, consider giving the distributor an advertising and promotion allowance. This often takes the form of a reimbursement for advertising space in local media and booth-space costs at a product trade show in the foreign market. While much of a company's advertising in U. S. publications does actually reach overseas markets, the messages in them which are geared to U.S. markets, do not always come across well in foreign countries. Advertising directly in overseas media may be too costly and not always practical nor available. Consider asking your distributors to explore local media for advertising and promotional possibilities. Reimbursing the distributors for one-half the space costs for an advertisement in a local magazine, trade journal or newspaper (a very popular medium in many countries), or the booth-space cost at a local trade show, is a very inexpensive way for a company to promote its products and give an important public relations boost to its local distributors. Many companies supply free art work, slides or transparencies for advertisements and posters, and samples or giveaways to be used at a booth at a trade show.

Art work may also be supplied free so a distributor can produce a brochure or other product literature in the local language, tailoring the message to local usage, customs and appeals.

The practice of granting reimbursements for advertising and promotion can be easily controlled. The company can authorize payments only after receipt from the distributor of a copy of a vendor's invoice (translated or in English) showing the expense involved, and attaching a copy of the advertisement itself. You should obtain from the distributor a quarterly or yearly list of advertisements or promotions he plans to use and estimates of their costs. Actually, this should be part of the marketing plan he presents to you each year. This will give you the opportunity to budget for your own expense and approve or reject the proposals.

10. Provide company history and product/application videos for distributor's use with prospective customers

These are especially important with engineered, special products or those which are difficult to carry to a prospect's premises for demonstration. They make things much easier for both the distributor and the customer. Be sure videos are produced in the correct format(s) for viewing in overseas markets. They should be in color and of a professional quality.

11. Make sales and other market reporting easy for the distributors

Let them know the basic facts and figures you want. They do not have to write a volume of prose. Some companies provide printed forms for distributors to fill in quickly so responding does not become a difficult chore.

12. Sales bulletins and selling tips should be supplied regularly

These will help the distributor sales force to stay fresh and on their toes when working with customers. They also help highlight important product features or special applications pertinent to customer presentations.

13. Provide customer samples

Supply your distributors with attractive, quality giveaways and samples to leave with customers. They do not have to be expensive, but they should not be "cheap" or flimsy creating an opposite effect to that which you intended.

14. Provide realistic facts on delivery of distributors' orders

If you know production is behind schedule, say so in your order acknowledgements. If your deliveries have historically been good and your distributors have become accustomed to receiving prompt deliveries, you must let them know if you now expect delays in shipment. Avoid leaving them in a bad inventory position or one in which they have to tell a customer he will not receive his goods when promised.

15. Return Goods Policy

Distributors must have some assurance they will be allowed to return damaged, obsolete, defective or incorrectly shipped products. Company's should formulate an equitable policy for the handling of such goods. While most companies do allow distributors to return products in these categories for credit, they require that the distributor obtain prior authorization. Distributors usually pay the return freight, except on products incorrectly shipped by the manufacturer. Sometimes a distributor may have ordered items which he later finds he cannot sell, and will want to return those also. Not all manufacturers allow return of these products. However, sometimes it is good "public relations" to accept them to keep the distributor happy.

16. Warranties

A good warranty (guarantee) policy does much to give a distributor confidence that he can sell a company's product with full protection for himself and his customers should the product fail or not perform properly. Manufacturers should not try to evade responsibility in dealing with warranty claims. The buyer wants to know that he runs little or no risk in purchasing the item. The distributor wants to protect the company's and his own reputation and goodwill in the market by promoting and selling products which he knows the manufacturer will repair or replace at no cost to him or the customer.

Summary

The key to a successful relationship between a principal and its distributors is the formation of a solid basis of mutual confidence recognizing the respective role each party plays in what is in reality, a partnership. The principal's role is the manufacturer and supplier of goods and services. The distributor promotes and sells the goods and services. For the partnership to survive and flourish, each partner must respect the position of the other and comply not only with all contractual agreements, but also relate to each other with goodwill and understanding.

Many and varied problems can arise between a distributor and a manufacturer. Thinking ahead and anticipating these problems, misunderstandings or conflicts, the manufacturer should formulate a definite policy of how it will address each situation when and if it does arise. It can often be too late to make the best decision after the fact.

Anticipating problems means being aware of what distributors want from principals; what makes distributors loyal to companies; and what makes them happy, beneficial partners.

Each of the sixteen items discussed in this chapter are important factors although not all need be applied to every market.

Obviously, other items covering unique situations could be added to this list. Anticipate what might be needed and implement the solution before it becomes crucial.

Communicate frequently by letter, fax, telephone and personal visits. Develop a feeling of trust and confidence, and treat your distributors as equal partners. Learn as much as possible about your distributor's markets, not only from a sales and marketing point of view, but also to understand them and their customers in the context of their varied and interesting cultures. This will not only give you greater insight and awareness of the many diverse markets with which you are dealing, but also offers a fascinating, rewarding personal experience.

Chapter 13

SELLING AND PROMOTING PRODUCTS OVERSEAS

Your early market research and analysis showed that your products can be sold overseas. You now have distributors in place in your chosen markets and you are ready to introduce and sell those products. As you learned earlier, you are aware that your products may have to be modified in some way to be acceptable in foreign markets, either physically or in their packaging. Now you have to consider carefully how you and your distributors will introduce, promote and sell your products in a given market. You cannot assume that this can be done in the same way as your domestic marketing group sells your products in the U.S. market.

Together with your distributor, you should now develop specific marketing plans for launching your line in each foreign market. The steps taken will depend in large part on the nature of your products and whether they are consumer goods, industrial items, automotive, etc. In any case, there will be some common factors to be considered which can apply to any class of products. For example, examine customer needs and attitudes, buying and using habits, customer's level of technology, local selling methods, and types of distribution outlets.

One of the most important things to consider is whether your company and your products are already known and recognized in the market. If they are, the task of introducing and selling will be much easier. If they are not well-known, your primary job will be to let your potential customers know who your company is and its reputation in the industry, what your products are and how they can satisfy customer's needs, and why you believe they are better than a competitor's products.

Getting The Message Across

Advertising

Decisions must now be made on how to get these messages to all potential buyers and users of your products. The first method to be considered is advertising, one of the primary elements to be included in your marketing plan.

You must decide on the strategy to use in an advertising program as well as focus on the specific media in which to implement that strategy. In both of these areas, your distributors can be of great help to you. They will know, for example, the buying influences peculiar to their local markets, the motivation needed, the preference of local buyers, who the key buyers are in local industries and businesses, and most importantly, they will know how to make a sales appeal for your products in the local language and idioms.

Your company may do a lot of advertising in the U. S. market, and some of it may reach foreign markets when the advertisements appear in industry trade-journals or magazines which circulate overseas. However, while the appeals used in U.S. advertising media may be successful in your domestic markets, they may turn off foreign buyers for a variety of business or cultural reasons. While there is, of course, some merit in domestic advertisements being circulated in overseas markets, direct appeals, preferably in the local language, will be much more acceptable and most cost-effective than most U. S. advertisements. Many foreign markets are too small to have specific trade magazines or industry journals of their own, so this medium cannot be used in those markets. In many countries however, the local newspapers are widely used and accepted as media for all types of advertising of consumer and industrial goods and services. An added benefit is their economical costs when compared to some of the "slick" magazines.

It would be a good idea to consult with your company's U.S. advertising agency about your plans for advertising in overseas markets. Many U.S. agencies have their own overseas branches staffed by local account executives, or work with foreign agencies located in some of your markets. The principal benefit in working with them is that the U.S.agency knows your company and products, and can transfer the knowledge to their foreign counterparts who can then devise a local strategy and appeal. Keep in mind also, the strategy suggested earlier, to have your foreign distributor take care of local advertising under a reimbursement plan incorporated in your contract.

Overseas Trade-Shows

Some of the same principals outlined above can apply to trade-shows held in overseas markets. Some of these are of world-wide importance, such as those held in Frankfurt or Hanover, Germany, the Vienna Trade Fair, the Paris Air Show or others covering many different industries held in other major cities around the world. Many trade-shows are also sponsored by the U. S. Department of Commerce in a large number of cities and countries, some of which focus on specific industries or services, while others are mounted to show a variety of U.S.-made products. Some overseas-sponsored trade-fairs receive the special endorsement or certification of the U. S. Department of Commerce which enhances a company's promotional efforts.

In many countries, the U. S. Department of Commerce's U.S. and Foreign Commercial Service maintains U.S. Trade Centers in which trade-shows are held. Companies can also participate in Catalog and Video-Catalog shows by sending complete sets of product literature to the trade centers where local potential customers can learn about your company and products.

A word or two about international trade-fairs (as they are commonly called overseas). In many countries, the trade-fair is one of the most important business events of the year for companies which participate in them. It is of equal importance to much of the rest of the business community which constitutes the buyers of the many diverse products shown at these fairs.

The Europeans have made trade-fairs an experience not to be believed or forgotten by a first-time American participant or attendee! The booths (or "stands" as Europeans call them), are larger and much more elaborate than those at U.S. trade-shows. Almost every stand will have a hospitality section, at least partially private, for conferences and meetings. In addition, many of the stands include a small, enclosed kitchen area from which hot and cold drinks and snacks are served. Some exhibitors will even serve sandwiches or, yes, bratwurst and beer!

Often, at the end of the day, notably at the Frankfurt Fair, one or two companies will bring in German "Oompah" bands who will play German drinking-songs while exhibitors and potential customers wind up the day's negotiations and deals and socialize over steins of cold beer. Similar, if not quite so elaborate, activities take place at fairs in many other parts of the world, and emphasize the importance placed on these business events by both exhibitors and visitors.

A good number of exhibits at foreign trade-fairs show locally-made products, or those of other foreign countries. But there are usually many U.S. companies exhibiting their products.

When considering trade-shows, don't overlook the fact that many shows mounted in the United States are characterized as "international." There will be, not only foreign exhibitors, (maybe even some foreign competitors!) but there are usually many foreign visitors who could be potential customers in their home markets. Discuss these shows with your domestic marketing people and make plans to attend some of them yourself. It may surprise you how many sales you will be able to make, and how many contacts you can refer to your overseas distributors. At one U.S. show the author attended, fully 15 percent of the visitor or lead-cards collected were filled in by overseas visitors; many of whom eventually bought the company's products from their home market distributors.

Before you make a decision about participating in an overseas trade-fair, discuss it with your distributor. He is sure to know which shows in his country can provide the best exposure for your product and which will draw a sizeable attendance. You and he should research the market before committing to exhibit, to be sure the "trade" will show up. A good trade-fair organizer usually advertises widely to attract visitors who are in the business and are good potential buyers.

A good distributor will already have advised you about trade-shows, and he will have analyzed their potential in the marketing plan he presented to you during your search for and evaluation of him. In your contract with the distributor, you may have established a partial reimbursement plan for his participation in a trade-fair. In either case, both of you should be at the booth so visitors will meet not only the local distributor and one or more of his sales people, but also an executive of the U.S. company. You may even decide to have colleagues from your home office, sales or technical department to help with "demos" and respond to technical questions.

Whatever the manner or extent of your participation—alone or with a distributor—a great deal of planning must proceed any action you take.

If you are new to the market, the objective of exhibiting obviously is to introduce your product. You must be sure it will be presented in its best light, and that all of the activity at the stand by your people is directed toward pointing out the benefits this new product will bring to the market.

Regarding the stand or booth itself, much planning and thought must be put into making it attractive and eye-catching—one in which your products can be seen, shown and used easily (especially if "demos" will be given). The booth must draw people to it, and make them stop, look at your products, and ask questions about them. It is only when people stop, that you and your colleagues can "go into your act" and get the visitor interested enough to either place an order or set up an appointment with your distributor to find out more about your product.

In addition, your booth for any show, but especially for your first show, must be a "class-act." A "chintzy" or sloppy-looking one will make people think your company and your products aren't first-class either, so put on the best display you can within your budget.

You should also plan to have cards available on which visitors who stop at your booth can fill in their name, address, company, type of business, and give an indication of their interest in your product. After the show, you or your distributor should call or write to these leads to thank them for stopping at your booth and showing an interest in your product. Your distributor will then have a prospect and mailing list to be followed up later by a salesman to determine if there is real interest, and perhaps take orders.

You will find that many of the visitors to a trade-fair will be upper-level management—the decision-makers and buyers of the very companies you want to attract, and to which you want to sell. Most fairs attract visitors from many foreign countries. This is an additional reason why it's important to have your booth manned by the best-trained and most competent people from your office or that of your distributor. The show will be your best opportunity to meet and talk to many potential customers face-to-face with your distributor and your product all in one place. Competence and a good image as shown by your display can work wonders for your sales effort.

Another advantage of participating is the opportunity to see and assess your competition, local, U.S.A. or foreign. You probably will have received a list of participants from the show organizers, so you'll know which of them will be in attendance. If you don't already know as much about them as you should, this could be an opportunity to learn more about their products, pricing and how they are working in the local market. Your competitors may know you or your colleagues personally, so you can bet your life they won't be anxious to give you any helpful information.

The way one company got around this was to have its French distributor, (unknown to his competitor) who was attending a trade-fair in another country, stop at several competitor's stands under the guise of a user of those products who just happened to be at the Fair. To complete the subterfuge, he had somehow managed to obtain several visitor badges with different names, each to be worn as he stopped at the different competitor's stands. He was thus able to see many "demos," to compare their products with those he distributed. He also obtained price information and found out some of the competition's future product and business plans, all of which he promptly reported back to his principals. Needless to say, he didn't spend too much time afterward at his principal's stand. Dominique, of course, was also able to use the information gathered to help him in his own country as well.

There are several other factors to consider when planning participation in an international trade-fair. Follow the check-list below to make sure you don't overlook any important ones.

1. Check on the services provided by the organizer to exhibitors

Experienced fair organizers offer a variety of services and, except for some specialized ones, they are usually included in the registration fee.

Look For:

a. Shipping Arrangements for your products and booth to the country in which the Fair is held. These matters should be taken care of well ahead of the opening day of the Fair. Give yourself at least two months. Don't forget to take into account the Export License Requirements for your product. A special validated license can usually be obtained quickly for products to be returned. There is also a special-request form giving you permission to sell these products at the Fair.

b. You'll need to know how and to whom to consign the products so clearance at destination will not be delayed. The organizer, even if he is foreign-based, works with a U. S. freight forwarder who will advise you and take care of many details and documentation.

The U.S. forwarder usually works in tandem with customs brokers in the foreign country to clear the arriving shipments under bond. The same broker and forwarding company combination will also arrange for return of the shipment to you.

c. Timing of the shipment is most important. Your shipment of products to be displayed, literature, promotional items, and any special equipment you might need, to use your equipment in a foreign country, should arrive at destination about two weeks before show-time. If you're working with a distributor, be sure he is aware of all the details so he can check things on-site, and ensure that everything will be ready to install, mount and tryout before the start of the Fair. If you're working the Fair on your own, you or a colleague should arrive well before the show date to set up the booth and products.

2. Some Special Needs
a. Extra tables, chairs or lighting for the stand.

b. Longer-than-standard extension cords.

c. Power conversion equipment.

d. Interpreters—allow extra time before the Fair starts to train your interpreter on your products so he/she can properly interpret them to local visitors.

e. A telephone at the stand can be very useful.

3. Hospitality areas at the Fair
If the size of your stand doesn't allow for the seating or discussion areas referred to earlier in this chapter, determine where you will be able to hold private discussions with prospective customers.

4. Check with the U. S. Embassy

Check in with the Embassy or consulates in the country to let them know you will be at a Fair in their post. Their commercial officers can help by notifying their contacts who may be prospective customers for the products that you will be exhibiting at a particular show.

Most trade-fair organizers are very competent and provide many different services before, during and after each Fair they arrange. They or their representatives are always available to help, and they can make your show enjoyable and successful.

After The Fair

Do a good job of analyzing everything that happened during the Fair—or didn't happen. Collect all your visitor cards and classify them as to the type of industries, the degree of potential for buyers (hot or cold prospects), number and value of sales made. Also analyze any positive or adverse comments you had from people you talked to, either about your stand, your "demos" or your product. Review all the information you have gathered about your competition so you will be better prepared to confront their efforts against you in the marketplace. Use all of this data to help improve your position in the market and to do a better job at the next Fair.

Personal Travel To Markets

One of the most successful ways to promote a line of products, is to get to know your customers and to let your customers get to know you, and through you, your company. Personal trips to all of your international markets are most important. On each trip, be sure to meet as many actual and potential customers as possible. Personal contact creates an excellent impression because an executive from the company is taking time to visit a customer who lives thousands of miles away. Your meetings with customers should emphasize your desire to be of service, and you should project sincerity, credibility, commitment (yours and the company's) and friendship, all of which helps to build up the "trust-factor" discussed earlier.

Learn from the customer why he likes your product and how it has helped him. Find out if he has any ideas on how to improve it, or better adapt it to his market, or if he has ideas for any new products your company might be interested in developing.

You will make a lasting impression if prior to your visit you have found out as much as possible about the country you are visiting. Learn about the culture, geography, literature, arts, religions, music, politics, sports, currency and other important things. Not only will you please your customer with your knowledge of his country, you will also derive much pleasure in knowing each country intimately, and in the long run, it will help you to sell better because you know the appeals your products have in the country's cultural pattern.

Above all, recognize how and why business practices, sales appeals and negotiating habits differ from country to country.

A full chapter (Ch. 17) is devoted to overseas business travel.

Chapter 14

PRICING THE PRODUCT FOR EXPORT

The name of the game is profit. Export sales, just as domestic sales, must produce a profit for the company. The success or failure of this exercise will depend largely on how the exported products are priced in foreign markets. Each company must, therefore, establish its own basic policy on how it will price its products.

In order to formulate an export pricing policy, the company must first clearly define its pricing objectives. Different companies have different objectives when it comes to pricing products for export markets; for example–is it the main objective to maximize profits, or are you trying to break into a market and capture a large share of it with low prices?

Some companies may find their competitor's prices quite low, so to remain competitive, they feel they too, must establish similar low price levels. Others feel their export prices should be the same as their U.S. domestic prices. Many will argue that a uniform price structure should be maintained in the U. S. and foreign markets so that all customers are treated alike. There are laws and regulations in the United States and in most foreign countries which can have an impact on how you formulate your pricing strategy, so you must be careful to avoid any appearance of price discrimination or price fixing.

Whatever your objective might be, the international executive responsible for implementing pricing policies for the company should receive input from other corporate managers—accounting, manufacturing, treasury and legal.

Close coordination among all members of the corporate structure is most important in determining and analyzing all of the factors which go into making a realistic export price structure.

There can be no fixed mechanical methods of working out a pricing policy and arriving at just the right price. There are too many variable factors involved to arrive at any set formula. Among those you should take into account are:

- Your manufacturing and other direct costs.
- Local practices regarding distributor margins
- Local fair trade laws
- How products are moved in distribution channels, e.g. manufacturer to wholesale distributor to jobber, to retail user.
- Appeals to customers (is price or service most important?)
- How customers perceive the value of your products and what they might be willing to pay for them.
- Customer relations (avoid the perception of over-charging)
- The market demand for your products.
- The cost of export sales terms—offering more extended terms to export customers is, in effect, a loan to them, and can cost you money and tie up your funds.

A number of other factors must also be examined to determine if you should maintain uniform pricing worldwide, but cost factors are primary considerations. The U. S. cost of sales versus foreign cost of sales can vary widely, so you must determine the exact cost to your company of your export sales to arrive at a final selling price to overseas customers. In many cases, some costs normally associated with domestic sales can be eliminated from foreign sales costs. These could include advertising and promotion which, by contract, you may be allowing your distributors to handle locally. You must however, retain in your calculations the portion of cost, if any, related to whole or partial reimbursement to the distributor. Transportation and other shipping allowances granted to U. S. customers can be eliminated if terms of the export sales are f.o.b. factory, since the overseas customer pays the in-land freight to the pier and some other costs associated with the export shipment. Many manufacturers give U. S. customers freight allowances which often equals the total transportation costs.

Some companies do not add to their export pricing calculations costs which they feel are adequately covered by domestic pricing, or take into consideration only small pro-rated percentages of those costs.

Very important in calculating costs to arrive at pricing levels, is the direct cost of manufacturing additional product to satisfy the export markets. You must calculate if the additional production required to fill export orders means lower manufacturing costs through economy of scale. If the domestic product must be changed or modified, will such changes increase manufacturing costs which must be recovered?

Other fixed costs can include: research and development, over-head, and some administrative and general expenses. Some marketing and product service expenses, (such as advertising and promotion noted above) are handled in whole or in part by foreign distributors, and costs of these services to the international marketing group can be either very low or non-existent.

The actual costs of selling in overseas markets is also an important factor. Items such as the international executive's salary and overseas travel expenses, credit costs, new packaging designs created expressly for export markets and export boxing or crating for shipment must also be considered.

To complicate matters a little more, you will also have to consider in establishing price schedules, whether you should have one price for all classes of trade within a given market. Many times you will be constrained to offer lower prices to O.E.M. accounts who purchase in large quantities, to government entities who just simply demand lower prices than those given to other users, or to all customers in a highly competitive market regardless of purchasing volume.

Consider too, that price is not always the deciding factor in successful selling in a market. If your product has no competition; if it is of higher quality or performance than similar products in a market; if the competition cannot adequately supply the market; if you and your distributors provide exceptional warranties and service on the products, then a price level which gives you and the distributor higher profit margins may well be in order.

As you have seen, there is no one standard set of rules for establishing a pricing strategy or policy. The majority of companies involved in international trade will use their domestic prices as the base level for export prices. They will then exclude or add as appropriate, the variable factors discussed in this chapter.

Since many, or most, of a company's distributors have occasion to meet each other and will discuss their mutual relationship with their common principal, pricing will certainly be one of the subjects raised. Therefore, most companies will, subject to unusual circumstances, have a uniform price policy to all overseas distributors to avoid claims of discrimination or unfairness. The company must use a lot of pure instinct, judgement, and common sense in setting its prices. For this reason, the input by several corporate executives must be carefully analyzed and judiciously applied.

Another thought on international pricing is that the international executive should establish come control features to assure that correct pricing is being adhered to by the overseas distributors. You will have taken into account in setting prices to distributors, that the distributor's cost of "landing" your products must be added to his purchase price from you. You must find out what these added costs are (freight and forwarding charges, insurance, customs duties, taxes, surcharges, pier charges, currency exchange costs etc.) and, adding in the distributor's normal margin, calculate what his selling price should be.

During your periodic evaluation, you should check on the prices at which he has been selling to be sure he is not overcharging his customers and thereby losing sales. Over the long run, this practice could have an adverse effect on your total volume and profit in that market. There are problems also in a distributor cutting prices, especially to certain customers. This practice can seriously damage the company's reputation and erode the customers' confidence.

The whole question of establishing an export pricing policy is, as you have seen in the foregoing discussion, a very complicated one with many unknown and unforeseeable variables. If there is one universal basis that should be applied to establishing a price structure, it is probably that you have to calculate a break-even point. You then establish the low-end of your price range to cover all of your fixed costs with enough of a profit to make it worth the effort to sell. You then calculate the high-end of the price range based on the profit you really want to obtain. Compare the low and high ends of the range and use your knowledge of your markets to arrive at a sense of what the markets will pay. Remember that customers won't pay beyond their perception of what they consider the real value of your product.

It is always best to maintain flexibility (in both directions) in your pricing policy in order not to lock yourself into a losing or too-low profit situation. You must also guard against a too-high price which yields exorbitant margins and puts you at risk of losing the market to competition because buyers simply won't pay the prices you are asking.

Terms of Sale

In addition to consideration of pricing your product correctly for foreign sales, you also have to be concerned with quoting your overseas customers the correct terms of sale. These terms will define at what point all costs and risks are for the account of the customer. Since there are a variety of costs which are not usually included in the base price of the product, it is most important that a clear understanding be reached by both the seller and the buyer as to which party is responsible for these added costs in shipping, and which party bears a risk at which point in the process of shipping.

Among these various costs could be:

- Export packing
- Inland freight from your plant to the port of export
- Cartage cost from the inland carrier's terminal to the pier itself. Note that there are sometimes very high waiting-time charges.
- Reconsignment costs if you have consigned the shipment to a party other than the vessel on which it is to be loaded.
- Loading charges onto the vessel or special equipment or handling charges for loading.
- Ocean freight (or air freight) costs.
- Fees charged by the Freight Forwarder.
- Consular Fees.

The "understanding" noted above is simplified by a group of standardized Terms of Sale, the use of which clearly defines to both parties which is responsible for what. These standard terms are found in two published compilations: *American Foreign Trade Definitions of 1941*, the most commonly used by U.S. exporters; and the *International Commerce Terms (INCOTERMS)*, revised in 1990.

The International Chamber of Commerce and most foreign trade specialists now recommend that *INCOTERMS 1990* be used instead of the *American Foreign Trade Definitions.* See Appendix "F" for an updated glossary of these terms.

- FOB Factory (Pinewood, Ct.) (Free on Board inland carrier and named point of origin). The customer pays for all charges over your invoice value for the goods.
- FOB Port (New York), (Free on Board inland carrier at named port of exportation). The shipper quotes a price that includes inland freight to the pier; customer pays separately for all other charges.
- FOB VESSEL or FAS VESSEL, (Free on Board vessel or Free Alongside Vessel at the port of exportation. The shipper quotes a price including charges incurred until the goods are actually placed on board the vessel (FOB), or alongside of it (FAS); customer pays all other charges.
- CIF Foreign Port (cost, insurance and freight), The shipper quotes the buyer a price which includes cost of the goods, insurance and all transportation and miscellaneous charges to the port in the foreign country.
- C & F FOREIGN PORT (cost and freight), The same as CIF above except insurance is to be obtained by the customer.

The above are but a few of the many variations of sales terms which can be applied to export orders. Foreign customers usually prefer the CIF or C&F because they can then easily figure their landed cost by adding in their import duties. If you do quote on either of these terms, be sure you have found out and added all the miscellaneous costs involved in the shipment.

Chapter 15

TERMS OF PAYMENT AND FINANCING EXPORTS

In either domestic or foreign operations, a sale is not a sale until payment is received by the seller. This is most emphatically true in export sales when dealing with many customers and countries all over the globe. Many of the markets you will work in have debt-ridden or depressed economies, high inflation and cost of living, and strictly controlled currencies. Also, there is always the worry that some customers somewhere will delay paying their bills. How can a company ensure that it will receive timely payment in U.S. dollars for goods and services exported by them?

Before accepting an order or shipping it, good businesses will always establish the credit-worthiness of its customers. While it may be a little more difficult to run credit-checks on foreign customers than on U.S. customers, there are many ways to obtain thorough and reliable information about a foreign firm's credit and payment history.

The most obvious place to start is with the customer's bank. You can also ask your own bank to check on a firm through the bank's branch or foreign correspondent bank in the customer's country. Dun and Bradstreet International is also an excellent source of information, and can provide in-depth financial and credit reports on customers throughout the world. The Foreign Credit Interchange Bureau can supply information about terms which are normally extended to customers in different markets as well as data on current payment conditions in most countries. Also, marine insurance brokers can often give credit information to their customers. You can also obtain from many U.S. banks, current economic and financial trends in many markets overseas through newsletters and bulletins which they publish regularly. These publications will give you a feel for what is happening in the economic and financial sectors and thus allow you to make realistic decisions on trading terms.

Other excellent sources from which to find out how a customer has handled his payment obligations are the customer's other U.S. or foreign suppliers or principals. A telephone call or short note that you are starting to work with a distributor or customer and would like to know the supplier's credit experience with him, is usually answered with full details by your international counterpart. Always be sure to tell the source you will keep the information confidential and will be happy to reciprocate with any information he may need from you.

Credit terms can often be of utmost importance in selling in overseas markets. A sale can be made or lost depending upon the generosity, or lack thereof, of the terms granted. Credit-worthiness and past history are, of course, the prime factors to consider in granting terms of sale, however, there are many other things to consider at this crucial stage.

One of these, which we discussed previously as a non-tariff barrier to trade, is foreign currency restrictions and resulting local government regulations as determinants of credit terms. Many countries, especially so-called Third World Countries, require imports to be paid for on extended terms, sometimes as long as 180 days. This is usually done to discourage imports of non-essential products as well as to conserve what may be the country's low or dwindling hard currency reserves. The exporter will have to take a long look at such a transaction to determine if he is willing to take the risk or to wait for such a long time for his money. While there are ways to minimize the risk, the long wait may not be acceptable, at least not without imposing some interest charge on the invoice value for the period beyond normal 30-day terms. However, this may not always be possible because some countries have laws which prohibit charging interest for credit terms. A strategy some exporters use successfully, is to add such interest to the selling price when negotiating the sale.

Remember, interest rates on credit in many foreign countries can exceed U.S. interest rates by 10 or 20% or more. Therefore, a buyer might be willing to accept standard U.S. interest rates added to his cost as a price for longer payment terms.

Another factor to consider is the political stability of the country with which you are dealing. If the country is at war, is part of, or close to a war zone or terrorist-prone area, subject to guerilla attacks or frequent coups d'etat, credit terms must then be as risk-free as possible. You should require all sales in these areas to be subject to terms of either cash-in-advance, or irrevocable letter of credit confirmed by a U.S. bank. Letters of credit can be negotiated by presenting either sight or time drafts, that is, drafts drawn for payment at either sight, 30, 60 or 90 or more days after sight or date of the draft. This term will depend on the sale negotiations. Cash-in-advance is a most extreme situation which you would exact only in the most unusual circumstances such as indicated above.

After consideration of the credit-worthiness of the customer and all of the economic, political and legal factors affecting business in the country with which you are dealing, you are in a position to consider credit terms you will offer.

As in the matter of setting pricing policies, the granting of credit terms is, in many companies, a joint exercise among several senior managers, very often including the president. The international executive will have to be aware of the company policy regarding payments, how the president and financial officers feel about extended terms of payment, and how such terms might impact on the company's own financial situation.

Proforma Invoices

In some situations, a customer will ask you to quote him for a quantity of your goods and requests that the quotation be in the form of a Proforma Invoice. This is a type of formal quotation which he requires either to present to his bank for opening a Letter of Credit, or to his government's exchange control officials to obtain an import license for the goods being ordered.

In both cases, the total expenses to be incurred by the customer (for which foreign exchange must be granted to pay you, the seller, in U.S. dollars) must be known before hand. The L/C must be drawn so all your costs will be reimbursed. The import license must also be made out to show all costs for which foreign exchange, must be allocated.

The proforma therefore, should itemize product cost, export packing charges, inland freight cost to piers, freight forwarders' handling fees, ocean freight, insurance charges, and any other surcharges or fees which you know may be imposed on the shipments.

A sample proforma is included among the exhibits later in this chapter.

Credit Terms You Can Offer

Usually, a company wants to obtain payment for sales in the shortest possible time, so the international marketer must keep the rest of management closely informed about factors in his territories which may demand something more than the normal thirty-day payments to which the other executives may be accustomed. No doubt there will be some customers to whom you will grant open account or 30-or-60 day terms, but these will usually be offered only to those who have impeccable credit ratings or histories with other known suppliers, or those with whom you have already had some good experience.

A. Cash-in-Advance

Cash-in-Advance terms, while possible, is not a practical term in current international business practice. In many countries, because of local bank restrictions, customers cannot obtain the foreign currency required for advance payments. In most countries, foreign currency is released for payment to principals only after the customer gives proof to the central bank that the merchandise ordered has been "nationalized", i.e. cleared through customs and received by the customer. The most common use of cash-in-advance terms is in cases where an exporter requires a down-payment for custom-made products, or an "up-front" payment for very costly equipment. In such cases it may be possible, with specific documentation supplied to central banks, for the customer to obtain the required currency to effect the payment.

B. Letter of Credit (L/C)

L/C terms are often used when you or the management team perceive problems, as discussed earlier in this chapter. Letter of credit terms are not usually demanded except in high-risk countries, or when dealing with poor or bad credit risk customers. It is unusual for example, to require a letter of credit from customers in Western Europe, or many other stable countries in which customers normally buy on open account with terms up to 30 days or more from date of invoice. In many countries, a request for such terms would be taken as an insult to the company or individual. In addition, your customer must pay a fee to open a letter of credit and make a deposit equal to some or all of the value of the credit. This will tie up his funds for the period of time it will take to ship his order and negotiate the credit.

Basically, an L/C is the assumption by a bank of a customer's credit liability to you, the seller. The bank opening the L/C guarantees that it will honor your draft drawn in compliance with the terms of the L/C. These terms are spelled out in the copy of the L/C you receive from the opening bank, and should be studied carefully since terms must be fulfilled precisely in order for you to receive your payment. Letters of Credit must be negotiated as soon as possible after shipment, but always before the expiration date of the L/C.

To be even more certain that you will receive your payment, you should request that the L/C opened by your customer at his local bank, be confirmed by a U. S. bank which takes on the liability for the foreign bank. Also, request that the L/C be irrevocable—that is, once issued, it cannot be changed or be cancelled by the customer. This may be very important if you are not sure of the stability or credit-standing of the foreign bank opening the credit. Banks have been known to fail!

One of the most important terms of the L/C is how you will be paid. The L/C will usually state the payment will be made by "your draft drawn on us". We will discuss drafts fully later, but basically, drafts can be drawn for payment at sight or at a specified time after its date. The usual method with L/Cs is to draw a sight draft, which means the bank will remit payment to you in a matter of a few days after it has checked that you have complied with all L/C terms.

C. Sight Draft (S/D)

S/D terms are comparable to C.O.D. terms in the United States and are a very common method of obtaining payment from export customers. A sight draft, usually designated as "Sight Draft-Documents Against Payment", is drawn by the seller when payment is wanted promptly, since it is payable on presentation. Original shipping documents are attached to the draft and the set is presented to the overseas customer by the collecting bank. The original bill of lading giving title to the goods is attached to the draft and is made out to the order of the shipper and is endorsed by him either in blank or to the order of the collecting bank. This procedure assures that the importer cannot obtain the shipment without first paying the bank the full amount due since he cannot obtain possession of the original documents needed to clear the shipment until he has paid the sight draft. The exporter thus retains control of the goods shipped until the buyer has paid for the shipment. The bank then notifies the drawer of the draft that payment has been made and remits the payment through normal banking channels.

It should be noted that, "to order" bills of lading are not available with air freight shipments, therefore, if a shipper wishes to retain control of the goods shipped, he must consign the airway bill to a third party, e.g., a customs house broker, or, with prior permission, to the collecting bank.

Depending upon the country, proceeds of sight draft payments will be received in the exporter's account anywhere from ten to as much as forty-five days after the customer has paid.

D. Time Drafts

Time Drafts are similar to sight-drafts, differing only in that they are drawn to mature for payment in a certain number of days, (30, 60, 90, etc.) after a specified date, e.g. at 30 days after date of the draft or date of acceptance. As with sight drafts, original documents are attached to a time draft and presented by the bank in the same manner, except in this case the exporter specifies on the draft that the documents are to be given to the importer upon his signing the draft with his "acceptance" to pay on the specified date. This gives the exporter a written, signed commitment that payment will be made on a certain date. The bank holds the draft for re-presentation for payment on the maturity date. Time drafts do represent more of a risk than drafts at sight, because the customer is able to obtain the shipment before he pays for it. You do have "his word" he'll pay at the specified time, but you do wait longer for the proceeds, and you do run the risk he might delay payment. Time draft terms should therefore be granted only to those customers with whom you've had some prior history of on-time payments and who have proven to be credit-worthy.

Financing For Export Sales

While few export transactions can be completely risk-free, there are ways to minimize and control financial risks. There are many public and private sources of export financing which can help you when you need to receive your money faster, require working capital to finance exports, or to help you protect yourself from the risk of non-payment.

A. Commercial Banks

Commercial Banks can provide assistance by discounting time drafts, that is, a bank will purchase the draft at a discount, keep it until its maturity date, then collect its full value. Meanwhile, you receive payment for the shipment, less the "discount" fee. In many cases this is a practical alternative to carrying a large accounts receivable balance extending over a lengthy period of time. It probably ends up costing you less than waiting the full term of the draft when you consider the cost of having your money tied up.

B. The Export-Import Bank of the U.S.A. (EXIM BANK)

EXIM BANK is a U.S. government agency whose purpose is to facilitate U.S. exports by offering export finance programs which are particularly useful to small and medium-sized businesses and to new-to-export companies. There are four main programs currently available to small businesses.

1. The Working Capital Guarantee Program is designed to assist new exporters obtain access to working capital loans from commercial lenders to finance pre-export activities. The guarantee may be used for a single transaction, or a revolving line of credit to help support marketing or production activities for potential export sales.

Eximbank's guarantee covers 90 percent of the loan and requires that the loan not exceed 90 percent of the collateral required to secure the loan. There is a one-time, up-front guarantee fee of 1.0 percent of the loan amount if it is for six months or less, 1.6 percent for six months to one year, or, for longer terms, 0.5 percent is added for each additional six month period or part thereof.

If an exporter qualifies as a small business, his bank may request a guarantee for loans up to $1 million under the Small Business Administration's Export Revolving Line of Credit Program. Eximbank participates by guaranteeing half of such loans in excess of $200,000. Look into this with your regional SBA office.

2. Export Credit Insurance provides some protection against the risk that some overseas customers will not, or cannot, pay for shipments made. These non-payments could be for a variety of reasons ranging from poor economic or market conditions, devaluation of currencies, natural disasters, etc. Eximbank will cover 90 percent or more or such risks. If the foreign customer cannot pay because of political actions such as confiscation of assets, diversion of shipments, cancellation of import licenses, or lack of access to foreign exchange, then Eximbank assumes 100% of the risk. These risks are covered by the Foreign Credit Insurance Association (FCIA) through insurance policies they sell and service. FCIA is a group of U. S. insurance companies acting as agent for Eximbank. Single or multi-buyer policies are available on short term (up to 180 days) or medium term (181 days to five years). A special policy with greater coverage is available for new-to-export companies that had export sales averaging less than $750,000 a year in the last two years and haven't used FCIA programs during that time.

3. Commercial Bank Guarantees are also given by Exmibank to cover repayment of loans on which a foreign buyer defaults. This guarantee encourages commercial banks to make such loans by reducing the bank's risk. This program can be used to guarantee export sales of U.S. capital equipment and coverage is available to buyers in more than 140 countries.

4. The Small Business Credit Program enables U.S. Banks to offer medium-term, fixed rate export loans to finance sales of products manufactured by small U.S. companies. Rates are the lowest permitted by the Organization For Economic Cooperation and Development (OECD) guidelines. This program can be a big help in supporting sales of heavy equipment up to a maximum value of any single contract of $2.5 million.

The foregoing programs are a few of the 15 or so available through Eximbank's Finance and Insurance Service. While they are current at this writing, for up-to-date details on these and information and additional programs available to U. S. exporters call Eximbank's Advisory Service at 800-424-5201 or (202) 566-8860, or write to the Marketing Department, Eximbank, 811 Vermont Avenue, N.W., Washington, D.C. 20571.

C. Other Sources for Export Financing:

1. For financing large projects in the construction or engineering industries, the Overseas Private Investment Corporation (OPIC) offers direct or guaranteed loans for medium to long-term financing for private U.S. investors involved in developing country investments. OPIC also has programs to provide financing for U.S. companies whose distributors sell and service U. S. equipment. It also offers insurance against expropriation, local currency inconvertibility and losses caused by wars or revolutions. Companies which make large capital investments in developing countries, usually also export equipment and other goods to back up their investment so those exports are also covered.

2. Another possibility for U. S. exporters to obtain export sales financing is through use of various programs offered by the Private Export Funding Corporation (PEFCO). Working with Emibank, PEFCO makes loans to public and private borrowers in foreign countries when they cannot obtain local financing to buy U.S. products. PEFCO loans are covered by unconditional guarantees of Eximbank for principal and interest.

These are but a few of the many financing programs offered by private, government or quasi-government agencies designed to assist U.S. companies enter or expand their business in overseas markets. Since some of the programs and services offered may change and new ones become available, close contact should be maintained with the local field offices of the Department of Commerce.

Don't let these financial issues intimidate you or keep you from going ahead with an export marketing and sales program or, as you grow in the international arena, keep you from considering other foreign operations. Make it a practice to do a constant financial review and up-dating of all of your foreign markets and customers at regular intervals to forestall any surprises in the area of foreign credits, payments and financing. If any phase of this important part of export operations gives you a problem, take comfort in the fact that there are many places to seek help and advice. In addition to the agencies and government departments discussed in this chapter, many banks, freight forwarders, shipping companies, foreign trade associations and clubs, colleges, and universities all over the country give seminars and special classes on the subject of letters of credit, drafts and all phases of international payments, financing and collection problems. Take comfort too, that the majority of companies involved in international sales and marketing have lost less money through bad credit than their counterparts dealing in the U. S. domestic market.

PROFORMA INVOICE

A.B.C. Manufacturing Co.
4 Porter Road
Pinewood, Ct. 06051

TO: X.Y.Z.Distribution Co.
5 Woochow Road
Hong Kong, B.C.C.

Shipment: FOB Pinewood, Ct.
Ocean freight prepaid and
added to invoice

Quantity	Model	Description	Unit Price In U.S. $	Total U.S.$
10	X-14	Graphic Design Machine	9,500	95,000
3	G-14	Spare Parts Kits	1,250	3,750
		Export Boxing	_____	250
		Total: FOB Factory Pinewood, Ct.		U.S.$ 99,000
		Inland freight to New York pier		195
		Pier delivery (by N.Y. Cartage Company)		75
		Forwarders Handling Fee (May include consular invoice and certificate of origin fees)		35
		Ocean Freight		3,000
		Insurance		250
		Total C.I.F. Hong Kong		U.S.$102,555

Terms of Shipment: F.O.B. Pinewood, Ct.

Terms of Payment: Irrevocable Letter of Credit
Confirmed by a New York Bank
and negotiable by our drafts
at sight

Shipment: Subject to approval of U.S.Export License

Sample ProForma Invoice

214

IRREVOCABLE COMMERCIAL LETTER OF CREDIT

International Banking Department

BANCO BRAZILIA

Avenue Bernardo 3315
Rio De Janiero, Brazil

IRREVOCABLE COMMERCIAL LETTER OF CREDIT

ADVISING BANK

Citytrust
961 Main St.
Bridgeport, Conn. 06602

OUR NO.
1234 E

DATE
October 1, 1980

APPLICANT (Accountee)

Calzado La Torre, S.A.I.C.
Ave. Portuguese, 667
Rio De Janiero, Brazil

BENEFICIARY

American Exporter Co., Inc.
670 Park Ave.
Bridgeport, Conn. 06608

AMOUNT

US$5,265.00

EXPIRY
December 15, 1980

GENTLEMEN: YOU ARE AUTHORIZED TO VALUE ON Citytrust

DRAFTS AT Sight FOR 100% INVOICE WHEN ACCOMPANIED BY THE FOLLOWING BY DRAWING

DOCUMENTS:

1. Commercial invoice in triplicate covering footwear articles per order No. 105 and 106, C & F Buenos Aires.

2. Complete set of clean on board ocean bills of lading to the order of Banco Brazilia notify Freight Forwarders Inc. marked "Freight Prepaid"

COVERING:

Pebble chain sandles

THE AMOUNT OF ANY DRAFT DRAWN UNDER THIS CREDIT MUST BE ENDORSED ON THE REVERSE OF THE ORIGINAL CREDIT. ALL DRAFTS MUST BE MARKED, "DRAWN UNDER BANCO BRAZILIA LETTER OF CREDIT NUMBER 1234E DATED Oct. 1, 1980

THIS CREDIT IS SUBJECT TO THE UNIFORM CUSTOMS AND PRACTICE FOR DOCUMENTARY CREDITS 1983 REVISION, INTERNATIONAL CHAMBER OF COMMERCE PUBLICATION NO. 400

SHIPMENT FROM: Bridgeport

TO: Buenos Aires

PARTIAL SHIPMENTS
Permitted

TRANS-SHIPMENT
Permitted

SPECIAL CONDITIONS:

Citytrust confirms this credit and thereby undertakes that all drafts drawn and presented as above specified will be duly honored by us.

We hereby agree with you that drafts drawn under and in compliance with the terms of this credit that such drafts will be duly honored on due presentation if presented on or before the expiration date.

SPECIMEN

AUTHORIZED SIGNATURE

Sample Irrevocable Letter of Credit

Herman J. Maggiori

CAPITAL BANK

INTERNATIONAL DIVISION

P.O. BOX 522800, MIAMI, FLORIDA 33152, UNITED STATES OF AMERICA
TELEPHONE: (305) 536-1740/CABLE: CAPITALBN
TELEX: RCA 264245

FEBRUARY 11, 1991

BENEFICIARY
REMINGTON ARMS CO. INC.
1007 MARKET STREET
WILMINGTON, DELAWARE 19898

APPLICANT
PEDRO WORMS Y CIA. S.R.L.
SARMIENTO 377
(1041) BUENOS AIRES
ARGENTINA

ISSUING BANK
BANCO DE GALICIA Y BUENOS AIRES
ESQ. RECONQUISTA 1038
BUENOS AIRES, ARGENTINA

OUR ADVICE NO. E908382
THEIR L/C NO. 75096

GENTLEMEN:

IN ACCORDANCE WITH INSTRUCTIONS RECEIVED FROM THE ISSUING BANK,
ABOVE LETTER OF CREDIT HAS BEEN AMENDED AS FOLLOWS:

AMOUNT INCREASED BY : USD 3,245.00 NEW CREDIT AMOUNT
USD 89,564.00
MERCHANDISE NOW READS:
AS PER AMDN. #1
97,500 UNIDADES RDS 21204-1522 AND R 22 LR HV RN PRECIO
UNITARIO USD 0.03215 NOW THE AMOUNT OF THE PRESENT CREDIT
IS DISCRIMINATE AS FOLLOWS:
FOB USD 86,535.00
CONSULAR FEES USD 3,029.

THIS IS AMENDMENT NO. 001
ALL OTHER TERMS REMAIN UNCHANGED.

YOURS TRULY,

AUTHORIZED SIGNATURE

AUTHORIZED SIGNATURE

ORIGINAL

Sample of an Amendment to a Letter of Credit

WILMINGTON, DELAWARE 3-15 19 86
BILL OF EXCHANGE OR DRAFT NO.
"DRAWN UNDER DOCUMENTARY CREDIT NO.86(02)13 OF BANCOLAT,BANCO DE LATINO AMERICA PANAMA 5,PANAMA DATED FEBRUARY 17,1986 AND FIRST PENNSYLVANIA BANK PHILADELPHIA,PA REF.NO.68067 DATED MARCH 4, 1986."
ON 60 DAYS B/L DATE 3-15-86

pay to the order of WACHOVIA INTERNATIONAL BANKING CORP. N.Y.

U. S. DOLLARS ***23,397.70***
PAYABLE IN U. S. DOLLARS FOR FACE AMOUNT.

FIRST PENNSYLVANIA BANK VALUE RECEIVED AND CHARGE TO THE ACCOUNT OF
P.O. BOX 13616
PHILADELPHIA, PA. 19101
REMINGTON ARMS COMPANY,INC.
E. I. DU PONT DE NEMOURS & COMPANY

By _Victor Fernandez_

Customer A/R No. 027 6450

To:
FIRST PENNSYLVANIA BANK
P.O. BOX 13616
PHILADELPHIA, PA. 19101

WIBCO NO. 9046645
IN ALL COMMUNICATIONS INCLUDING TRANSFER OF PROCEEDS MENTION THIS NUMBER

ATTN: LETTERS OF CREDIT
INTERNATIONAL OPERATIONS

We enclose for collection draft No. _____ and other documents listed below: U.S. $ 23,397.70

BILLS OF LADING		CONSULAR INV.		COM'L INV.	PACKING LISTS	CERT. OF ORIGIN		INSURANCE CERT.		P. P. RECEIPT		
ORIG.	COPIES	ORIG.	COPIES			ORIG.	COPIES	ORIG.	COPIES	ORIG.	COPIES	
3	4	1	1	1/6	3							1 orig. L/C

1 draft in dupl
1 orig.official

DRAWING UNDER LETTER OF CREDIT—HANDLE IN ACCORDANCE WITH FOLLOWING INSTRUCTIONS
Refer discrepancies to JAY C. LYONS _____ phone no.(203)368-1666
Do not forward documents on an approval basis without Du Pont Credit Division's authorization.
Retain acceptance for payment upon maturity. DO NOT DISCOUNT.

TIME LETTER OF CREDIT—Hold accepted draft until maturity "UNDER ADVICE TO WACHOVIA INTERNATIONAL BANKING CORPORATION", New York, 620 Fifth Avenue, New York, NY 10020
Attn: L/C Dept.
* receipt

REMITTANCE INSTRUCTIONS: (ALWAYS REFERENCE WIBCO NO.)—Remit proceeds by wire (in New York via CHIPS) to Wachovia International Banking Corp., New York, 620 Fifth Avenue, New York, NY 10020, Attn: L/C Dept. For account: E. I. du Pont de Nemours & Co. A/C# 10100-031 (UID #79520)

DO NOT MAIL FUNDS

SPECIAL INSTRUCTIONS
WILLIAM A. MARSHALL
FREIGHT FORWARDING
P. O. BOX 128
BRIDGEPORT, CONN. 06601   EXW#86-93

BUYER:
EL CAZADOR
APARTADO 6877
PANAMA 5, PANAMA

S/S AM. LARK
SHIPPED ON   3-15-86
DATE
Advising Bank

REMINGTON ARMS COMPANY, IN
E. I. du Pont de Nemours & Company
INCORPORATED

Sample Draft and Bank Transmittal Letter Drawn under a Letter of Credit

Herman J. Maggiori

Wilmington, Delaware	JUNE 7,	19 89	BILL OF EXCHANGE OR DRAFT NO.

At **90 DAYS AFTER DATE OF BILL** OF LADING

pay to the order of **THE KYOWA BANK** U.S. $ ***30,614.51***

U.S. DOLLARS **THIRTY THOUSAND SIX HUNDRED FORTEEN AND 51/100------------------**

VALUE RECEIVED AND CHARGE TO THE ACCOUNT OF

TO

NIKKO SANGYO COMPANY LTD.
MUSASHINO BLDG. 6F
13-10, SHINJUKU 2-CHOME
SHINJUKU-KU, TOKYO JAPAN 106

E. I. DU PONT DE NEMOURS & COMPANY

By _Janet Murphy_
Authorized Signature

CUSTOMER A/R NO.

NCNB
National Bank of North Carolina
International Division T21-3
Charlotte, N. C. 28255

Via Airmail To—

THE KYOWA BANK
SHINJUKU BRANCH
1-15, SHINJUKU 3-CHOME
SHINJUKU-KU
TOKYO 160, JAPAN

IMPORTANT
DP 92841
In All Communications Including Transfer of Proceeds Mention This Number.

Gentlemen:
We enclose for collection the above draft and documents subject to the instructions given below. Please handle for account of NCNB National Bank of North Carolina, Charlotte, NC, to whom you should direct your acknowledgement of receipt of this collection and all communications. In all your correspondence regarding this item please refer to collection number above.

Subject to uniform rules for the collection of commercial paper (1979 revision) International Chamber of Commerce, brochure number 322 or succeeding revisions.

	CONSULAR INV.		COM'L INV.	PACKING LISTS	CERT. OF ORIGIN		INSURANCE CERT.		P. P. RECEIPT	
ORIG. COPIES	ORIG.	COPIES			ORIG.	COPIES	ORIG.	COPIES	ORIG.	COPIES
1 A.W.B.			4							

HANDLE IN ACCORDANCE WITH INSTRUCTIONS MARKED [X]

[X] Deliver documents against payment in U.S. dollars if sight draft or against acceptance if time draft. If dollar exchange is not immediately available you are authorized to accept a provisional deposit in local currency under drawee's written obligation to remain liable for all exchange differences.

[X] All collection charges including stamp taxes, etc. of country of destination for account of drawee. Include NCNB National Bank of North Carolina's commission of $25.00.

[X] In case of need, non-acceptance or non-payment, refer promptly to

E.I.DUPONT DE NEMOURS & CO., INC.
ATTN: CREDIT DIVISION, EXA#918106
WILMINGTON, DELAWARE 19898

[X] Do not protest.

[X] whose instructions you are authorized to follow.

[ ] who is authorized only to obtain honoring of draft as drawn.

[X] Remit proceeds by telex or S.W.I.F.T. at drawer's expense to NCBANK, Charlotte, N.C., Telex 575-297, S.W.I.F.T. NCNBUS 33.

[X] SPECIAL INSTRUCTIONS

TIME DRAFTS ADVISE DATE OF ACCEPTANCE AND CORRESPONDING MATURITY.

Janet Murphy
Authorized Signature

Sample Time Draft and Letter of Instructions to Bank

Chapter 16

EXPORT DOCUMENTATION
AND SHIPPING

Yes, there is a lot of paperwork required in exporting. No, it's not mysterious or difficult once you get the hang of it. Most of the documentation required is logical and necessary to protect you and your customers, to make sure each shipment overseas gets to its destination in good time and in good condition, and, most importantly, that you get paid promptly for your goods.

The best part is that you don't have to do a lot of the work yourself in preparing most of the required documentation. It can be given to a foreign freight forwarder to do. This would be especially advantageous to the start-up export department which would not have to hire an experienced export traffic and documentation person, usually at a substantial salary. Later on, of course, as your volume grows and you make some good profits, you may want or need to have a full-time person to do the actual documentation and coordination with your freight forwarders.

Let's take a look at all this paperwork, piece by piece, so we can understand why each is necessary. We'll also see how to prepare, pack, mark, insure and ship those export orders which you have now received after much hard work establishing your new export sales program. We'll also take a look at who is out there who can help you through the haze and hassle or what some people have called the "paper pollution" in international trade.

The Foreign Freight Forwarder

A good freight forwarder can be an exporter's best friend and ally. Basically, the forwarder handles export shipments, but he can, and very often does, act as an agent and export traffic department. You can use his services as little or as much as you want. He charges a fee for each service he performs, but you may find that even though you pay for several different services, it will be more economical to use him than hiring one or more people to perform those functions.

International freight forwarders are highly-trained and experienced professionals who keep abreast of all the laws and regulations governing the movement of freight to foreign destinations. In addition, they are knowledgeable about conditions in many world markets, and can offer advice and information on many aspects of selling and working in those markets.

The average foreign freight forwarder provides exporters with many basic services in connection with the movement of ocean and air freight. Since they work in close cooperation with inland carriers, steamship and air freight companies, banks and U.S. Customs, they can:

1. Coordinate your shipment to the steamship company piers.
2. Arrange space on a vessel and follow-up to departure.
3. Clear your export shipment with U.S. Customs
4. Prepare documents and send overseas by registered mail or courier.
5. Prepare banking documents as required by the letter of credit to effect payment.
6. Prepay and audit any inland and ocean freight charges.
7. Arrange marine insurance through their Open Marine Policy.
8. Offer traffic coordinators and managers personal service enabling them to better control their shipments.

Among the many documents an experienced forwarder is able to prepare for you are:

1. Export declarations.
2. Department of Commerce or Department of State licenses.
3. Ocean bills of lading.
4 Marine Insurance certificates.
5. Dock receipts for pier delivery.

6. Delivery instructions.
7. Drafts for either direct collections or letter of credit transactions.
8. Beneficiary's certificates.
9. Certificates of Origin
10. Consular invoices (for certification and/or legalization).
11. Insurance notifications.
12. Special Certificates of Value and Origin.
13. Additions to commercial invoices such as charges and necessary clauses that may be required either by the country of importation or letter of credit.
14. Any other export documentation necessary for proper handling of a shipment or bank presentation.

At the start of your export program, you should interview several freight forwarders to find one you can be sure will perform all the services you will require. Forwarding is a very competitive field, so look carefully for one you feel will do a good job for you at good prices, and who will be available when you need him. Usually all you need to do when you have a shipment ready, is send a Shipper's Letter of Instruction to your forwarder. He will take care of the rest.

The Export Documents (Shipping and Collection)

Let's take a typical export shipment and work through the documents that will be required. These include the actual shipping documents, and documents needed for collection to receive your payment for the shipment. In some cases, the shipping documents become the collection documents—you will know which are which in the following discussion of each.

1. The Inland Bill of Lading (B/L)

This is needed to transport your shipment from your factory to the point of embarkation—a pier for ocean freight or a terminal for air shipment.

Consignment can be made to the steamship company, showing the name of the vessel on which the shipment will be loaded, the pier number and port name. The B/L should also show the number of packages, their gross weight, description of the goods, shipping marks (see later discussion), sailing date of vessel or departure of flight, and the latest delivery date. Note also if dock receipts are attached or lodged at the pier.

2. The Dock Receipt (D/R)

The Dock Receipt shows most of the same information as on the inland B/L. It is a document permitting a trucking or cartage company to deliver the shipment to a pier for loading on a vessel. When you have a shipment ready, you call your freight forwarder to arrange the shipment and book space on the next vessel going to your customer's overseas port. The forwarder will tell you the vessel's name, give you the booking number, pier number, sailing date, and last date for pier delivery. He will then prepare a D/R and mail it to you. To save time however, forwarders frequently supply blank D/Rs to their clients, who complete the form after obtaining the details as above.

3. The Ocean Bill of Lading

This document comes in two forms: the Straight, or the Order Bill of Lading. The straight B/L is a non-negotiable document; the order B/L is a negotiable instrument. The straight B/L shows the shipment consigned directly to the buyer. Since this document gives the buyer title to the goods on arrival at his port, you would issue it only to customers with whom you are dealing on an open account basis. In other words, you are passing title to the goods to the customer before he pays you.

On the other hand, if your terms are letter of credit or sight or time draft, you must have a "to order" ocean B/L. This shipment is then consigned to someone other than the customer, e.g. in your own name (to order of shipper) or to order of the bank (with their permission), negotiating the collection. This document then becomes part of the set attached to the LC or draft sent to the bank for collection. Usually, "to order" B/Ls are stamped "On Board," or "Clean On Board," and are signed or initialed, indicating the goods are actually on board the vessel, and there is no apparent damage to the shipment.

4. Air Waybills

A word about air freight bills of lading. They are called Air Waybills (AWB) and are always designated as Straight, i.e., non-negotiable. Consignment on other than open account shipments must therefore be made to a third party at destination, usually the customer's bank who will turn over the air waybill only after payment by the customer.

5. The Shipper's Export Declaration ("Export Dec")

The Export Dec serves many functions and is a document which must accompany all export shipments. This form (7525-V), issued by the Department of Commerce, serves two important functions. It is used as a census form in the sense that it is used by Commerce to collect data about all products being exported from the United States. The data collected includes a description of the product (classified under its Schedule B commodity number). the quantity shipped, the dollar value and the country (port) of destination. These data are then published by Commerce in various reports valuable to exporters as marketing and research tools.

Another vital use of the Export Dec is as a regulatory document by means of which the U. S. Export Administration Laws are enforced. (See Chapter III under Export Licensing).

An entry must be made on line 21 showing the validated export license number or the general license symbol. On line 22, the ECCN number (Export Commodity Control Number) must be entered if a validated license is applicable.

The Export Dec is submitted to the carrier along with the Ocean B/L or Air Waybill who then files them with the U. S. Customs Service.

6. The Insurance Certificate

The Insurance Certificate shows that shipment has been insured for certain types of loss or damage. Insurance must be considered on all overseas shipments; in fact, on those covered by an L/C, insurance is always one of the terms specified. There are many possibilities for loss or damage to your shipments from the time they leave your plant until they arrive at a customer's warehouse.

There are different ways you can obtain insurance coverage. The most common for small or new exporters is to insure through freight forwarders. This can be arranged when you contact them to take care of your shipment(s). Another method is to insure under your company's own Open Policy. Under this type of policy, which remains in force until it is cancelled, you report successive shipments to your insurance company. Your worldwide coverage is spelled out in the basic policy. The special certificate of insurance needed for documenting collections (L/C's and drafts) can be obtained by your forwarder through your insurance company. You would consider purchasing this type of policy once your volume grows and you ship on a regular basis. It will be more economical since you can negotiate with insurance companies for a better rate than you would get from a forwarder.

In some cases, your customer will have his own insurance policy, or he may be required by his country's laws to obtain and pay for insurance locally. In such cases, you should obtain "contingency" insurance to protect yourself should the customer's insurance not cover all risks.

7. Commercial Invoices

Commercial Invoices for export orders are basically the same as domestic invoices, so this is one of the company resources and support systems you can use in your export sales program. Some countries require additional information on the invoice such as a verification that prices are the same as for any other export customer. Often such statements must be in the language of the country, but you can get the standard set from your billing department and have the additional items typed on them.

The export invoice should also show a clause, which can be rubber-stamped, stating that the merchandise covered is licensed by the United States for export to (name of country) and diversion contrary to U. S. law is prohibited. If a validated export license has been issued, its number and date of expiration should be shown. Shipping marks should also be typed in. Finally, all commercial export invoices must usually be signed by the shipper.

8. Consular Invoices

Consular Invoices are a special form of invoice required by some countries. They can be taken care of by your forwarder who submits a copy of your invoice to the nearest consulate which then translates your invoice into the language of the country. It is then visaed (signed and sealed) by the consul. There is a charge for this—sometimes quite a stiff one. It has been said that this job is often given to a relative or close associates of the head of state and that he or she gets to keep the proceeds of the sale of consular invoices. Nice work if you can get it! Actually, consular invoices do serve some purpose as they are used for statistical control of imports and other such purposes.

9. Certificate of Origin

Commercial invoices usually show the origin of the goods being shipped. Nevertheless, many foreign governments require submission of a separate certificate attesting to the origin of the goods.

10. Inspection Certificates

Inspection Certificates are required by some customers who purchase certain food products, live animals, or grains. The U.S. Department of Agriculture issues these certificates attesting that the products meet with U.S.D.A. standards. Other products may also require either the customers' or countries' acceptance, and may need to be inspected and certified. These inspections are often done by a U.S. Laboratory (Underwriter's Laboratories—U.L. for Electrical Products), or an engineering firm for machinery or heavy equipment.

11. The Export Packing List

The Export Packing List is a very important document, usually quite different from a packing list used in domestic shipments.

This is especially true when making multiple-package shipments. Each package in the shipment should be numbered. For example: No. 1/10 (number 1 of 10) and so on. The packing list will then include:
- The consecutive package numbers.
- The dimensions of each package.
- The gross, legal and net weights in pounds and kilograms.
- An itemized listing showing the quantity and description, or part number of every item packed in each box.

The Export Packing List is used by the customs inspectors at the customers' ports of entry to verify what is being imported and some, if not all, packages may be opened. In addition, the packing list is of great value in the event of loss or damage to any or all of the packages in the shipment— the insurance company will demand it as a proof of shipment and the actual contents of the lost package(s).

12. Harbor Maintenance Fee—Customs Form 349

This fee has been in effect since 1987 and must be paid to the U. S. Customs on every export shipment which requires a shipper's Export Declaration. The fee paid, based on the value declared on the Export Dec less certain exemptions, is used to maintain and improve U.S. ports and harbors. Fees must be paid quarterly and a summary sheet of all export shipments made during that quarter must be sent with the payment.

Export Packing

According to CIGNA, one of the nation's largest insurance organizations with affiliates handling large volumes of marine and aviation insurance, about 75 percent of all cargo losses are preventable.* The last thing any exporter wants is to find out from an overseas customer that his shipment arrived damaged, in unusable condition, or that it was lost due to pilferage or inadequate marking.

Too often, not enough attention is given to how an export shipment is prepared, packaged or marked for either identification or special handling.

Keep in mind that in most, cases you cannot and should not use the same shipping packaging for export as you do for domestic shipment. Your cargo will be subject to a variety of hazards which do not exist in domestic shipping. Cargo moving on ocean-going vessels could be damaged by the various, and often violent, motions of the ship or the impact of waves washing over deck-stowed containers. Even air shipments are subject to damage from air turbulence or poor handling. In both modes of transport, improper storage can cause damaging movements or crashing of packages if they are improperly stacked. On the ground, export shipments face unusual hazards. Facilities at many ports around the world and the people who handle freight, range

*CIGNA Property and Casualty Companies

226

from primitive to good, and from unskilled or illiterate to professional.

In addition, many world ports are notorious for the amount of pilferage which occurs on a daily basis. CIGNA has estimated that roughly one-third of preventable losses are attributable to theft or pilferage.*

In many ports, there is no enclosed area in which to store discharged cargo; therefore, it is subject to heavy rains, scorching sun, extremes of temperature and flooding, contamination or spoilage along with strong possibilities for pilferage.

With all of these possible losses, an export shipper should, at the very least, take reasonable precautions to protect his shipment, not only to prevent losses, but also to keep his customers happy. Nothing is so frustrating to a customer who has waited weeks or months for his order to shipped, than to hear that his shipment has been lost, stolen, or damaged beyond repair.

You should learn some of the basic principles of packing for export, starting with the various types of outer container and inner protection materials available. Deciding to ship your products in domestic cartons because you will export them in an intermodal container is no assurance they will not be damaged. Although container shipments are somewhat more protected than those stored in a ship's hold, they can move around inside the container if the packages are not stored properly or damaged by stacking heavier cargo on the top of weaker cartons.

There are many types of good, strong exterior packing containers, many of which are made expressly for export shipping.

Air Versus Ocean Freight

You should look into and compare the cost of using air freight versus ocean freight for your export shipments. Everyone assumes that air shipments are automatically more expensive than shipping by ocean freight. This is not necessarily true! Let's look at some of the cost factors involved in each mode of shipping.

• Packing Costs. Depending upon your product, your export packing could be quite expensive. Many companies when pricing or quoting on their products include the cost of export packing. The landed cost to your customer will be higher because of it. Since the cost of packing for air freight

*CIGNA Property and Casualty Companies

is usually much lower, this represents a savings to both parties.

• Insurance Premiums are lower on air freight shipments since the likelihood of damage is lower.

• Customs Duties which the customer pays would be lower. Many countries levy duties on the gross weight of the imported goods, so without the heavy export packing, some savings accrue.

• Inventory Costs for both parties are minimized because with the faster air freight delivery, stocks move faster.

• Customer Satisfaction is increased since his order is delivered faster, he can sell the goods faster, and you'll be paid much more quickly.

Put all of these factors together and you may be pleasantly surprised to find that shipping your products by air is cheaper than by slow ocean freight.

A. N. DERINGER, INC.

727 Honeyspot Road
STRATFORD, CONNECTICUT 06497
Telephone: 203-378-5006
FAX 203-386-0202

FMC Lic. No. 1853

U.S. Customs Brokers
Ocean Forwarders
Air Forwarders
IATA Agents

Freight Brokers
Insurance Agents
Bonded Warehousing
Warehousing

Serving Importers, Exporters and the Transportation Industry Worldwide

NEW HAVEN, CONN. - HARTFORD, CONN. - NEW LONDON, CONN.

SERVICES OFFERED

OCEAN FREIGHT * EXPORTS

1) MAIL EIGHT COPIES OF YOUR COMMERCIAL INVOICE WITH A COPY OF OUR OCEAN
    FREIGHT INSTRUCTION SHEET (SEE ATTACHED) TO OUR ABOVE ADDRESS. WE WILL
    RETURN DOCK RECEIPTS TO YOU TO ACCOMPANY YOUR SHIPMENT TO THE PIER VIA
    YOUR INLAND CARRIER.

    > ASK US TO EXPLAIN HOW YOU CAN SHIP
    > YOUR WATER FREIGHT EXPORT THE SAME DAY IT
    > IS PACKED.

2) PREPARE OCEAN BILLS OF LADING, EXPORT DECLARATIONS, DOCK RECEIPTS, AND
    DELIVERY INSTRUCTIONS. CUSTOMS AND CONSULAR DOCUMENTS ARRANGED AS
    REQUIRED BY THE COUNTRY OF IMPORTATION.

3) HOUSE TO HOUSE INSURANCE ARRANGED UNDER A.N. DERINGER, INC. OPEN CARGO
    POLICY. RATES PROVIDED UPON REQUEST.

4) ALL SHIPMENTS BOOKED WITH STEAMSHIP LINES TO GUARANTEE LOADING ON THE
    FIRST AVAILABLE VESSEL.

5) DOCUMENTS DISTRIBUTION AS FOLLOWS:
    a) LETTER OF CREDIT - SHIPPING DOCUMENTS HAND-DELIVERED TO YOUR U.S.
        ADVISING/NEGOTIATING BANK BY OUR MESSENGERS.

    b) SIGHT DRAFT - ORIGINAL DOCUMENTATION SPEEDILY DISPATCHED TO YOUR
        CUSTOMER'S OVERSEAS BANK VIA REGISTERED AIR-MAIL.

    c) OPEN ACCOUNT/CASH IN ADVANCE-DOCUMENTS ARE REGISTERED AND AIR-
        MAILED DIRECTLY TO YOUR CUSTOMER OR HIS BROKER.

    YOUR CONSIGNEE IS ALWAYS NOTIFIED OF SHIPMENT BY THE SEPARATE AIR-
    MAILING OF A COPY OF YOUR COMMERCIAL INVOICE AND A COPY OF THE OCEAN
    BILL OF LADING.

6) CALL (203)378-5006 FOR ALL RATE QUOTATIONS, SAILING SCHEDULES, AND
    PICK-UP APPOINTMENTS.

    WE HAVE ATTACHED A COPY OF OUR OCEAN FREIGHT INSTRUCTION SHEET FOR YOUR
    CONVENIENCE. CALL US FOR ADDITIONAL COPIES.

Our Service Recommends Us

Grand Rapids, MI
Detroit, MI
Port Huron, MI
Sault Ste. Marie, MI
Buffalo, NY
Niagara Falls, NY
Lewiston, NY
Watertown, NY
Alexandria Bay, NY
Ogdensburg, NY
Fort Covington, NY
Massena, NY

Trout River, NY
Mooers, NY
Champlain, NY
Rouses Point, NY
Syracuse, NY
Alburg, VT
St. Albans, VT
Highgate Springs, VT
Burlington, VT
Richford, VT
Newport, VT

Derby Line, VT
Norton, VT
Jackman, ME
Houlton, ME
Fort Kent, ME
Madawaska, ME
Van Buren, ME
Limestone, ME
Fort Fairfield, ME
Bridgewater, ME
Vanceboro, ME

Calais, ME
Bangor, ME
Bar Harbor, ME
Portland, ME
Portsmouth, NH
Gloucester, MA
Boston, MA
Windsor Locks, (Hartford) CT
Bridgeport, CT
Jamaica, NY (JFK Airport)
New York, NY

Also serving the above port: through our subsidiary, W. R. FILBIN & CO., Inc. (FMC Lic. No. 803)

Services Offered by Freight Forwarders

Herman J. Maggiori

A. N. DERINGER, INC.

727 Honeyspot Road
STRATFORD, CONNECTICUT 06497
Telephone: 203-378-5006
FAX 203-386-0202

FMC Lic. No. 1853

U.S. Customs Brokers
Ocean Forwarders
Air Forwarders
IATA Agents

Freight Brokers
Insurance Agents
Bonded Warehousing
Warehousing

Serving Importers, Exporters and the Transportation Industry Worldwide

OCEAN FREIGHT INSTRUCTION SHEET

SHIPPER'S NAME & ADDRESS: _____

REFERENCE NO. _____

CONSIGNEE'S NAME & ADDRESS: _____

REFERENCE NO. _____

NOTIFY PARTY (IF ANY): _____

REFERENCE NO. _____

NAME OF INLAND CARRIER: _____

PORT OF LOADING: _____ DISCHARGE: _____

OCEAN FREIGHT: PREPAID: _____ COLLECT: _____

MARKS & NUMBERS: _____

DESCRIPTION & NO. OF PIECES: _____

COMMODITY (AND LABEL IF ANY:) _____

GROSS WEIGHT: _____

VOLUME OR DIMENSIONS: _____

INSURANCE: _____

OTHER: _____

F.A.S._____ F.O.B._____ C & F _____ C.I.F._____ OTHER: _____

*LETTER OF CREDIT:_____ *DRAFT_____ OPEN ACCOUNT:_____ OTHER: _____

* IF LETTER OF CREDIT OR DRAFT IS INVOLVED, PLEASE CONTACT OUR OFFICE FOR FURTHER
  INSTRUCTIONS. PHONE # 203-378-5006

Grand Rapids, MI	Trout River, NY	Derby Line, VT	Calais, ME
Detroit, MI	Mooers, NY	Norton, VT	Bangor, ME
Port Huron, MI	Champlain, NY	Jackman, ME	Bar Harbor, ME
Sault Ste. Marie, MI	Rouses Point, NY	Houlton, ME	Portland, ME
Buffalo, NY	Syracuse, NY	Fort Kent, ME	Portsmouth, NH
Niagara Falls, NY	Alburg, VT	Madawaska, ME	Gloucester, MA
Lewiston, NY	St. Albans, VT	Van Buren, ME	Boston, MA
Watertown, NY	Highgate Springs, VT	Limestone, ME	Windsor Locks, (Hartford) CT
Alexandria Bay, NY	Burlington, VT	Fort Fairfield, ME	Bridgeport, CT
Ogdensburg, NY	Richford, VT	Bridgewater, ME	Jamaica, NY (JFK Airport)
Fort Covington, NY	Newport, VT	Vanceboro, ME	New York, NY
Massena, NY			

Our Service Recommends Us

Also serving the above port: through our subsidiary, W. R. FILBIN & CO., Inc. (FMC Lic. No. 803)

Sample of Forwarder's Ocean Freight Instruction Sheet

A.N. DERINGER, INC.
FREIGHT FORWARDER
P.O. BOX #128
BRIDGEPORT, CONNECTICUT 06601
FMC# 1853
FAX#(203)386-0202 TEL:(203)378-5006
OUR REFERENCE NO. EXW#_____

DATE DELIVERED TO YOU_____

J. COTY MESSENGER SERVICE, INC.
33 CEDAR STREET   STREET LEVEL
NEW YORK, NEW YORK 10006

GENTLEMEN:

PLEASE ATTEND TO THE LEGALIZATION OF THE ENCLOSED DOCUMENTS WITH THE
CONSULATE OF_____.

_____COMMERCIAL INVOICE IN_____COPIES

_____OCEAN BILLS OF LADING IN_____COPIES

_____COPY LETTER OF CREDIT

_____AIR WAYBILL IN_____COPIES

_____COPY IMPORT PERMIT NUMBER_____

_____CERTIFICATE OF ORIGIN IN_____COPIES

_____

_____

_____

SPECIAL INSTRUCTIONS ARE AS FOLLOWS:

Sample of Instructions to Forwarder's Messenger

Herman J. Maggiori

A. N. DERINGER, INC.

FMC Lic. No. 1853

727 Honeyspot Road
STRATFORD, CONNECTICUT 06497
Telephone: 203-378-5006
FAX 203-386-0202

U. S. Customs Brokers
Ocean Forwarders
Air Forwarders
IATA Agents

Freight Brokers
Insurance Agents
Bonded Warehousing
Warehousing

Serving Importers, Exporters and the Transportation Industry Worldwide

NEW HAVEN, CONN.-HARTFORD, CONN.-NEW LONDON, CONN.

SERVICES OFFERED
AIR FREIGHT * EXPORTS

1) Arrange for common carrier to pick-up the shipment at your plant-
SAME DAY SERVICE

2) Prepare International Air Waybill and Export Declaration. Customs
and Consular Documents arranged for the country of importation.
Banking services and insurance policies are available.

3) Book the cargo with International Airlines and furnish the shipper
with flight information and air waybill number the same day as the
pick-up.

4) Prepay all charges and add to shipper's invoice if the shipment
is prepaid. If the shipment is collect, air freight and forwarding
fees will be collected by the airline from your customer overseas.

5) Attach to International Airbill Invoices, Packing List, Certificate
of Origin etc...For customer or his Custom House Broker to clear
goods thru customs.

*Note- a phone number would be helpful if you have one.

6) Call (203)378-5006 for all rate and flight informaton and pick-up
appointments.

AN INSTRUCTION SHEET IS ATTACHED FOR FOR YOUR CONVENIENCE

Grand Rapids, MI	Trout River, NY	Derby Line, VT	Calais, ME
Detroit, MI	Mooers, NY	Norton, VT	Bangor, ME
Port Huron, MI	Champlain, NY	Jackman, ME	Bar Harbor, ME
Sault Ste. Marie, MI	Rouses Point, NY	Houlton, ME	Portland, ME
Buffalo, NY	Syracuse, NY	Fort Kent, ME	Portsmouth, NH
Niagara Falls, NY	Alburg, VT	Madawaska, ME	Gloucester, MA
Lewiston, NY	St. Albans, VT	Van Buren, ME	Boston, MA
Watertown, NY	Highgate Springs, VT	Limestone, ME	Windsor Locks, (Hartford) CT
Alexandria Bay, NY	Burlington, VT	Fort Fairfield, ME	Bridgeport, CT
Ogdensburg, NY	Richford, VT	Bridgewater, ME	Jamacia, NY (JFK Airport)
Fort Covington, NY	Newport, VT	Vanceboro, ME	New York, NY
Massena, NY			

Our Service Recommends Us

Also serving the above port through our subsidiary, W. R. FILBIN & CO., Inc. (FMC Lic. No. 803)

Sample of Forwarder's Air Freight Services

232

A. N. DERINGER. INC.

FMC Lic. No. 1853

727 Honeyspot Road
STRATFORD, CONNECTICUT 06497
Telephone: 203-378-5006
FAX 203-386-0202

U. S. Customs Brokers
Ocean Forwarders
Air Forwarders
IATA Agents

Freight Brokers
Insurance Agents
Bonded Warehousing
Warehousing

Serving Importers, Exporters and the Transportation Industry Worldwide

AIR FREIGHT INSTRUCTION SHEET

AIRPORT OF DEPARTURE: _____

AIRPORT OF DESTINATION: _____

NAME & ADDRESS OF SHIPPER: _____

NAME & ADDRESS OF CONSIGNEE: _____

NOTIFY PARTY (IF ANY): _____
REFERENCE NO. OF SHIPPER: _____
REFERENCE NO OF CONSIGNEE: _____
REFERENCE NO OF NOTIFY PARTY: _____

VALUE: _____
INSURANCE: YES: _____   NO: _____
AIR FREIGHT: _____
DESCRIPTION & NO. OF PIECES: _____
COMMODITY: _____
GROSS WEIGHT: _____
VOLUME OR DEMENSIONS: _____
F.A.S.   F.O.B.   C.& F. C.I.F.   OTHER: _____

IF LETTER OF CREDIT, ATTACH THE ORIGINAL LETTER OF CREDIT.
IF BANK DRAFT, GIVE TENOR INSTRUCTIONS & NAME OF FOREIGN BANK.
PLEASE ATTACH EIGHT (8) COPIES OF YOUR COMMERCIAL INVOICE & FOUR (4)
COPIES OF YOUR PACKING LIST (IF AVAILABLE).

Our Service Recommends Us

Grand Rapids, MI	Trout River, NY	Derby Line, VT	Calais, ME
Detroit, MI	Mooers, NY	Norton, VT	Bangor, ME
Port Huron, MI	Champlain, NY	Jackman, ME	Bar Harbor, ME
Sault Ste. Marie, MI	Rouses Point, NY	Houlton, ME	Portland, ME
Buffalo, NY	Syracuse, NY	Fort Kent, ME	Portsmouth, NH
Niagara Falls, NY	Alburg, VT	Madawaska, ME	Gloucester, MA
Lewiston, NY	St. Albans, VT	Van Buren, ME	Boston, MA
Watertown, NY	Highgate Springs, VT	Limestone, ME	Windsor Locks, (Hartford) CT
Alexandria Bay, NY	Burlington, VT	Fort Fairfield, ME	Bridgeport, CT
Ogdensburg, NY	Richford, VT	Bridgewater, ME	Jamaica, NY (JFK Airport)
Fort Covington, NY	Newport, VT	Vanceboro, ME	New York, NY
Massena, NY			

Also serving the above port: through our subsidiary, W. R. FILBIN & CO., Inc. (FMC Lic. No. 803)

Sample of Forwarder's Air Freight Instruction Sheet

SHIPPER'S LETTER OF INSTRUCTIONS

1a. EXPORTER (Name and address including ZIP code)		**SHIPPER: PLEASE BE SURE TO COMPLETE ALL BLUE SHADED AREAS.**
	ZIP CODE	

b. EXPORTER'S EIN (IRS) NO.	c. PARTIES TO TRANSACTION ☐ Related ☐ Non-related	**A. N. DERINGER, INC.**
4a. ULTIMATE CONSIGNEE		727 Honeyspot Road
		Stratford, Connecticut 06497
b. INTERMEDIATE CONSIGNEE		Telephone: 203-378-5006
		Fax: 203-386-0202

5. FORWARDING AGENT

A. N. DERINGER
727 Honeyspot Road
Stratford, Connecticut 06497

SHIPPER MUST CHECK

8. LOADING PIER (Vessel only)	9. MODE OF TRANSPORT (Specify)
10. EXPORTING CARRIER	11. PORT OF EXPORT
12. PORT OF UNLOADING (Vessel and air only)	13. CONTAINERIZED (Vessel only) ☐ Yes ☐ No

☐ PREPAID ☐ COLLECT C.O.D. $_____

☐ AIR ☐ OCEAN ☐ CONSOLIDATE ☐ DIRECT

SHIPPER'S INSTRUCTIONS IN CASE OF INABILITY TO DELIVER CONSIGNMENT

AS ASSIGNED ☐ ABANDON ☐ RETURN TO SHIPPER

SHIPPER REQUESTS INSURANCE ☐ No ☐ Yes $

☐ DELIVER TO

14. SCHEDULE B DESCRIPTION OF COMMODITIES, (Use columns 17–19) 15. MARKS, NOS., AND KINDS OF PACKAGES				SHIPPER'S REF. NO. DATE	VALUE (U.S. dollars, omit cents) (Selling price or cost if not sold)
D/F (16)	SCHEDULE B NUMBER (17)	CHECK DIGIT	QUANTITY – SCHEDULE B UNIT(S) (18)	SHIPPING WEIGHT (Kilos) (19)	(20)

SHIPPER NOTE:

IF YOU ARE UNCERTAIN OF THE SCHEDULE B COMMODITY NO. DO NOT TYPE IT IN – WE WILL COMPLETE WHEN PROCESSING THE 7525V.

WE HAVE FORWARDED TO YOU, THE SHIPMENT DESCRIBED BELOW VIA:
☐ YOUR TRUCK, OR
☐ OTHER CARRIER (LISTED BELOW)
TRUCK LINE NAME _____

RECEIPT (PRO) NUMBER _____

DECLARED VALUE FOR CARRIAGE
$

21. VALIDATED LICENSE NO./GENERAL LICENSE SYMBOL	22. ECCN (When required)	PLEASE SIGN THE FIRST EXPORT DECLARATION IN BOX 23 WITH PEN AND INK.

23. Duly authorized officer or employee	The exporter authorizes the forwarder named above to act as forwarding agent for export control and customs purposes.	DOCUMENTS ENCLOSED:
24. I certify that all statements made and all information contained herein are true and correct and that I have read and understand the instructions for preparation of this document, set forth in the "Correct Way to Fill Out the Shipper's Export Declaration." I understand that civil and criminal penalties, including forfeiture and sale, may be imposed for making false or fraudulent statements herein, failing to provide the requested information or for violation of U.S. laws on exportation (13 U.S.C. Sec. 305; 22 U.S.C. Sec. 401; 18 U.S.C. Sec. 1001; 50 U.S.C. App. 2410).		
Signature	Confidential - For use solely for official purposes authorized by the Secretary of Commerce (13 U.S.C. 301 (g).	SPECIAL INSTRUCTIONS:
Title	Export shipments are subject to inspection by U.S. Customs Service and/or Office of Export Enforcement.	
Date	25. AUTHENTICATION (When required)	

NOTE: The Shipper or his Authorized Agent hereby authorizes the above named Company, in his name and on his behalf, to prepare any export documents, to sign and accept any documents relating to said shipment and forward this shipment in accordance with the conditions of carriage and the tariffs of the carriers employed. The shipper guarantees payment of all collect charges in the event the consignee refuses payment. Hereunder the sole responsibility of the Company is to use reasonable care in the selection of carriers, forwarders, agents and others to whom it may entrust the shipment.

Sample of Shipper's Letter of Instruction to Freight Forwarder

FORM 503 WHSE. NO. 0852
APPERSON BUSINESS FORMS, INC.
(800) 438-0162 (1-1-88)

U.S. DEPARTMENT OF COMMERCE • BUREAU OF THE CENSUS - INTERNATIONAL TRADE ADMINISTRATION

FORM **7525-V** (1-1-88)

SHIPPER'S EXPORT DECLARATION

OMB No. 0607-0018

1a. EXPORTER (Name and address including ZIP code)			
	ZIP CODE	2. DATE OF EXPORTATION	3. BILL OF LADING/AIR WAYBILL NO.

b. EXPORTER'S EIN (IRS) NO.	c. PARTIES TO TRANSACTION ☐ Related ☐ Non-related

4a. ULTIMATE CONSIGNEE

b. INTERMEDIATE CONSIGNEE

5. FORWARDING AGENT

A. N. DERINGER
727 Honeyspot Road
Stratford, Connecticut 06497

6. POINT (STATE) OF ORIGIN OR FTZ NO.	7. COUNTRY OF ULTIMATE DESTINATION

8. LOADING PIER (Vessel only)	9. MODE OF TRANSPORT (Specify)
10. EXPORTING CARRIER	11. PORT OF EXPORT
12. PORT OF UNLOADING (Vessel and air only)	13. CONTAINERIZED (Vessel only) ☐ Yes ☐ No

14. SCHEDULE B DESCRIPTION OF COMMODITIES,
15. MARKS, NOS., AND KINDS OF PACKAGES

(Use columns 17 – 19)

D/F (16)	SCHEDULE B NUMBER (17)	CHECK DIGIT	QUANTITY – SCHEDULE B UNIT(S) (18)	SHIPPING WEIGHT (Kilos) (19)	VALUE (U.S. dollars, omit cents) (Selling price or cost if not sold) (20)

21. VALIDATED LICENSE NO./GENERAL LICENSE SYMBOL	22. ECCN (When required)

23. Duly authorized officer or employee	The exporter authorizes the forwarder named above to act as forwarding agent for export control and customs purposes.

24. I certify that all statements made and all information contained herein are true and correct and that I have read and understand the instructions for preparation of this document, set forth in the "Correct Way to Fill Out the Shipper's Export Declaration." I understand that civil and criminal penalties, including forfeiture and sale, may be imposed for making false or fraudulent statements herein, failing to provide the requested information or for violation of U.S. laws on exportation (13 U.S.C. Sec. 305; 22 U.S.C. Sec. 401; 18 U.S.C. Sec. 1001; 50 U.S.C. App. 2410).

Signature

Title

Date

Confidential - For use solely for official purposes authorized by the Secretary of Commerce (13 U.S.C. 301 (g).

Export shipments are subject to inspection by U.S. Customs Service and/or Office of Export Enforcement.

25. AUTHENTICATION (When required)

The "Correct Way to Fill Out the Shipper's Export Declaration" is available from the Bureau of the Census, Washington, D.C. 20233

Sample Shipper's Export Declaration

U.S. DEPARTMENT OF COMMERCE — BUREAU OF THE CENSUS — INTERNATIONAL TRADE ADMINISTRATION

FORM **7525-V** (1-1-88)

SHIPPER'S EXPORT DECLARATION

OMB No. 0607-0018

1a. EXPORTER (Name and address including ZIP code)			2. DATE OF EXPORTATION	3. BILL OF LADING/AIR WAYBILL NO.
Brown and Company 123 Samantha Road Toledo, OH	ZIP CODE 43264	1-10-88		00—1234—5678

1b. EXPORTER'S EIN (IRS) NO.	c. PARTIES TO TRANSACTION
12—345678901	☐ Related ☒ Non-related

4a. ULTIMATE CONSIGNEE
Kirk Sales, LTD
162 Belva Street
London, England

b. INTERMEDIATE CONSIGNEE
Tim Service Company
3456 Fred Lane
London, England

5. FORWARDING AGENT
Sharyn Exports
P.O. Box XYZ
New York, NY 10047

6. POINT (STATE) OF ORIGIN OR FTZ NO.	7. COUNTRY OF ULTIMATE DESTINATION
OH	England

8. LOADING PIER (Vessel only)	9. MODE OF TRANSPORT (Specify) Air
10. EXPORTING CARRIER Fairway Air	**11. PORT OF EXPORT** Kennedy Airport
12. PORT OF UNLOADING (Vessel and air only) Gatwick, England	**13. CONTAINERIZED** (Vessel only) ☐ Yes ☐ No

14. SCHEDULE B DESCRIPTION OF COMMODITIES. (Use columns 17—19) 15. MARKS, NOS., AND KINDS OF PACKAGES				VALUE (U.S. dollars, omit cents) (Selling price or cost if not sold)
D/F (16)	SCHEDULE B NUMBER (17)	CHECK DIGIT	QUANTITY – SCHEDULE B UNIT(S) (18)	SHIPPING WEIGHT (Kilos) (19)	(20)

2 Boxes (B/1 and B/2) of Model 525 Signal Generators					
D	8543.20.0000	3	2	6 Kg	2,375
1 Box (B/3) of Parts for Model 525 Signal Generator (probes, tees, defectors, and defector mounts)					
D	8543.90.9500	4	X	31 Kg	1,854

21. VALIDATED LICENSE NO./GENERAL LICENSE SYMBOL A 123456	22. ECCN (When required) 1529

23. Duly authorized officer or employee   *H. Green*   The exporter authorizes the forwarder named above to act as forwarding agent for export control and customs purposes.

24. I certify that all statements made and all information contained herein are true and correct and that I have read and understand the instructions for preparation of this document, set forth in the "Correct Way to Fill Out the Shipper's Export Declaration." I understand that civil and criminal penalties, including forfeiture and sale, may be imposed for making false or fraudulent statements herein, failing to provide the requested information or for violation of U.S. laws on exportation (13 U.S.C. Sec. 305; 22 U.S.C. Sec. 401; 18 U.S.C. Sec. 1001; 50 U.S.C. App. 2410).

Signature *S. Sharyn*
Title President
Date 1-10-88

Confidential - For use solely for official purposes authorized by the Secretary of Commerce (13 U.S.C. 301 (g)).

Export shipments are subject to inspection by U.S. Customs Service and/or Office of Export Enforcement.

26. AUTHENTICATION (When required)

Sample of Completed Shipper's Export Declaration

U.S. DEPARTMENT OF COMMERCE - BUREAU OF THE CENSUS - INTERNATIONAL TRADE ADMINISTRATION		CONFIDENTIAL - For use solely for official purposes	OMB No. 0607-0152
M 7525-V-ALT. (Intermodal) (1-1-88) SHIPPER'S EXPORT DECLARATION		authorized by the Secretary of Commerce (13 U.S.C. 301(g)).	DO NOT USE THIS AREA

1. EXPORTER (Principal or seller license and address including ZIP Code)
REMINMGTON ARMS COMPANY
1007 MARKET STREET
WILMINGTON, DELAWARE 19898
ZIP CODE

5. DOCUMENT NUMBER
220-47331874

5a. B/L OR AWB NUMBER

6. EXPORT REFERENCES
TD#057   IATA #01-101431/050
845135   IW SHOW

AUTHENTICATION (When required)

29. THE UNDERSIGNED HEREBY AUTHORIZES
A.N. DERINGER, INC.
TO ACT AS FORWARDING AGENT FOR EXPORT CONTROL AND CUSTOMS PURPOSES.
EXPORTER (BY DULY AUTHORIZED REMINGTON ARMS CO. OFFICER OR EMPLOYEE)

2. CONSIGNED TO
HELMUT HOFFMAN, GMBH
POSTFACH 38
8744 MELLRICHSTADT
WEST GERMANY

7. FORWARDING AGENT (Name and address - references)
A.N. DERINGER, INC.
727 HONEYSPOT ROAD
STRATFORD, CONN. 06497

8. POINT (STATE) OF ORIGIN OR FTZ NUMBER

30. METHOD OF TRANSPORTATION (Mark one)
☐ Vessel   ☐ Other - Specify
☒ Air

31. ULTIMATE CONSIGNEE (Give name and address if this is a different than # 2 or # 3)
SAME AS #3

3. NOTIFY PARTY/INTERMEDIATE CONSIGNEE (Name and address)
HANS WAGNER CONTAINER DIENSTE
GMBH& CO.
BREITEWEG 32 - 2800 BREMEN 1,
WEST GERMANY

9. DOMESTIC ROUTING/EXPORT INSTRUCTIONS

32. DATE OF EXPORTATION (Not required for vessel shipment)
3=9-91

33. COUNTRY OF ULTIMATE DESTINATION
GERMANY

4. PRE-CARRIAGE BY

13. PLACE OF RECEIPT BY PRE-CARRIER

34. EXPORTER'S E.I.N. (IRS) NUMBER
51-0246028-00

12. EXPORTING CARRIER
LUFTHANSA

15. PORT OF LOADING/EXPORT
JFK, NEW YORK

10. LOADING PIER/TERMINAL

35. PARTIES TO TRANSACTION
☐ Related   ☐ Non-related

16. FOREIGN PORT OF UNLOADING (Vessel and air only)
FRANKFURT

17. PLACE OF DELIVERY BY ON-CARRIER

11. TYPE OF MOVE

11a. CONTAINERIZED (Vessel only)
☐ Yes   ☐ No

Export shipments are subject to inspection by U.S. Customs Service and/or Office of Export Enforcement.

MARKS AND NUMBERS (18)	NUMBER OF PACKAGES (19)	DESCRIPTION OF COMMODITIES in Schedule B detail (20)	GROSS WEIGHT (Kilos) (21)	MEASUREMENT (22)	D OR F	CD - Check digit / Value - Selling price or cost if not sold (U.S. dollars, omit cents) Quantity - Schedule B unit(s)
						21. SCHEDULE B NO.		CD
HELMUT HOFFMAN GMBH POSTFACH 38 8744 MELLRICHSTADT WEST GERMANY		FREIGHT PREPAID				**25a. QUANTITY 1**	**25b. QUANTITY 2**
						26. VALUE	
	1	CTN. CONSISTING OF; HUNTING & SPORTING EQUPMENT-CENTER FIRE RIFLES	3.54k/10#	-------	D	**24. SCHEDULE B NO.** 9303.30.8050 **25a. QUANTITY 1** 1PCS.	CD **25b. QUANTITY 2**
						26. VALUE 961.00	
STATE DEPT. EXPORT LICENSE #463820-EXPIRES 7-18-93						**24. SCHEDULE B NO.**	CD
THESE COMMODITIES LICENSED BY THE US FOR ULTIMATE DESTINATION, BIXXRSIEXXX GERMANY. DIVERSION CONTRARY TO US LAW PROHIB8ITED.						**25a. QUANTITY 1**	**25b. QUANTITY 2**
						26. VALUE	

27. VALIDATED LICENSE NO./GENERAL LICENSE SYMBOL

28. ECCN (When required)

36. I certify that all statements made and all information contained herein are true and correct and that I have read and understand the instructions for preparation of this document, set forth in the "Correct Way to Fill Out the Shipper's Export Declaration." I understand that civil and criminal penalties, including forfeiture and sale, may be imposed for making false or fraudulent statements herein, failing to provide the requested information, or for violation of U.S. laws on exportation (13 U.S.C. Sec. 305; 22 U.S.C. Sec. 401; 18 U.S.C. Sec. 1001; 50 U.S.C. App. 2410).

Sample of Completed Alternate Shipper's Export Declaration

CORRECT WAY TO FILL OUT THE SHIPPER'S EXPORT DECLARATIONS
(Follow Carefully to Avoid Delay at Shipping Point)

1. Purpose

The Shipper's Export Declarations (SEDs), Forms 7525-V and 7525-V-Alternate (Intermodal) and the Shipper's Export Declaration for In-Transit Goods, Form 7513, are joint Bureau of the Census — International Trade Administration documents used for compiling the official U.S. export statistics and administering the requirements of the Export Administration Act, as provided for in the Foreign Trade Statistics Regulations (FTSR) (15 CFR, Part 30) and the Export Administration Regulations (15 CFR, Parts 368—399).

2. Forms

The SED, Form 7525-V, its continuation sheet, and the in-transit SED, Form 7513, may be purchased from the Superintendent of Documents, Government Printing Office, Washington, D.C. 20402, local Customs District Directors, or privately printed. Form 7525-V-Alternate (Intermodal) and its continuation sheet must be privately printed. Sample copies may be obtained from the Bureau of the Census, Washington, D.C. 20233. When privately printing SEDs, the forms must conform in every respect to the official forms in size, wording, color (black ink on buff paper — Form 7513 on pink paper), weight of paper stock (not less than 16 nor more than 20 pounds commercial substance), and arrangement including the Office of Management and Budget Approval Number printed in the upper right-hand corner of the face of the form. The SEDs are designed to allow their inclusion as part of a set of documents so that an exporter can prepare several shipping documents at the same time. Form 7525-V (See page 8.) aligns with the Canadian invoice, air waybills, and other vertically oriented documents. Form 7525-V-Alternate (Intermodal) aligns with the ocean bill of lading and other horizontally oriented documents. Either form may be used regardless of method of transportation or destination.

The Bureau of the Census has a program whereby exporters, carriers, or freight forwarders may submit monthly reports via electronic medium or summary declaration in lieu of filing an individual Shipper's Export Declaration for each shipment.

3. When Required

SEDs are required to be filed for virtually all shipments, including hand-carried merchandise, (see Section 9 for exemptions, particularly if the shipment is valued $1,500 or less) from the United States (50 states and the District of Columbia); Puerto Rico; U.S. or Puerto Rican Foreign Trade Zones (FTZs); and the U.S. Virgin Islands to all foreign countries or areas (including FTZs located therein).

SEDs are also required to be filed for shipments between the United States and Puerto Rico and from the United States or Puerto Rico to the U.S. Virgin Islands.

SEDs are not required for shipments from the United States or Puerto Rico to U.S. Possessions (except the U.S. Virgin Islands) or from a U.S. Possession to the United States, Puerto Rico, or another U.S. Possession.

The SED for in-transit merchandise (Form 7513) is required to -oe filed for:

(a) merchandise destined from one foreign country to another which transits the United States, Puerto Rico or the U.S. Virgin Islands and is exported by vessel regardless of the method of transportation by which the merchandise entered. If a validated export license is

required this form must be filed regardless of the method of transportation for the export;

(b) merchandise exported from General Order Warehouses; and

(c) imported merchandise which has been rejected by government inspection and is being exported. (Form 7513 is not to be used for the reexport of imported merchandise, except rejected merchandise.)

4. Number of Copies Required

(a) One copy for shipments to Canada, Puerto Rico, and the U.S. Virgin Islands

(b) One copy for exports through the U.S. Postal Service

(c) Two copies for all other shipments

Additional copies may be required for export control purposes by the International Trade Administration, other Government agencies (when authorized), Customs Directors, or the Postmaster.

5. Preparation and Signature

The SED shall be prepared in English in a permanent medium with the original signed (signature stamp acceptable) by the exporter or his duly authorized agent. The agent's authority to sign the SED must be executed by a power-of-attorney or as authorized on the SED.

6. Requirement for Separate SEDs

Separate SEDs are required for each shipment from one consignor to one consignee on a single carrier (including each rail car, truck, or other vehicle). However, Customs Directors may waive this requirement if multiple car shipments are made under a single loading document and cleared simultaneously. Also, merchandise requiring a validated export license shall not be reported on the same SED with merchandise moving under general license.

7. Presentation

(a) Postal Shipments — the SEDs shall be delivered to the Postmaster with the packages at the time of mailing.

(b) Pipeline shipments — the SEDs shall be submitted to the Customs Director within 4 working days after the end of the calendar month.

(c) All other shipments — the SEDs shall be delivered to the exporting carrier prior to exportation.

(d) Exporting carriers are required to file SEDs and manifests with Customs — See Sections 30.20 through 30.24 of the FTSR.

Shipments from an interior point — SED may accompany the merchandise being transported to the exporting carrier or the port of exportation, or it may be delivered directly to the exporting carrier.

Shipments exempt from SED filing requirements — a reference to the exemption must be noted on the bill of lading, air waybill, or other loading document for verification that no SED is required.

Sample of Instructions for Completing Shipper's Export Declaration

8. Corrections

Corrections, amendments, or cancellations of data may be made directly on the originally filed SED, if it has not been forwarded to the Bureau of the Census. If the SED has been forwarded to the Bureau, corrections, amendments, or cancellations should be made on a copy of the originally filed SED (marked "Correction Copy") and filed with the Customs Director or the Postmaster where the declaration was originally presented.

9. Exemptions

A. Shipments (excluding postal shipments) where the value of commodities classified under each individual Schedule B number is $1500 or less and for which a validated export license is not required and when shipped to countries not prohibited by the Export Administration Regulations (15 CFR, Parts 368—399).

B. Shipments through the U.S. Postal Service that do not require a validated license when the shipment is: (1) valued $500 or under, (2) either the consignee or the consignor is not a business concern, or (3) the shipment is not for commercial consideration.

C. In-transit shipments not requiring a validated export license and leaving for a foreign destination by means other than vessel.

D. Shipments from one point in the United States to another point thereof by routes passing through Canada or Mexico, and shipments from one point in Canada or Mexico to another point thereof by routes passing through the United States.

E. Shipments to the U.S. Armed Services
   (1) All commodities consigned to the U.S. Armed Services, including exchange systems.
   (2) Department of Defense Military Assistance Program Grant-Aid shipments being transported as Department of Defense cargo.

F. Shipments to U.S. Government Agencies and Employees
   (1) Office furniture and supplies for use in Government offices.
   (2) Household goods and personal property for the use of U.S. Government employees.
   (3) Food, medicines, and related items and other commissary items for use by U.S. Government employees and offices.
   (4) Government shipments of books, charts, maps, and so forth, for use by libraries or similar institutions.

G. Miscellaneous Exemptions
   (1) Diplomatic pouches and their contents.
   (2) Human remains and accompanying appropriate receptacles and flowers.
   (3) Shipments of gift parcels moving under General License GIFT.
   (4) Shipments of interplant correspondence and other business records from a U.S. firm to its subsidiary or affiliate.
   (5) Shipments of pets as baggage, accompanying or unaccompanying persons leaving the United States.

H. Conditional Exemptions

SEDs are not required for the following if they are not shipped as cargo under a bill of lading or air waybill and do not require a validated export license.

   (1) Baggage and household effects and tools of trade of persons leaving the United States when such are owned by the person, in his possession at the time of departure and intended for his use only.
   (2) Carriers' stores, supplies, equipment, bunker fuel, and so forth, when not intended for unlading in a foreign country.
   (3) Usual and reasonable kinds and quantities of dunnage necessary to secure and stow cargo. (For sole use on board the carrier.)

If the shipments indicated above are shipped under a bill of lading or air waybill, the SED should show in the description column in lieu of a description, a statement that the shipment consists of baggage, personal effects, and so forth, and Schedule B Commodity Numbers should not be shown.

If these shipments require a validated export license, the SED must identify the shipment as baggage, personal effects, and so forth, and must contain all of the information required on the SED.

10. Retention of Shipping Documents

The Bureau of the Census, the International Trade Administration, and the U.S. Customs Service may require the exporters or their agents to produce copies of shipping documents within 3 years of exportation.

11. Administrative Provisions

SEDs and the information contained thereon are confidential and used solely for official purposes authorized by the Secretary of Commerce in accordance with 13 U.S.C. Section 301(g). Neither may be disclosed to anyone except the exporter or his agent by those having possession of or access to any official copy.

Information from SEDs (except common information) may not be copied to manifests or other shipping documents. Exporters may not furnish SEDs or their information to anyone for unofficial purposes.

Copies of the SEDs may be supplied to exporters or their agents when such copies are needed to comply with official requirements as authorization for export, export control requirements, or U.S. Department of Agriculture requirements for proof of export in connection with subsidy payments. Such copies will be stamped certified, and not for any other use and may not be reproduced in any form.

When the Secretary of Commerce or delegate determines that the withholding of information provided on an individual SED is contrary to the "National Interest," the Secretary or delegate may make such information available taking safeguards and precautions as deemed appropriate.

A SED presented for export constitutes a representation by the exporter that all statements and information are in accordance with the export control regulations. The commodity described on the declaration is authorized under the particular license as identified on the declaration, all statements conform to the applicable licenses, and all conditions of the export control regulations have been met.

Sample of Instructions for Completing Shipper's Export Declaration

11. Administrative Provisions — Continued

It is unlawful to knowingly make false or misleading representation for exportation. This constitutes a violation of the Export Administration Act, 50. U.S.C. App. 2410. It is also a violation of export control laws and regulations to be connected in any way with an altered SED to effect export.

Commodities that have been, are being, or for which there is probable cause to believe they are intended to be exported in violation of the Export Administration Act are subject to seizure, detention, condemnation, or sale under 22 U.S.C. Section 401.

To knowingly make false or misleading statements relating to information on the SED is a criminal offense subject to penalties as provided for in 18 U.S.C. Section 1001.

Violations of the Foreign Trade Statistics Regulations are subject to civil penalties as authorized by 13 U.S.C. Section 305.

12. Regulations

Detailed information regarding the SED and its preparation is contained in the Foreign Trade Statistics Regulations (FTSR) (15 CFR, Part 30). Also, the FTSR should be consulted for special provisions applicable under particular circumstances. Copies may be purchased from the Bureau of the Census, Washington, DC 20233. Information concerning export control laws and regulations of the International Trade Administration is contained in the Export Administration Regulations, which may be purchased from the Superintendent of Documents, Government Printing Office, Washington, DC 20402.

Reference Schedules

Schedule B — Statistical Classification of Domestic and Foreign Commodities Exported from the United States. For sale by the Superintendent of Documents, U.S. Government Printing Office, Washington, DC 20402 and local U.S. Customs District Directors.

Schedule C — Classification of Country and Territory Designations for U.S. Foreign Trade. Free from the Bureau of the Census, Washington, DC 20233. Also included as part of Schedule B and USTSA.

Schedule D — Classification of Customs Districts and Ports. Free from the Bureau of the Census, Washington, DC 20233. Also included as part of Schedule B and USTSA.

Schedule K — Classification of Foreign Ports by Geographic Trade Area and Country. Free from the Bureau of the Census, Washington, DC 20233.

Foreign Trade Statistics Regulations. For sale by the Bureau of the Census, Washington, DC 20233.

Export Administration Regulations. For sale by the Superintendent of Documents, U.S. Government Printing Office, Washington, DC 20402 and U.S. Department of Commerce District Offices.

NOTE: This is an instructional pamphlet summarizing the preparation of the SED. It is in no way intended as a substitute for either the *Foreign Trade Statistics Regulations* or the *Export Administration Regulations*.

Sample of Instructions for Completing Shipper's Export Declaration

INFORMATION TO BE REPORTED ON SEDS

Data	FTSR Reference	SED Item Number		
		7525-V	7525-V Alternate (Intermodal)	7513
Commodity Description — A sufficient description of the commodity to permit verification of the Schedule B Commodity Number or the description shown on the validated export license.	30.7(l)	14	20	14
Schedule B Commodity Number — The commodity number as provided in Schedule B — Statistical Classification of Domestic and Foreign Commodities Exported from the United States. The "check digit" as shown in Schedule B shall be reported immediately after the commodity number. When form 7513 is used, report only the first six digits of the Schedule B commodity number.	30.7(l) 30.8(a)	17	24	15
Gross Shipping Weight — (For vessel and air shipments only) The gross shipping weight in kilograms, including the weight of containers but excluding carrier equipment (1 kilo = 2.2 lbs. Report whole units.)	30.7(o)	19	21	13
"D" (Domestic) or "F" (Foreign) (a) Domestic exports — merchandise grown, produced, or manufactured (including imported merchandise which has been enhanced in value) in the United States. (b) Foreign exports — merchandise that has entered the United States and is being reexported in the same condition as when imported.	30.7(p)	16	23	NA
Net Quantity — The amount in terms of the unit(s) specified in Schedule B with the unit indicated or the unit as specified on the validated export license. (Report whole units.)	30.7(n)	18	25	16
Value — Selling price or cost if not sold, including inland freight, insurance, and other charges to U.S. port of export, but excluding unconditional discounts and commissions (nearest whole dollar, omit cents).	30.7(q)	20	26	17
Export License Number or Symbol — Validated export license number and expiration date or general license symbol.	30.7(m)	21	27	14
Export Control Commodity Number (ECCN) — (When required) ECCN number of commodities listed on the Commodity Control List (commodities subject to U.S. Department of Commerce export controls) in the Export Administration Regulations.	30.7(m)	22	28	15
Bill of Lading or Air Waybill Number — The exporting carrier's bill of lading or air waybill number.	30.22(b)	3	5(a)	NA
Date of Exportation — (Not required for vessel and postal shipments) The date of departure or date of clearance, if date of departure is not known.	30.7(r)	2	32	NA
Designation of Agent — Signature of exporter authorizing the named agent to effect the export when such agent does not have formal power of attorney.	30.7(s) 30.4	23	29	NA
Signature — Signature of exporter or authorized agent-certifying the truth and accuracy of the information on the SED.	30.7(s) 30.4	24	35	18
Additional Information Required Only on Form 7513				
U.S. Port of Arrival — The U.S. port at which the merchandise arrived from a foreign country.	30.8(a)	NA	NA	9
Country from Which Shipped — The foreign country where the merchandise was loaded on the carrier that brought it to the United States.	30.8(b)	NA	NA	10
Date of Arrival — The date on which the merchandise arrived in the United States.	30.8(c)	NA	NA	11
Country of Origin — The country in which the merchandise was mined, grown, manufactured or substantially transformed. If the country of origin is not known, show the country of shipment designated as "Country of Shipment."	30.8(d)	NA	NA	12

Information Required on Shipper's Export Declaration

		SED Item Number		
Data	FTSR Reference	7525-V	7525-V Alternate (Intermodal)	7513
Exporter — The name and address of the principal party responsible for effecting export from the United States. The exporter as named on the validated export license. Report only the first five digits of the ZIP code.	30.7(d)	1(a)	2	5
Exporter Identification Number — The exporter's Internal Revenue Service Employer Identification Number (EIN) or Social Security Number (SSN) if no EIN has been assigned.	30.7(d)	1(b)	34	NA
Related Party Transaction — One between the U.S. exporter and the foreign consignee, that is, an export from a U.S. person or business enterprise to a foreign business enterprise or from a U.S. business enterprise to a foreign person or business enterprise, when the person owns (directly or indirectly) at any time during the fiscal year, 10 percent or more of the voting securities of the incorporated business enterprise, or an equivalent interest if an unincorporated business enterprise, including a branch.	30.7(v)	1(c)	35	NA
Agent of Exporter — The name and address of the duly authorized forwarding agent.	30.7(e)	5	7	4
Ultimate Consignee — The name and address of the party actually receiving the merchandise for the designated end-use or the party so designated on the validated export license.	30.7(f)	4(a)	3 31	8
Intermediate Consignee — The name and address of the party in a foreign country who effects delivery of the merchandise to the ultimate consignee or the party so named on the export license.	30.7(g)	4(b)	4	NA
Exporting Carrier — The name of the carrier transporting the merchandise out of the United States. For vessel shipments, give the vessel's flag also.	30.7(c)	10	14	1
U.S. Port of Export (a) Overland — the U.S. Customs port at which the surface carrier crosses the border. (b) Vessel and Air — the U.S. Customs port where the merchandise is loaded on the carrier which is taking the merchandise out of the United States. (c) Postal — the U.S. Post Office where the merchandise is mailed.	30.7(a) 30.20	11	15	2
Method of Transportation — The mode of transport by which the merchandise is exported. Specify by name, i.e., vessel, air, rail, truck, etc. Specify "own power" if applicable.	30.7(b)	9	30	NA
Loading Pier — (For vessel shipments only) The number or name of the pier at which the merchandise is laden aboard the exporting vessel.	30.7(c)	8	10	NA
Containerized — (For vessel shipments only) Cargo originally booked as containerized cargo and that placed in containers at the vessel operator's option.	30.7(u)	13	11(a)	NA
Point (State) of Origin or Foreign Trade Zone (FTZ) Number (a) The two-digit U.S. Postal Service abbreviation of the state in which the merchandise actually starts its journey to the port of export, or (b) The state of the commodity of the greatest value, or (c) The state of consolidation, or (d) The Foreign Trade Zone Number for exports leaving a FTZ.	30.7(t)	6	8	NA
Foreign Port of Unloading — (For vessel and air shipments only) The foreign port and country at which the merchandise will be unladen from the exporting carrier.	30.7(h)	12	16	7
Country of Ultimate Destination — The country in which the merchandise is to be consumed, further processed, or manufactured; the final country of destination as known to the exporter at the time of shipment; or the country of ultimate destination as shown on the validated export license.	30.7(i)	7	33	6
Marks, Numbers, and Kinds of Packages — Marks, numbers, or other identification shown on the packages and the numbers and kinds of packages (boxes, barrels, baskets, etc.).	30.7(j) 30.7(k)	16	18 19	12 14

Information Required on Shipper's Export Declaration

DELIVERY INSTRUCTIONS

2. EXPORTER (Principal or seller-licensee and address including ZIP Code)	5. DOCUMENT NUMBER	5a. B/L OR AWB NUMBER
	6. EXPORT REFERENCES	
ZIP CODE		
3. CONSIGNED TO	7. FORWARDING AGENT (Name and address - references)	
	8. POINT (STATE) OF ORIGIN OR FTZ NUMBER	
4. NOTIFY PARTY/INTERMEDIATE CONSIGNEE (Name and address)	9. DOMESTIC ROUTING/EXPORT INSTRUCTIONS	
12. PRE-CARRIAGE BY	13. PLACE OF RECEIPT BY PRE-CARRIER	
14. EXPORTING CARRIER	15. PORT OF LOADING/EXPORT	10. LOADING PIER/TERMINAL
16. FOREIGN PORT OF UNLOADING (Vessel and air only)	17. PLACE OF DELIVERY BY ON-CARRIER	11. TYPE OF MOVE

11.a CONTAINERIZED (Vessel only) ☐ Yes ☐ No

MARKS AND NUMBERS	NUMBER OF PACKAGES	DESCRIPTION OF COMMODITIES in Schedule B detail	GROSS WEIGHT (Kilos)	MEASUREMENT
(18)	(19)	(20)	(21)	(22)

DATE ISSUED	DOCUMENTS ATTACHED		
	☐ DOCK RECEIPT ARRIVAL NOTICE ☐ DELIVERY ORDER ☐ CHECK FOR $		

PICK UP FROM:

DELIVER TO: ☐ CARRIER @ PIER ABOVE
☐ OTHER:

CARTAGE ACCOUNT

Sample Delivery Instructions Form

DOCK RECEIPT

		5a. B/L OR AWB NUMBER
2. EXPORTER (Principal or seller-licensee and address including ZIP Code)	5. DOCUMENT NUMBER	
	6. EXPORT REFERENCES	
ZIP CODE		
3. CONSIGNED TO	7. FORWARDING AGENT (Name and address - references)	
	8. POINT (STATE) OR ORIGIN OR FTZ NUMBER	
4. NOTIFY PARTY/INTERMEDIATE CONSIGNEE (Name and address)	9. DOMESTIC ROUTING/EXPORT INSTRUCTIONS	

12. PRE-CARRIAGE BY	13. PLACE OF RECEIPT BY PRE-CARRIER	
14. EXPORTING CARRIER	15. PORT OF LOADING/EXPORT	10. LOADING PIER/TERMINAL
16. FOREIGN PORT OF UNLOADING (Vessel and air only)	17. PLACE OF DELIVERY BY ON-CARRIER	11. TYPE OF MOVE	11a. CONTAINERIZED (Vessel only) ☐ Yes ☐ No

MARKS AND NUMBERS	NUMBER OF PACKAGES	DESCRIPTION OF COMMODITIES in Schedule B detail	GROSS WEIGHT (Kilos)	MEASUREMENT
(18)	(19)	(20)	(21)	(22)

DELIVERED BY:

RECEIVED THE ABOVE DESCRIBED GOODS OR PACKAGES SUBJECT TO ALL THE TERMS OF THE UNDERSIGNED'S REGULAR FORM OF DOCK RECEIPT AND BILL OF LADING WHICH SHALL CONSTITUTE THE CONTRACT UNDER WHICH THE GOODS ARE RECEIVED, COPIES OF WHICH ARE AVAILABLE FROM THE CARRIER ON REQUEST AND MAY BE INSPECTED AT ANY OF ITS OFFICES.

LIGHTER ....
TRUCK
ARRIVED— DATE .... TIME ....

UNLOADED—DATE .... TIME ....

FOR THE MASTER

CHECKED BY............

BY ....
RECEIVING CLERK

PLACED ON DOCK IN SHIP LOCATION............

DATE ....

502 (1-1-88)
WHSE. NO. 0848

ONLY CLEAN DOCK RECEIPT ACCEPTED.

Sample Dock Receipt Form

VOTAINER CONSOLIDATION SERVICES USA Inc.
Member of the VAN OMMEREN CETECO Group

ORIGINAL

BILL OF LADI!
not negotiable unless consigned "to orc

Shipper/Exporter (Complete Name and Address)

71074 HUBBELL INCORPORATED
STATE STREET & BOSTWICK AVENUE
BRIDGEPORT   CT 06605
U.S.A.

B/L Number
NYCKEE155/12

Export References
INV#35587 D/B
551-1018766-7

Consignee (Complete Name and Address)

TAIAN ELECTRIC
7TH FLOOR 156-2, SUNG CHIANG ROAD,
TONG YUON BUILDING
TAIPEI, TAIWAN
REPUBLIC OF CHINA

Forwarding Agent - References (Complete Name and Address)
2869   A N DERINGER FMC 1853 BHC#22
P.O. BOX 128
BRIDGEPORT   CT 06610

Point and Country of origin

Notify Party (Complete Name and Address)

TAIAN ELECTRIC
7TH FLOOR 156-2, SUNG CHIANO ROAD,
TONG YUON BUILDING
TAIPEI, TAIWAN
REPUBLIC OF CHINA

For Cargo Arrival & Information Apply To
GENERAL MERCHANDISE CONSOLIDATORS
7FL MANHATTAN BLDG 132 CHUNG SHIAO
RD SEC 3
TAIPEI
TAIWAN ROC

Pier

Vessel/Voy #
S/L FREEDOM   112

Place of Receipt

Port of Loading
NEW YORK

Port of Discharge
KEELUNG

For Trans Shipment To

On Carriage To/Onward Inland Routing (Place of Delivery)

ON BOARD 12/17/90
VOTAINER CONSOLIDATION SERVICES (NY) INC.

PARTICULARS FURNISHED BY SHIPPER

Marks and Numbers	No. and Kind of Packages	Description of Goods	gross weight/kilos	measurement/ct
TAIAN ELECTRIC 7TH FLOOR 156-2 SUNG CHIANG ROAD TONG YUON BUILDIN G TAIPEI, TAIWAN REPUBLIC OF CHINA #1	1 PALLET	CONTAINING: 850 PIECES ELECTRIC WIRING DEVICES WITH SURGE PROJECTION	159.7	0.844
		FREIGHT COLLECT THESE COMMODITIES LICENSED BY THE U.S. FOR ULTIMATE DESTINATION TAIWAN DIVERSION CONTRARY TO U.S. LAW PROHIBITED.		

Freight Charges Payable At:

Declared Value   R..id Clause 6 (4) b & c HereoF concerning
Extra Freight and C..riers Limitation of Liability

SEAU4843080
Loaded into container number

RECEIVED FOR SHIPMENT in apparent good order and condition except as otherwise noted the total nu
of containers or other packages or units enumerated below (*) for transportation from the place of accep
to the place of delivery subject to the terms hereof including the terms on the reverse side hereof and the
of the C.T.O.'s applicable tariff. One of the original Bills of Lading must be surrendered duly endors
exchange for the Goods or Delivery Order.
IN WITNESS whereof : Bills of Lading stated below have been signed

Total Number of
Packages or Units   1
(in words)   (** ONE **)

Freight & Charges	Quantity Based on	Rate	Per	Prepaid	Collect
					TOTAL

By VOTAINER CONSOLIDATION SERVICES (NEW YORK) INC.
As Agent For The Carrier

Dated at Port of Loading Shown Above

Sample of an Original Ocean Bill of Lading

Herman J. Maggiori

Sample of a Straight Air Waybill (1)

220 | 4733 1885 *Straight B/L*

220-4733 1885

Shipper's Name and Address	Shipper's Account Number		
REMINGTON ARMS COMPANY 1007 MARKET STREET WILMINGTON, DELAWARE 19898	TD#060	Not negot...le **Air Waybill***	**⊘ Lufthansa**

Issued by
Deutsche Lufthansa AG,
D-5000 K... n 21, Von-Gablenz-Straße 2—6

Member of International
Air Transport Association

Copies I... and 3 of this Air Waybill are originals and have the same validity

VIA JAMAICA

Consignee's Name and Address	Consignee's Account Number	It is agreed that the goods described herein are accepted for carriage in apparent good order and condition (except as noted) and SUBJECT TO THE CONDITIONS OF CONTRACT ON THE REVERSE HEREOF. THE SHIPPER'S ATTENTION IS DRAWN TO THE NOTICE CONCERNING CARRIER'S LIMITATION OF LIABILITY.
HELMUT HOFFMAN GMBH POSTFACH 38 8744 MELLRICHSTADT W.GERMANY		

Issuing Carrier's Agent Name and City	Accounting Information
A.N. DERINGER, INC. 727 HONEYSPOT ROAD STRATFORD, CONN. 06497	

Agent's IATA Code	Account No.
01-1-1431/050	

Airport of Departure (Addr. of First Carrier) and Requested Routing

JFK NEW YORK

To	By First Carrier	Routing and Destination	To	By	To	By	Currency	CHGS Code	WT/VAL PPD COLL	Other PPD COLL	Declared Value for Carriage	Declared Value for Customs
							$US	X		NVD		961.00

Airport of Destination	Flight/Date	Flight/Date	Amount of Insurance
FRANKFURT	FIT 4223-3-5-91		INSURANCE — If Carrier offers Insurance, and such Insurance is requested in accordance with the conditions thereof, indicate amount to be insured in figures in box marked 'Amount of Insurance'

Handling Information

ATTACHED; COMMERCIAL INVOICES, EXPORT DECLARATION & COPY OF STATE DEPT.
LICENSE #463820-EXPIRES 71893
NOTIFY; HANS WAGNER CONTAINER
DIENSTE GMBH & CO., BREITEWEG 32 2800 BREMEN 1, W.GERMANY

No. of Pieces RCP	Gross Weight	kg lb	Rate Class	Commodity	Chargeable Weight	Rate / Charge	Total	Nature and Quantity of Goods (incl. Dimensions or Volume)
1	10	l			10#	MIN.	70.00	HUNTING & SPORTING EQUIPMENT
								STATE DEPT. EXPORT LICENSE #463820-EXPIRES 71893
								SHIPMENT DOES NOT FALL UNDER GERMANY WEAPON LIST - NOT MORE THAN 5 RDS
								THIUS IS FOR A SHOW IN GERMANY

Prepaid	Weight Charge	Collect	Other Charges
	70.00		

Valuation Charge

Tax

Total Other Charges Due Agent

Shipper certifies that the particulars on the face hereof are correct and that insofar as any part of the consignment contains dangerous goods, such part is properly described by name and is in proper condition for carriage by air according to the applicable Dangerous Goods Regulations.

Total Other Charges Due Carrier

Lee Cappello

Signature of Shipper or his Agent

Total Prepaid	Total Collect

A.N. DERINGER, INC
BRIDGEPORT, CONN.

Currency Conversion Rates	CC Charges in Dest. Currency

MARCH 4, 1991

Lee Cappello

For Carrier's Use only at Destination	Charges at Destination	Total Collect Charges

Executed on (date) at (place)

Signature of Issuing Carrier or its Agent

220-4733 1885

Luftfrachtbrief (nicht beaobbar) — eine verbindliche Übersetzung dieses Frachtbriefformulars (einschlließlich

Sample of a Straight Air Waybill (2)

Herman J. Maggiori

COMMERCIAL INVOICE	FACTURA COMERCIAL

SOLD TO: Negev Ceramic Materials Ltd.
............26 Yair Street............
VENDIDO A P.O. Box 21
      Beer-Sheba, Israel

DATE: 12/7/90

FECHA

ustomer Order No. __FG/904145__   Our Order No. __NBXR19411__   Invoice No. _____
rden De Compra NU   Nuestra Orden NU _____   Factura NU _____

CARTON NOS. NUMEROS DE LAS CAJAS	PESO EN KILOGRAMS / WEIGHT IN KILOGRAMS			QUANTITY CANTIDAD	DESCRIPTION / COUNTRY OF ORIGIN: UNITED STATES OF AMERICA / DESCRIPCION / PAIS DE ORIGEN: ESTADOS UNIDOS DE AMERICA	UNIT PRICE PRECIO POR UNIDAD	TOTA NET TOTA NET(
	NET NETO	LEGAL LEGAL	GROSS BRUTO				
					Industrial Shotshell		
1/10			28.76	2,500	0081B SP 8 MAG 3OZ LD BRSHD	824.70	2,061.
10			287.6		FIS New York		2,061.

Total weight - 634 lbs.
Total cu.ft. - 5.55
Powder - 36.25 lbs.

Payment Terms: S/D-D/P thru Bank Hapoalim Ltd.
                          Branch 361
                          Ha-Atzmaut Street
                          Beer=Sheba, Israel

These commodities licensed by the United
Stat=s for ultimate destination Israel.
Diversion contrary to United States
law prohibited.

Linda McFeury

E.I. Dupont de Nemours & Co., Inc.
Remington Arms Division

Sample of a Manufacturer's Commercial Invoice (1)

03/01/91   14:01   002

Remington.

REMINGTON ARMS CO., INC.
1007 Market Street
Wilmington, Delaware 19898
Tel: 302-773-5324
TELEX: 964201REMARMSWIL
FAX: 302-774-4893

COMMERCIAL INVOICE	FACTURA COMERCIAL

SOLD TO:	Helmut Hofmann GMBH	DATE:	3/1/91
VENDIDO A	Postfach 38	FECHA	
	8744 Mellrichstadt		
	W. Germany		

Customer Order No. _____ 1/18/91 _____   Our Order No. _____ PMMR15120A01 _____   Invoice No. _____

cen De Compra NU _____   Nuestra Orden NU _____   Factura NU _____

CARTON NOS. LIMEROS DE LAS CAJAS	PESO EN KILOGRAMS WEIGHT IN KILOGRAMS			QUANTITY CANTIDAD	DESCRIPTION COUNTRY OF ORIGIN: UNITED STATES OF AMERICA DESCRIPCION PAIS DE ORIGEN: ESTADOS UNIDOS DE AMERICA		UNIT PRICE PRECIO POR UNIDAD	TOTAL NET TOTAL NETO
	NET NETO	LEGAL LEGAL	GROSS BRUTO					
					Center Fire Rifle			
1			3.54	1	6000	40XC KS 7.62MM NATO	961.00	961.00
						CIF Frankfurt		961.00
					Total weight - 10 lbs.			
					Total cu.ft. - 1.0			
					Serial NO. 057608C			
					Export License #463820 expires 7/18/93			

Payment Terms: Net60 Days

These commodities licensed by the United
States for ultimate destination W. Germany.
Diversion contrary to United States
law prohibited.

E.I. Dupont de Nemours & Co., Inc.
Remington Arms Divison

Sample of a Manufacturer's Commercial Invoice (2)

Herman J. Maggiori

U.S. CERTIFICATE OF ORIGIN
FOR EXPORTS TO ISRAEL

1. Goods consigned from exporter's business (name, address): REMINGTON ARMS COMPANY, INC. BRANDYWINE BUILDING 1007 MARKET STREET WILMINGTON, DELAWARE 19898	Reference No. U.S.– ISRAEL FREE TRADE AREA CERTIFICATE OF ORIGIN (Combined declaration and certificate)
2. Goods consigned to (consignee's name, address) NEGEV CERAMIC MATERIALS LTD. 26 YAIR STREET P.O. BOX 21 BEER-SHEBA, ISRAEL	(See notes over leaf)
3. Means of transport and route (as far as known) EL AL AIRLINES 114-2729 4540	4. For official use

5. Item number	6. Marks and numbers of packages	7. Number and kind of packages, description of goods	8. Origin criterion (see notes over leaf)	9. Gross Weight or other quantity	10. Number and date of invoices
	NEGEV CERAMIC MATERIALS LTD. 26 YAIR STREET P.O. BOX 21 BEER-SHEBA, ISRAEL				
1.	NEXR19411	INDUSTRIAL SHOTSHELL (10) CTNS.	P	287.6K 634#	NEXR19411 12/7/90

| 11. CERTIFICATION

The NEW YORK CHAMBER OF COMMERCE
a recognized chamber of commerce, board of trade, or _____
_____ under the laws of the State of _____
NEW YORK _____ has examined the manufacturer's
invoice or shipper's affidavit concerning the origin of the
merchandise and, according to the best of its knowledge and
belief, finds that the products named originated in the United
States of America.

_____
Certifying Official | 12. DECLARATION BY THE EXPORTER

The undersigned hereby declares that the above details and
statement are correct; that all the goods were produced in the
United States of America and that they comply with the origin
requirements specified for those goods in the U.S.—Israel Free
Trade Area Agreement for goods exported to Israel.

Janet Murphy
Signature of Exporter

Sworn to before me this 13th
day of December 19 90

William A. Marshall
Signature of Notary Public

WILLIAM A. MARSHALL
NOTARY PUBLIC
MY COMMISSION EXPIRES MARCH 31, 1994 |

Form 10-380P (R2(7) 190 Baldwin Ave., Jersey City, NJ 07306 • (800) 631-3098 • (201) 795-5400

Sample of a Special Destination U.S. Certificate of Origin

CERTIFICATE OF ORIGIN

2. EXPORTER *(Principal or seller-acct'd and address including ZIP Code)* REMINGTON ARMS COMPANY, INC. BRANDYWINE BUILDING 1007 MARKET STREET WILMINGTON, DELAWARE ZIP CODE 19898	5. DOCUMENT NUMBER 5A. B/L OR AWB NUMBER 120870956 6. EXPORT REFERENCES IATA # 01-1-1431/050 845101 TD#045 KRCR10455
3. CONSIGNED TO ETS RIVOLIER PERE & FILS 21-23 RUE CESAR BERTHOLON 42100 ST. ETIENNE, FRANCE	7. FORWARDING AGENT *(Name and references)* A.N. DERINGER, INC. 727 HONEYSPOT ROAD, SUITE 202 STRATFORD, CONNECTICUT 06497
	8. POINT (STATE) OF ORIGIN OR FTZ NUMBER WE USE COTY MESSENGER SERVICE
4. NOTIFY PARTY/INTERMEDIATE CONSIGNEE *(Name and address)* TRANSPORTE RIVOIRE 4 RUE DE LA TAULAUDIERE 42004 ST. ETIENNE CEDEX, FRANCE	9. DOMESTIC ROUTING/EXPORT INSTRUCTIONS THESE COMMODITIES LICENSED BY THE U.S FOR ULTIMATE DESTINATION, FRANCE. DIVERSION CONTRARY TO U.S. LAW PROHIBITED

12. PRE-CARRIAGE BY	13. PLACE OF RECEIPT BY PRE-CARRIER J.F.K. NEW YORK	
14. EXPORTING CARRIER AIR FRANCE AIRBORNE	15. PORT OF LOADING/EXPORT J.F.K. NEW YORK	10. LOADING PIER/TERMINAL
16. FOREIGN PORT OF UNLOADING *(Vessel and air only)* LYONS	17. PLACE OF DELIVERY BY ON-CARRIER	11. TYPE OF MOVE 11.a CONTAINERIZED *(Vessel only)* ☐ YES ☐ NO

MARKS AND NUMBERS (18)	NUMBER OF PACKAGES (19)	DESCRIPTION OF COMMODITIES *in Schedule B detail* (20)	GROSS WEIGHT *(Kilos)* (21)	MEASUREMENT (22)
ETS RIVOLIER PERE & FILS 21-23 RUE CESAR BERTHOLON 42100 ST. ETIENNE, FRANCE		"FREIGHT PREPAID"		
	1	CARTON CONTAINING: CLOTHING	11.75#	

The undersigned..A.N..DERINGER, INC.,..(Owner or Agent), does hereby declare for the above named shipper, the goods as described above were shipped on the above date and consigned as indicated and are products of the United States of America Dated at...STRATFORD, CONN.................. on the....20TH day of.....FEBRUARY.................................19 91

Sworn to before me this ...24th.. day of...February................. 19...7..

.....Fauher Joirah........................ .......O.N. Deringe Inc.......
Leopoldine T. Belovich   SIGNATURE OF OWNER OR AGENT
My commission expires............................. INDUSTRY

The..... 1 BATTERY ...., N.Y. 10004.................

under the laws of the State of ...., a recognized Chamber of Commerce concerning the origin of the merchandise, and, according to the best of its knowledge and belief, finds that the products named originated in the United States of America.

Secretary ....
AURORA DIAZ SIMONE

Form X-501-A Whse. No. 0863
Apperson Business Forms, Inc.
(800) 438-0162 Rev. 1-1-88

Sample of a U.S. Certificate of Origin

Herman J. Maggiori

DA 59

Supplier (name, address, country)	DECLARATION OF ORIGIN— for the export of goods to the REPUBLIC OF SOUTH AFRICA
Consignee (name, address, country)	**NOTE TO IMPORTERS** This declaration, properly completed by the supplier, must be furnished in support of the relative bill of entry where goods qualify for and are entered at the rate of duty lower than the general rate
Particulars of transport	Customs date stamp

1 Item No	2 Marks and numbers	3 No. and desc. of packages	4 Description of goods	5 Country of origin	6 Gross Mass	7 Invoice No./ Ref.

I, (name and capacity)
duly authorised by the supplier of the goods enumerated above hereby declare that—

1. the goods enumerated opposite item(s)   in column 1 above have been wholly produced or manufactured in the country stated in column 5 in respect of such goods from raw materials produced in that country;

2. the goods enumerated opposite item(s)   in column 1 above have been wholly or partly manufactured from imported materials in the country specified in column 5 in respect of such goods; and

   2. 1 the final process of manufacture has taken place in the said country;

   2. 2 the cost to the manufacturer of the materials wholly produced or manufactured in the said country plus the cost of labour directly employed in the manufacture of such goods is not less than   per cent of the total production cost of such goods;

   2. 3 in calculating the production cost of such goods only the cost to the manufacturer of all materials plus manufacturing wages and salaries, direct manufacturing expenses, overhead factory expenses, cost of inside containers and other expenses incidental to manufacturing, used or expended in the manufacture of such goods have been included and profits and administrative, distribution and selling overhead expenses have been excluded.

Place   Date   Signature of Deponent

Form No 10-639   Printed and Sold by Unz & Co., Division of Scott Printing Corp., 190 Baldwin Ave. Jersey City N J 07306 — N J (201) 795-5400 / N Y (212) 344-2270

Sample Declaration of Origin for Exports to South Africa

252

WM. A. MARSHALL INC.
CUSTOM HOUSE BROKER
FOREIGN FREIGHT FWD.
P. O. Box 128
BRIDGEPORT, CONNECTICUT 06601
TELEPHONE (203) 335-0187 • (203) 368-1666
TELEFAX (203) 367-0459

IMPORTS – EXPORTS
I A T A – AGENT
NEW HAVEN, CONN. — HARTFORD, CONN. — NEW LONDON, CONN.

C H B 3676

F M C 1068

TO: _(BANK)_____

DATE:

SUBJECT: _(SHIPPER)_____

OUR REF. NUMBER: _____

GENTLEMEN:
ON BEHALF OF THE ABOVE MENTIONED SHIPPER WE ARE ENCLOSING THE FOLLOWING DOCUMENTS:-

—— COMMERCIAL INVOICE
—— COPY OCEAN BILL OF LADING
—— COPY AIR WAYBILL
—— ORIGINAL OCEAN BILL OF LADING
—— ORIGINAL AIR WAYBILL
—— INSURANCE CERTIFICATE (ORIGINAL)
—— INSURANCE CERTIFICATE (COPY)
—— COPY LETTER TO INSURANCE COMPANY
—— ORIGINAL CERTIFICATE OF ORIGIN
—— OTHER

—— PACKING LIST
—— CONSULAR INVOICE (ORIGINAL)
—— CONSULAR INVOICE (COPY)
—— INSURANCE DECLARATION (ORIGINAL)
—— ORIGINAL LEGALIZED INVOICE
—— COPY LEGALIZED INVOICE
—— SPECIAL CUSTOMS INVOICE
—— STEAMSHIP CERTIFICATE (ORIGINAL)
—— COPY CERTIFICATE OF ORIGIN
—— OTHER

IN THE EVENT THE ORIGINAL SHIPPING DOCUMENTS ARE NOT ATTACHED, PLEASE BE ADVISED THAT WE HAVE EFFECTED DISTRIBUTION OF SAME IN ACCORDANCE WITH THE SHIPPER'S INSTRUCTIONS AS FOLLOWS:-

—— FORWARDED TO BANK
—— RETURNED TO SHIPPER

—— FORWARDED TO BROKER
—— (OTHER)_____

—— (SPECIAL REMARKS/INSTRUCTIONS)

TRUSTING SHIPMENT HAS BEEN HANDLED TO YOUR ENTIRE SATISFACTION, WE ARE
VERY TRULY YOURS,

WILLIAM A. MARSHALL

Sample of Forwarder's Letter of Document Transmittal to a Bank

Herman J. Maggiori

DEPARTMENT OF THE TREASURY
UNITED STATES CUSTOMS SERVICE

HARBOR MAINTENANCE FEE
QUARTERLY SUMMARY REPORT

19 CFR 24.24

1. IDENTIFYING NUMBER		EIN or IRS No.		Customs No		SSN

2. NAME OF COMPANY OR INDIVIDUAL

3. COMPLETE MAILING ADDRESS

SEND TO: U.S. CUSTOMS SERVICE
P.O. BOX 70915
CHICAGO IL 60673-0915

Check here if address has changed since last filing

REPORTING PERIOD	QUARTER ► (one only)	1 Jan. 1 - Mar. 31	2 Apr. 1 - Jun. 30	3 Jul. 1 - Sep. 30	4 Oct. 1 - Dec. 31
YEAR ► 19____					

TYPE OF SHIPMENT	5 VALUE OF SHIPMENTS	6 VALUE OF EXEMPTIONS (From Corresponding Columns A to D of Line 14)	7 NET VALUE (Column 5 less column 6)
EXPORTS			
DOMESTIC MOVEMENTS			
FTZ ADMISSIONS			
PASSENGERS			
TOTAL NET VALUE ON WHICH HMF IS TO BE CALCULATED (Sum of Column 7 Lines A to D)			
HMF DUE (Multiply the amount on line E by .0004)			

ITEMIZATION OF EXEMPTIONS	A. EXPORTS	B. DOMESTICS	C. FTZ's	D. PASSENGERS	E. TOTAL
EXEMPT PORT					
INLAND WATERWAY FUEL TAX					
INTRAPORT					
U.S. MAINLAND: STATE/POSSESS					
OTHER					
TOTALS (Also enter amounts in 14A thru 14D in 6A thru 6D above)					

CERTIFICATION

I hereby certify under penalties provided by law that the above information regarding the Harbor Maintenance Fee is complete and accurate to the best of my knowledge.

Please
Sign
Here ►

_____   _____
Signature   Date

TYPE OR PRINT NAME OF PERSON WHO PREPARED THIS REPORT (If same as block 2, write "Same")

17. TELEPHONE NO. INCLUDING AREA CODE
(   )

Customs Form 349 (120789)

Sample of Quarterly Report for Harbor Maintenance Fee

FORM INSTRUCTIONS

(See also: Customs Publication No. 548, "Preparation of Harbor Maintenance Fee Forms"; and 19 CFR 24.24.)

The following are specific instructions for most of the items on the form. Items that have no instructions are self-explanatory. Exports, domestic movements, foreign trade zone (FTZ) admissions, passengers, or any combination of these, may be declared on one form provided the name of the company and identifying number are the same for all movements declared. (See Customs Publication No. 548 for additional instructions)

Item 1. IDENTIFYING NUMBER—Individual summary reports may contain only one identifying number. This does not preclude filing more than one summary report for one identifying number. The identifying number must correspond to Item 2. Name of Company or individual. Check the appropriate box to indicate the kind of identifying number being used. Enter the following information:

— Exports—Internal Revenue Service (IRS) Number, or Employer Identification Number (EIN) listed on the Shipper's Export Declaration (Census Bureau Form 7525-V-Box 1b., or equivalent). Exporters without EIN's may enter their Social Security Number.

— Domestic Movements—Shipper's Internal Revenue Service (IRS) Number listed on the Vessel Operator Report (U.S. Army Corps of Engineers Form 3925).

— FTZ Admissions—Applicant For Admission to a Foreign Trade Zone's Internal Revenue Service (IRS) Employer Identification Number (EIN).

— Passengers—Vessel Operator's Internal Revenue Service (IRS) Employer Identification Number (EIN).

Item 2. NAME OF COMPANY OR INDIVIDUAL—Enter the following information:

— Exports—Exporter listed on the Shipper's Export Declaration (Census Bureau Form 7525-V-Box 1a., or equivalent: 7525-M, 7525-V-ALT. INT.. 7513).

— Domestic Movements—Shipper listed on the Vessel Operator Report (U.S. Army Corps of Engineers Form 3925).

— FTZ Admissions—Applicant or Firm Name listed on the Applicant for Foreign Trade Zone Admission and/or Status Designation (Customs Form 214-Box 24).

— Passengers—Operator of the Passenger Carrying Vessel.

Item 3. ADDRESS—Street Address or P.O. box number, city, and state, and zip code where company or individual may be contacted.

Item 4. REPORTING PERIOD—Check only one box. A separate summary report is required for each quarter reported.

Item 5. VALUE OF SHIPMENTS—Figures inserted in Items 5A. through 5D. shall represent quarterly totals.

(5A.) Exports—Total value listed on Shipper's Export Declaration (7525-V-Block 20, or equivalent).

(5B.) Domestic Movements—Total value at the time of loading (Free Alongside Ship (FAS) value, which includes selling price, inland freight, insurance, and all other charges to transport the cargo to the dock alongside the vessel).

(5C.) FTZ Admissions—Total entered value listed on the Applicant for Foreign Trade Zone Admission and/or Status Designation (Customs Form 214-Total of Block 21).

(5D.) Passengers—Actual charge for transportation paid by the passengers, or the prevailing charge for comparable service if no actual charge is paid. The HMF is paid only once per journey for each passenger. Crew members are not subject to the HMF.

Item 6. VALUE OF EXEMPTIONS

Exemptions are to be itemized in Items 9. through 13. Totals shall be inserted in Items 6A. through 6D.

Item 7. NET VALUE

Net value shall be calculated by subtracting Items 6A. through 6D. from Items 5A. through 5D. Enter the total net value (sum of lines A–D, column 7) on line E, column 7.

Item 8. HMF DUE

The HMF is to be calculated by multiplying Item 7E, times 0.0004 (or .04%). Remit a check or money order payable to U.S. Customs Service.

U.S. GPO: 1990-743-005/00644

ITEMIZATION OF EXEMPTIONS

Only one exemption per movement may be claimed. (See definition of "movement" in Item 5 of the General Instructions in Customs Publication No. 548). Figures inserted in Items 9. through 14. shall represent quarterly totals.

9. Exempt Port—Total value of shipments, for each type of movement (e.g. exports, domestics, etc.), loaded and/or unloaded at an exempt port. See Customs Publication No. 548 "Preparation of Harbor Maintenance Fee Forms" for list of non-exempt ports.

10. Inland Waterway Fuel Tax—Total value of shipments transported by vessels using fuel subject to the Inland Waterway Fuel Tax. Applies only to domestic movements.

11. Intraport—Total value of cargo moved within a single Customs port. Applies only to domestic movements.

12. U.S. Mainland-State/Possession/Territory—Total value of the following:

· Cargo, other than Alaskan crude oil, loaded on a vessel in Hawaii, Alaska, or Puerto Rico, and unloaded in the state or territory in which loaded.

· Cargo, other than Alaskan crude oil, transported from the U.S. Mainland to Alaska, Hawaii, Puerto Rico, or the U.S. Possessions for ultimate use or consumption; and/or

· Cargo, other than Alaskan crude oil, transported from Alaska, Hawaii, or any U.S. Possession to the U.S. Mainland, Alaska, Hawaii, or such possession for ultimate use or consumption in the mainland, Alaska, Hawaii, or such possession.

— U.S. mainland includes the 48 contiguous states, and the District of Columbia.

— The U.S. Possessions and Territories include the following:

American Samoa
Baker Island
Guam
Howland Island
Jarvis Island
Johnston Atoll
Kingman Reef
Midway
Northern Mariana Islands including:

Agrihan
Aguijan
Guguan
Pagan
Rota
Saipan
Tinian

Palmyra Island
Puerto Rico
U.S. Virgin Islands
Wake Island

13. Other—The total value of cargo, for each type of movement, subject to the following exemptions:

· Cargo entering the U.S. in-bond for transportation and direct exportation to a foreign country. (Does not include cargo for which a formal entry or warehouse entry is filed, or cargo which is admitted into a foreign trade zone.)

· Fish and other aquatic animal life caught by a U.S. vessel, and not previously landed on shore, regardless of the extent to which it has been processed.

· Donated export cargo which Customs certifies as intended for use as humanitarian or developmental assistance.

· Passengers transported on ferries. Ferries are defined as vessels engaged primarily in the transport of passengers and their vehicles between ports in the U.S., or between ports in the U.S. and ports in Canada or Mexico. The vessel must arrive in the U.S. on a regular schedule during its operating season.

Item 15. CERTIFICATION

Insert signature of Importer, Exporter, Shipper, Applicant for FTZ Admission, or Operator of Passenger Carrying Vessel.

Customs Form 349 (120789) (Back)

Instructions for Preparing Harbor Maintenance Fee Form

Herman J. Maggiori

The following pages, are reproduced with permission of the Loss Control Service Group of the CIGNA Property and Casualty Companies of Philadelphia, Pennsylvania. They describe and illustrate the many types of exterior packing currently common for export shipping by ocean and air freight. Also described and illustrated are the various types of containers in use, and how to pack your merchandise for proper storing and shipping via ocean or air.

EXTERIOR CONTAINERS

Fiberboard Boxes (Cartons)

The most common economical container continues to be the fiberboard box. This is understandable as shippers seek efficient, but inexpensive and lighter weight containers.

It comes closest to fitting the description of the ideal shipping container, which is light in weight, of low cost, but able to withstand normal transportation hazards and protect the contents against loss or damage. The fiberboard box frequently measures up to most of these requirements in domestic transportation, but fails frequently in overseas movements when proper selection procedures are not followed. It must be recognized that all commodities cannot be suitably packed in fiberboard boxes. Moreover, all fiberboard boxes are not suitable overseas containers. This is particularly true because increases in moisture content of corrugated fiberboard adversely affect its stiffness and compressive strength.

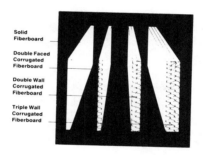

Solid Fiberboard

Double Faced Corrugated Fiberboard

Double Wall Corrugated Fiberboard

Triple Wall Corrugated Fiberboard

NOTE: Compressive strength may be reduced to approximately one-half normal strength by high humidity (90 percent r.h. +). Impregnation of coating of the fiberboard will delay but not completely prevent this loss.

First, the shipper must determine whether or not a fiberboard container is a suitable one for the particular commodity to be shipped, bearing in mind the item's vulnerability as well as the handling and transportation hazards to be encountered. If the answer is "Yes," he must then proceed to select the fiberboard container subject to the following

1. The underlying factors in the selection of the fiberboard box are resistance to compression, resistance to puncture, strength on the score lines, and probably the most important—resistance to moisture absorption. Impregnated and multi-wall boxes are the most practical. Never use corrugated fiberboard boxes with a bursting test strength of less than 275 lbs. per square inch (for exporting).

2. Flaps should be stapled or glued with a water resistant adhesive applied to the

entire area of contact between the flaps. For further protection, all seams can be sealed with a water resistant tape.

3. Keep weight of contents within load limits specified in the box maker's certificate which appears on the box.

4. Reinforce with two tension straps applied at right angles, and criss-crossing at top and bottoms, or with two girth straps of filament tape.

5. When the nature of the contents permits, the load should support the walls of the container. Otherwise, the container selected should have sufficient resistance to compression to prevent collapse when placed in the bottom tier of a pile of similar boxes. NEVER OVERLOAD.

6. Full height partitions should be utilized to separate fragile items within the same fiberboard box and/or to increase the stacking strength of the box.

7. Do not overlook economies and additional security offered by unitizing or palletizing, or by overpacking several fiberboard boxes in consolidation containers.

8. Remember, highly pilferable merchandise is rarely sate in fiberboard boxes.

Nailed Wood Boxes

The nailed wood box is one of the most satisfactory containers for overseas shipment of moderate weight commodities.

Among its particular advantages are: its ability to support superimposed loads, its ability to contain difficult loads without undue distortion or breaking open, the protection it affords contents from damage due to puncture, breakage or crushing and, finally, the fact that it permits interior blocking to hold the contents in place, thus allowing the container to be turned on its side or upside down. The following recommendations should be considered in selecting the nailed wood box:

1. Boxes should be made up of seasoned lumber with moisture content between 12 percent and 19 percent. Knots should not be over one-third the width of the board and specifically should not interfere with nailing. Severe cross graining should also be avoided.

2. Boxes with two or four cleats on each end are particularly recommended for overseas shipment.

3. Many a well-designed box fails because the load is not properly fitted or secured in the container. If necessary, use proper blocking and bracing to adequately secure the board. A properly fitted or secured load should not move when the container is roughly handled.

Boxes with two or four cleats on each end are particularly recommended for overseas shipment.

If the load must be kept upright, equip the box with lift handles, skids, top peaks or gables, or some similar device to assure the box being stowed and handled in an upright position. AVOID OVERLOADING.

4. Reinforce the boxes with adequate tension metal straps placed one-sixth of the distance from the ends, unless containers are in excess of 48 inches in length or over 250 pounds. Then, three or more straps should be used, with one for each additional 24 inches. Staples should be used to hold strapping in place when boards are five-eights of an inch in thickness or greater.

5. DO NOT USE SECONDHAND BOXES. They are deficient in strength and do not permit detection of pilferage.

6. Boxes should be equipped with corrugated fasteners or similar devices where contents are substantially valued and susceptible to pilferage.

7. Boxes should be lined with a waterproof barrier material, sealed at the edges with a waterproof tape or adhesive, to protect both the contents and the interior packing material.

There are two general types of crates—the open or skeleton crate and the fully sheathed crate. Both types are dependent upon properly constructed frame works. While the drawings in this section illustrate the comparative strength of frame members of open crates under vertical compression, the same principles apply to sheathed crates, as they also require diagonal bracing to make them rigid. Keep in mind that sheathing is provided to protect the contents against exposure to the elements.

The open crate can be used where contents are virtually indestructible and packing is required only to facilitate handling and stowage. It also serves well as an overpack to consolidate fiberboard boxes or to provide unit pack stiffness to resist crushing. Three-way corner construction should be reinforced with diagonals.

3-way corner... the strongest, most rigid corner construction for a crate

Consider these points in sheathed crate construction.

1. Provide a SUBSTANTIAL framework, i.e., corner posts or vertical end struts, edge or frame members, intermediate struts and diagonal braces.

2. Large crates are usually stowed in lower holds, hence must bear great superimposed weights. Insure top strength by frequent top joists under sheathing

(never more than 30" apart). DON'T depend on end grain nailing ALONE to hold these joists. Provide joist support positioned directly under the joists' ends.

3. Reinforce floor at load-bearing points when between skids or sill members.

4. Design for vertical sheathing: sides and ends.

5. On skid type crates terminate end sheathing at flooring to permit entry of forklifts. Terminate side sheathing 1/2" short of skid bottoms to prevent tearing away of sheathing when crate is dragged sideways. The use of rubbing strips facilitates handling by forklift trucks.

6. On sill-type crates provide lengthwise rubbing strips at base to facilitate handling and prevent tearing adrift of sheathing when the crate is dragged.

7. Where skids are used, be sure they are of sufficient dimensions and an adequate number provided. Skid ends should always be cambered, sling points provided and marked to facilitate loading aboard ship.

8. Reduce cube and interior bracing problems by providing maximum disassembly of the carried item. Spares and disassembled parts should be adequately secured to the crate interior. In so doing, aim at a low center of gravity.

9. Supplement weak end grain nailing of interior bracing by back-up cleats.

10. Line crate interiors (except bottom) with a good grade water proof barrier material. Ventilate crates containing machinery or other items susceptible to damage from condensation with baffled vents or louvre plates covering ventilation hole clusters at ends or sides. Also, space floor boards 3/8" apart. Consider use of crate top coating where open freight car or open storage may be encountered.

11. Corners of all crates should be reinforced with lengths of 1" flat nailed

strapping applied so as to tie together all their faces at each corner.

12. Assure yourself that handling facilities are available for your crate at

destination and at intermediate points. Provide consignee with opening instructions to reduce accidental damage during unpacking.

Wirebound Boxes and Crates

Wirebound boxes and crates have shown themselves useful for a large variety of products not affected by minor distortions of the container. It is an ideal container for overpacks of solid or corrugated fiberboard boxes (cartons). If the wirebound container is not completely filled or if the contents may be affected by-possible distortion of the container, properly applied interior blocking and bracing is recommended. The

ends of wirebound containers should be reinforced to adequately resist the forces that may be applied during handling, thus preventing damage to contents.

Shippers should AVOID OVERLOADING and should not use boxes too large for their contents. Other considerations are:

1. Veneer and cleats should be full thickness, straight grained and sound, free from knots, decay, mildew or open splits. Sound knots not more than 1-1/2" in diameter and less than one-third the width of the piece of veneer are allowable. Wire should be free from rust and scale.

2. Ideal staple spacing is 2-1/2" on crates—2" on boxes. A minimum of two staples per slat is recommended.

3. Observe care in effecting closures to avoid wire fatigue. Use special closure tools.

4. Consult appropriate tables and your box supplier for export type container specifications.

5. Where contents are susceptible to pilferage or exceed 150 lbs., apply one tension strap around top, bottom, and ends. If over 250 lbs., apply two additional straps 3" from each end around top, bottom and sides. Also consider applying straps over intermediate cleats.

6. Line box interior with good grade of waterproof barrier material, properly sealed.

Cleated Plywood Boxes

Properly assembled and used, cleated plywood panel boxes have many uses in foreign trade. Their lightness and comparative strength particularly recommend them for air freight shipments. Shippers may abuse these containers, however, by using second-hand units, overloading, applying strapping improperly, allowing long unsupported panels or failing to

properly nail the box closed. Thin panels invite damage to contents through punctures. Follow these points in plywood shipments.

1. Consult appropriate tables to avoid overloading, to determine proper nail spacing and to find correct dimensions of plywood and cleats.
NEVER USE SECOND-HAND BOXES.
2. Reject rotted, split or otherwise defective cleats.
3. Apply intermediate cleats to all panels in excess of 24".
4. Apply strapping only over edge and/or intermediate cleats for maximum support. Strapping which spans unframed areas is easily broken; may injure handlers. Employ stapling to hold banding in place on the cleats.
5. Don't overlook lining with adequate waterproof or vaporproof barrier material, where contents are susceptible to water damage.

Steel Drums

New steel drums are generally excellent for export. Second-hand drums, unless thoroughly reconditioned and tested, may give trouble because of fatigue caused by dents at the chime and previous damages to closures. Also consider the following:
1. Closures must be made as prescribed by the manufacturer. Back up friction type covers of drums, as well as cans or pails, with soldering or spot welding at three or more points.
2. Be sure adequate seals are used on locking levers and sealing rings of open end drums. Failure of seals may result in accidental opening of covers.
3. Consider use of tamperproof seals at filling and dispensing holes.
4. Make frequent spot checks of automatic filling machinery by weighing filled drums. Shortages may occur at the source.
5. Do not re-use single or one-trip containers.
6. For hazardous/dangerous goods, be sure the drums meet DOT/IMO/IATA-ICAO, or appropriate standard-making group specifications, and are properly labeled for carriage of the intended cargo.

Fiber Drums

Fiber drums are gaining importance in the export picture. Before using, however, it should be determined that open storage enroute is not contemplated. Considerations for fiber drums include:
1. High density materials should not be packed into fiber drums.
2. Fiber drums should be filled to the top in order to add rigidity to the package. If contents are such that weight limits will be exceeded if filled to the top, smaller drums should be used. Avoid empty spaces at top of the drum.

3. It is advisable to settle or deaerate materials—particularly light fluffy powders—during the filling operations. Use of a vibrator or mechanical settler is recommended. Bag-lined drums can be deaerated simply by manually compressing the filled bag.

4. Keep size of drum compatible with weight of contents to avoid overloading.

5. Closures are important. Be sure sealing rings and locking levers are properly in place and will not be accidentally jarred or pulled loose.

6. Handle with mechanical equipment or roll on bottom chimes. Fiber drums are not designed to roll on sidewalls. Avoid cutting and chafing of sidewalls.

7. If possible, palletize fiber drums to facilitate mechanical handling in warehouses or on docks.

8. Never use a drum that has sidewall damage (cuts, dents) as stacking strength is lost.

Barrels, Casks or Kegs

The wooden barrel has been a workhorse of overseas trade, dating back to ancient times. Selection of the wrong barrel for your product can result in leakage, contamination, breakage and many other headaches. The following are basic recommendations:

1. Tight (liquid) barrels should be stored bung up. Request stowage on bilges. Slack (dry) barrels should be stored on ends. Never store or ship slack barrels on their side.

2. Provide reinforcing head cleats running from chime to chime at right angles to headpieces. Cleat thickness should never be greater than chime depth .

3. Use tongue and groove staves with a suitable liner where contents, such as dry chemicals and powders, may sift. Make sure barrel wood and liner material will not contaminate contents.

4. Keep voids in slack barrels to a minimum. Use headliners (strips of coiled elm fastened inside chime) to give barrel heads added strength.

5. Where tight barrels are employed, hoops should be fastened with not less than three fasteners (dogs) per hoop. Provide for inspection at interim transit points, where practicable, to check for leakage. If contents are carried in brine, re-brining at interim points may save contents of leaking units.

Multi-wall Shipping Sacks

Multi-wall shipping sacks or bags are being used more and more for packaging of powdered, granular and lump materials, particularly dry chemicals. These sacks are flexible containers generally made up from two walls or plies of heavy duty kraft paper to a maximum of six. Often, they are made in combination with special coating, laminations, impregnations, or even plies of textile material such as burlap to give them additional strength and added protection to their contents. Because of the flexibility of these containers, special attention must be given to the use of flexible waterproof or moisture-proof barriers in their construction.

There are several types of bags used, the most common being the pasted bottom or sewn bottom open-mouth, and the pasted valve or sewn-valve. The pasted bottom and sewn bottom open mouth type bags are closed after filing, by sewing through all plies with a strip of tape incorporated into the sewn end in such a way that it folds over the end of the sack to control sifting. They can also be closed by gluing. The valve type bags are closed by manually folding over an external paper sleeve or by the checkvalve action of an inner paper sleeve when the bags are full. The internal pressure of the contents causes this, and care must be taken that the bags are sufficiently filled to exert this pressure. It must be recognized that slight leakage will nevertheless occur, particularly when the bags are handled.

The use of these bags for overseas shipments should be limited. This type of container, more than any other, must be adapted to the requirements of the commodity they contain.

This requires careful research and intelligent selection. It is recommended that the loaded bag does not exceed 50 lbs. Consideration must be given to the value of the product as well as to its hygroscopic properties and chemical and physical characteristics. Utmost consideration must be given to in-transit hazards, such as atmospheric conditions or exposure to the elements, number of transfers and handlings, warehouse facilities, etc. Of major importance is the question as to whether the contents of the sack will be subjected to contamination if the bags are ruptured or if foreign matter can filter in through stitching holes.

A good practice for the shipper is to include a supply of open mouth refill or overslip sacks with each shipment.

The number of refill sacks should not be less than one percent of the number of sacks in the shipment and preferably three percent. The refill sacks should be imprinted with instructions for their use as well as identification of the commodity which they will carry. Overslip sacks should be slightly larger than the original sack and constructed of the same number and kind of plies.

Palletizing of a number of sacks, adequately shrink-wrapped and/or banded to the pallet, has been particularly effective in reducing damage and pilferage, and forces use of mechanical handling equipment.

Bales

A well-made bale may be expected to outturn reasonably well in most export trades. Bear in mind, however, that all bales are subject to pilferage, hook holes and water damage. They are,

therefore, not recommended for highly valued commodities. To minimize losses, follow these recommendations:

1. Where contents may be subject to damage from strapping pressure, use a primary wrap of fiberboard material.

2. Use an inner wrap of creped or pleated waterproof paper. This type paper is necessary to provide moisture protection and to give with bale distortions without tearing.

3. Provide heavy outer wrap of burlap or similar cloth able to withstand heavy abrasions in transit.

4. Provide "ears" at corners of small bales to facilitate handling without hooks. Bale weights under 300 lbs. are less apt to be handled with hooks.

5. A minimum of four flat tension bands should be used. Apply tightly at the maximum bale compression to avoid slipping of end bands.

6. Stencil all shipping and cautionary marks on bale. Do not use tags.

Cushioning

Fragile and brittle items must be suspended or protected against shock and vibration by a cushion that gradually increases resistance against item movement. Selection of the correct cushioning material depends on the item's size, weight, shape, surface finish and the built-in shock resistance.

Unitizing Cargo

Assemble individual items into one unit by bolting, nailing, or strapping together.

Provide unit load with skids to facilitate handling by forklift.

Provide vertical cleats on sides of load to facilitate handling by cargo slings.

Provide water damage protection by using plastic shrink wrap or stretch wrap on individual items before assembly into unit load.

Apply shrink wrap or stretch wrap to entire load.

Use waterproof paper or plastic film overwrap.

The American National Standards Institute (ANSI) publishes a guide to aid manufacturers, consumers and the general public on unit-load and transport-package sizes to efficiently fit within the truck trailer, freight container or railroad boxcar. Unit load stacking patterns are also presented. ANSI can be contacted at 1430 Broadway, New York, NY 10018. Reference ANSI MH10. IM-1980.

Suggestions for Valuable Shipments (Air)

In planning the shipment of valuable cargo, seek a level of security comparable to the security you know you require for your own premises.

Select a tariff designed for the movement of valuable goods and abide by its recommendations.

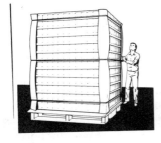

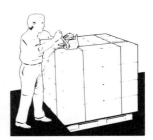

unitizing cargo

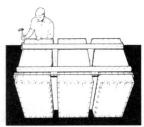

Make advance booking with a carrier for shipment so consignees may be on alert for arrival.

Tender shipment to carrier not more than three hours prior to the scheduled departure of the flight for which advance arrangements have been made.

Notify the consignee to accept delivery of the shipment at destination within three hours after scheduled arrival time of flight.

Avoid shipping when consignment will arrive at destination on weekends or holidays. (Some carriers will refuse shipments tendered between 1 p.m. Friday and 8 a.m. Monday.)

When delays in acceptance of valuable merchandise are anticipated, e. g., when weekend or holiday arrivals are unavoidable, arrange for special handling such as transportation via an armored vehicle or placement in a suitable repository such as provided by Purolator at Kennedy Airport. (Some carrier tariffs provide for special handling charges which are assessed against the shipment when consignee fails to pick up the shipment within three hours of scheduled arrival time of flight.)

Adhere to minimum package dimensions. Most tariffs provide for minimum package size of one cubic foot.

Use only new, well-constructed packaging for your product.

Clear and complete delivery and handling instructions should appear on at least three surfaces of the exterior shipping package.

Eliminate all product identification on the exterior of shipping package.

Avoid shipping on a routine schedule; report suspected theft quickly.

Security

Cargo security world-wide must be improved if theft and related losses are to be reduced. Studies conducted into this area have fixed the dollar losses—all transportation modes, i.e., air, truck, rail and ocean from a conservative $1 billion to a figure in excess of $5 billion. Whether the true picture is at either end or somewhere in-between is not as important as the acknowledgment that it constitutes a major drain on international trade.

The losses range from the pilferage of individual items of cargo to the theft of a 40-foot container or the highjack of a tractor/trailer. Although the latter cannot be ignored, the majority of incidents involve cargo taken from transportation facilities by personnel authorized to be there and on vehicles controlled or similarly authorized by management.

The task at hand is to establish and maintain a cargo security program, providing organizational, physical and procedural standards. To aid industry management in this undertaking, the Department of Transportation has developed a handbook entitled: "Guidelines for the Physical Security of Cargo" (DOT P 5200.2). As a corollary, U.S. Customs has issued "Standards for Cargo Security" (0-623485/771).

In some cases, attaining and implementing these standards may entail substantial expense. They are also effective. Conversely, "bargain basement" measures provide an open invitation to theft/pilferage. The false economy created by scrimping on security must be eliminated. Experience demonstrates that the decrease in cargo loss, i.e., loss of profit dollars, far outweighs the cost.

In addition, several organizations are working to make the ports of the world safe and secure.

• The Port Security Committee of the American Association of Port Authorities is attempting to combat cargo theft by initiating discussions between the transportation industry, insurance carriers, port management, and law enforcement on the present state of affairs in cargo security.

It has been concluded that cargo theft can be controlled effectively only when all concerned parties communicate with each other, and understand that cargo theft damages the profit potential, prestige, and credibility of everyone within the industry.

• The International Association of Chiefs of Police is also strongly committed to the cargo crime battle. The Cargo Security Committee of this association has provided training seminars, and other aids to law enforcement and industry personnel involved in cargo security. They are working to develop specialized training courses through the United States Federal Law Enforcement Training Center.

• On the global scene, the International Association of Airport and Seaport Police has addressed the problem by developing a truly international team of port law enforcement managers and directors capable of coordinating cargo theft investigations around the world. The IAASP is also committed to assisting the United Nations on the world's cargo security situation, and has offered its services, expertise and other resources to help all nations deal with the problem.

The organizations above have pledged their support to this effort and stand by ready to recommend various approaches which may be implemented by members of the transportation industry. Contact can be made by writing to the following addresses: ATTN: Port Security Committee, American Association of Port Authorities, Suite 990, 1612 K Street NW, Washington, DC 20006.

ATTN: Cargo Security Committee, International Association of Chiefs of Police, Eleven Firstfield Road, Gaithersburg, MD 20760.

ATTN: General Secretariat International Association of Airport Seaport Police Maritime House, No. 1 Linton Road, Barking, Essex 1G11 8HG United Kingdom.

Over the past few years, numerous incidents of maritime fraud have come to light, and many traders, particularly buyers in the Middle East, West Africa and South East Asia, have lost millions of dollars. Sellers, shipowners, insurers and bankers, both in these regions and other areas of the world, have also suffered major losses.

Although as a percentage of the value of all international seaborne trade transactions, the incidence of maritime fraud would not be considered high, the problem is very serious, appears to be increasing and, if not checked, will undermine the whole system of maritime trading.

In 1980 the International Chamber of Commerce (ICC), with the support of commercial interests world-wide, embarked on a major program to prevent and control marine fraud and related suspect practices. The culmination of the work was the establishment of the ICC International Maritime Bureau (IMB) by the ICC Council on 2 November 1980. The IMB officially began operations in London on 1 January 1981.

The United Nations maritime agency, IMO, has taken a close interest in the formation of the IMB and has drafted an appeal for all parties concerned, both government and private, to cooperate fully with it.

THE BUREAU'S OBJECTIVES ARE:
• to receive information provided by commercial and other interests relating to fraudulent or other suspect practices and to collate this information as a basis on which to determine appropriate measures;
• to suggest avenues of procedure to those who are involved in a transaction which they suspect may be fraudulent;
• to contribute to the provision of advice in setting up or improving operational and commercial systems to reduce their vulnerability to fraudulent or suspect practices;

• to contribute to the design and provision of educational services relating to the above and to provide a reference point concerning relevant information.

The IMB offers practical services to member associations, companies and individuals of both a preventive (general information, education, trading records) and remedial (general advice, deviation searches) nature. Additional information can be obtained by contacting:

Director,
International Maritime Bureau
Maritime House,
No. 1 Linton Road
Barking, Essex 1G11 8HG,
England
Telephone 01-59 1-3000
Telex: 8956492 IMB LDNG

Hazardous Materials

Unilateral state regulation of international commerce is impractical in today's interdependent world. Procedures that are acceptable in one country and forsaken in another inhibit world trade through embargo or unacceptable delay in cargo reaching its ultimate destination. The labels shown on these pages are the hazardous material (dangerous goods) identifications adopted by many IMO (United Nations) member countries to smooth the flow of these type materials in waterborne commerce. The color coding, symbol, and the class number (when displayed) are universal.

These labels simply provide a visual signal of dangerous goods in transport. They will cause special handling along the transport path, including embargo, if the commodity is not authorized for carriage. Dangerous goods regulations almost always require special documentation and packing under strict criteria. Routing through named entry ports is also a frequent requirement. Consequently, negotiating for entry into foreign trade of these items, always requires a complete explanation of the applicable rules.

IMPORTANT—Do not assume that compliance with domestic regulations will automatically qualify a shipment for passage through enroute countries and entry into the destination port. Requirements that are not met can easily be the difference between profit and loss.

If the material may be hazardous, then, in addition to all known required markings and labels, furnish pertinent chemical or physical data. This will expedite foreign freight relabeling by forwarders.

As of 1 January 1983, a new set of regulations apply to international shipments of hazardous goods by air. The new International Civil Aviation Organization (ICAO) Regulations deal with shipping papers, classifications, marking, labeling, packaging, and quantity limitations. However, existing packaging can be used until 1 January 1988.

Shippers will be permitted to continue to use the Code of Federal Regulations (CFR), Title 49, CAB 82 and Circular 6-D for all domestic shipments. However, the new ICAO Regulations are MANDATORY for all international shipments originating, terminating, or in transit through the United States.

Hazard Classes

The following refers to the number displayed at the bottom of the label.

1. **Explosives** (Class 1.1, 1. 2 and 1.3) **Explosives** (Class 1.4 and I .5)
2. **Non-Flammable and Flammable Gases**
3. **Flammable Liquids**
4. **Flammable Solids** (Readily combustible) **Spontaneously Combustible Substances Water Reactive Substances**
5. **Oxidizing Materials** (Oxidizing matters and/or organic peroxides)
6. **Poisonous Materials** (Class A, B & C poisons or toxic substances) **Poisonous Materials** (Harmful-stow away from foodstuffs)
7. **Radioactive Materials** (White I, Yellow II or Yellow III)
8. **Corrosive Materials** (Acids, corrosive liquids/solids & alkalines)
9. **Miscellaneous Hazardous Materials** (Those materials which present a danger in transport. No specific label authorized.)

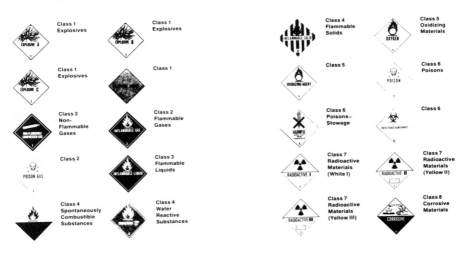

EXPORT GUIDE

Shipper

Cargo moves on paper! The part you play is shown in the following steps.

1. Prepares Domestic Bill of Lading for movement of cargo to pier, and sends copy to his forwarder along with packing list.
2. Checks Bill of Lading:
   - number of packages
   - marks and numbers
   - description of cargo
   - foreign destination
   - gross weights of each package shipped
   - local party to be notified
3. Marks cargo plainly to show:
   - gross and net weights
   - cubic measurement
   - foreign destination
   - identification marks
   - country of origin

Motor Carrier

4. Secures interchange agreement with steamship company on containers.
5. Accepts cargo for transit to the port.
6. Advises freight forwarder or shipper's local representative of cargo's arrival.
7. Obtains the following information from forwarder or representative:
   - name of vessel
   - sailing date
   - pier number and location
   - location of any special permits needed to clear hazardous or oversize cargo for acceptance by ocean terminal
8. Obtains Dock Receipt from forwarder or other representative to accompany cargo.
9. Contacts terminal operator to make appointment for special handling or equipment, if required, at least 24 hours before delivery.

Forwarder

10. Provides Dock Receipt and special permits, if any, to delivering motor carrier.
11. Checks Dock Receipt for completeness:
    - name of shipper
    - name of vessel

- ports of loading and discharge
- number and type of packages
- description of cargo
- gross weight, dimensions, and cubic measurement of each package
- marks and numbers
- shipper's export declaration number, if required

Driver
12. Moves his truck on line upon arrival at pier.

Terminal Operator
13. Issues pass to driver at gate house.
14. Assigns driver a checker and an unloading spot.

Driver
15. Unloads his vehicle (using extra pier labor is optional, at rates specified in the Terminal Conference tariff).
16. Obtains signed copy of Dock Receipt, and receipt for extra labor, if used.

Terminal Operator
17. Retains original of Dock Receipt.

Driver
18. Surrenders gate pass at gate house.

Terminal Operator
19. Forwards Dock Receipt to steamship company.

Steamship Company
20. Issues Ocean Bill of Lading to shipper or his agent.

LOSS CONTROL—CONTAINERIZED CARGO
The use of intermodal containers for the transport of a great variety of cargo has become increasingly popular in recent years. Intermodalism—a concept which embraces the movement and transfer of standardized cargo containers by sea, air and land—has reduced cargo handling, particularly in Door-to-Door shipments. Development of specialized containers with a wide range of types, sizes and configurations permits containerization of most cargo.

Prompt, undamaged arrival of the complete shipment at destination is the primary objective of the shipper.

INTERMODAL VARIATIONS

The popular intermodal container, adaptable to carriage by truck chassis, railcar, barge and oceangoing vessel is the most common form of containerization. The considerations governing preparation and stowage of the cargo in these containers are no less applicable to other methods of cargo transport.

Trailer-on-Flatcar (TOFC)—"Piggybacking" highway trailers on specially equipped rail flatcars.

Container-on-Flatcar (COFC)—Carriage of intermodal containers detached from their highway chassis and "bogie" on rail flatcars.

The TOFC and COFC variations mainly involve movements between the U.S. East and West Coasts. These movements are often referred to as "the land bridge."

Air Cargo Containerization—The unique aspects of cargo carriage via air and the application of containerization to this transport mode are treated separately in this publication (see Air Cargo discussion).

CONTAINER SERVICES

Door-to-Door (House-to-House)—The greatest benefits of containerization are realized when the shipper uses the container to carry goods directly from his premises to his customer's location. Perhaps the only time the container will be opened while enroute is for Customs inspection. Reduced susceptibility to pilferage and theft, elimination of multiple handling of individual items of cargo and the least possible exposure to the elements are all attractive features of Door-to-Door service. In utilizing this type of service, the shipper accepts the additional responsibility of ensuring that his cargo is properly stowed and secured in the container, precluding damage to the cargo, container, or transport vehicle.

The tendency to reduce packing protection of cargo destined for Door-to-Door container shipment must be resisted. The ocean leg of the voyage will still subject the cargo to severe motion stresses, considerably greater in force than during highway or rail movement. Reduction of packing protection must be carefully evaluated and implemented only after due consideration of the hazards of ocean transport, including the lifting force at transshipment points.

Port-to-Port (Pier-Pier)—When cargo volume does not provide for a full container load or when the shipper or consignee does not have the facilities to load or unload the cargo into the container at his premises, he can utilize the services of forwarders, consolidators, or the carrier to stow his goods in containers at the port of departure. This service is less attractive than Door-to-Door service. Since the cargo is not in a container for the entire journey, it is subject to the same degree of exposure to weather, handling and stowage damage, and theft and pilferage as break-bulk cargo. MAXIMUM EXPORT PACKING STANDARDS ARE RE-QUIRED WHEN SHIPPING PORT-TO-PORT.

Door-to-Port/Port-to-Door—Combinations of Door-to-Door and Port-to-

Port service are possible, depending on the desires of the shipper and the facilities available. While these combinations are more advantageous than Port-to-Port service, the cargo will still be exposed to the hazards of theft, weather and additional handling during part of the journey.

AS IN PORT-TO-PORT SERVICE, THE CARGO MUST BE PACKED TO THE HIGHEST EXPORT STANDARDS.

LCL (Less Than Container Load)—On LCL shipments, the shipper can still stow the container himself, but the container will be delivered to a consolidation point at the pier where other shippers' goods will be stowed in the container. What this means is that the smaller, low-volume exporter can still have his cargo containerized, although this is not as desirable as a sealed House-to-House container.

SELECTING THE RIGHT CONTAINER

Consultation with the carrier will permit selection of the type and size container most suitable for the cargo.

Many types and sizes are available to the shipper. The most common is the dry cargo container which may be used for a great variety of general cargo. Specialized containers should be used for goods or commodities requiring special environments.

  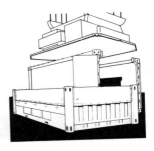

end loading,	*side loading,*	*open top,*
fully enclosed	*fully enclosed*	*Opentop/hard top*

DRY CARGO CONTAINERS

End Loading Fully Enclosed—The basic intermodal containers, with end doors, suitable for general cargo not requiring environmental control while enroute.

Side Loading, Fully Enclosed—Equipped with side doors for use in stowing and discharge of cargo where it is not practical to use end doors, as when the container must remain on a railcar while cargo is placed in or removed from the container.

Open Top—Used for carriage of heavy, bulky or awkward items where loading or discharge of the cargo through end or side doors is not practical. Most open top containers are equipped with fabric covers and are often termed "soft" or "rag" top containers. Some open top versions are fitted with removable hatch type panel covers or a detachable full-size metal roof.

Ventilated—Equipped with ventilating ports on ends or sides, and used for heat generating cargo or cargo requiring protection from condensation (sweat) damage. Versions with powered air-circulating fans are available. Vents are normally fitted with bars to prevent entry of sea or rainwater.

Insulated—For cargo which should not be exposed to rapid or sudden temperature changes. Available in ventilated or nonventilated versions. Some carriers provide containers with heating systems for special applications.

SPECIAL PURPOSE CONTAINERS

Refrigerated: insulated and equipped with a built-in refrigeration system, powered by direct electrical connection or by diesel or gasoline generator. It is used primarily for foods or other commodities requiring a temperature controlled environment.

Liquid Bulk: tank-type containers for carriage of liquids. Some have been designed to high level specifications for carriage of certain hazardous materials.

Dry Bulk: designed for carriage of bulk cargo; such as dry chemicals and grams.

Flat Rack: available in a variety of sizes and models, the flat racks are used for lumber, mill products, large, heavy or bulky items, or machinery and vehicles. Some are equipped with removable sides and fabric covers.

ventilated   *refrigerated*   *liquid bulk*

Auto: used for carriage of vehicles and available in enclosed or open versions.

Livestock: configured for the nature of livestock carried; containers are available for transporting poultry, cattle, and other livestock.

Sea Shed: experimental open top container developed by MARAD and U.S. Navy. This cargo-handling system is designed to adapt container-ships to the carriage of heavy, outsized equipment (notably military). The "work-through" floor construction (floor sections opened by a self-contained winch) can reduce unloading time and pierside storage space since they need not be removed at destination.

flat rack

sea shed

Containers are categorized into six groups based on original usage, locale or ownership. They are not limited to use in any particular area, and may be found in any port of the world. Dimensions given here will vary due to construction materials used, minor modifications and design differences.

Category I—Standard Accepted as Standard by U.S. Standards Institute.

Category II—Standard Accepted as Standard in Common Use in Europe.

Category III—Accepted as Standard Sizes—Used by Two of the Largest Commercial Containership Operators.

Category IV—U.S. Government Ownership— Used Primarily for Military Cargo—Commonly Called "Conex" Containers.

category V—U.S. Government Owned/Developed Sea Sheds.

Category VI—U.S. Government Ownership.

Category	Exterior Dimensions (W - H - L)			Interior Dimensions (W - H - L)			Cube Capacity (cu. ft.)	Cargo Capacity (lbs.)
I Standard	8′	8′	40′	90″	85″	39′4″	2,090	50,000-55,000
	8′	8′	30′	90″	85″	29′4″	1,560	45,000
	8′	8′	20′	90″	85″	19′4″	1,040	38,000-44,800
	8′	8′	10′	90″	85″	9′4″	490	22,000
II Standard	8′	8′	6′8″	90″	85″	73¹/₂″	329	16,000-18,000
	8′	8′	5′	90″	85″	54³/₄″	248	12,000
III Sea Land	8′	8′6″	35′	92″	93¹/₄″	34′7″	2,088	45,000
Matson	8′	8′6¹/₂″	24′	93″	94¹/₄″	23′6″	1,415	42,000-46,000
IV CONEX	6′3″	6′10¹/₂″-4′3″		71³/₄″	72³/₄″	46⁵/₈″	135	9,000
	6′3″	6′10¹/₂″-8′6″		71³/₄″	72³/₄″	97⁵/₈″	295	9,000
V Sea Shed	25′	12′6″	40′	24′6″	12′6″	39′4″	12,180	220,000
VI Milvans	8′	8′	20′	92″	87″	19′3″	1,010	44,800
Seavans	8′	8′	35′	92″	87″	34′6″	1,810	45,000

CERTIFICATION OF INTERMODAL CONTAINERS

The International Convention for Safe Containers, effective 6 September 1977, makes certain structural requirements mandatory for containers moving in international trade. Under the Convention, periodic examination of containers in accordance with procedures prescribed or approved by signatory governments are required. Approved units are issued safety plates, which are affixed to the containers.

A number of independent firms provide testing and inspection services for intermodal container operators. Certification of adequacy of construction occurs prior to delivery of the new container to the carrier, and periodically after delivery.

A ship at sea may move in six different directions simultaneously

This container may travel 70 feet with each roll; as much as 7-10 times/minute

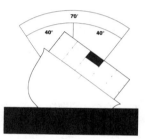

The shipper should look for the certificate seal on containers supplied for his use as evidence the container has met adequate construction and maintenance standards.

Presence of this seal is not, however, a guarantee that the container is presently free from defects, as damage may have occurred since the last certification inspection.

The shipper must make a personal inspection of the container before use to be absolutely certain that it is in condition to adequately protect his goods.

An understanding of the hazards to which a container may be exposed (as depicted in the two adjacent illustrations) is essential. This knowledge will permit intelligent inspection of the container and also provide the background necessary for adequate preparation and stowage of the cargo.

INSPECTING THE INTERMODAL CONTAINER

The following checklist will assist you in inspecting the container to be sure it will properly protect your cargo. Containers that leak or have inherent defects which endanger the cargo or pose a safety hazard to personnel must be rejected.

Interior

Must be free from splinters, snags, dents or bulges. These may interfere with loading. Serious defects indicate the container is structurally unsound.

- **Watertight Integrity**— "Light" tests whereby you enter the container, have the doors closed and look for light leaks in the roof, side and door panels and deck are a must. Also, previous patches and repairs must be checked to ensure they are watertight. Hose (water) or smoke tests are alternative methods of discovery.
- **Fittings**—Cargo tie-down cleats or rings should be in good condition and well-anchored. If ventilator openings are present, be sure that they have not been blocked off, and that they are equipped with bars to prevent rain or sea water entry.
- **Cleanliness**—Free of residue from previous cargo particularly odors which may taint your cargo.

Exterior

Must be free from dents, bulges or other damages; all may interfere with handling.

- **Doors**—Be sure doors can be securely locked and sealed. Check that door gaskets are in good condition and watertight when closed. Inspect door hardware closely. If bolts or nuts can be easily removed from the outside with simple tools, it means that the container can be opened without breaking the seal or lock—an attractive invitation to the pilferer.
- **Fittings**—A quick look at the lifting fittings at each corner of the container will reveal those which are obviously damaged or unsafe. Check the fittings that secure the container to the trailer chassis; they should all be in working order and in use.
- **Covers/Hatch Panels**—If an open-top container, be sure that the fabric cover supplied with the container is in good condition and can be properly secured. Check hatch panels for close, watertight fit.

The following is a partial check list of typical types of damage.

Front End

Front Panel—Dented, torn, holed or punctured.

Patches—Loose, not of same material as panel, not sealed or riveted with waterproof Customs-approved rivets, poor welds, not primed or painted.

Top Rail—Bent, cut, crushed or fractured.

Bottom Rail—Bent, cut, crushed or fractured.

Corner Posts—Bent, broken, cut, gashed or distorted.

Upper and Lower Corner Fittings and Attachments—Fractured or distorted fittings, cracked attachment welds.

Rivets—Loose or missing.

Welds—Improperly made, not primed or painted.

Right and Left Sides
Panels—Dented, torn, holed, or punctured.
Corner Posts—Bent, broken, cut, gashed or distorted.
Upper and Lower Corner Fittings and Attachments—Fractured or distorted fittings, cracked attachment welds.
Door Holdbacks—Damaged or missing.

Rear End
Doors—Difficulty in opening and/or closing.
Doors Panels (plymetal or other)—Torn, cut, holed or punctured .
Door Locking Bars (rods)—Seized, bent, broken or twisted.
Door Locking Bar Cams—Bent or broken.
Door Handle and Retainers—Broken, bent or missing.
Door Cam Lock Retainers (keepers)—Bent or broken.
Door Hinges—Broken, torn, twisted, binding or seized.
Door Seals (gasket and attachments)—Cut, torn or loose.
Door Header—Cut, broken, distorted or dented.
Door Sill—Cut, fractured or distorted.
Anti-Rack Device (if any)—Bent, cut, damaged or broken.
Rain Gutter—Bent, broken or crushed.
Roof
Panel—Punctured, dented or distorted.
Upper Corner Fittings and Attachments—Fractured or distorted fitting, cracked attachment welds.
Corner Protection Plate (where provided)—Punctured, dented or distorted.

Under Structure
Cross Members and Attachments—Crushed, cut, bent, distorted or broken loose from bottom side rails or floor.
Tunnel Recess (if any)—Cut, dented, distorted, cracked weld attachments.
Forklift Pockets (if any)—Cut, dented, distorted, bottom straps broken or bent.

Interior
Roof Sheet—Punctured dented or distorted.
Roof Bows (if any)—Bent, cut or broken loose from roof.
Floor—Torn, gouged, broken, shrunken, warped, stained excessively.
Sides—Dented, torn, holed or punctured.
Logistic Track (side walls or floor)—Torn, loose, bent, missing or cracked welds.
Cargo Securing Rings or Strips (floor or sides)—Torn, loose, bent or missing.

Liners (where provided)—Torn, punctured, gouged, pulled loose, stained excessively.

Cleanliness—Debris, spillage, etc.

Odors—Objectionable, contaminable.

Light leaks.

SPECIALIZED CONTAINERS

If you are utilizing a refrigerated tank, or other special purpose container, inspect for the following:

Motors/Compressors—Check to see that they are in good operating condition and perform as required. Be sure that adequate fuel has been supplied.

Valves/Piping—They must be free of leaks with tight fittings. Valves should operate smoothly and seal tightly.

Electrical—Wiring and connections should be clean and free of corrosion. Switches should operate properly. Be alert for potential shock hazards.

Barges

When using intermodal barges to transport your cargo, pay particular attention to:

Hull—The exterior should not show evidence of serious hull damage. The interior hull should be dry and tight.

Hatches—They should fit tightly, with watertight seal at the edges. Securing lugs and bolts must be in good condition.

PREPARING THE CARGO

An intermodal container or barge is essentially a ship's hold on a reduced scale. When the containers and barges are placed aboard ship for an ocean voyage, the cargo stowed in them is subject to the same motion forces and damage hazards while at sea that affect cargo shipped in break-bulk fashion.

The same principles and techniques which govern export packing and cargo stowage of break-bulk shipments are equally valid when preparing cargo for intermodal shipment and when stowing the same in the container or barge.

PACK FOR THE TOUGHEST LEG OF THE JOURNEY!

Refer to the *Basic Packing Guide* section for guidance in selection of packing containers.

Be certain that goods cannot move within the fiberboard box, wood crate or other container in which it is packed. Immobilize the contents by blocking or bracing, and/or provide adequate cushioning.

Fiberboard boxes or wood crates must be able to withstand the weight pressure of cargo stacked up to an eight foot height. They must be able to survive lateral pressures exerted by adjacent cargo—up to 7/10 of the vertical stacking weight pressure. This will help to prevent crushing as the container is tilted (up to 45°) during handling or at sea.

Heavy items, machinery and items not uniform in shape or dimension should be crated, boxed and/or provided with skids to permit ease of handling and compact stowage.

Where possible, cargo should be unitized or palletized. Cargo handlers are then required to use mechanical handling equipment to move cargo.

Provide adequate water damage protection. Use of desiccants (moisture-absorbing materials), moisture or vapor barrier paper or plastic wraps, sheets or shrouds will protect cargo from water leakage or condensate damage. Susceptible machine parts should be coated with a preservative/rust inhibitor.

Bonded block stowage method alternates blocks on each layer

WOOD CRATES

Wood Boxes and Crates

Crates of uniform size and weight should be stacked directly one atop another.

Separate groups of crates with different weights or dimensions by use of partitions, dividers, or auxiliary decking.

Fill voids at top, sides, or ends by use of partitions or fillers.

If large voids are present, block, brace, and tie down cargo to prevent movement in any direction.

When contents are susceptible to water damage, provide plastic or water-repellent paper shrouds over the top and sides of the load.

Use dunnage on container deck to provide sump area for condensate drainage if crates are not skidded.

When bracing crates, apply bracing to strength members only, not to panels or sheathing.

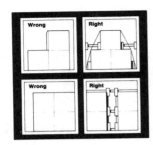
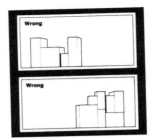

weight distribution—heavy loads

Machinery and Heavy Items

Distribute weight by proper placement and use of cradles or skids.

Use deck cleats and bracing to prevent lateral and fore-and-aft movement. Use the downs of metal strapping to prevent vertical movement.

Extremely heavy, dense items should be through bolted to the container deck. Consult with carrier or container leasing operator for approved method(s).

Top-heavy items should be shored and braced to prevent toppling. Do not brace against the side panels of the container. All bracing must bear on a structural member of the container.

Provide plastic or water-resistant paper shrouds over the top and sides of the item to prevent water damage.

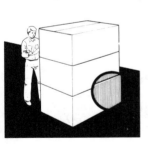

vertical positioning of corrugasted flutes provides best support

keep voids in center and immobilize

fill end voids to prevent movement of cargo

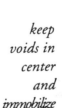

1. Roll paper on deck to eight block length, then up wall

282

2. Stow 1st 2 blocks to full height, 2nd 2 to half height, fold roll over 1st 2 then down and over 2nd 2 then to deck.

3. Complete stow of 2nd 2, then anchor paper with 3rd 2 to healf-height.

4. Repeat 1, 2,3.

AIR CARGO

Air Cargo service has become more and attractive to shippers as aircraft capacity, frequency of lifts, handling facilities, and the number of points served have been improved/ increased.

Air cargo losses can be controlled with the shipper himself as the key figure in effective loss control. Recognition of the hazards involved, packing cargo to survive the toughest leg of the journey, and prudent selection of transportation services will assist the shipper in realizing successful, loss-free delivery of his goods.

Inadequate packing and improper marking of cargo are the leading causes of air cargo losses. It is these areas in which the shipper can effectively influence the sound arrival of his goods.

THE AIR CARGO ENVIRONMENT HAZARDS

In the Aircraft

Acceleration/Deceleration— Fore-and-aft pressures are exerted on cargo during takeoff and landing. Compression forces are exerted during rough landings.

Turbulence—Rough or "bumpy" flight conditions subject cargo to rapid alternating vertical movements, imposing heavier pressures one moment, and almost weightless conditions the next.

Altitude—As altitude increases, atmospheric pressure decreases, subjecting liquid cargo to leakage hazards and pressurized cargo to increased internal pressure.

Temperature—Aircraft cargo compartment temperatures normally range between 30°F and 70°F (–1°C and 21°C). If the aircraft is parked with cargo aboard in freezing or very hot weather, cargo will be subjected to unusual cold or heat conditions.

Cargo Compartments—The main cargo compartments of air freighters are normally well equipped for adequate stowage. Passenger aircraft belly compartments, however, are often loaded without provision for adequate restraint of cargo, permitting its movement during flight and inviting damage from adjacent cargo.

283

In Terminals

Handling—Many large terminals are equipped with conveyor systems and mechanical cargo handling gear, permitting rapid and safe movement within the terminal. Overcrowded conditions contribute to handling damage as facilities are overtaxed. Manual handling is common as cargo is stacked on pallets and in containers ("igloos"). In smaller terminal facilities, it is the rule.

Storage—Modern terminals are equipped with segregated security areas for high-value cargo, and some have cold storage (reefer) facilities for perishables. Terminals not so equipped are subject to increased theft, pilferage, and deterioration loss hazards. Overcrowded conditions may require storage of some cargo outdoors, exposed to the elements.

Ramps—Cargo is commonly exposed to the weather while enroute to loading ramps. If cargo transfer carts, pallets and containers are not adequately covered (tarped), water damage may result. High-value cargo is particularly susceptible to theft when not in the aircraft or the terminal.

Security—Security conscious carriers provide maximum physical measures to protect cargo from theft or pilferage. Restricting working areas to employees, applying modern locking and alarm devices, and enforcing strict cargo documentation procedures are examples. When these measures are not used, cargo security is jeopardized.

Restricted Articles—Only trained personnel should handle dangerous goods. Consult appropriate Hazardous Materials regulations, such as the IATA's Restricted Articles Guide.

Most cargo is delivered to both carrier and consignee by truck. Air carriers have only limited control over trucking firms providing these services.

Often, air cargo is stored in warehouses or on transfer docks before forwarding, increasing exposure to loss through theft pilferage and handling damage.

"Hijackings"—the theft of entire truckloads of air cargo—continues as a serious problem in recent years.

INSIST ON PROMPT PICKUP AND DELIVERY OF YOUR CARGO! This is the most effective means of reducing exposure to theft, pilferage and hijacking.

Preparing Cargo for Air Shipment

Pack For The Toughest Leg Of The Journey: Truck or rail transport to air terminal, handling in terminals, stowing in aircraft, in flight, unloading aircraft, transfer to terminals, rail or truck transport to consignee.

Cargo Should Be Packed To Withstand: Stacking up to eight feet high, pressure from adjacent cargo, crushing action of tiedown straps, manual handling, exposure to the elements.

Unitize, Palletize, Containerize to: Minimize manual handling, reduce incidence of lost or stray items, limit exposure to theft and pilferage, minimize stowage damage, provide water-protective coverings which will accompany pallet and unit loads on entire journey.

Liquid Cargo

Do not fill containers completely—provide expansion space to compensate for temperature and/or pressure variations.

Be sure all caps, valves and seals are tightly closed.

Put orientation marks (arrows) on all sides of package.

Hazardous Cargo

Consult with your carrier to obtain the most recent regulations, restrictions, and labeling requirements. See *Hazardous Materials* section.

Large, Heavy or Awkward Cargo

Check with carrier to determine allowable aircraft floor weight concentrations.

Provide skids for ease of mechanical handling.

Check dimensions to be sure cargo will pass through aircraft loading doors.

Provide adequate locations for application of tie-down straps.

Water Damage Protection

Pack cargo in wooden crates with waterproof paper or polyethylene liners.

Line non-impregnated fiberboard boxes with waterproof paper or polyethylene.

Large items can be shrouded with polyethylene sheeting. Be sure there are drain holes in the base of the crate.

Use desiccants (moisture absorbent materials) in conjunction with waterproof barrier wrapping when packing moisture sensitive items. Use shrink wrap, stretch wrap or plastic shrouds on unit and pallet loads.

Perishable Cargo

Provide adequate package ventilation where required.

Furnish appropriate instructions (e.g., carrying temperatures, handling requirements, etc.) to carriers.

Use direct flights where possible.

Delivery and pick-up should be closely timed with aircraft departure and arrival.

Marking

Avoid marks and advertising which reveal that contents are of a valuable or desirable nature.

Apply appropriate coded identification marks to at least three sides of item.

Use international handling symbols.

Include handling instructions in both English and the language of the country of destination.

Use indelible inks and waterproof labels.

AIR CARGO CONTAINERIZATION

Shippers can realize savings and minimize cargo loss by containerizing their air cargo shipments. Airlines encourage use of containers by providing special tariffs for containerized FAK (Freight-All-Kinds) shipments on many routes.

Certain commodities are excluded from air cargo FAK special rates. Consult with your carrier or forwarder for specifics on excluded items and on articles prohibited by IATA "Restricted Articles Regulations."

Air carriers prefer containerized shipments for a number of reasons:

Reduces the number of individual pieces of cargo which must be handled in terminals.

Provides for most efficient use of cubic capacity of aircraft.

Permits use of mechanical handling systems and equipment to best advantage.

Speeds loading and unloading of aircraft.

Minimizes exposure of cargo to weather, theft, pilferage, and handling damage while in custody of the carrier.

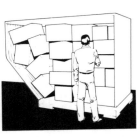

Provide dunnage or shelving to prevent crushing of cargo into recessed end of lower deck container.

Air Cargo Containers Fall into Three Basic Categories

1. AIR CARGO PALLETS— Designed for use with conveyor systems in terminals and in aircraft. The low-profile flat pallet is equipped with fittings for securing the pallet firmly to the aircraft deck.

Cargo is normally secured to the pallet by use of cargo nets, tightened over cargo by the application of tensioned straps.

Contoured, semi-structural covers called "igloos," "hulahuts," or "cocoons" are used with pallets to provide protection for cargo and keep cargo within safe dimensions for loading in aircraft. Igloos may be attached to the pallet by use of cargo nets over the exterior, or the igloo may be permanently attached to the pallet.

These containers may have one side (front) open, with cargo secured by nets or have metal or fiberglass removable doors which are capable of being sealed.

2. LOWER DECK CONTAINERS—Developed for use in the lower deck cargo spaces of high-capacity aircraft; they are fully structured and completely enclosed.

Cargo is loaded into the container which may be equipped with shelves for accommodation of small or irregularly shaped cargo.

The container doors of metal, fabric or a combination of both are closed and sealed.

Containers are locked directly into aircraft restraint systems without need for nets or tiedowns.

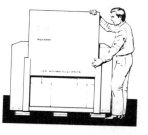

Provide dunnage or shelving to prevent crushing of cargo into recessed end of lower deck container.

3. BOX-TYPE CONTAINERS—Developed in standard sizes to facilitate establishment of uniform shipping rates, they are used to consolidate shipments.

Available from various manufacturers, they may be purchased by the shipper or used by freight forwarders to consolidate the shipper's cargo into one easily handled and rated unit.

Constructed of wood, fiberglass, plywood, fiberboard, metal or combinations of these materials, all must conform to the basic standards prescribed by the Air Transport Association (ATA) for domestic use, or the International Air Transport Association (IATA) for international shipments.

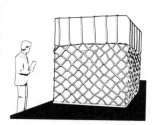

Contoured Box—(igloo configurations) are handled and loaded aboard aircraft in the same manner as the pallet-igloo combinations.

Air/Land Containers—Introduction of the 747-class freighter has permitted adding the air dimension to the intermodal container. Lightweight 20- and 40 foot containers permit land and air freight transportation without rehandling or reloading.

Square-sided box-type containers are normally loaded on pallet-igloo combinations by the carrier for stowage aboard the aircraft .

The following table lists standard IATA & ATA containers. Minor variations in internal dimension and cube will occur due to differences in the construction techniques and materials used.

Air Cargo is a popular mode of transportation for live animal shipments. Consult the applicable IATA/ATA guide for specific requirements and restrictions. Equally important check on the import regulation and quarantine laws that can affect the shipments.

Dimensions (inches)	Description	IATA Type	ATA Type
96 × 238.5 × 96	20-Ft Main Deck Container	1	M2
96 × 125 × 96	10-Ft Main Deck Container	2	M1
88 × 125 × 96	10-Ft Main Deck Container	2A	M3
88 × 125 × 88	Main Deck Container	2AA	M4
96 × 125 × 72	Main Deck Container	2B	—
96 × 125 × 118	10-Ft-High Main Deck Container	2H	M1H
96 × 125 × 118	10-Ft-High Main Deck Pallet	2H	M5
96 × 238.5 × 118	10-Ft-High Main Deck Pallet	—	M6
88 × 125 × 86	Main Deck Container	3	A1, 2, 3
88 × 108 × 86	Main Deck Container	4	A4
88 × 108 × 80	Main Deck Container	4A	A4
88 × 125 × 64	Lower Deck Container	5	LD-7, LD-9
60.4 × 125 × 64	Lower Deck Container	6	LD-5, LD-10, LD-11
88 × 61.5 × 86	Half-Size Main Deck Container	7	—
60.4 × 61.5 × 64	Lower Deck 1/2 Width Container	8	LD-1, LD-3
58 × 83 × 76	Half-Size Main Deck Container	CO3	B
58 × 83 × 75	Half-Size Main Deck Container	CO4	B
58 × 83 × 61	Half-Size Lower Deck Container	CO5	B
42 × 83 × 75	Mini-Half-Size Main Deck Container	CO6	—
54 × 54 × 56	Lower Deck Container Insert	CO7	LD-N
58 × 41 × 45	Quarter-Pallet-Size Container	CO8	C, D, D₂
40 × 48 × 40	Nonaircraft Container	CO9	—
40 × 48 × 27	Nonaircraft Container	COO	—
42 × 29 × 25.5	Nonaircraft Container	COS	E

Palletizing and Unitizing

Many products or commodities can be economically palletized or unitized to facilitate their handling, stowage and protection. Often, packing costs can be significantly reduced by palletizing and unitizing. Pallet and unit loads offer the following additional advantages:

Requires use of mechanical handling equipment—reducing the manual handling damage hazard.

Eliminates the multiple handling of individual items—further reducing possible damage from manual handling.

Reduces opportunity for pilferage and theft and permits early detection of tampering .

Speeds loading and unloading of trailers, boxcars, intermodal containers, barges, ships and aircraft.

Facilitates application of waterproofing protection to the load, the overwrap applied accompanies the load for the entire journey.

Reduces incidence of lost or astray items.

Facilitates checking and inventory of shipment.

PALLETIZING is the assembly of one or more packages on pallet base and securing the load to the pallet.

UNITIZING is the assembly of one or more items into a compact load, secured together and provided with skids and cleats for ease of handling.

Palletizing Cargo

There are four "standard" pallets that accommodate the various modal/intermodal containers presently used in international commerce. The nominal sizes, in inches, of these pallets are 54 x 45, 45 x 45, 49 x 41, and 48 x 40. In addition, other dimensions frequently utilized include 52 x 44, 44 x 44, 35 x 44, 33 x 44, 36 x 45, and 34 x 45.

Select the pallet that:

1. Best utilizes the space of the intermodal transportation to be used.

2. Best utilizes the uniform unit package dimensions of the item to be shipped.

3. Limits the weight of the palletized load to 2,200 pounds (1,000 kg).

Assemble the individual unit packages on the pallet base without an overhang. The load pattern should minimize voids and be interlocking.

Insert spacers between the rows or layers of irregularly shaped items. Adhesives can be used between cartons in a uniform load.

Secure the load tightly and firmly by using horizontal and vertical strapping. Plastic shrink wrap can be used to stabilize and protect palletized loads.

Provide stacking protection to the top of the pallet by using a lumber, plywood or fiberboard cap. Loads that are susceptible to compression must also be supported with vertical framing.

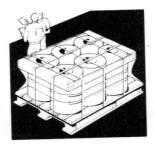
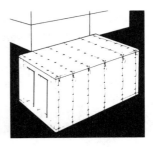

Palletized loads susceptible to water damage can be protected by shrink wrap or stretch wrap, overwrapping with barrier material, or consolidated shipping in a weathertight container.

MARKS

The primary purpose of marking is for the identification of the shipment, enabling the carrier to forward it to the ultimate consignee. Old marks, advertising and other extraneous information only serve to confuse this primary function for cargo handlers and carriers. Follow these fundamental marking rules:

1. Unless local regulations prohibit, use blind marks; particularly where goods are susceptible to pilferage. Change them periodically to avoid familiarity by handlers. Trade names, consignees' or shippers' names should be avoided as they indicate the nature of the contents.

2. Consignee (identification) marks and port marks showing destination and transfer points should be large, clear and applied by stencil with waterproof ink. They should be applied on three faces of the container, preferably side, and/or ends, and top.

3. If commodities require special handling or stowage, the containers should be so marked, and this information should also appear on the bills of lading.

4. Cautionary markings must be permanent and easy to read (use the languages of both the origin and destination countries). The use of stencils is recommended for legibility—do not use crayon, tags or cards. An example of marking on an export pack is illustrated.

Non-Hazardous Pictorial Markings

It is recommended that handling instructions be printed on the exterior pack in the language of the destination country. It is not unusual for a shipment to be handled by another country along the transport path or by cargo handlers that cannot read. These potential problems can best be overcome by pictorial markings. The symbols depicted under the heading of "International" represent markings that have been accepted as standards.

A new form, "Shipper's Declaration of Dangerous Goods" has been developed by IATA/ ATA. International hazardous material/dangerous goods shipments MUST be accompanied by this new form. Members of the Air Transport Association will be required to use the new form for all domestic shipments.

The ICAO *Technical Instruction for the Safe Transport of Dangerous Goods by Air* has been published. In addition several courses are available through the Hazardous Materials Advisory Council (HMAC) and the National Committee on International Trade Documentation (NCITD).

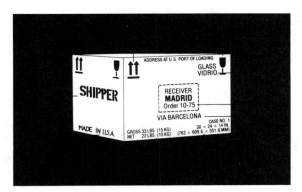

PLAN THE STOW

Observe Weight Limitations

Do not exceed rated capacity of container or barge.

Do not exceed permissible weight concentrations per square foot of deck.

Check highway weight-axle limitations on 'both sides of the' ocean voyage because some containers have total capacities which exceed local permissible limits.

Distribute Weight Equally

Avoid concentrating heavy weights at one side or one end.

Stow heaviest items on the bottom.

Heavy, dense items should be boxed, crated or placed on cradles or skids to distribute weight.

Avoid Mixing Incompatible Cargo

Cargo which exudes odor or moisture should not be stowed with cargo susceptible to tainting or water damage.

Items with sharp projections or of awkward or unusual shape should be segregated from other cargo by boxing, crating, padding or use of partitions.

Cargo subject to leakage or spillage should not be stowed on the top of other cargo.

Observe Hazardous Material Regulations

Consult with carrier for regulations and restrictions on shipping:
• combustibles
• explosives
• flammable liquids
• flammable solids
• gaseous material
• radioactive material
• magnetized material
• corrosives
• poisons
• oxidizers
• etiologic agents

After receiving information from carrier, proceed as follows:

Label and mark hazardous material properly. (See *Hazardous Materials* section.) Affix warning placards to container exterior. Note that placards vary throughout the world. What is acceptable at origin may not be in compliance with enroute or destination countries' regulations. Check before shipment to avoid embargo or delay.

Record the nature of the cargo on all shipping documents.

Have all Cargo and Materials Ready before Stowage Begins

This facilitates proper placement, stacking, and weight distribution. Additionally, it precludes removal of cargo already stowed to accommodate unexpected items and permits installation of blocking, bracing and filling of voids as stowing operations progress.

Plan for Ease of Unloading

Stow cargo in reverse order of desired cargo discharge.

Be sure that cargo for multiple consignees is physically separated by partitions, dividers, or other suitable means.

Make sure that forklift openings in pallets or skids face doors.

Provide lift clearance at top of container for items to be handled by forklift.

Fill the voids, but avoid wedging or jamming cargo in container.

Cosmetic Damage

The exterior packing of your commodity is often the first representative the consignee sees of your company. A package showing exterior damages, although perhaps only cosmetic in nature, can cause loss of market, poor shipper/consignee relationships, and more importantly cause the goods to be rejected and/or not paid for even though the commodities inside may arrive without damage. Repackaging commodities can be very costly as well as time consuming.

Cosmetic damages can be prevented by referring to the *Basic Packing Guide* section of this booklet. Remember, the appearance of your product is in many cases as important as the product itself.

DUNNAGE AND STOWAGE MATERIALS

Lumber

Should be clean and dry (not above 19 percent moisture content).

Most common sizes used as dunnage and for bracing are nominal 2" x 4" and 4" x 4".

Should be free from significant splits.

Use as filler, decking, blocking, bracing, and for constructing partitions/dividers.

Plywood

Should be clean and dry.

Use for partition faces, dividers, auxiliary decking, and blocking in limited spaces.

Inflatable

Available in paper, fabric, rubber or plastic; in both reusable and disposable versions.

Use it for filling voids; light and medium duty bracing.

Be sure cargo facing inflatable dunnage will not cause punctures. Also, a check for sharp edges and/or protrusions of packaging, pallet or containers, etc. must be made.

Patented Systems

Various patented cargo control and dunnage systems are available. Pre-built partitions, shelves, straps, laminated liner board bulkheads, and dunnage bars facilitate stowage and securing of cargo.

Fiberboard

Available in sheets, rolls and in prescored structural shapes for light-duty bracing.

Use sheets for dividers, decks, partition facings and auxiliary decks.

Use rolled fiberboard sheets (solid or corrugated) for linings or facings and for filling voids.

Strapping

Heavy duty metal strapping is used to separate cargo units and for tying down heavy or awkward items.

Nonmetallic strapping is used to separate and tie down light cargo units.

Nonmetallic strapping has only a fraction of the strength of similar steel material and would not resist shearing on a sharp edge as well. Furthermore, it will stretch as much as nine percent under heavy loads.

Metal and plastic straps must be firmly anchored and properly tensioned. Be sure not to puncture container panels when attaching strapping anchors. The use of corner (anti-chafing) pads is recommended.

STOWING THE CARGO

Fiberboard Boxes

Fiberboard boxes containing tightly packed, dense items which support sides and ends of the box are stowed using the "bonded block" method.

Fiberboard boxes containing lightweight or fragile items which provide little or no support to the box surfaces are stowed by stacking directly one atop the other. This method takes advantage of the vertical rigidity of the side walls and corrugations in each box.

Use plywood or lumber dunnage, or fiberboard dividers as auxiliary decking sheets to segregate tiers of different sized fiberboard containers.

Provide plastic or water-repellent shrouds over top and sides of load to protect against damage from water (ship's sweat or holed containers).

Use dunnage or pallets on the container deck to provide a condensate sump area, protecting lower tiers from moisture.

Fill all voids by bracing or using fillers to prevent sliding or shifting of cargo.

Fill end voids to prevent movement of cargo.

Use of Retaining or Dunnage Paper in "Bonded Block" Stowage

Use rough dunnage paper between stowage blocks of fiberboard containers with smooth exteriors to prevent sliding or shifting.

Bags, Sacks and Bales

Use "crosstier" method of stacking bags and sacks. (Refer to illustration.)

Use sufficient dunnage layer on container deck to provide sump area for condensate drainage.

Separate bags, sacks and bales from other cargo by using partitions or auxiliary decks.

When stowing bales, provide dividers between rows and tiers to prevent chafing and friction between metal bands or strapping.

Liquid Cargo (Drums)

Provide adequate dunnage on container deck to prevent leakage or spillage from damaging lower tiers.

Stow liquid cargo below the other cargo.

Separate liquid cargo from the other cargo by use of partitions and auxiliary decks.

Stow liquid cargo with containers full and bung holes up.

Use dividers to protect drum rims from chafing damage.

COMPLETING THE STOW

Isolate Cargo From Container Doors

Construct partition across rear of stowed cargo to prevent it from contacting doors and falling out when doors are opened.

Provide Water Damage Protection—Cover cargo adjacent to doors with plastic or waterproof paper sheets to protect cargo from possible leakage at door gaskets.

Ventilated Cargo—Be sure air flow in container is unrestricted and that vents are open and clear.

Close and Seal Container—Be sure all locking lugs are engaged.

Affix locks and seals. (On containers with side and end doors—be certain to check both.)

Record seal numbers and enter on shipping documents.

Herman J. Maggiori

Summary

If you have been thinking there is a lot involved in exporting products to foreign countries, you're right! There is a lot to learn—forms, documents, letters of credit—all the ins and outs of getting your products shipped abroad.

The author remembers (barely!) when, as a young international marketing graduate, he was first given a stack of orders and was told to get them invoiced and ready for shipment, and to prepare the necessary documentation. I was ready to quit right then! Foreign trade really seemed "foreign."

In a reasonably short time however, I learned how to do it all, one day at a time. Eventually I was able to teach other scared young men and women the intricacies of export shipping and documentation as I moved up the ladder in my 35-year love affair with sales and marketing and the fascinating world of international operations.

Everything is important! Everything is logical! It can all be done, and in the end, it will all be very profitable.

Chapter 17

OVERSEAS BUSINESS TRAVEL

In the preceding chapters, reference has been made to the need for, and the importance of making personal visits to each of the foreign markets you've chosen to enter for the sale of your products. Overseas travel is very important to international trade. You need to make these visits to conduct your on-site market research, interview, appoint and evaluate distributors, attend and participate in trade shows, and meet personally with customers. Close personal relationships between principals and distributors, agents and customers, play a most important part in the eventual success of your efforts to penetrate overseas markets.

You will be working with many people who have totally different business philosophies and methods from those with whom you may have been accustomed to dealing. They will speak different languages and belong to different cultures in which many, many situations are looked at and treated in a variety of ways which may appear alien to you. It is important that you learn to understand and cope with all of the differences you will encounter in the 20, 50, 80, 100 or more different markets in which you may eventually work.

The only way you can acquire the knowledge and understanding which will enable you to work at peak performance levels with your foreign distributors, agents and customer network, is to visit them on a regular and continuing basis. It is impossible to carry on your international sales program without leaving your office, relying only on correspondence or telephone communication. Issues and problems tackled in face-to-face discussions during personal visits can often be easily resolved in minutes instead of days or weeks.

Domestic sales executives would not think of not being "on the road" on a regular basis to establish and cement personal relationships. In view of the differences existing between American and foreign business connections, how much more important it becomes that the international manager be ready to do as much or more to strengthen his overseas connections with associates who are, and will be, so vital to the execution and fulfillment of his global marketing plan!

Travel to foreign markets and meeting personally with distributors, agents, customers, government agencies and others with whom you should have regular contact in order to conduct your business properly must become one of the major functions of the international sales and marketing executive and any of his staff who have regional sales responsibilities. Remember, your competitors, especially those from foreign countries, will be out there traveling and fighting to get their share of the available business. You must do likewise for your company—and your country.

Planning Your Overseas Trip

There are probably as many different concepts of how to plan and implement a foreign business trip as there are people who take them. Nevertheless, there are basic views and principles that are common to any trip to visit overseas markets. Keep in mind that traveling to, and working in even the most developed countries can be an arduous and strenuous experience. You will often travel for many hours to arrive at your first destination, and probably take several additional long flights as you proceed on your itinerary. Some people like to fly all night, arriving at their first destination in the early morning hours, then take a short nap, freshen up, and start their day's work. Others prefer to take daytime flights and get a good night's sleep before starting work the next morning. In almost all cases you will be working long hours with people who speak a different language and work under very different business ethics and culture. You will be eating strange and different foods, and sometimes have not-so-great accommodations at the end of your long day. It is therefore important that you plan your trip with an awareness of some of the physical limitations foreign travel imposes on you. You must have a clear understanding of your goals and priorities and how you expect to accomplish all that needs to be done. Overseas travel is expensive, so you must consider many things, even minor things, when arranging your trips in order to obtain maximum value for the money and time you will be investing.

Much can be accomplished before the trip begins to ensure that you make the best possible use of your time abroad. Not the least of these is arranging appointments with your distributor for visits to customers or officials in government agencies, obtaining names and titles of people to be visited, mailing ahead quantities of new or needed literature, and writing to U.S. embassies with copies of your itinerary so they can set up appointments for you on arrival.

Experience has shown that at least the following preparations should be carefully planned and carried out for any overseas trip.

1. Work out the travel itinerary

a. Decide on the length of the trip, the cities to be visited, the number of travel days it will take to get to each destination, and the number of working days you will need in each place. Then fix the actual dates for departure and the length of time you expect to stay in each place. Try not to squeeze too much activity into a short two or three day visit to a city. Allow enough time to do a good job with the major issues you need to cover so that you are not exhausted by trying to accomplish too much in a short time.

b. Try to keep some flexibility in the schedule to allow for unexpected situations which may arise. You would not want to miss taking advantage of a good sales opportunity which might require a day's travel to another city.

c. In planning your itinerary, be aware of geography. Try to form your itinerary so you will be visiting contiguous territories in sequence. This will help avoid having to take unduly long flights and the trip will also be more economical if you don't have to backtrack.

d. Problems such as a flight delay may also arise. Be sure your itinerary is not too tight. Most businessmen and women try to schedule departures over a weekend when possible so if a delay occurs, they have extra time to travel to the next destination.

e. When finalizing dates, be sure to check for normal business days, business hours and local holidays. You don't want to be caught by surprise arriving in a city shut down due to a local holiday, or where the practice is to have short work hours. In some countries, the work week may start on Sunday and end on Friday (Israel), or it may start on Saturday and end on Thursday, (Moslem countries). There may typically be long lunch breaks when everyone goes home for two or three hours for lunch, which may also include a siesta. Because of this two-or-three=hour lunch/siesta, the work day can often end at eight or nine o'clock in the evening.

Obtain a list of holidays observed around the world so you can be aware of them. Such lists are available from many U.S. banks and the Department of Commerce field offices. You should also confirm your final itinerary with your distributor as well.

g. As soon as you have a fairly sure idea of your travel plans and dates, advise your distributor or other contacts to arrange appointments and meetings. On an exploratory market survey trip (before having appointed distributors), you should write to the prospects you have selected for interview and to the U. S. Embassies and U.S. Foreign Commercial Service offices so they can schedule interviews through their commercial officers with local prospects.

h. It would be a good idea to schedule travel plans to take advantage of any trade fairs put on by local industry groups, your distributor, or the U.S. Department of Commerce. Schedules of international trade fairs around the world are readily available. In addition, you can get valuable assistance from the Department of Commerce and Department of State Desk Officers in Washington, D. C. who can give you much information about fairs and promotions in many countries.

i. Some international traders may also want to take advantage of participating in trade missions to certain countries sponsored by the Department of Commerce as an aid to U. S. companies wanting to enter or improve their positions in foreign markets or in specific industries in those markets. Trade missions are of various types. There are seminar missions at which U. S. businessmen and women may present scientific or technical papers on their products to potential customers or distributors, after which private meetings with prospects can be arranged.

There are also specialized trade missions led by Department of Commerce officers for participants in specific industries, while other missions are sponsored and led by trade associations or state international trade development agencies.

j. When all of your travel plans are complete, consult and work with either your corporate travel personnel, or an experienced travel agent, to arrange your flights and hotel reservations. Before starting any trip overseas, you should learn as much as possible about the countries you will be visiting since, more than likely, you will be working in unique business and cultural environments. It will help you get along in business and personally if you are aware of such things and know how to react to them.

2. Travel Documents

a. A valid U.S. passport is required for all travel outside the U. S. and Canada, and should be obtained at least two or three months before travel is to start. If you already have a passport, be sure it remains valid for the duration of your trip. Passports can be obtained from some local post offices, local passport offices or the Passport Office in Washington, D.C.

b. Many countries require a visa for entry. Visas can only be obtained from the consulate of the country to be visited. An application form must be completed, and usually two or more recent photographs and your passport are also required. You can apply for your visa personally or through your travel agent. You can send your application, photographs and passport to one of the many visa services who specialize in obtaining visas for travelers at a nominal cost.

You should determine if you will need a business or tourist visa. Different countries have different rules for each type, and some countries require additional documents accompanying the application. For a business visa, some require a letter from your company or an invitation from an association or business contact in the country you wish to visit. It is best to apply for a multiple-entry visa since most visas otherwise limit the validity of the visa to one entry, often to within three or six months of its issue. You may have to go back to the country in a hurry after your first visit. Since visa requirements change from time to time, be sure to check with your travel agent when working on your plans. Some countries allow visitors to obtain a visa at a point-of-entry; however, it can be risky to rely on this because of frequent changes in the rules which may occur without your being aware of them. In any case, most airlines will want to see your visas at check-in and may not allow you to board your flight without a valid visa

c. Another travel document which may be most useful is an ATA carnet. This is a document allowing duty-free entry of product samples. Some countries have high import duties on samples, and importing them may subject the traveler to annoying and time-consuming customs procedures. With a carnet, samples are allowed free entry for a short period of time simply by making a quick stop at the customs counter on entry where the carnet is stamped but no duty need be paid. Upon departure, another short stop at customs is required to stamp the carnet evidencing the sample has been taken out of the country. Full details for using the carnet system can be obtained from the U.S. Council for International Business, 1212 Avenue of the America, New York, New York, 10036.

d. Aside from product samples, the traveler must also be aware that other items which he carries may be subject to customs duties. These include tobacco products, liquor and food products. Check on the limitations and/or permissibility allowed on these items in each country to be visited to avoid any problems or confiscation on entry. For example, many Moslem countries strictly prohibit the importation of any alcoholic beverages and certain publications which may be considered pornographic or anti-religious.

e. Be sure to carry a good supply of business cards. Aside from the obvious need for them, the exchange of business cards is a very important part of the introductory meeting. It is a nice touch to have business cards printed in the language of the country being visited, especially where the local language is written in other than Roman letters (Japan, China, Soviet Union, etc.)

United States Council for International Business
ATA Carnet
Application Package Containing:

- Complete Application, Bonding and Insurance Information
- Instructions on how to complete your Application and General List Forms

---

How to apply for your ATA Carnet...

The applicant for an ATA Carnet will save time and money by proceeding in this order:

1. Read Terms, Definitions, Abbreviations.
2. Read Processing Time, Security Requirements.
3. Read "General List" Instructions (complete enclosed "General List" Form.)
4. Read and complete Bonding/Insurance Instructions and Forms.
5. Read and complete Carnet Processing Fees with example of calculation and your Carnet Fee Worksheet.
6. Read Carnet Application Instructions (complete enclosed "Carnet Application" Form.)

IMPORTANT! After completing all instructions, RETURN the "General List" Form, all "Continuation Sheets," the Guarantee/Bond Form (if applicable) and the Application Form, together with the proper fees in the envelope provided, to the nearest U.S. Council Regional Carnet Issuing Office listed below.

Obtaining a Carnet does not relieve you of the obligation to comply with U.S. export controls. Some articles for reasons of national security, foreign policy and short supply may require an export license. An export license is a U.S. Department of Commerce legal authorization for U.S. companies to export commodities that are controlled by U.S. Export Administration Regulations. If you are in doubt as to what type of license you need before shipping, consult with the U.S. Department of Commerce, Office of Export Administration, (202) 377-4811.

Note: All shipments over $2,500 will require a U.S. Department of Commerce "Shippers Export Declaration" (Form 7525V). Note on your application if you wish the U.S. Council to provide a "S.E.D." with your Carnet.

Description and Instructions for Application and Use of ATA Carnet

Our Issuing Office Locations are:

New York City Headquarters:
1212 Avenue of the Americas, 21st Floor
New York, New York 10036
(212) 354-4480
Telex: 820-864, Fax: (212) 575-0327

New York City—Downtown Office:
39 Broadway, Suite 1915
New York, New York 10006
(212) 747-1800
Telex: 12-5722, Fax: (212) 747-1948

21 Custom House Street, Suite 240
Boston, Massachusetts 01220
(617) 737-1800
Telex: 94-0387, Fax: (617) 951-1468

16 Green Meadow Drive, Suite 117
Timonium, Maryland 21093
(310) 561-0438, Fax: (301) 561-0974

8725 N.W. 18th Terrace, Suite 402
Miami, Florida 33172
(305) 592-6929
Telex 51-4779, Fax: (305) 592-9537

1930 Thoreau Drive, Suite 101
Schaumburg, Illinois 60173
(708) 490-9696
Telex 20-6830, Fax: (708) 885-8710

5300 Memorial Drive, Suite 460
Houston, Texas 77007
(713) 869-5693, Fax (713) 880-4335

3345 Wilshire Boulevard, Suite 502
Los Angeles, California 90010
(212) 386-0767
Telex: 67-4679, Fax (212) 3840363

353 Sacramento Avenue
San Francisco, California 94111
(415) 956-3356, Fax: (415) 394-8758

Now let's get started!

Terms, Definitions and Abbreviations—

ATA Carnet: (Admission Temporaire-Temporary Admission) French and English acronym for the international Customs document used for temporary admission.

ATA Carnet Conventions: Conventions have been established to allow for the temporary importation of different categories of merchandise. The three basic categories which account for most merchandise traveling under Carnet are Commercial Samples (CS), Professional Equipment (PE) and Exhibitions & Fairs (EF). If your merchandise does not fall within these categories, call USCIB Headquarters, in New York, to determine if your merchandise falls within another category.

Claim: A notice from the foreign Customs Authority of the country you have entered that a violation of the Carnet system has occurred.

Counterfoil/Voucher Sheets: The top section of one of these sheets is known as the counterfoil and the bottom section is known as the voucher. Sheets are issued in sets. A yellow set for leaving and re-entering the U.S., a white set for entering and exiting a foreign country and a blue (transit) set for passing through or stopping over in one country in order to enter another. A set of counterfoil/vouchers must be issued for every country you intend to visit, for each exit and re-entry into the U.S., and for each transit.

CS (Commercial Samples): Items for showing or demonstrating in the country of importation for the pupose of soliciting orders.

EF (Exhibitions and Fairs): Means trade, industrial, agricultural or crafts exhibition, fair or similar show or display; exhibition organized for a charitable purpose or to promote learning, craft, scientific or cultural activity, friendship between people, religious knowledge or worship. Does not include exhibits for private purposes in shops or premises with a view to selling.

Expiration Date: This is the formal date for re-exportation given you by the U.S. Council at the time your Carnet was issued. All merchandise must leave the country of importation before midnight on that date.

Final Date for Re-Exportation: The U.S. Council will set an expiration date at the time your Carnet is issued. However, a foreign Customs Authority does have the right to restrict any shipment and require that the goods leave prior to the date granted by the U.S. Council. If a Customs Authority does limit your stay, this will be noted on the importation counterfoil at the time you enter.

General List: A detailed list of all merchandise you intend to ship under a Carnet.

Guarantee/Bond: A form of security to the U.S. Council which will be drawn upon in the event a claim is issued against your Carnet and we must pay a penalty on your behalf to a foreign Customs Authority.

Guaranteeing Association: An association set up in every country within the Carnet system to guarantee to the Customs Authority of a country that all import duties, taxes and penalties will be paid for any claim issued against a Carnet that was not properly utilized. The U.S. Council was authorized by the U.S. Treasury to act as a guaranteeing association for all Carnets that originate in, and enter, the United States.

Holder: A corporation or individual on whose behalf the Carnet has been issued will be known as the Holder. A Holder must have a beneficial interest in the merchandise being exported; therefore, a Customs Broker or Freight Forwarder cannot be listed as a Holder of a Carnet when they are acting in their professional capacity on behalf of someone else.

Import Duties: Means Customs duties and all other taxes and charges payable on or in connection with an importation.

Issuing Association: An association or organization authorized by a guaranteeing association to issue Carnets under its direction.

L/C (Letter of Credit): A form of security (must have prior approval from USCIB Headquarters).

PE (Professional Equipment): Equipment for the press or television broadcasting; cinematographic equipment; equipment for testing or repair of machinery; other equipment for the exercise of the calling, trade or profession of a person visiting abroad to perform a specific task.

Penalty: A duty, tax or charge levied by a foreign Customs Authority against a Carnet which has not been utilized in conformance with all conditions of the Carnet system.

Premium: A non-refundable fee paid by a Holder to a bonding company whenever a Holder elects to post a Guarantee/Bond instead of cash or L/C as Carnet security.

Security: A cash deposit, L/C, Guarantee/Bond or Written Agreement deposited with the U.S. Council to insure the U.S. Council against any loss for penalties it may be called upon to make on behalf of a Carnet holder.

USCIB: United States Council for International Business

Written Agreement (W/A): A form of security (only available to U.S. Council members).

Processing Time Requirements—

Standard Carnet processing time is five (5) working days. We reserve the right to direct applications to any of our offices for processing. However, if faster turnaround time is required, Carnets may be completed and ready for pickup or shipment in less than five working days. Expedited Service rates are: **24 hours-$100, 48 hours-$75, 72 hours-$55, 96 hours-$35.**

Standard Processing Time starts when all required documents are presented to an Issuing Office in acceptable form. Processing time will begin on the next business day for documents received after 3:00 p.m. If Expedited Service is necessary, you must confirm with the Issuing Office that such service is available and/or possible. The Expedited Service fee should be included in your Carnet processing fee check.

Security Requirements—

All Carnet applicants must furnish the U.S. Council with a security deposit. The amount of the deposit will vary according to the country visited. The deposit is used to reimburse the Council in the event it incurs a liability or loss in connection with the issuance of your Carnet, or its use. The security is returned providing the original Carnet has been returned to the U.S. Council at the conclusion of the last covered trip, is in proper order, and no claims or costs are anticipated. When returning your Carnet, request in writing that your security be returned or cancelled. Note, that while Carnets are good for one year only, it may be necessary to hold security for up to 30 months or until any claim has been resolved since it can take that long for claims or costs to reach the Council. The amount of your deposit is based on the total value of all items shown on the General List form, and may be in the form of: A **Certified Check, a Surety Bond, or a Letter of Credit.** Note: Letters of credit are accepted only on application and approval by the U.S. Council Carnet Department Headquarters Office, New York. A non-refundable Letter of Credit processing fee of $75 will be charged. There will be no security required for merchandise valued up to $499.99 (except for Israel and Republic of Korea). Note: Security will not be required for Federal, State and Local Government Agencies. In lieu of security these agencies are to remit a Refundable Claim Deposit of $250 per Carnet which will be returned if the Carnet is returned to the USCIB within 30 days of the expiration date and has been properly validated by each foreign Customs. The deposit is in addition to the Carnet fee and should be remitted on one check. To determine the amount of security you will require see the enclosed Bonding Information and Insurance Packet .

Carnet Processing Fees—with Calculation Example The Carnet processing fee will be a total of: A. **Basic Fee Schedule Determined By Total Shipment Value:**

Shipment Value	Fee	Shipment Value	Fee
Under $5,000	$120	$50,000-199,999	$200
$5,000-14,999	$150	$200,000-499,999	$225
$15,000-49,999	$175	Over $500,000	$250

B. **Expedited Service Fee (if necessary):** See Processing Time Requirements for rate schedule if you elect to use our Expedited Service.

C. **Additional Counterfoil/Voucher Sets:** The Basic Fee includes up to eight sets of the counterfoil/voucher forms. The total number of sets in a Carnet will vary with the number of the countries you plan to visit or transit and the number of U.S. exits und returns. Additional sets of counterfoil/voucher forms are supplied without limit at the rate of $5.00 per set ($20.00 minimum).

D. **Additional General List Pages (Continuation Sheet):** The Basic Fee also includes the first General List (original) page. There is a charge of $5.00 for each Continuation Sheet that you return with your application. (As explained in General List Instructions.)

E. **Shippers Export Declaration:** All shipments over $2,500 will require a completed U.S. Department of Commerce Shippers Export Declaration (Form 7525V) prior to departing. USCIB will provide S.E.D. forms at $5.00 each.

How To Calculate Your Carnet Fee: EXAMPLE: A Carnet applicant submits the General List (original) and three Continuation Sheets of merchandise with a total value of $17,500.00. The applicant plans to leave the U.S., visit seven Carnet countries, und then return to the U.S. Later, the applicant plans to visit Canada four times. This total of 11 visits to member countries and five U.S. exits/ entries will require a total of 16 sets of counterfoil/vouchers. The applicant also requires completion within 48 hours, and has verified that expedited service is available.

CALCULATION	Example	Worksheet
A. **Basic Carnet Fee:** (According to total shipment value)	$175.00	$_____
B. **Expedited Service Fee:** (For 48 hour processing time)	75.00	_____
C. **Additional Counterfoil/Voucher Fee:** For 8 sets (in addition to the 8 which are put of basic fee) 8 x $5.00 = S40.00	40.00	_____
D. **Additional "Continuation Sheets" Fee:** For three sheets (in addition to the original General List which is put of the basic fee) 3 X $5.00 = $15.00	15.00	_____
E. **"Shippers Export Declaration:** (If required)	5.00	_____
Refundable Claim Deposit*:	($250.00)	_____
Total:	$310.00	$_____

*If you are a Federal, State or Local government agency your "Refundable Claim Deposit" will be $250.00

Payment for the total Carnet fee must accompany your application. Make checks payable to the U.S. Council for International Business .

Instructions on How to Complete Your "General List" Forms—

Careful completion of this form is essential, ensuring entry and departure from foreign countries with a minimum of time and trouble. The entire shipment to be covered by the Carnet must be itemized, with each item accurately described and accompanied by a stated value. If your list of merchandise will require more than the first General List page, you must use Continuation Sheets. Number your Continuation Sheets and put the total number used at the bottom of the first General List page. The individual applying for the Carnet, or applying on behalf of a corporation must sign the original General List page and any Continuation Sheets" in the space marked Holder s Signature. Only typed listings are acceptable! Do not list consumable items such as bottle fluids, foods, paper goods, giveaways, etc. Carnets cannot be issued for consumables. A General List form has been included in this application package. If you feel you will require Continuation Sheets simply make photocopies of the General List" form prior to its use.

Your ATA Carnet Application Instructions—

Before completing this application you must first complete your original General List and any Continuation Sheets. You must then determine the type and amount of your security. (See Bonding/Insurance information packet.)

In order to ensure that you will receive your Carnet on time, you must return the ATA Carnet Application fully completed and signed. Read carefully and thoroughly Sections E and F.

Correlate the line item on the Application Form to the line item on these instructions.

A. Applicant Information

1. The corporation, partnership or individual on whose behalf the Carnet is being issued. If a Customs Broker, Freight

Forwarder or agent is completing and signing the Application on behalf of a corporation or individual, a Power of

Attorney must accompany the Application.

2. If a corporation, this is your Federal I.D. number; if an individual, your social security number.

3. If the Holder is a subsidiary, the Parent Company's name and IRS number must be included.

4. Person authorized to sign the Application on behalf of a corporation or partnership. If the Holder is an individual or

Sole Proprietorship enter same. (Also enter Title if appropriate.)

5. Individuals or agents in the U.S. and abroad who, on behalf of the Holder, will be authorized to handle any Customs

clearance transaction.

B. Carnet Preparation Information

6. The category of your merchandise will determine which country will accept your Carnet. If your merchandise is not for PE, CS, EF call USCIB Headquarters in New York to determine if your merchandise falls within another category and if your country of destination accepts that category.

7. Providing the date you intend to leave the U.S. allows us to schedule delivery of your Carnet prior to your departure.

8. If the country you wish to enter under a Carnet is not listed, call your local Carnet representative to confirm if that country is part of the ATA Carnet System.

9. Enables the U.S. Council to issue the correct number of yellow counterfoil/voucher sheets.

10. Enables the U.S. Council to issue the correct number of blue transit sheets. Transit sheets are used when your merchandise is conveyed by land, and must pass

through, or stop over in a country that lies between the country you are leaving and the next country you intend to enter...e.g. leaving France to go to the Netherlands but having to pass through or stop over in Belgium.

C. Shipping Instructions for Completed Carnet

11. When your date of departure will allow ample time to have your Carnet sent to you by U.S. Mail.

12. When you intend to have your own messenger service pick up your Carnet. Your local Carnet representative will call you when your Carnet is ready for pick-up. Make sure your messenger asks for the name listed on your Carnet and not his messenger service s name.

13. When you intend to have us send your Carnet by courier service. Include a completed Airway Bill with your account number. All courier service requests must be billed to your account number.

D. Fees

14. thru 19. use as your guideline the example in How To Calculate Your Carnet Fee on Page 4.

E. Security and F. Obligation

20. Indicate if you elect to post a cash deposit as security. Only Certified Checks are acceptable. Refer to the Bond and Insurance Information Packet for security amount.

21. Indicate if you elect to post a Guarantee/Bond as security. Refer to the Bond and Inswance Information Packet for security amount and Guarantee/Bond requirements.

22. Include your W/A if you are a USCIB member or your L/C if you have received prior approval from USCIB Headquarters.

23. All Applications must be signed and dated.

(Retain a copy of the ATA Carnet Application, General List, any "Continuation Sheets" and Bond, if used, for your records.)

United States Council for International Business
1212 Avenue of the Americas, New York, New York 10036, (212) 354-4480

ATA Carnet Application

A. Applicant Information:

1. Carnet Holder (Corporate or Individual)_____ABC Corporation_____

   Address_____123 Anywhere Lane, Our Town, Illinois 12345-6789_____ Phone No. (123) 456-7890

2. IRS No./SS No.___123456789___

3. Parent Company_____SAME_____ IRS No.___SAME___

4. Person Duly Authorized & Title___John Doe, President___ Phone No. (123) 456-7890

5. Authorized Representative:___Joseph Doe, Sales Manager, XYZ Customs Broker, Freight Forwarder___

B. Carnet Preparation Information:

6. Goods to be exported for: [X] Commercial Samples,   7. Date of departure from U.S.___2/14/91___
   ☐ Professional Equipment, ☐ Exhibitions and Fairs, ☐ Other

8. Check the box next to all countries to be visited and indicate the number of expected visits on the line provided beside each:

☐ _ Australia (AU)	☐ _ Gibraltar (GI)	☐ _ Korea (KR)	☐ _ Senegal (SN)
☐ _ Austria (AT)	☐ _ Greece (GR)	☐ _ Luxembourg (LU)	☐ _ Singapore (SG)
☐ _ Belgium (BE)	☐ _ Hong Kong (HK)	☐ _ Malaysia (MY)	☐ _ South Africa (ZA)
☐ _ Bulgaria (BG)	☐ _ Hungary (HU)	☐ _ Malta (MT)	☐ _ Spain (ES)
☐ _ Canada* (CA)	☐ _ Iceland (IS)	☐ _ Mauritus (MU)	☐ _ Sri Lanka (LK)
☐ _ Cyprus (CY)	☐ _ India (IN)	☐ _ Netherlands (NL)	☐ _ Sweden (SE)
☐ _ Czechoslovakia (CS)	☐ _ Ireland (IE)	☐ _ New Zealand (NZ)	☐ _ Switzerland (CH)
☐ _ Denmark (DK)	☐ _ Israel (IL)	☐ _ Norway (NO)	☐ _ Turkey (TR)
☐ _ Finland (FI)	☐ _ Italy (IT)	☐ _ Poland (PL)	☐ _ U.K. (GB)
[X] _ France (FR)	☐ _ Ivory Coast (CI)	☐ _ Portugal (PT)	☐ _ Yugoslavia (YU)
☐ _ Germany (DE)	[X] _ Japan (JP)	☐ _ Romania (RO)	☐ _ Other

9. Number of times leaving and re-entering U. S:___2___   *Only Certain PE items will be admitted.

10. Countries Transiting:___0___

C. Shipping Instructions For Completed Carnet:

11. ☐ Regular Mail   12. [X] Messenger Pick-up   13. ☐ Courier Service (Completed Airway Bill attached or enclosed.)

D. Fees:

14. Basic Carnet Fee $___175.00___

15. Refundable Claim Deposit $___0.00___
    (Federal, State and Local Gov't Agencies Only)

16. Expedited Service Fee $___75.00___

17. Additional Counterfoil/Voucher Fee $___0.00___

18. "Continuation Sheets" Fee $___5.00___

19. S.E.D. Fee $___5.00___

     Total $___260.00___

E. Security:

20. ☐ Cash--Amount $_____ 21. [X] Bond--Amount $_6,000.00_____ 22. ☐ Other--Amount $_____

In connection with this security, I, as Carnet Holder, agree that the security I have posted as guarantee may be drawn upon to reimburse the U.S. Council for such duties, taxes, charges, and costs incurred by the U.S. Council as a result of my failure to comply with all U.S. Customs or foreign Customs conditions as required by all ATA Conventions, and with all instructions issued by the U.S. Council on the use of my ATA Carnet, or as a result of any breach of the Carnet system. I further agree to reimburse the U.S. Council for any payments made on my behalf that may exceed my security amount. I also understand that if the Carnet is surrendered to the U.S. Council with all used and unused counterfoils/vouchers and the U.S. Council has determined that it has been correctly utilized, the U.S. Council may release me from the guarantee I have furnished prior to the 30 month period.

F. Obligation:

In connection with the use of this Carnet, I as the Holder of Carnet and my representative(s) undertake to timely repatriate under Carnet all of the goods taken abroad, to produce satisfactory and timely evidence to cancel or mitigate any claim issued against my Carnet by a foreign guaranteeing association, to comply with all Customs regulations and requirements both in the United States and abroad, and to accept responsibility for the results of the negotiations or proceedings with any Customs Authority conducted by me as Holder or by the U.S. Council on my behalf. I further agree to return the Carnet to the U.S. Council with all used and unused counterfoils/vouchers within 15 days after my final trip by receipted mail and to retain a copy for my records.

I declare that I have read all of the contents of this application package and that all my statements in connection with this application, and the descriptions and items on the General List, are true and correct.

23.___John Doe, President___   Date___1/23/91___
     (Duly Authorized Signature)

(7)

ATA Carnet Application Form

Herman J. Maggiori

| | INTERNATIONAL GUARANTEE CHAIN | C.I.C | INTERNATIONAL GUARANTEE CHAIN |
| | CHAINE DE GARANTIE INTERNATIONALE | B.I.C.C | CHAINE DE GARANTIE INTERNATIONALE |

GENERAL LIST/*LISTE GENERALE*
(May be used for Continuation Sheets / *Feuille Supplementaire*)

X..X

Signature of Holder / *Signature du titulaire*

Signature of authorized official and stamp of the issuing Association /
Signature du delegué et timbre de L'association emettrice

VOUCHER No............................
VOLET DE No.

CONTINUATION SHEET No.............
FEUILLE SUPPLEMENTAIRE No.

A.T.A. Carnet No.
Carnet A.T.A. No.

Item No./ No. d'ordre	Trade description of goods and marks and numbers, if any/ Désignation commerciale des marchandises et, le cas échéant, marques et numéros	Number of Pieces/ Nombre de Pièces	Weight or Volume/ Poids ou Volume	Value/* Valeur	* Country of origin Pays d'origine	For Customs Use/ Réservé à la douane
1	2	3	4	5	6	7
TOTAL CARRIED OVER / REPORT						

General List includes_____ (number) "Continuation Sheets".

TOTAL or CARRIED OVER/*TOTAL ou A REPORTER*

* Commercial value in country of issue and in its currency, unless stated differently./ *Valeur commerciale dans le pays d'emission et dans sa monnaie, sauf indication contraire*
** Show country of origin if different from country of issue of the Carnet, using ISO country codes./ *Indiquer le pays d'origine s'il est différent du pays d'emission du carnet en utilisant le code international des pays ISO.*

ATA Carnet "General List" Form

312

SECURITY REQUIREMENTS

The amount of security you must deposit with the USCIB is based on:
(1) A percentage of the total value of your merchandise as shown on the General List form.
(2) The countries you intend to visit.

Use the following list to ascertain the percentage required for your country(s) of destination:

Country	Security Amount	Country	Security Amount
Algeria	40%	Korea	100%
Australia	40%	Malaysia	40%
Austria	40%	Mauritis	40%
Belgium/Luxembourg,.	40%	Malta	40%
Bulgaria	40%	Netherlands	40%
Canada	40%	New Zealand	40%
Cyprus	40%	Norway	40%
Czechoslovakia	40%	Poland	40%
Denmark	40%	Portugal	40%
Finland	40%	Senegal	40%
France	40%	Singapore	40%
Germany	40%	South Africa	40%
Gibraltar	40%	Spain	40%
Greece	40%	Sri Lanka	40%
Hong Kong	40%	Sweden	40%
Hungary	40%	Switzerland	40%
Iceland	40%	Turkey	40%
India	40%	United Kingdom	40%
Ireland	40%	Yugoslavia	40%
Israel	100%		
Italy	40%		
Ivory Coast	40%		
Japan	40%		

For instance, if you are travelling to France, Germany and Italy, and the total value of your merchandise is $10,000.00 you must deposit 40% of $10,000.00 to cover all three entries. If you are traveling to Israel and France you must deposlt 100% of the value of your merchandise to cover your entry to Israel. The percent required for each country has been estimated according to the rates of duty and taxes assessed by these countries in the event of claim.

INSTRUCTIONS FOR COMPLETING ENCLOSED CARNET GUARANTEE/BOND

Each Carnet applicant must furnish the U.S. Council for International Business with security. This security may be used to reimburse the U.S. Council for any penalties we must pay on your behalf. Security can be either certified check or Surety guarantee/bond.

For your convenience, a Carnet guarantee in the required form is enclosed. You may submit a guarantee from any Surety of your choice that is included on the list of sureties approved by the Department of the Treasury. All guarantees **must** contain the same text as the attached guarantee form. If you decide to use the form provided the name of the Surety company will be inserted by your Carnet Issuer.

Guarantee Amounts and Premium
1. Every guarantee must be in the penalty amount of 40% of the total value of your merchandise as listed on your general List. (Carnets going to Israel and Korea must have a penalty amount of 100% of the value of your merchandise due to high duty and taxes.)
2. The premium for posting a Carnet guarantee instead of a certified check is 1% of the amount of the guarantee. This 1% premium is of the bond amount and not the value of your merchandise. The premium is not refundable and covers the full 30 month Carnet period. Your returned check will act as your receipt.
3. There is a $50.00 minimum premium for all guarantees, i.e. guarantees with a penalty amount up to $5,000 require the minimum premium of $50.
4. All premium checks for guarantees provided by this office should be made payable to the Corporation for International Business.

Required Applicant Information for Corporations
1. Place Federal ID No. (IRS No.) where indicated.
2. Type Holder's name, (Corporate name) street address, city, state, and zip code.
3. Type in penalty amount of guarantee in words and numbers where indicated (following the words "in the amount of")
4. Date, sign, and seal where indicated at bottom of guarantee. An authorized officer of the corporation must sign on behalf of the Corporation (holder). Affix the Corporate seal (if applicable) next to the officer's name.
5. Complete the Certificate As To Corporate Principal/holder at the bottom of the guarantee. A different officer of the Corporation must complete this section then sign, and again affix the Corporate seal next to his/her name.

Required Applicant Information for Sole Proprietorship/Partnership
1. Place Federal ID No. (If Individual, Social Security number) where indicated.
2. Type holder's name (individual or company's name), street address, city, state, and zip code.
3. Type in penalty amount of guarantee in words and numbers where indicated.
4. Date and sign where indicated.
5. It is not necessary to complete the Certificate As To Corporate Principal/Holder.

Application and completed surety guarantee/bond should be returned to:

UNITED STATES COUNCIL FOR INTERNATIONAL BUSINESS
1212 AVENUE OF THE AMERICAS
NEW YORK, N.Y. 10036
Tel: (212) 354-4480

ATA CARNET GUARANTEE

CARNET NO. _____   Federal I.D.No. _____

KNOW ALL MEN BY THESE PRESENTS: That _____

_____

as Principal (hereinafter called Principal) and certain underwriters at Lloyd's, members of a market organized under the laws of the United Kingdom located in the city of London, England as Surety (hereinafter called Surety) are held and firmly bound unto the UNITED STATES COUNCIL FOR INTERNATIONAL BUSINESS, INC., as Obligee (hereinafter called Obligee) in the amount of, _____ Dollars ($ _____) for payment whereof Principal and Surety bind themselves, their heirs, executors administrators, successors and assigns, jointly and severally, firmly by these presents.

WHEREAS, Obligee has issued the Carnet as numbered above to the Principal; and

WHEREAS, the terms and conditions of said Carnet enable the Principal to enter the goods described therein into the countries specified therein on a temporary basis and require the Obligee to make payment to said countries of any customs duties, excise taxes or charges which may be due as a result of Principal's failure to re-export said goods within the time period allowed; and

WHEREAS, Principal, by written application, has agreed to indemnify the Obligee against loss caused by Principal's failure to so re-export said goods, and to reimburse Obligee for any payments made by Obligee for customs duties, excise taxes and charges resulting from said failure, for which losses or payments Obligee shall be legally liable,

NOW, THEREFORE, THE CONDITION OF THIS OBLIGATION is such that if Principal shall re-export said goods in accordance with the terms of said Carnet, and shall reimburse the Obligee for any payments of customs duties, excise taxes or charges which may be imposed and for which the Obligee is legally liable, resulting from Principal's failure to so re-export said goods, then this obligation to be null and void; otherwise to remain in full force and effect,

SUBJECT, HOWEVER, TO THE FOLLOWING CONDITIONS:
(1) Notice of claim hereunder must be mailed by the Obligee or otherwise transmitted in a manner agreed upon, to the Home Office of the Surety within ninety (90) days from the date the Obligee shall receive its notice of a claim from any country specified in said Carnet.
(2) Regardless of the number of countries specified in said Carnet, and regardless of the periods of time spent in each said country, the liability of the Surety shall not extend to any temporary importation transactions occurring after the expiration of said Carnet, or after one (1) year from the effective date hereof, whichever occurs first.
(3) All suits at law or proceedings in equity to recover on this bond must be instituted within two (2) years of the date Obligee received notice of claim from any specified country.
(4) regardless of the time for which this bond is in effect and regardless of the number of payments hereunder, the maximum liability of the Surety shall not exceed the penalty hereof.
(5) No right of action shall accrue upon or by reason hereof to, or for the use or benefit of, anyone other than the Obligee herein named.
(6) Payment by Surety of claims hereunder shall be due within 30 days from date demand amount shall be determined to be fixed and undisputed.

Signed and sealed this _____ day of _____ ,19 _____

BY: _____ TITLE: _____ BY: _____
(Signature of Authorized Officer or Individual)   (Authorized Signatory for Underwriters at Lloyds)

CERTIFICE AS TO CORPORATE PRINCIPAL/HOLDER

I, _____
_____ certify that I am the * _____
in the within bond; that _____ of the corporation named as Principal
_____ who
signed the said bond on behalf of the Principal was then _____ of said corporation; that I know
his signature, and his signature thereto is genuine; and that said bond was duly signed, sealed, and attested for in behalf of said
corporation by authority of its governing body.
                                         _____
                                         Signature of Certifying Officer

*May be executed by any other officer of the corporation.

315

3. Timing and Length of the Trip

When to travel and for how long, will depend mostly on the business need for the trip and how long you can afford to be away from your office. It is a "given" that the international sales executive's job entails frequent overseas travel, especially if he has a sizeable and far-flung distributor/agent network, and perhaps some sales offices, subsidiary companies or joint-venture partners scattered around the world. The average international businessman takes two or three, four-to-six-week trips, and perhaps several additional one-or-two-week trips during the year.

While this sort of travel cannot always be made during the most pleasant time of the year with respect to favorable climatic conditions in foreign countries, the trips should be planned with an eye to avoiding travel during secular or religious holiday periods. Holidays in foreign countries are very different from those in the U.S.A. Some religious holidays can shut down the entire country for as long as an entire week or more; for example, Holy Week and Easter in most Latin American countries. The weeks before and after Christmas are also a bad period when businesses in many foreign countries are either totally shut down, or at least partially so, and no one is anxious to see foreign visitors. The Muslim Feast of Ramadan, which lasts for a month, during which most of the Middle East population fasts all day, would certainly not be a good time for business visits to that area. Many countries celebrate several religious holidays which vary in dates from year-to-year, so it is wise to check these in advance of any trip-planning.

Most experienced overseas travelers feel that about four to six weeks is the longest trip that should be planned. Beyond that, most people find their efficiency decreases, and they become quite tired. Remember, you have to be "turned on" for as much as ten to fourteen hours a day during your visits with distributors and customers. But as the days and weeks go by, some of the glow of working at top form in different cultures and languages wears off. A shorter trip is more advantageous.

Allow yourself enough time to do a good job in each country you visit. Do not plan to visit more countries than you can comfortably cover competently. On an exploratory trip, when you are seeking distributor prospects and must interview several candidates in each country, you should probably limit the number of countries visited to six or seven in a six-week trip.

After you have established your distributor network, you can probably cover a few more countries in a shorter time on trips made to reinforce relationships, to evaluate or motivate distributors, and to resolve a few problems.

4. Beware Circadian Dyschronism! (Jet Lag)

One of the real "hazards" of foreign travel is the effect on body rhythms when crossing three or more time zones on long, eastward or westward flights. The body's circadian rhythms become "misaligned." It tries to realign its various rhythms to the destination clock, but until they all catch up with each other, you suffer what is commonly called "jet lag." People feel its effects in different ways. Some experience an out-of-sorts feeling. Others experience extreme fatigue, sleeplessness, loss of appetite or some form of disorientation. The more time zones crossed, the more symptoms one feels. Circadian research, which studies the rhythms of sleep and wakefulness, has found that sunlight can have a beneficial effect on resetting one's body clock to the time at the foreign destination. According to this research, after crossing up to six time zones in an eastward direction, you should spend some time out-doors in the morning; in the evening if you have traveled westward. After crossing more than six time zones, you should get some midday sun if you have traveled eastward or westward. Avoid morning sun or late-afternoon sun if you are traveling westward. Many experts support the theory that internal body rhythms of all life on earth can be advanced or delayed by out-door light.

Plan to allow time in your itinerary for adjusting to the time zones you will enter so that you can do your most effective work. Don't plunge right into your work as soon as you arrive. It takes a couple of days for your body and reflexes, thinking and reactions, to adjust to the new schedule.

5. Choosing Hotels

Hotel reservations should be made well in advance of your departure, preferably at the same time your travel agent or corporate travel people confirm your flight schedules. If your trip will coincide with the heavy tourist-travel season, it is extremely important that all reservations be made early.

The choice of hotels is a matter of personal preference. Because of the nature of overseas travel however, you would be wise to select deluxe or first class hotels. Throughout your trip you will be working at top physical and emotional capacity. Having a comfortable and pleasant room in which to rest, relax and work in your off-hours will do much to recharge your energies. Having a nice, well appointed room, can also be an asset if you will be conducting interviews or other business meetings here.

You also need a hotel which offers fast laundry service and prompt room service, and which features the additional services required by businessmen, such as fax, telex, translators and interpreters. The staff in top quality hotels will probably be bi-lingual, which will make your life much easier in many ways.

In many countries the top hotels are often the social centers of the major cities, and in many cases house the best restaurants and bars. This will facilitate your entertainment chores and probably delight your local business contacts to be invited there for drinks or dinner.

Many hotel chains now have "frequent stay" programs which feature room upgrades, (often to suites) and many other amenities. Take advantage of them! In strange countries, and after long, tiring days of hard work, you will want and appreciate some of the "comforts of home" which these programs provide.

The location of the hotel in relation to the location of your business associates and customers should be considered so you and your distributor will not waste a lot of time traveling to and from the part of the city in which you will be working. You will save on taxi fares also.

If, on a particular trip, you will be working on a long-term project, perhaps for several weeks, you should consider renting a small apartment or cottage for the length of your stay. Rental prices could be 25 to 40 percent less than hotel rates and would give you an opportunity to learn what it's like to live in a foreign city since you could eat at local restaurants or shop at local stores for some meals you might want to have "at home."

One of your best sources of information and assistance at most top-rated hotels will be concierge; the man (or sometimes woman) wearing crossed golden keys in both jacket lapels. Whether you need business information, the name of a good restaurant, theatre tickets, or assistance in selecting flowers to bring to your distributor's wife who has invited you to dinner, the concierge will always have ready answers. Most of them are storehouses of information about the city, its banks, stores, entertainment and travel information, and will perform many small tasks for you which could otherwise take you hours to do.

6. Packing For the Trip

Travel light! Aside from having to pay stiff excess baggage charges on airlines, you may, in some places, have to carry your own bags without benefit of carts or porters. Also, the more you carry, the less organized you will be when you have to repeat the packing and unpacking process. Unless absolutely necessary, do not lug quantities of catalogs, samples, displays etc. with you. Ship them to your various destinations, but make sure to allow time for them to arrive and clear customs before you do. Ship personal things addressed to yourself at your hotel or your distributor's office marked "Hold for Arrival on (list date)."

Experienced travelers carry one three-suiter suitcase, an attache case for business papers and small personal articles, and a small carry-on with an extra set of toiletries, a shirt, underwear, and any medications which you cannot be without. The carry-on can be a lifesaver should your checked baggage be lost or delayed. (More about that later.)

What you actually pack will be determined by how long you will be traveling, and the climate(s) you will encounter. Sometimes you may be in both tropical or cold climates on the same trip, so you will have to pack separate clothing for each. Following is an example of what to pack for a four to six week trip.

- Two suits (conservative) plus the one you wear traveling.
- One sports jacket and a pair of slacks
- Eight dress shirts plus a couple of sport shirts. (Try to coordinate suits, shirts, ties and socks so you don't have to carry too many different "matches" of each article of clothing.)
- Two pairs of comfortable shoes, plus a pair of running or casual shoes. (Never take brand new shoes. Make sure you have worn them for a while and that they are comfortable. You don't want blisters or tight shoes.)

- Four or five neckties.
- Eight sets of underwear and socks
- A sweater
- Four or five coordinated neckties
- Pajamas
- Handkerchiefs
- A raincoat (a light-weight one for tropical areas)
- Swim trunks—(most good hotels have pools which are great foreunwinding after a busy day and for relaxing on free weekends.)
- Toilet articles
- A good book (for long plane rides or long waits in airports.

For the Woman Executive
- Two or three suits plus a travel outfit
- Four or five blouses which can be washed and drip-dried.
- One dressy dress (not cocktail), plus a dressy skirt and blouse.
- Two pairs of shoes, plus the one you wear for travel. One pair should be heels. (use basic colors to go with everything). Also one basic color handbag and one evening bag.
- Three sets of underwear which can be washed daily.
- Pantyhose (6 pairs)
- A sweater or light jacket
- A raincoat
- Make-up and toilet articles
- Basic jewelry (never leave jewelry in your room. If it is valuable, leave it in the hotel safe along with your traveler's checks and passport).
- One nightgown—drip dry which can be washed daily.
- A good book for long plane rides or waits in airports.

There are also a few other indispensable items you will need to pack:
- A travel alarm clock (wake-up calls in hotels are not always totally dependable.)
- Camera and film (it's expensive overseas)
- If your personal grooming accessories do not have dual-voltage,

carry a voltage converter which transforms the overseas power on shavers, hair dryers, or other electrical accessories from 220/240 volts to 110 volt U.S. power.

- Adapter plugs. Since wall outlets in most foreign countries do not take the flat pin plugs used on U.S. appliances, take along adapter plugs so you can connect your items. These can be purchased in a set of four different-shaped and length pins to fit most outlets around the world. If you come upon an odd one, your hotel concierge can probably loan you one which will fit.
- A few plastic bags, scotch tape, small scissors and a pocketknife with a corkscrew.
- An extra set of luggage keys—carried separately.

While there might be many other items you consider indispensable, don't go overboard and load up with a lot of "gimmicks" you won't use. After a couple of trips you will learn just which items you cannot do without....everyone has different needs.

A good rule to follow before packing is to make a check-list of everything you think you will need for the trip for business and personal needs. Then go over the list carefully and eliminate everything you honestly do not feel is essential. Strive to keep your luggage light. Not all airports or train stations have baggage carts or porters, and in some places you may have to carry your own bags for a considerable distance.

7. The Anxiety of Lost, Misrouted or Delayed Baggage

As a frequent traveler, your chances of facing a lost baggage problem will be proportionately higher than the average traveler's. Last year, about seven airline passengers of every 1,000 filed claims for lost, damaged or pilfered baggage. While these odds do not appear too bad when you consider the millions of pieces of baggage annually checked onto airlines around the world, you could be one of a substantial number of passengers who have to endure the inconvenience of arriving in a strange city while their baggage is on its way to another.

Most lost luggage eventually turns up. But there can be a lot of anxiety and discomfort before you actually get it back. When it does come back to you, the bag itself may be damaged or its contents may have been pilfered.

Short of traveling with only carry-on baggage, which is usually impractical for a long overseas trip, there are several things which can be done to minimize the chances that your bags will find their way to Buenos Aires while you land in Caracas.

- Put your name and address on a secure tag on the outside of the bag as well as on a label inside.
- Use your company address, especially on the outside of the bag. There are people who make a "business" of collecting names and addresses from baggage at airline counters or luggage carousels, and pass them on to associates to burglarize travelers' homes.
- Check in at the airline counter at least an hour before international fight times.
- Make sure the correct three-letter destination airport code is on the ticket attached to your bag, and also on the baggage claim check given to you. Hang on to this as it is your only proof of checked baggage.
- Put essentials in a carry-on bag — "just in case" (see "Packing for the Trip")
- Luggage is most often lost or delayed when you are traveling on an interline trip—transferring en route from one line to another, or even when changing aircraft on the same airline. It is important that you allow ample time between connecting flights for your baggage to be transferred.
- Many travelers compile a list of the contents (and their costs) of each checked bag, and some even carry a photograph of the bag to help process a claim if it is lost.
- If a bag is lost or damaged, file a written claim with the airline baggage office immediately, before you leave the airport! If the bag cannot be found shortly after your arrival, some airlines may give you some sort of compensation, but this is subject to negotiation, depending upon the airline. Often the most you can expect is a toiletry kit or a small sum for some essentials.
- If your bag is not located in a "reasonable" time, usually two or three weeks, and is considered lost, you will probably have to fill

out a more detailed claim form which then becomes your financial claim. The usual wait to receive compensation can be another two months.

- Do not expect to recover 100% of your loss. When you file a claim for loss, you will have to itemize the contents and note each item's age and cost (include the cost of the lost suitcase too.) Worn or used items will be depreciated, and no airline accepts liability for cash, jewelry or other valuables claimed to have been in the suitcase. Liability of airlines for lost baggage on international flights is drastically less than on domestic U.S.A. flights, and is based on an old (circa 1929) international treaty called the Warsaw Convention. In accordance with this treaty, you may receive only a maximum of about US$360 for a bag weighing 40 pounds, regardless of the possibly higher value of its contents, or the bag itself!

- Several types of insurance are available to cover lost baggage. Before purchasing any other policy, check your homeowner's policy which may also cover loss or theft of your personal property (luggage) while you are traveling. Many of the major credit card companies provide what is called "supplemental baggage insurance" when you charge your flight tickets on their card. "Supplemental Coverage" gives you compensation for claims which the airline disallows (although they will usually not cover you for jewelry, cash or other such valuables in the lost baggage.) One major card also covers losses if your bags arrive late. In most cases the supplemental coverage is optional for a small fee for each trip. There are also many private insurers who sell baggage-loss protection at airports and through travel agencies.

If your luggage is lost, be sure to follow up regularly with the airline's claim department so your claim doesn't get lost in the shuffle.

You are also entitled to file a claim if your suitcase or its contents are damaged. The airline should pay for its depreciated value, or if it is repairable, give you a list of shops which they authorize to repair your bag at their expense.

8. Business Gifts

Should you take business gifts along with you on your overseas trips? Most international businessmen do take small, inexpensive gifts such as pens, knives, small desk accessories, or key chains, often with their company name or logo on them. Some bring more expensive gifts, such as pictorial books of the region or state in which the U.S. company is located, for distributors or valued customers with whom they have had a long and successful business relationships.

Gifts are always welcomed, especially if they are personalized for the recipients. They should not, however, be overly expensive so they take on the aspect of a bribe, nor should they be so cheaply made as to be considered "junk." In some countries, exchanging gifts is a ritual, but you must be careful not to outdo your host while still giving him an appropriate gift. Giving business gifts is a nice thing to do and helps to establish friendly, pleasant feelings during your visits.

9. You and Your (Company's) Money

Overseas business travel is costly, but it is necessary and can be very profitable if you do your job properly. Your company will get to keep most of those profits if you are sensible about watching how you spend its money while traveling. Many companies have established policies and guidelines for overseas travelers regarding the class of air travel, hotels, rental cars, and the types and amount of entertainment.

Unfortunately, most business travelers cannot take advantage of the many low airline rates available to tourists because of the restrictions which usually apply to these special fares. These include having to make reservations (which cannot be changed) many weeks before departure date, departure and return limited to certain days of the week, total travel limited to perhaps seven or 14 days, number of stopovers limited to one or two days etc. etc. It is, of course, worth checking for any special airline deals when you are planning your trip, but unless you happen to be going to one or two contiguous markets where you will stay for a designated time, and will be there at the prescribed dates, you will have to travel at the so-called unrestricted fares.

Many companies will allow business-class air travel for flights of six or more hours; very few authorize first-class air travel.

When renting a car overseas, be aware that foreign car rental companies have different policies from U. S. firms. Even foreign branches of U.S. car rental firms may not offer the same deals as they do at home. This is especially true of one-way rentals where the drop-off charges can be super high. Drop-off charges on one-way rentals often vary, based on whether it is returned in the country in which it was rented, or in another country. In some European countries however, some companies allow you to return cars in certain cities in another country with no drop-off charge. Since rental-car companies policies are subject to frequent changes, it is best to check all policies carefully based on your driving plans and itinerary. When checking rates and drop-off charges in Europe, don't forget to take into account the often costly VAT (value-added tax) levied throughout Europe. The VAT on car rentals ranges from a low of 12% in Spain, to a high of 33% in France. While the tax is refundable on certain purchases over specified values, it is not refundable for car rentals. The VAT is levied in the country where the car is picked up, not where it is dropped off!

Exchanging your dollars for local currency can be tricky and could cost you more than you might expect if you are not careful of when and where you do it. Most countries have stringent currency control regulations and many have "official" rates of exchange. No matter what the rate may be, it will cost you a service charge to exchange your dollars into local currency.

How well you do in exchanging your dollars will depend upon the current strength or weakness of the dollar. If the dollar is rising, do not change your dollars to foreign currency ahead of time, nor should you change too much when you arrive at your destination. Try to estimate how much you will need for small expenses (taxis, tips, incidentals etc.) and charge everything else on a credit card. These charges are not converted to U. S. dollars until the issuer of the card records the charge. Even if the card company charges a nominal 1% fee, you could still come out ahead when you are billed.

If the dollar is falling, you should consider changing a little more of your money and using it to pay most bills. This, however, could mean you would have to carry more traveler's checks (you should not carry too much cash in any case!) and charge less on your credit cards.

Whether the dollar is going up or down, you should not exchange your dollars for a lot of the currency of the first country you are visiting and expect to change it for currency of the next country (or countries) when you arrive there. You would do much better to change just the dollars you need in each country you are visiting in order not to keep losing money through excessive service charges and the different (usually lower) values for other foreign currency exchanges which you would be receiving. Keep your exchange receipts as you may need to show them at a bank when you want to exchange your remaining currency into dollars when you leave a country.

In many countries, hard currencies, such as the U.S. dollar, are greatly sought after. You will, no doubt, run into many taxi drivers, hotel porters or local people on the street who will want to buy your dollars at much higher rates than you could get at your hotel or even at a bank. Do not be tempted to do this. It is against the law of all countries and you could get into serious trouble and jeopardize your company and your business. Do all your currency exchanging at a local bank where you get the best rate, or at your hotel, which is an authorized exchange agency. Check with each to see which will give you the best rate.

Another concern of the overseas traveler is the daily living expense in foreign countries. Regardless of the position of the dollar the time you are traveling, don't be surprised to find that your "living costs" in most countries are high for hotels, meals, laundry, dry cleaning and entertainment—the basic expenses of an international businessman.

An additional expense to keep in mind is that some 50 or so countries charge a departure tax payable at the airport before boarding a flight. While some require payment of this tax in local currency, most will accept payment in dollars. These taxes range from a low of $2.00 in Yugoslavia, to $15.50 in Japan, the average being about $8.00. Check before you leave your hotel or exchange your local currency back to dollars.

As suggested earlier, don't carry large sums of money even in traveler's checks. You should take an "advance" from the company against your small or daily expenses and charge everything else on a major credit card. You will be safer in case of loss. You won't have to pay the service charges for exchanging dollars frequently or in large amounts, and your company will have the benefit of deferred payment of your larger bills until after you have submitted your expense account or been invoiced by the credit card company.

10. The Fine Art of Tipping

There are several types of "tippers" ranging from the big spender to the tightwad. Everyone has his or her style of tipping for the variety of situations that seem to require additional "payment" for services rendered. Most traveling executives fall somewhere in the mid-range when it comes to tipping. The amount of a tip should be based on the quality and type of service given, but you must also consider the local customs and the country you are in. In the Peoples Republic of China, tipping for anything is frowned upon. A tip is not expected in Tokyo for a bellman carrying your bags, for a head waiter or a taxi driver. (The same is true for taxi drivers in Australia.)

In some countries a service charge (read tip) of 10–15% is added to your bill in hotels and restaurants. If this is done in restaurants, the custom is usually to round off the bill leaving a few small (but not too small) coins for the waiter. It is helpful also to figure out which local coin or bill is worth about fifty cents or one dollar and tip that amount for services such as carrying your luggage, checking your coat etc. If someone, for example the concierge, gives you some special service such as booking seats at a theatre or a special event, or making phone calls in the local language, or giving some other form of special assistance, a tip should be given. It is always a good idea to ask the concierge what the appropriate tips should be in the country you're visiting. Common sense helps too.

11. The Great Telephone Rip-off!

Calling home from overseas can be hazardous to your wallet and your temper. Many hotels around the world are reaping huge profits from what is really an outright scam—the telephone surcharge added to your bill when you place a direct-dial, long-distance telephone call. Most hotels charge something for telephone calls, local or long-distance—usually $1.00 or less. But a few years ago many started adding charges from as low as 40% up to 200-300% or more to calls made from the hotels on a direct-dial basis. No amount of arguing or cajoling has been successful in cancelling such charges once they appear on your bill.

There are, however, ways to avoid the surcharges. Direct dialing should be your last resort to placing a call to your office. Before doing so, you should try to make your calls by credit card or collect using either AT&T's "USA Direct," or MCI's "Call USA." These are "express call" services which connect you by means of special access numbers to a U.S. operator who can then place your call. You are then billed (in the U.S.A.) by AT&T or MCI at their rates while the hotel charges you only for a local call. AT&T's "USA Direct" can be reached from over 50 countries including 13 in Europe. MCI's service is available in seven European countries and Australia. If you're in a country where you cannot reach either "USA Direct" or "Call USA," you can still avoid the surcharges by placing a collect call through the hotel operator. If the operator delays giving you a line for the collect call (hoping you will direct-dial), keep calling the operator until you get through. If things get too annoying, (and they can) arrange to have your office call you at a specified time.

12. Traveling Healthy

Try to be as fit and rested as possible before you start your trip. You don't need to be a traveling drug store to stay healthy on a trip overseas. If you are taking any prescription medications, be sure to take an extra quantity with you in case your trip is extended or you lose them. Pack one lot separately. Also take with you a duplicate prescription, (have your doctor type it for legibility) which includes the generic and trade names of the medication. The dosage should be clearly noted. Names and doses of drugs may differ in many countries.

The average person needs only an anti-diarrheal (Lomotil is one commonly prescribed) and an antibiotic (for example, Keflex) for severe cases or other infections. Talk to you doctor before leaving to learn how and when to take these and any other medications he might recommend and prescribe. Be sure to pack a supply of aspirin, band-aids and antacids. For many countries an insect repellent is very important, not only for your comfort, but to guard against the many diseases transmitted by mosquitoes and other bugs.

Should you need a doctor while overseas, the best advice is to call the American Embassy or Consulate and ask for the name of a reputable English-speaking doctor (or dentist). If this is not possible, ask the concierge to contact the hotel doctor for you.

There are some basic precautions you should take while working and traveling. You will soon discover that working overseas for long hours in strange countries, in hot, tropical climates and perhaps high altitudes, eating strange foods and taking off every few days for a new destination, soon begins to take its toll on you. Do your best to get as much rest as possible. In high altitudes take it easy the first couple of days, and also go easy on alcoholic beverages. At 7,000 feet or so they pack twice the wallop as at sea level! Don't eat a heavy meal just before going to bed. Pace yourself when walking around a high-altitude city. You can find yourself panting and your heart thumping even when you are not moving around! Above all, do not drink the water from any tap—not even in hotels where a tap is marked "potable water." You risk contracting any number of parasitic diseases, including typhoid fever or cholera. You should drink only bottled water or soda and without ice, which is probably made from the tap water. You'll find that in many countries, even the "locals" drink only bottled water.

For the same reasons, don't eat any uncooked foods. Peel your own fruits, and be very careful about eating raw or undercooked shellfish, especially in Third World countries. Make sure it is steaming hot when served to you.

Some weeks before starting your trip, check with your doctor and the nearest U.S. Public Health Center or the Federal Centers for Disease Control in Atlanta (404-332-4559 or 404-332-4455) for information about health conditions in the countries you'll be visiting. Find out if they recommend any immunizations or other preventive medicine against cholera, yellow fever, malaria, etc. Also find out if some "shots" are required for re-entry into the United States or for entry from one foreign country into another. Some immunizations can cause severe reactions when given, so plan ahead since you don't want to start the trip feeling sick. In addition, some preventive treatments, such as that for malaria, are supposed to be started at least two or three weeks before departure, and some are given in a series a week or two apart.

If you are in a tropical country, even when fully clothed, you should be very careful about being out in the sun for too long, especially without a hat. If doesn't take long to get sun-stroke. If you are lying on a beach or at a pool, don't remain there too long. You can get a severe sunburn in a very short time which could be bad enough to cause you to lose working days. Invest in a good pair of sunglasses to block the ultraviolet rays of the sun. Use a good sunscreen on your face and neck, and on all exposed parts of your body.

Moderation is the key to staying healthy while traveling or working abroad. Don't eat too much. Watch carefully what you eat and drink, and get some rest whenever you can. Most foreigners are very hospitable and will entertain you constantly if you let them. It's o.k. to beg off diplomatically once in a while...order something from room service, plan your next day, read a book, and go to bed early. It will do you a world of good. Use your common sense and you will stay well.

13. How to Travel Safely

You should be aware of the potential problems and hazards of traveling overseas in order that you can plan how to avoid them or to cope with them should an untoward incident occur.

Learn as much as you can about local conditions and developments in the places you plan to visit. If the media are reporting demonstrations, strikes or other disturbances, you should stay away from areas where such things are taking place. Don't be curious and feel you want to see it happening. Read about it, or watch it on television the next day. Warnings are issued to U. S. travelers by the State Department which publicizes any dangerous situations including health risks, terrorism, or other civil disturbances. You can also call the State Department's Citizen's Emergency Center Hotline for information before you leave at 201-647-5225 on any weekday during office hours.

Keep in mind that U. S. Embassy or Consular offices cannot guarantee your safety overseas. All they can do is act as liaison between you, the traveler, and the U. S. Government. It is important therefore, that you recognize that you are not "protected" by U. S. representatives abroad even though they can help in some ways. If you arrive in a country where there is unrest or other serious problems, register in person with the nearest embassy or consulate so they know you are there. They can then reach you should your office or family not be able to get in touch with you because of local problems, or if you have become ill and possibly hospitalized. If you lose your money, or it is stolen, they can tell you how and when you can obtain some cash. A new passport can also be issued if you have lost yours.

Above all, familiarize yourself with local laws and rules. Just because you are an American citizen, you are not immune from prosecution if you break any laws. Don't get involved in any situations involving drugs or black market activities especially with currency. If you do get into any legal difficulties, contact a consular officer at once. Even though they cannot give you legal advice or act as your attorney, they can help you find legal representation. If you are arrested, consular officials can visit you, ensure you are held in good conditions, and advise you of your rights under local laws.

Following are a few additional tips and precautions to help you travel safely and assure your personal security.

- Dress and behave conservatively. Avoid drawing attention to yourself.
- Avoid dangerous areas, narrow alleys, poorly lit streets, and don't travel alone at night.
- Don't give your hotel room number to anyone you don't know well. Keep your door locked at all times. It is best to meet visitors in the lobby and escort those whom you know to your room for a meeting or visit.
- Use the hotel safety-deposit boxes (usually free) to safeguard your extra cash, traveler's checks, passport, airline tickets and other valuables. Do not leave any of these items in your room while you are not there.
- Be alert for street gangs operating in large cities. If confronted, don't fight attackers.
- If you are robbed of your valuables, report the loss to the police and keep a copy of the police report for insurance purposes. You should report the loss of your passport to the nearest U. S. Embassy or Consulate, airline tickets to the airline company, and traveler's checks to the office of the issuing company.
- If you can, take a room above the second and below the eighth floors to prevent easy entry at ground level and to assure fire equipment can reach your floor in the event of a fire.
- Make notes of the telephone numbers you may need in case of an emergency or illness—your distributor's home, police, fire, U. S. Embassy. Learn how to use local pay phones and have some change

or telephone tokens handy. Learn a few phrases in the local language to enable you to ask for help if necessary.

- If you use rental cars, it is wise to use the common types locally available. Make sure the care is in good condition, keep your doors locked, wear seatbelts, and don't pick up hitchhikers.

Many people overseas are concerned about the possibility of terrorism, hijacking or hostage-taking. The best advice in these situations is that given by the U. S. Department of State, Bureau of Consular Affairs, in its Publication 9493. Pertinent parts of that publication are reprinted below:

Protecting Yourself Against the Possibility of Terrorism

Terrorist acts occur in a random and unpredictable fashion which makes it impossible to protect oneself absolutely. The first and best way is to avoid travel to unsafe areas —areas where there has been a persistent record of terrorist attacks or kidnappings. The vast majority of foreign states have a good record of maintaining public order and protecting residents and visitors within their borders from terrorism. Most terrorist attacks are the result of long and careful planning. Just as a car-thief will first be attracted to an unlocked car with the key in the ignition, terrorists are looking for undefended, easily accessible targets who follow predictable patterns. The chances that a tourist, traveling with an unpublicized program or itinerary, would be the victim of terrorism are slight: the random possibility of being in the wrong place at the wrong time. In addition, many terrorist groups, seeking publicity for political causes within their own country or region, are not looking for American targets.

Nevertheless, the pointers below may help you avoid becoming an American "target of opportunity." They should be considered as adjuncts to the tips listed in the previous section for ways to protect yourself against the far greater likelihood of falling prey to ordinary criminal activity. The following are additional reasonable precautions which may provide some degree of protection, and can serve as practical and psychological deterrents to would-be terrorists.

- Schedule direct flights if possible. Try to minimize the time spent in the public area of an airport, which is a less protectable area. Move quickly from the check-in counter to the secured areas. On arrival, leave the airport as soon as possible.
- Be aware of what you discuss with strangers, or what may be overheard by others.
- Avoid luggage tags, dress, and behavior which may identify you as an American. While sweatshirts and T-shirts with American university logos are commonly worn throughout Europe, leave other obvious U.S. logos or apparel at home.
- Keep an eye out for suspicious abandoned packages or briefcases. Report them to airport security or other authorities and promptly leave the area.
- Avoid obvious terrorist targets and places where Americans and Westerners are known to congregate.

HIGH-RISK AREAS

If you must travel in an area where there has been a history of terrorist attacks or kidnappings, also make it a habit to:

- Discuss with your family what they would do in case of an emergency, in addition to making sure your affairs are in order before leaving home.
- Register with the U. S. Embassy upon arrival.
- Remain friendly, but be cautious about discussing personal matters, your itinerary, or program.
- Leave no personal or business papers in your hotel room.
- Watch for people following you or "loiterers" observing your comings and going.
- Keep a mental note of safe havens, such as police stations, hotels, and hospitals.
- Let someone else know what your travel plans are. Keep them informed if you make any changes.
- Avoid predictable times and routes of travel, and report any suspicious activity to local police, and the nearest U. S. Embassy or consulate.

- Select your own taxicabs at random—don't take a cab which is not clearly identified as a taxi. Compare the face of the driver with the one posted on his license.
- If possible, travel with others.
- Be sure of the identity of visitors before opening the door of your hotel room. Don't meet strangers at unknown or remote locations.
- Refuse unexpected packages.
- Formulate a plan of action for what you will do if a bomb explodes or there is gunfire nearby.
- Check for loose wires or other suspicious activities pertaining to your car.
- Be sure your vehicle is in good operating condition in case you need to resort to high-speed or evasive driving.
- Drive with the windows closed in crowded streets; bombs can be thrown through open windows.
- If you are ever in a situation where somebody starts shooting, drop to the floor or get down as low as possible and don't move until you are sure the danger has passed. Do not attempt to help rescuers and do not pick up a weapon. If possible, shield yourself behind or under a solid object. If you must move, crawl on your stomach.

HIJACKING/HOSTAGE SITUATION

While every hostage situation is different and the chance of becoming a hostage is very remote, some considerations are important.

The U. S. Government's policy not to negotiate with terrorists is firm— doing so only increases the risk of further hostage-taking by terrorists. When Americans are abducted overseas, we look to the host government to exercise its responsibility under international law to protect all persons within its territories and to bring about the safe release of the hostages. We work closely with these governments from the outset of a hostage-taking incident to ensure that our citizens and other innocent victims are released as quickly and safely as possible.

The most dangerous phases of most hijacking or hostage situations are the beginning and, if there is a rescue attempt, the end. At the outset, the terrorists typically are tense, high-strung, and may behave irrationally. It is extremely important that you remain calm and alert and manage your own behavior.

- Avoid resistance and sudden or threatening movements. Do not struggle or try to escape unless you are certain of being successful.
- Make a concerted effort to relax. Breathe deeply and prepare yourself mentally, physically, and emotionally for the possibility of a long ordeal.
- Try to remain inconspicuous, avoid direct eye contact and the appearance of observing your captor's actions.
- Avoid alcoholic beverages. Consume little food and drink.
- Consciously put yourself in a mode of passive cooperation. Talk normally. Do not complain, avoid belligerency, and comply with all orders and instructions.
- If questioned, keep your answers short. Don't volunteer information or make unnecessary overtures.
- Don't try to be a hero, endangering yourself and others.
- Maintain your sense of personal dignity, and gradually increase your requests for personal comforts. Make these requests in a reasonable low-key manner.
- If you are involved in a lengthier, drawn-out situation, try to establish a rapport with your captors, avoiding political discussions or other confrontational subjects.
- Establish a daily program of mental and physical activity. Don't be afraid to ask for anything you need or want—medicines, books, pencils, papers.
- Eat what they give you, even if it does not look or taste appetizing. A loss of appetite and weight is normal.
- Think positively; avoid a sense of despair. Rely on your inner resources. Remember that you are a valuable commodity to your captors. It is important to them to keep you alive and well.

14. Consider Using the Local Railways

In some parts of the world, notably in Europe, you should consider including some rail travel in your itinerary instead of using air travel. Traveling by train between cities and countries can be relaxing and interesting and will usually not take you any longer to arrive at your destination than flying.

Many countries have progressed much more than the United States in developing very fast, comfortable trains that are really a joy to travel on, e.g. the T.G.V. (Train A Grande Vitesse) in France or the Bullet trains in Japan. There are now express trains traveling between most cities in Europe at speeds of 100-plus miles per hour. The Euro-City System links every country in Europe (except Portugal) with trains averaging 98 m.p.h. including stops, and will soon have trains as fast as 140 m.p.h.

Trains usually leave from and arrive in the City Center; the train station is often within walking distance of your hotel.

On the way you will have relaxed, maybe have time to read, do your expense account, or write a report on your last visit. You will also have a chance to see the countryside at lot closer than you would from an airplane flying at 15,000 or 20,000 feet.

One of the most beautiful of such train rides is between Zurich and Milano. You travel through the Alps, through the 9.4 mile long St. Gotthard Pass and see some of the most spectacular mountain and valley scenery in the world.

Many trains also have dining cars serving excellent food, sleeping cars for overnight travel, and telephones for calling your business associates. First or second-class trains are very comfortable, although the latter tend to be more crowded.

Train departures in most European countries are very conveniently spaced so you can leave in early morning and arrive in many cities early enough to accomplish some work with your business contacts. An added benefit is that rail travel is considerably less costly than the one-way air fare or car rentals would be between most cities.

A word of caution though: Confine such travel to the more populated areas of the world rather than through the more remote areas of some countries—there are a few latter-day Jesse James boys still practicing the dubious art of holding up trains.

15. Minding Your Manners

Yes, you learned good table manners and the social graces from your parents. You are a civilized, educated person who can get along well with anyone and can be counted on to do and say the right thing. Right? Probably not. At least, probably not overseas, unless you've taken the trouble to learn how people in different cultures eat their food, meet and work with one another, socialize and react to a great variety of different situations— including how they react to an American businessman visiting them in their country.

As an international executive you must understand that people in foreign countries do many things that are very different from the way we might do them. In order not offend them in either social or business relationships, you will have to learn what these differences are and conform to their customs and behavior patterns.

A lot of business has been lost for American companies because an executive has been either too informal, brash, loud, or has asked a lot of personal questions. In many countries, these things are taken as a lack of respect and unacceptably boorish behavior.

You must take time to develop a good rapport with your overseas associates and not expect to jump right into business matters minutes after meeting someone for the first time. Your counterpart wants to get to know you first. As trust develops, he will eventually get down to the business at hand.

Be prepared to accept the slower pace of business dealings, the different philosophies of selling and buying, and the more formal or gracious social contacts. Remember that it matters a lot that you show by your words and actions that you are aware of how your various counterparts live, work and play. They will respect you for that even though you might make a faux pas at times. If they know you are at least trying to learn, it will go a long way to forming and cementing the good rapport which will bring success to the business relationship. Forming a strong personal bond can be even more important than having a legal contract.

Some foreign businessmen have stereotyped images of American executives as brash, know-it-alls who have come to save the country and show its people how business should be done. Do all you can not to be overbearing, offensive or arrogant. If your overseas distributors or customers don't like you, they will go to your foreign competitor.

There are so many things to be aware of in the many countries you will be visiting that an entire volume could be written about them. To give you an idea of some of the things you should be sensitive about in different parts of the world, consider the following:

- Body language is not the same everywhere. In many Asian countries, for example, when talking to someone, don't look deeply into the eyes of a customer. Don't slap him on the back or squeeze his arm. Also, cute as he or she might be, don't pat a child on the head. These things that we do as a matter of habit in the United States, are often taken as signs of hostility or disrespect.
- In parts of Asia and Arab countries, if you cross your legs when seated, don't expose the soles of your shoes. Also in these countries, never pass on object on to someone with your left hand.
- Don't be shocked if a Latin American or an Arab hugs or kisses you as a greeting. It's common and a sign of respect.
- Don't refuse coffee offered by an Arab or Latin American—it is considered an insult.
- Do not offer alcoholic beverages to anyone in the Middle-East. Muslims are forbidden to drink alcohol.
- Most Europeans think Americans have bad table manners and are amazed at our use of knife and fork—switching them several times to different hands when cutting, then laying down the knife and picking up the fork in the right hand to eat. In Europe it is customary to eat with the fork in the right hand, knife in the left, and to use both utensils simultaneously!
- In most countries, especially in Europe and Japan, businessmen are very reserved, especially about their private lives, so don't ask about their wives, children or other personal questions. The notable exceptions to this rule are Indians and Pakistanis who can get very personal, but this is their way of showing an interest in you.
- If invited to a colleague's home for dinner, you should take or send flowers to the hostess. Be careful though—don't send red roses as they are considered "too romantic." Yellow roses are for older

people. Chrysanthemums and gladioli are sent only for funerals or a death in the family. Ask your concierge what is proper or what other type of gift could be given.

- In some countries, usually in the Middle East and Japan, most entertaining is strictly "stag." Do not inquire why your host's wife is not present.

- You might not think so, but the British way of doing things is quite different from the American way. Because the British speak English, do not think you can do everything just as you do in the United States. Dress conservatively, don't use slang, especially in negotiating, and be aware of the nuances of English English.

- American businesswomen are more and more becoming accepted as good international executives, especially since the role of women increasingly becomes more liberal in many countries which previously kept women strictly in the home. Women executives should not attempt to look or act masculine, but be "themselves" and obey the rules of etiquette just as a man would.

- In most countries you should not go on a first name basis until your contact does. In many cultures, even life-long friends do not address each other by their given names.

- The American penchant for "business breakfasts" or "power lunches" is not an acceptable practice in many countries. In fact, discussing business at any meal is often considered a gross faux pas. Many foreigners feel that mealtime should be a quiet, social event.

- Especially in Spain and Latin American countries, be prepared to alter your mealtimes drastically. You will probably be at lunch from 2:00 p.m. until 4:00 p.m., work until 8:00 p.m. and not have dinner until at least 9:30 or 10:00 p.m. If you're alone and want to dine early in these countries, you will probably have to order from your hotel room service menu or pick up some cheese, cold meat or pastries at a local food market. Restaurants don't even open until after 9:00 p.m., and even then, you'll probably be the only one in the place.

This sample of some of the business, cultural and social differences you will find around the world, gives you only a small idea of what you will encounter as you broaden your foreign travels. Always travel with an open mind, and try to fit into the variety of customs and practices. Most of them are interesting, and can be fun. Be patient, accept them and you will make lasting and good friendships.

16. Taking Your Spouse Along

The very nature of foreign business travel means that couples have to put up with long separations. Unlike business travel in the United States, the international executive cannot usually limit a trip to only a few days and must often be away from home for anywhere from two to six weeks at a time. It is obviously impractical to come home for the weekend, then go back. These sometimes frequent separations can play havoc with even the best of marriages, so the matter of a spouse accompanying you on a long trip is a very personal one. Several factors come into play in making the decision to travel together.

- Expense—Most companies do not pay any part of an executive's spouse's travel costs. As discussed earlier, the international business traveler usually cannot take advantage of special air fares and must travel at higher unrestricted fares. This would apply to the spouse's fare as well. If the company allows the executive to travel on business class on long flights, he obviously wants his wife in the seat next to him, so travel costs can be high.

- The cost of hotel rooms is not too much of a problem since a double-room is often only a few dollars more than a single. In many cases, one of the benefits of membership in a "Frequent Stay" club is a double room for the price of a single. Some hotels associated with "Frequent Flyer" clubs also offer the same benefit.

Additional expenses such as meals, sight-seeing, and non-business entertainment, shopping and the like, should also be a consideration. Most companies (and the IRS) allow spouses to be included in the expenses reported for some business-related entertainment events. You pay for everything else, but the cost of your spouse's trip and expenses overseas are not normally deductible from your income tax return as legitimate business expenses. There have been many IRS tax court hearings and investigations on this matter, but very few have been decided in favor of the businessman-taxpayer.

It is a good idea to keep a careful, separate record of your expenses and those of your spouse if you travel together, especially those charged on a hotel bill. One way to do this is to annotate on the bill itself your spouse's expenses as "personal" and deduct them from what you charge the company on your expense report. Also, keep receipts for any such expenses in case you need them.

Being alone a lot of the time is something your spouse may have to cope with. If you are on an exploratory trip and visiting and meeting with many people every day, she will be alone a lot of the time. Unless she is a good traveler and can find interesting things to do and see during your working hours, and possibly late stag entertainment, she may wish she had not come.

Cementing relationships with foreign distributors and customers often comes a lot easier if your spouse is with you. This allows your associates to see and appraise the "other side" of you. They will feel more relaxed with you and often will invite you to their home to meet family and friends, giving you a further insight into them as "total persons" and not just another distributor. You will also see and learn how people in foreign countries live and socialize—something few tourists ever get to know.

Your spouse will learn exactly what it is that you do and have a better appreciation for your work and your company. If she has not traveled with you previously, she probably never understood why you were so tired when you returned home. Now she will know that you got your deep tan from schlepping the hot streets of Kuala Lumpur, Bombay and Djakarta, and not from lying on a beach or at a hotel poolside!

If your spouse is astute and perceptive, she can sometimes learn things about your business associates that you may have failed to notice. From other wives she will learn birthdates and the names of children in the family, special anniversaries, and sometimes, things that may later be useful to you in business.

17. Your Business Expenses

It is important to keep a daily diary of your expenses while traveling. On a multi-country trip you can get horribly confused as to what you spent where, what the exchange rate was two weeks ago in Pakistan, and did I take three, or was it five, long taxi rides? You can't always get receipts for taxis or other daily expenses, so jot them down as you go along. A small notebook, easily tucked in your shirtpocket, can be a lifesaver when you are confronted with an expense sheet later.

Many executives do at least a "working copy" of their expense reports every week. Arrange with your accounting department to give them your complete trip expense reports after you return.

18. The U. S. Customs Service

As a unit of the Department of the Treasury, the mission of the U. S. Customs Service is to stop the flow of narcotics into the United States, collect duty on items brought into the country, and protect U. S. agriculture by confiscating prohibited products such as fruits, vegetables, and fresh meats. The latter is to prevent the spread in the United States of insects or diseases harmful to the United States agricultural products or cattle.

In addition, they are on the lookout for products made from animals which are on the World Wildlife Fund's list of endangered species, such as turtles, jaguars, crocodiles, eagles, ocelots and many others. Also prohibited are items from certain countries, such as Cuban cigars and Iranian caviar as well as Pre-Colombian artifacts from Latin America which are forbidden to be taken out of the countries in the first place.

Generally, you have a $400 personal exemption from duties if you have been out of the United States for at least 48 hours and have not claimed an exemption within the last 30 days. A 10% duty is payable on the next $1,000 worth of items.

The Customs Service also protects owners of registered trademarks or tradenames, so you cannot import any foreign-made merchandise with registered trademarks or names without permission of the owner. There is, however, a law which allows a traveler to bring in one such article for personal use. Occasionally, the trademark holder may permit importation of more than one provided they will not be sold. Be aware that many products with well-known trademarks or names are counterfeited and sold overseas at bargain-basement prices. These include watches, cameras, electronic items, computer software, cosmetics, etc. Since Customs officers are highly-trained experts, they will recognize such counterfeits and can confiscate them.

You should not have any problems in clearing through customs inspection if you obey the basic rules. Don't try to bring into the United States any prohibited articles or try to declare something at a fraction of its cost. The inspectors know how much brand-name articles cost.

Up-dated information and advice is offered free by the Customs Service in a booklet "Know Before You Go." Write for it to 1301 Constitution Avenue, Washington, D. C. 20229. The Department of Agriculture (USDA, APHIS, Room G-110, Belcrest Road., Hyattsville, Maryland, 20782) offers a brochure called "Traveler's Tips" and the U. S. Fish and Wildlife Service of the Department of The Interior has a helpful brochure called "Buyer Beware" discussing products made from endangered animals. You can also call your local district Customs Office for answers to specific questions or problems.

19. Some Additional Tips

A few things you might not think about when preparing for your trip or while traveling are:

- If you are carrying a foreign-made camera, recording equipment or other such items, register them with your local customs unit before departure. You will receive a receipt of registration which you can show to the Customs inspector on arrival should you be questioned about where and when the items were purchased.
- Make a list of the numbers of all documents you are carrying with you in case you lose any of them. These include your passport, airline ticket serial numbers, traveler's checks, credit cards, reservations and cancellation numbers for hotels, car-rental confirmation numbers if you have reserved a car, Frequent Flyer and Frequent Hotel-Stay numbers, eyeglass prescriptions, and important telephone numbers. Having all of these numbers readily available will be of enormous help in obtaining replacements for any lost items.
- It is a good idea to make a photocopy of the pages of passport showing your passport number, name and address, date and place of issue, and your photograph. You should also make a copy of the

pages on which foreign-country visas have been registered. If your passport is lost or stolen, the copies of these pages will speed up your getting a replacement at a local U. S. Embassy or Consulate.

- Keep all of these copies separate from your documents or money and in a safe place. You should also leave a copy at home or your office, just in case.
- Learn at least something about the metric system of measure and weights which is used worldwide to measure length, distance, weight, volume and area. You may need it in discussing and selling your products or when buying food or other products. Remember too, that clothing sizes almost everywhere outside the U.S.A. are different. It is a good idea to carry a clothing size conversion chart if you are planning on buying things like shirts, shoes, sweaters, women's blouses etc. Temperatures (weather and bodily) are also measured differently overseas and recorded in degrees Centigrade (Celsius) so if you hear on a radio or TV that the weather outside is 0 degrees, that means it's 32 degrees Farenheit!
- When you arrive in a foreign city, get yourself a city map and note on it your hotel's location to orient yourself. Then, if it is a weekend, you can take a walk around the city, go into some stores, and get a feel for the place and lifestyle of the city before starting to work.
- If you plan to shop for local crafts, clothing or souvenirs, try to find out before you go what you'd like to look for to save time which may be tight. Your hotel concierge can help you find the best places to shop.
- Reconfirm your air or rail reservations in each country at least 72 hours before scheduled departure in case a flight may be rescheduled or cancelled. Be sure your reservation is recorded on the airline's computer.
- Carry a few of your company's letterheads should you need to write a memo confirming a point of discussion with a distributor or customer, or to write a letter after you have left about something you forgot to discuss, or some information you promised to send. You can also write thank-you notes as you go along. They will look

nicer on your company letterhead than on hotel stationery and your hosts will get them sooner than if you wait until you return home to write them.

- It is always interesting to look through the local yellow pages in each foreign city. Look for distributors and manufacturers of products competitive with or similar to yours. You may also find possible users of your products. You can discuss these with your distributor to be sure he has information about them in his marketing plan. You can also use the information from these pages to round out or confirm your own prior market research. It is also useful to find actual street address and telephone numbers of someone for whom you may have had only a post office box number.

SUMMARY

Don't let the myriad of do's and don't's, musts, watch-out-fors, and details noted and listed in this chapter give you the feeling that you'll never learn it all or be able to cope with overseas business travel. There are, of course, a lot of things to remember, to do and to think about, not only in preparing a trip, but also in the actual travel. As with almost everything else concerned with international business, attention to detail, common sense, and keeping an entirely open mind will serve you well when it comes to going abroad to study your markets, meet with and appoint agents and distributors and begin to put your company on the global map.

Traveling and working overseas does require a lot of hard work, psychological and physiological adjustments, and a real interest in people and their cultures. But the business and personal rewards for making these efforts can be great. You may not always do or say the right thing, you may mess up a deal now and then, but it it if is perceived by your overseas counterparts that you have tried to do things right, that you have been honest, ethical and forthright in your business and personal dealings and relationships, you'll be able to go back and try again—and succeed the next time.

Along the way, try to have some fun also. Take advantage of weekends, a few spare hours, or holidays to see the city and culture you are in. Learn what people do and think in their spare time. It will help you to work better with them and you will become a better person by understanding more about the world in which we live, work and play.

A FINAL THOUGHT

Your bright, new world of export trade should now be taking shape. You have discovered the economic and personal benefits of joining with the thousands of other American companies, small and large, who call "the world" their sales territory. You are working with foreign colleagues who no longer seem quite so "foreign." New names will soon be added to the list of countries to which you are selling. To continue growing in world trade, you and your company's senior executives, from your CEO down the management and support line, must continue to strengthen the initial commitment to the new business. There will be much hard, but gratifying, work to be done—a large portion of which will consist of staying "au courant" with everything that's happening everywhere in the world. At any given momement in time, some overseas markets are flourishing, while others are languishing. You must always know which is doing which, and why. Then you will always be ready to implement your market strategies and direct your efforts to take advantage of new opportunities or to protect your interests. Many exciting and historic events are taking place even as this is being written, and yes, even as you read these words. Every night as you read your newspapers, periodicals and watch television, you will learn about new events which may have serious impact on your international business. One of the nicest things about international trade is that you are not alone out there. There are a lot of people to help you and guide you along—banks, forwarders, colleagues in other exporting companies, shipping companies and others. Call on the Department of Commerce. In their U.S. export assistance programs through their district field offices, as well as through their network of specialists abroad, Commerce has helped many companies get into exporting and flourish. It was announced recently in the Journal of Commerce that the Commerce Department is adding $10 million to its budget this year to increase its overseas staff by 93 persons, representing a ten percent expansion. On a more personal note, I would like to point out that while times change, and things change, I have found that in 35 years of business travel to 76 countries, there has been one constant—the basic honesty, goodness and decency of the many hundreds of people with whom I have worked and who have helped me discover the joys and pleasures of their multiple and varied cultures. I hope that you too, will experience these pleasures as you build your overseas business. I think you will find that export gets in your blood—and you'll love every minute of it.

Appendix A

1992 International Trade Fairs

To assist U.S. exporters, *Business America* annually publishes a schedule of future international trade fairs. These exhibitions range from the general type, which promote sales in numerous product categories, to the highly specialized fair, designed to attract buyers of specific products.

Events are listed by country, city, date, and name, and are generally open to participation by any U.S. company in the related industry. Each firm must make arrangements for its own exhibit, including rental of space and utilities, transportation of products, and setting up and staffing of the booth.

Although few of the fairs listed have a U.S. Pavilion (organized in most cases by private companies), a visit can be productive even if the U.S. company does not exhibit, provided the visitor exploits the opportunity to conduct market research on a particular industry; all major companies, distributors/agents, and associations can often be found under one roof.

The listing of international trade fairs was compiled from information provided by U.S. and Foreign Commercial Service (US&FCS) officers at American embassies abroad. The US&FCS office in each country can provide interested U.S. exporters with addresses of fair management organizers. The US&FCS offices and their addresses are listed on pages 77–78. For countries where the US&FCS has no office, the telephone number of the Commerce Department Desk Officer, or the Embassy address, is provided as a source for the fair organizer's address.

The information is taken from the latest data available. However, the Department of Commerce cannot assume responsibility for accuracy of dates or for the outcome of any transactions with foreign fair managements.

The organizers of many exhibitions not listed on these pages would welcome the participation or attendance of U.S. firms.

Argentina
Buenos Aires
April 10-27. 18th International Book Fair.
May 7-16. International Machine Tool Show—Emaqh '92.
May 12-15. Cable TV Show/ 92.
June 15-18. Gas '92. Oil and Gas Production.
July 31-Aug. 19. 105th International Cattle, Agricultural Equipment and Industrial Exhibition— Rural '92.
Aug. 3-6. 4th International Custom Jewelry Show.
Aug. 24-28. 4th International Software Expo.

Australia
Melbourne
March 5-15. International Motor Show.

April 4-7. Interior Designex.
April 28-30. ATUG Telecommunications.
May 25-30. PAKPRINT '92.
Aug. 8-12. International Gift/ Jewelry.
Aug. 11-14. PC/Communications/ Office Technology.
Aug. 22-30. International Home Show.
Sept. 6-9. International Food Exhibition.

Sept. 29-Oct. 2. ELENEX AUTOMATE.

Oct. 21-25. International Airshow and Aerospace Expo.

Perth

May 13-15. Wamex Mining '92.

May 25-27. Petroleum Technology '92.

Aug. 26-27. Dowerin Machinery Field Days.

Sydney

Feb. 18-20. Hospitality Exhibition.

Feb. 22-26. International Gift/Jewelry.

May 11-15. International Engineering Exhibition.

May 15-18. Automotive.

May 26-29. HOSPMEDEX '92.

June 20-24. International Catering Trade Fair.

Aug. 15-23. International Home Show.

Sept. 8-10. LABEX Scientific.

Sept. 29-Oct. 3. CONBUILD '92.

Austria

Graz

April 25-May 3. Grazer Fruehjahrsmesse International (International Spring Fair Graz).

June 3-5. Technova International (high-tech and innovation trade fair).

Sept. 26-Oct. 4. Grazer Herbstmesse International (International Fall Fair Graz).

Linz

Nov. 17-19. UTEC—Absorga '92 (environmental fair).

Salzburg

Jan. 16-19. Autozubehoer und Werkstatt (service station equipment, tools, automotive accessories).

March 13-15. JIM—Er und Es (international young fashion).

March 13-15. OESFA—International (sporting goods, sportswear).

Sept. 11-13. JIM—Er und Es (international young fashion).

Sept. 11-13. OESFA International (sporting goods, sportswear).

Vienna

Jan. 26-29. ATB—Austrian Travel Business.

Jan. 30-Feb. 2. JASPOWA (hunting and sporting weapons, fishing, off-road).

March 18-22. Wiener Fruehjahrsmesse (international spring fair Vienna).

Aprll 2-4. Security and Safety.

May 12-16. IFABO and Programma (information technology, office organization and software).

June 10-12. Fachmesse Schweisssen '92 (welding fair).

June 11-15. Vinova (wines, wine growing, and cellar equipment).

Sept. 5-8. HIT (consumer electronics).

Sept. 29-Oct. 3. INTERTOOL Austria (metalworking, automation, and machine tools).

Bahamas

Nassau

April (date to be announced). Bahamas Chamber of Commerce Computer and Electronics Show.

May (date to be announced). Bahamas Chamber of Commerce Manufacturers' Exhibit.

Contact U.S. Embassy Nassau, U.S. Department of State, Suite H, 7415 NW 19th St., Miami, Fla. 33126, tel. (809) 322-1181; fax: (809) 328-7838.

Bahrain

Manama

Jan. 11-14. MEFEX '92. 7th Middle East Food and Equipment Show and Salon Culinaire.

April 25-28. Jewelry Arabia 92, incorporating Perfume Arabia '92.

May 11-14. MEDEF '92. Middle East Defense and Security Exhibition and Conference.

May 27-June 1. 5th Bahrain Fair '92. Tourism and Commercial Exhibition.

Contact Commerce Department Desk Officer for Bahrain at (202) 377-5545.

Belgium

Antwerp

March 8-28. FRIGOTEcH (cooling equipment).

Brussels

Jan. 15-26. Auto show.

Feb. 9-16. International Week of Agriculture.

Feb. 27-March 8. BATIBOUW (building and construction).
Feb. 18-23. Book Fair.
April 4-6. Stationery.
April 8-9. Trade Show for Telecommunications.
May 5-9. EUROTECH (seven simultaneous industry shows).
May 24-28. Ophthalmology Congress and Exhibition.
June 2-5. EUROSURGERY Congress & Exposition.
Sept. 6-9. DECOSIT (upholstery fabrics).
Sept. 23-30. BUREAU (office equipment).
Oct. 4-7. Hardware and Household Goods.
Nov. 8-12. Furniture Show.
Nov. 21-23. Brussels Travel Fair.
Nov. 25-27. EXPOMED (medical equipment).
Nov. 27-29. DENTEX (dental equipment).

Ghent
Jan. 25-28. TEXTIRAMA (textile machinery, clothing).
March 24-28. MICROTEX (microcomputers).
Oct. 19-23. INTERELECT (electronic computers, equipment).

Kortrijk
March 29-31. Fish Expo (fish trade).
Sept. 2-5. KANTOOR (office equipment).
Sept. 29-Oct. 1. Cad Cam.
Oct. 15-25. Interior (interior design).

Libramont
July 24-27. Foire Agricole (agricultural show).

Liege
October. Initiatives (exchange of technologies).

Belize
Belmopan
May 1-3. National Agriculture and Trade Show.
Contact U.S. Embassy Commercial Section, P.O. Box 286, Belize City Belize; tel. 011-501-2-77161; fax 011-501-2-30802.

Bolivia
Santa Cruz
Sept. 14-27. International Trade Fair—1992.
Contact Commerce Department Desk Officer for Bolivia at (202) 377-2521

Botswana
Gaborone
May. BITEX. Building Industries.
Contact Commerce Department Desk Officer for Botswana at (202) 377-5148.

Brazil
Belo Horizonte
May 6-10. Civil Construction Fair.
June 5-14. Furniture and Household Goods Show.

Rio de Janeiro
March 25-27. 1st International Exhibition on Optics, Cine, Photo and Sound.
June 1-12. United Nations Conference for Environment and Development—Rio '92.
Oct. 4-9. 4th International Seminar and Exhibition on Transfer of Technology.
Oct. 18-23. Oil and Gas Expo '92.
Nov. 4-7. 16th Inter-American Congress of Radiology and Exhibition of Radiology Equipment.
Nov. 17-Dec. 2. International Congress on Telecommunications and Exhibition of Telecommunication Equipment.

Sao Paulo
Jan. 29-Feb. 2. Audio, Video, Communications. and Telecommunications Fair.
Feb. 11-16. International Construction Fair.
Feb. 18-21. Refrigeration, Air Conditioner, Ventilation, and Air Treatment Fair.
March 26-27. Visit USA Travel Expo '92.
April 10-19. International Show on Household Goods.
May 4-9. Printing and Graphics Arts USA '92.
May 26-28. Electro/Electronics USA '92.
June 6-11. International Exhibition on Environmental Technology.
June 23-26. Food Processing and Packaging USA '92.
July 21-24. International Software Show.
Aug. 4-7. Productivity/Instrumentation USA '92.
Sept. 14-18. Comdex Sucesu South America '92.
Oct. 5-8. Surface Treating

Conference and Exhibition.
Oct. 6-11. International Musical Instruments Fair.
Oct. 15-25. Automobile and Auto Parts Show.
Nov. 14-20. Brazil International Trade Fair.

Bulgaria
Plovdiv
May 4-10. Plovdiv Spring Consumer Goods Fair.
Sept. 28-0ct. 4. Plovdiv Fall Trade Fair.
For information about this event, contact the Commerce Department's Bulgaria Desk Officer on tel. (202) 377-2645.

Burundi
July 5-15. Burundi's 6th Annual Trade Fair (to be confirmed).
Contact: Hermand Mununi, tel. 22 22 80, tlx. 5145 BDI; fax 22 78 95.

Canada
Calgary
June 9-10. National Petroleum Show.
Sept. 9-13. EQUI-FAIR '92 (Equine Industry).

Charlottetown
Feb. 13-15. International Potato Expo (Potato Growing and Processing Machinery, Equipment and Supplies).

Halifax
June 9-11. Halifax Industrial Exhibition.
Sept. 16-17. Atlantic Canada Computer Show.

Hamilton
Jan. 21-23. Landscape Ontario Annual Congress.

Moncton
March 14-16. Atlantic Building Materials Show.
March 29-31. APEX '92 (Hotel, Restaurant and Institutional Equipment and Supplies).
April 3-5. Fish Canada '92 (Onboard and Onshore Fish Harvesting and Processing Equipment and Supplies).

Montreal
Jan. 28-30. EXFOR '92 (Pulp and Paper).
Feb. 9-12. SALON RENDEX-VOUS '92 (Hotel and Restaurant).
Feb. 16-19. 75th CGSA Annual International Convention and Exhibition (Sporting Goods).
Feb. 23-25. Canadian International Menswear Show.
March 8-11. Montreal Spring Gift Show.
March 9-11. Action Expo (Municipal and Public Works Exhibition).
March 15-17. Canadian International Womenswear Show.
March 25-26. Automated Manufacturing Show.
April 12-14. CIAS '92—Canadian International Automotive Show (Automotive Aftermarket Parts, Accessories, Tools and Equipment).
May 11-14. Canadian Plant Engineering and Machine Tool Show.

May 24-26. SSA '92 INTERNATIONAL—Super Salon De L'Alimentation (Food Show).
June 3-5. SIIM '92— Montreal International Computer and Office Exhibition.
June 14-17. Montreal Furniture Market.
Sept. 24-26. International Environmental Economy Exhibition Crossroads.
Nov. 3-5. Canadian Computer/Office Technology Show (SCIB '92).

Ottawa
Jan. 7-8. Open System Show (Multi-User Computer Show).
April 28-29. Ottawa Business Show.
May 5-6. Canadian High Technology Show.
Sept. 30-Oct. 1. Ottawa Business and Government Computer Show.

Prince George
May 7-9. Prince George Forestry Exhibition.

Regina
June 15-20. Western Canadian Farm Progress Show (Farm Equipment).

St. John's
June 23-25. Offshore Newfoundland (Offshore Oil Development, Industrial and Construction Machinery, Equipment and Supplies).

Toronto

Jan. 26-30. Canadian Toy and Decoration Fair.

Feb. 9-11. Canadian Hardware/Housewares/Home Improvement Show.

Feb. 4-7. Canadian International Farm Equipment Show.

Feb. 12-14. Canadian Construction Show.

Feb. 16-18. Canadian Food and Beverage Show.

Feb. 23-26. Toronto Spring Gift Show.

April 6-8. Safety and Health Conference and Exhibition.

April 26-28. HOSTEX '92 (Hotel and Restaurant Equipment and Supplies).

May 11-14. PLAST-EX '92 (Plastics Materials, Machinery and Equipment).

May 14-15. Ontario Dental Association Conference and Exhibition.

June 2-3. Toronto Environmental Trade Show & Conference (Formerly Haztech Canada Eastern— Hazardous Materials/Dangerous Goods Equipment and Services).

June 17-18. Vardex Toronto (Value Added Reseller/Dealer Exposition).

Sept. 20-23. Toronto Fall Gift Show.

Sept. 23-25. TELECON '92 (Voice and Data Communications Products and Services).

Sept. 28-30. LOGISTECH 92— International Materials Handling and Distribution Show.

Oct. 2-3. REHABEX '92

(Health and Home Care Products).

Oct. 20-22. Canadian Integrated Manufacturing/Design Show.

Oct. 20-22. Canadian Environmental Technology Exhibition & Conference (CETECH).

Oct. 20-22. Canadian High Technology Show.

Oct. 20-22. Plant Maintenance & Design Engineering Show (PMDS).

Oct. 20-22. Weld Expo '92 Canada.

Oct. 26-28. Ontario Hospital Association Convention and Exhibition.

Oct.   30-Nov.   1. TRUCKCAN '92.

Nov. 7-9. Canadian Home Centre Show.

Nov. 16-19. Canadian Computer Show and Conference.

Nov. 19-21. IIDEX (International Interior Design Exposition).

Nov. 24-25. Process Equipment & Instrumentation Show.

Vancouver

Feb. 5-9. Vancouver International Boat Show.

March 8-10. Vancouver Spring Gift Show.

March 16-20. GLOBE '92 (Environmental Technology and Pollution Control).

April 22-25. INDEPENDENCE '92 (Equipment and Supplies For the Handicapped and Disabled)

Aug. 23-25. Vancouver Fall Gift Show.

Sept. 13-15. Canadian Sporting Goods Show.

Sept. 23-25. Wood Expo (Forestry, Sawmilling, Pulp and Paper and Logging Equipment).

Chile

Santiago

March 8-15. FIDAE '92.

May 12-16. Latin American Mining Show—EXPOMIN '92.

July 6-13. SOFTEL '92.

Oct. 28-Nov. 8. Santiago International Trade Fair, FISA '92.

China

Beijing

Feb. 26-March 2. Woodworking and Fur Fair.

March 26-31. Chinaplas '92.

April.   International Mechatronics Fair '92.

April 1-8. China National Machine Tool Fair '92.

April 7-11. Agro Expo China '92.

April 8-13. Cilotex '92.

April 24-29. International Logimachinery Expo '92.

May 13-19. Achemasia '92.

May 19-24. EP China '92— fourth international exhibit on energy and power.

June 3-9. China Print '92.

June 19-23. China Secure '92— international exhibition of police and civilian security and fire equipment.

June 24-29. IESFEI '92.

June 25-30. Construction China '92.

June 25-30. Auto China '92.

Sept. 4-9. Metal China '92.

Sept. 8-12. BICES—international construction machinery exhibition and seminar.
Sept. 8-13. IEIE '92—international educational instrument exhibition.
Sept. 22-26. MICONEX '92—5th multi instruments conference and exhibition.
Sept. 22-27. Mining China '92.
Oct. 21-25. ISEMI '92—third international symposium and exhibition on measuring instruments.
Oct. 30-Nov. 4. Expocomm China '92—international telecommunications/computer exhibition and conference.
Nov. 30-Dec. 4. International Forest '92 and Fire Prevention '92.
Dec. 5-10. First China International Industrial Safety, Protection, and Technology Exhibition.

Guangzhou
April 1-5. China International Accessories and Machinery Exhibition.
May 5-9. International Shoes and Leather Exhibition.
May 19-23. International Musical Instruments and Manufacturers Exhibition.
May 30-June 3. International Audio-Visual and Broadcasting Exhibition.
June 9-13. International Public Security and Technology Equipment Exhibition.
June 23-27. Fifth International Medical Institutions, Health Care Equipment, and

Pharmaceuticals Exhibition.
June 23-27. International Chemical Industry Equipment and Materials Exhibition.
Sept. 8-12. Second International Refractory Industry Exhibition.
Sept. 22-26. International Agrotechnology and Agricultural Food Processing Exhibition.

Shanghai
May 9-13. China Engines '92.
May 15-20. Die and Mold China '92.
May 18-23. Instrumentation '92.
June 10-15. Medical '92.
June 15-20. Hospital Expo China '92.
June 23-28. SICME '92—second Shanghai international clothing machinery exhibition.

Shenzhen
May 4-7. Fishery China '92.

Tianjin
Jan. 14-18. Tianjin International Exhibition for Agriculture Machinery & Technology.
March 1-10. Tianjin Export Commodities Fair '92.
April 21-25. International Trade Fair for Wine Products and Techniques.
May 19-23. Foodtech China '92—international exhibition for food processing technology and equipment.
May 26-30. China Optifibre '92—international exhibition

and conference on optical fiber technology.
June 18-22. China Medica '92—international exhibition on medical health equipment and pharmaceutical technology.
July 2-6. Energy Fair '92—international trade fair for energy industry and energy supply.
Sept. 1-5. China Plas '92.
Sept. 4-8. International Lighting Appliances and Production Technology Exhibition.
Sept. 15-19. China Construct '92—international exhibition for construction equipment and material.

Colombia
Bogota
Feb. 4-9. XVI Columbian Leather Show.
Feb. 19-22. Salon Internacional del Calzado (international shoe exposition).
March 13-23. Salon Internacional del Automovil, Nautico y Aereo (automobile, boat, and aircraft expo).
April 22-May 2. V Feria Internacional del Libro (international book fair).
May 19-23. Feria de Asona (auto parts show).
July 15-26. XIX Feria Internacional de Bogota (biennial Bogota international trade fair).
Aug. 11-16. XVII Colombian Leather Show (fall show).
Sept. 4-19. IX Feria del Hogar (housewares expo).

Sept. 28-Oct. 5. Mercado Internacional del Cine, Video y la Television (movies, video, and tv market show).
Oct. 22-28. X COMPUEXPO (computer show).

Costa Rica
San Jose
Feb. 21-March 1. FERCORO, 5th Costa Rican International Fair.

Cote D'Ivoire
Abidjan
April 23-26. USA-West Africa Expo '92.

Cyprus
Nicosia
Feb. 29-March 8. Sports and Leisure.
April 22-26. Property Development.
April 22-26. Tourism.
May 21-31. U.S. Products Pavilion at the 17th Cyprus International State Fair.
Oct. 14-18. OFFITEC (office equipment).
Nov. 4-8. HORECAMediterranean '92 (hotel, restaurant and cafe equipment).
Nov. 28-Dec. 6. DOMAP (domestic appliances). Contact U.S. Embassy, P.O. Box 568, Nicosia, Cyprus; tel. 011-357-2-465151; fax 011-3572-459571.

Czechoslovakia
Bratislava
April 27-30. DANUBIUSGASTRO '92. Tourism and Hotel Business.

May 19-23. CONECO '92. Construction Technology Fair.
June 9-12. COFAX '92. Computer Technology, Reprography.
June 23-27. INCHEMBA. Chemical Fair.

Brno
Jan. 1-12. GO '92. International Tourist Salon.
Feb. 12-16. INTECO. International Exhibition of Small Business and Public Catering.
March 3-6. ROBOT. International Exhibition of Industrial Robots.
March 3-6. Welding. International Exhibition of Welding Technology.
March 24-27. PIBEX. International Exhibition of Finance and Insurance.
April 12-16. INTERMODA. Fashion Fair.
June 16-21. AUTOTEC '92. International Exhibition of Road and Highway Construction Technology.
Sept. 16-23. International Engineering Fair.
Oct. 20-23. INVEX—Novelties. International Exhibition of Inventions and Know-How.
Oct. 20-23. INVEX—Computer.
Oct. 20-23. ENVIBRNO. Environmental Protection Technology.

Prague
Feb. 3-7. Repro '92. International Exhibition of Reprog-

raphy.
Feb. 12-12. TSL Market '92. Services and Goods for Tourism.
Feb. 26-March 1. CONEXPO '92. International Fair of Construction Technology and Materials.
March 12-15. Sport Prague '92. International Fair of Sporting Goods.
April 7-10. PRAGOMEDICA— Medical Engineering.
April 7-10. PRAGOREGULA— Measurement Engineering.
April 7-10. PRAGOPHARMA— Pharmaceuticals.
April 7-10. PRAGOORDATA— Electronics.
Nov. 10-13. PRAGOTHERM— Heating and Airconditioning.

Denmark
Copenhagen
Jan. 10-19. Biler I Bella— automobiles, motorbikes, and equipment.
Jan. 30-Feb. 2. FERIE '92. Travel and Tourism.
Feb. 28-March 8. Copenhagen International Boat Show.
March 6-8. Intershop 92— shopfitting, promotion, and design.
March 6-8. Service Station and Minimarket '92.
March 6-8. Scan Franchise '92. Franchising and Franchising Services.
Feb. 13-16. Future Fashions

Scandinavia.
March 11-13.
EUROMODAL '92. Combined rail, ship, and transport systems.
March 26-28. SCANDEFA '92. Dental Fair.
May 6-10. Scandinavian Furniture Fair.
May 26-30. World Fishing '92.
Aug. 20-23. Future Fashions Scandinavia.
Aug. 25-27. Image '92. Trade Fair for Marketing Activities, Company Gifts. and Clothing.
Sept. 17-20. Health, Fitness and Well-Being '92.
Sept. 30-Oct. 7. Kontor & Data '92. Business and Data Exhibition.
Oct. 27-30. DANITEK '92. Industrial automation electronics and robot technology.

Fredericia
March 10-13. Building '92.
May 19-23. Metal '92. Machine tool exhibition.
Aug. 17-20. ISAK '92. Civil Service Fair, Government Purchasing Fair.
Sept. 29-Oct. 3. TIMI '92. Wood Industries Buyers Fair.

Herning
Jan. 21-25. AGROMEK. International Exhibition for Agricultural Mechanization.
Feb. 7-10. Formland. Gift and handicraft.
March 28-30. Do-It-Yourself '92.
May 5-7. Cable and Pipe '92.
May 19-21. Cure and Care '92. Trade fair for hospitals

and nursing homes.
June 24-27. Danish Agricultural Fair.
Aug. 7-10. Formland. Giftware and handicraft.
Aug. 7-10. Lighting and Accessories Fair.
Aug. 26-30. Furniture Fair Denmark.
Sept. 10-13. Music '92. Nordic Music Fair.
Sept. 15-19. Building Trades Fair.
Sept. 26-28. Interfair '92. Food Fair.
Oct. 6-9. DANMILJOE '92. Environmental and process technologies.

Dominican Republic
Santo Domingo
April. Expo Piel.
May. Expo Textil.
October. Feriarte.
September. Compuexpo.
September. Repfind '92.
November. Expo Herrera.

Ecuador
Quito
Oct. 19-25. COMPU '92.

Egypt
Alexandria
Jan. 20-Feb. 2 (tentative). International Book Fair.

Cairo
Jan. 4-17. International Book Fair.
Jan. 29-Feb. 2. MEDEXPO (medical and analytical).
Feb. 9-12. COMPUEXPO V (computer exhibition).
Feb. 15-28. Cairo International Fair.

November. Cairo International Defense Equipment Exhibition.

El Salvador
Nov. 4-15. XV International Fair. *Contact Commercial Section, U.S. Embassy, San Salvador, APO AA 34023; 011-503-98-1666.*

Finland
Helsinki
Jan. 6-10. Medicine '92. Medicine/nursing/health care.
Jan. 16-19. Travel '92. Finnish International Trade Fair.
Feb. 7-16. Helsinki International Boat Show '92.
Feb. 28-March 1. Caravan '92. Caravans and motor caravans.
April 7-12. FINNBUILD '92 HEPAC.
Sept. 14-18. KT-92. Business machinery and equipment.
Oct. 6-10. PACTEC '92. Packing and materials handling.
Nov. 3-5. KEMIA '92. Finnish Chemical Congress.
Nov. 6-8. SKIEXPO '92. Skiing and winter tourism.
Nov. 12-15. EDUCA '92. Education and teaching materials.
Nov. 25-29. Helsinki International Trade Fair. Consumer goods.

Jyvaskyla
Jan. 29-31. Electrical Industry 92/ Communications 92/ Light '92. Specialized Exhibition.
Feb. 7-9. HEPACEL and

Building Exhibition/92.
Feb. 26-27. Environment '92.

Lahti
March 5-8. RAKSA '92. Building Fair.
Aug. 13-16. FURNIA '92. Furniture Fair.
Sept. 10-13. International Car Show '92.
Oct. 13-15. FINNCORR '92. Corrosion and Surface Techniques.

Tampere
May 18-22. Eureka Exhibition. Competitiveness through Technology.
May 20-22. ENTEC '92. Environmental technology.
Sept. 1-4. Network '92. Cable network construction.
Nov. 4-6. SPORTEC '92. Construction of sports and recreation centers.

Turku
March 28-29. ARS-ANTIK '92. Antiques, art, collecting.
Oct. 9-11. Music Fair '92.
Oct. 9-11. International Book Fair.
Oct. 15-18. H and R '92. Special fair for the hotel and catering business.
Oct. 24-25 and Oct. 30-Nov. 1. Turku Boat Fair.

France
Besancon
Sept. 22-26.
MICRONORA— Microtechniques International Trade Show.

Cannes
Jan. 19-23. MIDEM—International Record and Music Publishing Market Show.
May 10-15. MIP-TV—International Market of Television Programs.
June 3-7. SIFAG—General Aviation Show and Festival.
Sept. 10-14. Festival International De La Plaisance— Cannes Boat Show.
Oct. 12-16. MIPCOM—International Market of Film and Television Programs.

Deauville
Sept. 16-20. TOP COM— Annual Conference For Communication Directors.

Grenoble
March 15-18. SIG—International Winter Sports Fashion Trade Fair.
April 8-11. SAM—International Mountain and Ski Resorts Equipment Exhibition.

La Rochelle
Sept. 16-21. Grand Pavois De La Rochelle—La Rochelle Boat Show.

Lille
Nov. 31-Dec. 11. CONFORT MENAGER—Housewares and The Family.

Lyon
Nov. 3-6. POLLUTEC— Water, Air, Noise, and Waste Techniques and Industrial Cleaning.
Nov. 24-28
EXPOTHERM—Energy

Science and Technology Fair.
Nov. 24-28. EUROBAT— European Exhibition of Building and Construction.

Marseille
Oct. 20-23. PHIRAMA— Scientific and Technical Materials Exhibition.

Metz
May 19-21. MESURE ET REGULATION—Measure and Regulation Show.

Montpellier
Nov. 24-26. SITEV—Grape & Fruit Growing & Wine Making Equipment.

Orleans
Sept. 10-13. HORTIMAT ARHOMAPE—Horticulture Equipmem and Production Fair.

Paris
Jan. 9-14. Salon International Du Luminaire—International Lighting Exhibition.
Jan. 10-14. TAPIRUG— International Rug and Tapestry.
Jan. 10-14. BIJORHCA— International Show of Jewelry, Cold and Silverware, Clocks and Gifts.
Jan. 10-14. Paas International— International Home Decoration and Gift Show.
Jan. 10-14. Moving International—Decorative Goods.
Jan. 10-14. MIC—Professional Trade Show For Domestic Lifestyles.
Jan. 10-14. PARALLELE—

Professional Trade Show For Objects and Gifts.

Jan. 10-14. Salon International Du Meuble—International Furniture Exhibition.

Jan. 10-14. TAPIRUG—International Rug & Tapestry Exhibition.

Jan. 10-14. APPROFAL—International Furnishing Suppliers Exhibition.

Jan. 12-14. TEX STYLES—International Exhibition of Household Textiles.

Jan. 17-20. INVESTIR ET PLACER—Investment and Savings Show.

Jan. 27-Feb. 1. MANUTENTION— International Exhibition of Handling Materials & Systems For Products & Logistics.

Jan. 29-Feb. 4. Salon International Du Jouet—International Games and Toys Exhibition.

Jan. 30-Feb. 3. PAPETERIE SIPPA—International Stationery and Office Supplies Show.

Jan. 31-Feb. 4. Salon International Du Pret-A-Porter Feminin & "Boutique"—International Ladies Ready-To-Wear Clothing Exhibition and "Boutique" Show.

Feb. 1-4. Salon International De La Lingerie—International Lingerie Exhibition.

Feb. 1-4. Salon International De La Mode Enfantine—International Children's Fashion Exhibition.

Feb. 1-4. SEHM—International Men's and Boys' Wear Trade Show.

Feb. 1-4. SISEL HIVER—International Sports & Leisure Trade Show.

Feb. 1-4. INTERFILERE—Fabrics & Supplies for intimate garments.

Feb. 4-7. ASSURE EXPo—Insurance Exhibition.

Feb. 11-14. PC Forum Europeen—European PC Forum.

Feb. 15-20. INTERGLACES—International Show For Ice Cream Manufacturing Technology.

Feb. 15-20. INTERSUC—International Confectionery, Chocolate, Cookie and Pastry Making Exhibition.

Feb. 17-21. MECANELEM—Int ternational Mechanical Engineering Design.

March 1-5. Machine Agricole (SIMA)—International Farm Machinery Show.

March 1-8. Agriculture (SIA)—International Agricultural Show.

March 14-17. Premiere Vision—Fabrics.

March 15-17. MIDEC—International Footwear Show.

March 18-25. TOURISME ET VOYAGE SMTV—World Tourism & Travel Show.

March 20-23. Franchise Show.

March 24-26. Cadeau Et Entreprise—Incentive Premium and Business Gift Show.

March '92. FOURRURE—International Fur Industries Exhibition.

March '92. RESTAURATION RAPIDE—Fast Food Exhibition.

April 1-7. MACHINE OUTIL—Machine Tools, Tools, Metrology, Welding, Assembly, Computer Technologies In Manufacturing.

April 1-7. EUROFOUR EUROFONDERIE—Furnace, Industrial Heat and Foundry Equipment Exhibition.

May 19-26. TPG—International Exhibition of Paper, Printing and Graphic Arts.

June 11-16. ENTEX—International Textiles Cleaning Exhibition.

Sept. 4-8. BIJORHCA—International Show of Jewelry, Gold, Silverware, Clocks and Gifts.

Sept. 4-8. Moving International— Top Drawer.

Sept. 4-8. PRET-A-PORTER FEMININ PAPF—International Ladies Ready-To-Wear Exhibition.

Sept. 5-8. Salon International De La Mode Enfantine—International Children's Fashion Show.

Sept. 5-8. SEHM—International Men's and Boys' Fashion Show.

Sept. 5-9. PAAS International— International Home Decoration and Gift Professional Show.

Sept. 5-9. PARALLELE—Professional Trade Show For Objects and Gifts.

Sept. 5-9. Maison Des

Internationaux Createurs— International Gift Decoration Jewel and Object Show.

Sept. 5-8. MONDE DE L'ENFANT— Baby Care Nursery Juvenile Products and Permanent Toys.

Sept. 6-8. SISEL-SPORTS— International Sporting and Leisure Goods and Equipment Show.

Sept. 6-8. MIDEC—International Footwear Fashion Show.

Sept. 8-11. EXPOPROTECTION SECURITE—International Exhibition of Protection Security and Safety.

Sept. 19-22. SEMAINE INTERNATIONALE DU CUIR—International Leather Week Show.

Sept. 20-23. QUOIEM— Domestic and Garden Tools and Hardware.

Sept. 23-25. CADEAU ET ENTREPRISE—Premium and Business Gift Show.

Sept. 26-Oct. 4. Salon De La Caravane, Des Vehicules et Residences De Loisirs— Caravan Trailers and Motor Home Vehicles Exhibition.

September. Salon International De La Musique—International Music Fair.

Oct. 3-6. Premiere Vision— Fabrics.

Oct. 5-9. SICOB—International Trade Show For Data Processing, Telematics, Communications, and Office Equipment.

Oct. 25-29. SIAL—International Food Products Exhibition.

Oct. 26-30. MATIC—International Exhibition of Equipment and Techniques for the Meat Industry and Trade.

Oct. 26-30. EQUIPMAG— Equipment For Retail Industry.

Oct. 27-30. GIA—International Exhibition For Food Processing Equipment.

Oct. 2 7-30. EQUIPMENT LAITIER (SIEL)—International Exhibition of Dairy Equipment.

Oct. 27-30. PUBLICITE SUR LIEU DE VENTE— European Show For Point of Sales Communication.

Nov. 12   -18. EMBALLAGE— International Packaging Exhibition.

Nov. 13-16. SILMO—Spectacles, Ocular Instruments & Equipments For Opticians.

Nov. 17-20. PHYSIQUE— Physics Exhibition.

Nov. 17-23. EQUIP'HOTEL— International Hotel and Catering Equipment Show.

Nov. 30-Dec. 4. ELEC—International Electrical Equipment Exhibition.

Nov. 30-Dec. 4. PRONIC— Electronic Components and Equipment.

Nov. 30-Dec. 4. MIDEST— International Market of SubContracting.

Dec. 4-14. Salon Nautique International—International Boat Show.

Dec. 5-13. Salon Du Cheval et Du Poney—Horse and Pony Show.

Dec. 8-11. FORAINEXPOR AMUSEXPO—Amusement Park Materials Exhibition.

Villeurbanne

Sept. 15-18. INSA-TECHNOLOGIES—Exhibition of Industrial Scientific Equipment.

Gabon

Libreville

March 22-April 6. Libreville International Fair.

Dec. 15-30. Commercial Fortnight. *Contact U.S. Embassy Libreville via pouch Libreville 2270, Washington, D.C. 20521-2270; tel. 011-241-76-20-03; fax 011-24174-55-07.*

Germany

Berlin

Jan. 17-26, GRUENE WOCHE—International Green Week. International Fair For Food, Forestry Agriculture, and Wine.

March 7-12. ITB—International Tourism Exchange.

June 15-21. IIA—International Aerospace Technologies Exhibition.

Cologne

Jan. 14-15. It's Cologne (Spring)—International Trend Show For Fashion.

Jan. 21-26. International Moebelmesse—Furniture Fair.

Feb. 2-6. ISM—International Sweets and Biscuits Fair.

Feb. 7-9. HERREN MODE WOCHE— International

Spring Menswear Fair.
Feb. 18-21.
DOMOTECHNICA— International Fair For Home Appliances, Household Goods.
Feb. 21-23. Kind and Jugend— International Spring Baby To Teenager Fair.
March 8-11. International Eisenwarenmesse—International Hardware Fair.
April 6-11. IDS—International Dental Show.
May 1-15. OPTICA—International Trade Fair For Opthalmic Optics.
July 14-15. It's Cologne (Fall)— International Trend Show For Fashions.
Aug. 14-16. Herren Mode Woche—International Fall Menswear Fair.
Aug. 21-23. Kind and Jugend— International Fall Baby To Teenager Fair.
Aug. 30-Sept. 1 SPOGA— International Trade Fair For Sports Goods, Camping Equipment and Garden Furniture.
Aug. 30-Sept. 1. GAFA—International Garden Trade Fair.
Sept. 16-22.
PHOTOKINA— International Trade Fair For Video/Cameras/Photofinishing.
Sept. 30-Oct. 4. IFMA—International Bicycle and Motor Cycle Exhibition.
Oct. 22 -2 7. ORGATEC—International Computer and Office Equipment Trade Show.

Dortmund
Feb. 17-21.
INTERSCHUL— Educational Products Trade Fair.

Dusseldorf
Jan. 18-25. BOOT—International Boat Show.
March 8-11. IGEDO—International Fashion Trade Fair With Sections For Lingerie, Foundations, and Swimwear.
March 20-23. GDS—International Spring Footwear Fair.
April 6-10. WIRE—International Wire and Cable Trade Fair.
April 6-10. TUBE—International Tube and Pipe Trade Fair.
May 25-29. ENVITEC—International Trade Fair With Congress For Environmental Products and Technology.
Sept. 6-9. IGEDO—International Fashion Trade Fair With Sections For Lingerie, Foundations and Swimwear.
Sept. 18-21. GDS—International Fall Footwear Fair.
Sept. 22-26. GLASTEC—International Trade Fair For Glass Machinery, Equipment, Applications, and Products.
Oct. 5-10. INTERKAMA—International Trade Fair For Innovations In Measurement and Automation.
Oct. 29-Nov. 5. K—International Kunststoff Messe—Trade Fair for Plastic and Rubber.
Nov. 18-21. MEDICA & BIOTEC— International Medical and Biotechnology Trade Fair.
Nov. 30-Dec. 4.
HOGATEC—International Trade Fair For Hotels, Gastronomy, Catering.
Nov. 30-Dec. 4.
DISCOTEC—International Light and Sound Entertainment Fair.

Essen
Jan. 22-29. DEUBAU—Building Trade Fair.
Feb. 14-16. IPM—International Trade Fair For Plants, Horticultural Equipment, Florist's Supplies.
May 27-30. REIFEN—International Trade Fair For Tires and Tire Technology.
Sept. 26-Oct. 4. Caravan Salon— International Caravan Exhibition.
Oct. 13-16. Security—International Security Products Exhibition.

Frankfurt
Jan. 8-11. HEIMTEXTIL—International Trade Fair For Home and Household Textiles.
Jan. 22-25. IMA—International Amusement and Vending Machines Trade Fair.
Jan. 25-29. International Spring Trade Fair For Consumer Goods.
Feb. 15-19. AMBIENTE—International Spring Trade Fair For Consumer Goods.
March 11-15.
MUSIKMESSE—International Trade Fair For Musical Instruments and Accessories.

March 19-22. International Pelzmesse—Trade Fair For Fur and Fashion.
April 7-9. INTERSTOFF—International Spring Trade Fair For Clothing Textiles.
May 5-7. INFOUASE—International Trade Fair For Database Producers, Database Software, and Associated Products.
May 16-21. IFFA—International Trade Fair For the Meat Industry.
Aug. 22-26. International Fall Trade Fair For Consumer Goods.
Sept. 8-13. AUTOMECHANIKA—International Trade Fair For Automobile Aftermarket Products, Workshop, and Service-Station Equipment.
Sept. 24-27. PLANTEC—International Trade Fair For Horticulture.
Sept. 30-Oct. 5. Frankfurt Buchmesse—Frankfurt Book Fair.
Oct. 27-29. INTERSTOFF—International Fall Trade Fair For Clothing Textiles.
Nov 3-7. DLG-FOODTEC '92—International Exhibition For Dairy, Technology and Food Processing.

Friedrichshafen
Sept. 19-27. Interboot—International Water Sports Exhibition.

Hamburg
March 13-18. INTERNORGA—International Exhibition For The Hotel, Restaurant, Catering, Baking, and Confectionery Trades.
Sept. 29-Oct. 3. SMM—International Shipping and Marine Technology Market.
Oct. 31-Nov. 8. Hanseboot with EMTEC Trade Days—International Boat Show With European Marine Trade Exhibition and Congress.

Hannover
Jan. 6-9. DOMOTEX—International Trade Fair For Carpets and Floor Coverings.
Feb 7-12. CONSTRUCTA—International Exhibition For the Building Trades.
March 11-18. CEBIT—World Center For Office, Information and Telecommunications Technology.
April 1-8. Hannover Messe Industries—Hannover Industry Fair.
May 9-17. IAA—International Motor Show For Commercial Vehicles.
May 27-30. DACH & WAND— Trade Fair For Roof, Wall, and Insulation Techniques.
June 1-4. INTERHOSPITAL—International Exhibition For Hospital Equipment and Congress.
Sept. 15-17. Biotechnica Hannover—International Trade Fair For Biotechnology.
Oct. 27-31. BLECH—International Sheet Metal Working Exhibition.

Leipzig
March 5-10. Leipziger Messe— Spring Leipzig Fair (Technical Products).
March 21-23. Leipziger Messe— Spring Leipzig Fair (Consumer Goods).
Sept. 3-8. Leipziger Messe— Fall Leipzig Fair (Technical Products). *Sept. 12-15.* Leipziger Messe— Fall Leipzig Fair (Consumer Goods).

Munich
Feb. 7-10. INHORGENTA—International Spring Trade Fair For Watches, Clocks and Jewelry.
Feb. 16-18. MODE WOCHE—International Spring Fashion Fair.
Feb. 27-March 1. ISPO—International Spring Trade Fair For Sports Equipment.
March 14-22. IMM—International Light Industries and Handicrafts Fair.
April 6-12. BAUMA—International Trade Fair For Construction Machinery and Equipment.
May 5-8. ANALYTICA—International Trade Fair For Biochemical and Analytical Instruments.
Aug. 16-18. MODE WOCHE—International Fall Fashion Fair.
Sept. 1-4. ISPO—International Trade Fair For Sports Equipment.
Sept. 12-14. INHORGENTA—Interna-

tional Fall Trade Fair For Watches, Clocks and Jewelery.

Sept. 19-23. IMEGA—International Trade Fair For the Food Industry, With Technology For the Food Trade, Hotel, Restaurant and Catering.

Oct. 20-23. SYSTEC—International Trade Fair For Computer Integration in Industry.

Nov. 10-14. ELECTRONICA—International Trade Fair For Components and Assemblies In Electronics.

Nuremberg

Feb. 6-12. Spielwarenmesse—International Toy Fair.

March 13-16. IWA—International Trade Fair For Hunting and Sporting Arms and Accessories.

May 7 -10. INTERZOO—International Trade Fair For Pet Supplies.

Nov. 12-14. BRAU—European Trade Fair For Brewery and Beverage Industries.

Offenbach

Jan. 23-26. International Lederwarenmesse—Spring Leather Goods Fair.

Aug. 22-25. International Lederwarenmesse—Fall Leather Goods Fair.

Pirmasens

May 5 - 7. PLW—International Spring Leather Exhibition.

Nov. 3-5. PLW—International Fall Leather Exhibition.

Stuttgart

Feb. 22 -2 7. INTERGASTRA—International Trade Fair For Hotel Catering and Confectionery.

March 10-14. INTHERM—International Trade Fair For Heating, Air-Conditioning and Firing Systems.

March 21-24. IKOFA—International Trade Fair For the Food Industry, Specialities, Shopfitting and Equipment.

May 5-8. CAT—International Exhibition For Computer Aided Technology.

Sept. 1-5. AMB—International Exhibition For Metalworking.

Sept. 16-19. REINIGUNGTECHNIK—Exhibition For Cleaning Techniques, Cleaning Products, Maintenance, etc.

Oct. 10-14. INTERBAD—International Trade Fair For Swimming Pools, Medicinal Baths Sauna and Equipment For Baths.

Ghana

Accra

Feb. 29-March 14. Third Ghana Industry and Technology Fair. *Contact Karl Fritz, Commercial Attache, U.S. Embassy—Accra, Ring Road East, P. O. Box 194 Accra, Ghana; tel. 011-233-21775297/8, fax 011-233-21776008.*

Greece

Athens

Jan. 17-20. American High Technology Computer Exhi-

bition.

Peania, Attica

October (date not yet available). IDNEX Computer Show. *November (dates not yet available).* Multi-Index Industrial Equipment Show.

Piraeus

June 1-5. Posidonia International Exhibition for Shipping, Marine Equipment and Services.

Oct. 6-10. Defendory International Exhibition of Defense Systems and Equipment for Land Sea-Air.

Thessaloniki

Feb. 2-9. Agrotica Agricultural Equipment/Supplies Exhibition.

Feb. 21-25. INFACOMA Building Materials, Heating, Insulation, Solar Energy Exhibition.

April 11-19. International Boat Exhibition.

Sept. 12-21. Thessaloniki International Fair.

Oct. 1-5. INFOSYSTEM. Information/Computer Network Systems Exhibition.

Nov. 13-16. Hotelia Equipment/Catering for Hotels, Restaurants Bakeries, Pastry Shops, Hospitals and Shops.

Guatemala

Guatemala City

February (second week). V National Convention of Architecture.

Feb. 26-28. Apparel Sourcing Show.

March (last week). XII Registered Cattle National Exposition.

March 26. EXPODENTAL '92.

April (third week). National Fair of Folklore and Handcrafts.

April 26-28. Visit U.S.A. Trade Show.

Mid-June. Annual Work Session of the Guatemalan Dental Society.

July 15 (tentative). National Tourism Congress.

Mid-August. Computer/Data Processing Convention.

October-November. National Fair

Oct. 9. Furniture Salon.

November. National Medical Congress.

November. National Gynecology Congress.

November. VII National Radiology Congress.

November (second week). National Cattle Exposition—EXPOGANA.

Nov. 22-25. Automobile Salon.

November. Agritrade V—International Convention.

Quetzaltenango

March 5-7. First International Guatemalan Handicrafts Expositions and Convention, Folklore

Honduras
San Pedro Sula

March. ISTMOFER (Feria del Istmo).

Hong Kong

Jan. 13-16. Hong Kong Fashion Week.

March 7-10. 3rd INTERPLAS Asia.

March 31-April 3. COMMTEL Asia.

May 6-9. ELENEX '92, SECURITEX '92, LUMINEX '92, and AIRVEX '92.

May 12-15. Computer '92.

May 22-26. Asian Industrial Expo.

June 10-13. International Building Exhibition '92.

June 14-17. Cosmetics Hair and Beauty '92.

July 11-14. GARMENTEC '92.

August. Food Expo '92.

August. Hong Kong Book Fair.

Oct. 14-17. Hong Kong Electronics Fair.

Oct. 23-26. Homestyle '92.

Nov. 4-6. INTERSTOFF Asia International Fabric Show.

Hungary
Budapest

March 19-22. Travel '92.

April 7-10. SECUREX (labor safety and security).

April 7-10. CONSTRUMA (building, construction).

April 23-26. Beauty and Health.

April 27-30. IFABO (computer, telecommunications).

May 20-27. BNV Budapest Industrial Fair.

Sept. 18-27. BNV Consum Goods Fair.

Sept. 18-27. HOVENTA

(catering).

Oct. 12-17. Europa Telecom.

Oct. 27-30. BUDATRANSPACK.

Nov. 7-11. AUTOMOBIL '92.

Nov. 25-29. FOODAPEST (food processing, drinks).

India
Bombay

Jan. 14-19. Offshore and Energy '92. 6th International Exhibition and Conference on Offshore Oil Gas, and Energy Development.

Jan. 17-21. Textile Festival '92 (textile/garments exhibition).

August-September (exact dates not yet set). Food Equipment '92 (food, food processing, hotel and restaurant equipment and supplies).

Nov. 27-Dec. 6. India ITME '92 (textile machinery).

New Delhi

Feb. 4-10. WISITEX '92 (instrumentation, computer hardware and software, telecommunications, electronics products and test equipment, electronic components, industrial electronics, process controls, and medical electronics).

March 7-16. IMTEX '92. Indian Machine Tool Exhibition.

Indonesia
Jakarta

Jan. 22-25. Airportech 2000

Jan. 25-Feb. 2. Indo Product.

Feb. 28-March 7. Industry,

Trade & Tourism Expo '92. *March 26-29.* International Robotic Technology. *April 22-25.* Exportel '92. *May 6-10.* Nusatex & Garmet '92. *May 19-23.* Indotex '92. *Aug. 5-8.* Machine Technology Indonesia. *Sept. 2-5.* Banking & Office Equipment Technology Indonesia Informatics Technology Indonesia, and Unix Forum Indonesia. *Sept. 22-26.* Building and Construction Indonesia, and Hotel, Catering & Tourism Indonesia. *Sept. 23-26.* Elmitech Indonesia. *Oct. 20-24.* Woodworking and Forestry Indonesia and Agriculture and Food Indonesia. *Nov. 10-14.* Manufacturing Indonesia.

Ireland
Dublin
Jan. 22-26. Holiday World. *Jan. 29-30.* Garden Leisure and Groundsmanship Expo. *Feb. 14-16.* Fish Industries Exhibition. *Feb. 16-18.* LEISUREQUIP. *Feb. 23-26.* Furniture Fair. *March 12-14.* ELEX (electrotechnical exhibition). *March 24-26.* PLASTEX. *March 25-27.* COMPUTEX/ IBETA. *April 10-12.* Motor Trade Show. *April 28-30.* IFEX (food and drink industry). *May 6-10.* Spring Show. *Sept. 13-15.*

FOODPROCESS '92. *Oct. 6-10.* Building Exhibition. *Oct. 21-24.* ENQUIP (engineering and industrial equipment).

Israel
Jerusalem
Nov. 2-5. MEDAX—hospital supplies and medical technology.

Tel Aviv
Feb. 3-6. ISRACHEM— chemical engineering and industrial processing. *Feb. 3-6.* ANALIZA—laboratory equipment. *May 11-14.* RAX—electrical engineering and instrumentation. *June 2-4.* COMPUTAX— computer systems, equipment, and software. *June 2-4.* GRAFIX—equipment and supplies for graphic architects and draftsmen. *Nov. 23-26.* FIS—office equipment. *Dec. 7-10.* KITEX-HOTEX— food processing, hotel, and restaurant equipment.

Italy
Bari
Feb. 13-17. International computers and related office equipment. *Sept. 11-21.* International general trade exhibition.

Bologna
March 25-29. International exhibition of interior fittings

and finishings. *April 8-11.* Children's books. *April 24-27.* Perfumery and cosmetics. *May 6-8 and Nov. 18-20.* Shoe and leather industry supplies. *Sept. 11-14.* Health foods. *Oct. 21-25.* Building industrialization. *Dec. 5-13.* International motor show.

Carrara
May 27-31. Marble and machinery.

Florence
Feb. 7-10 and Sept. 11-14. Florence Gift Mart. *April 24-May 1.* International handcrafts show.

Foggia
April 30-May 5. International agricultural exhibition.

Genoa
Feb. 17-21. The automated factory show. *May 27-31.* Exhibition on renovation, restructuring maintenance in the building industry. *Oct. 15-25.* International boat show and underwater equipment exhibition. *Nov. 9-13.* International exhibition of the furnishing and technologies for hospital industry

Messina
Aug. 16. International fair.

Milan
Jan. 17-20 and June 5-8. Gift

articles, fancy goods, perfumery items, smokers' accessories.
Jan. 24-29. International toy exhibition.
Feb. 14-17 and Sept. 4-7. Crystalware, ceramics, jewelry, silverware, gift articles, etc.
Feb. 26-March 1. International tourism exhibition.
March 5-9. Environmental and pollution control equipment.
March 21-26. Packaging machinery, mechanical handling equipment.
April 10-15. Furniture and accessories.
May 8-11. International exhibition of optics, optometry, and ophthalmology.
May 25-29. Electronics and electrotechnics.
Oct. 1-5. Equipment computers, telecom, and furniture.
Oct. 6-10. Equipment for trade, tourism, and catering; and equipment, beverages, and food products.

Naples
Jan. 31-Feb. 6. International exhibit of hotel industry.
March 7-15. International boats and marine equipment.
Nov. 11-15. International computers & related equipment.

Padua
May 16-24. International samples

Palermo
May 23-June 7. International general consumer goods show.

Parma
May 7-11. International good fair.

Rimini
Jan. 18-23. Confectionery and ice-cream exhibition.
Nov. 28-Dec. 2. Hotel equipment exhibition.

Rome
May 23-June 7. International general trade exhibition.
Nov. 11-15. International electronic space energy exhibition.

Turin
April 23-May 3. International automobile show.

Verona
March 10-15. International agricultural exhibition.

Vicenza
Jan. 12-19. International exhibit of gold, jewelry, and silverware

Japan
Fukuoka
April 16-17. 6th American Electronics Show.
Sept. 24-26. Kyushu International Techno Fair '92.
October (Planned). 3rd U.S. Japan Construction and Design Seminar Meeting.
Nov. 28-29. American Medical Seminar and Hospital Show '92.

Itakyushu
March 19-22. Western Japan Total Living Show.
April 16-18. Nishinihon Techno Exhibition.
May 22-25. Western Japan General Machinery Show and CAD/CAM/CG Show.
Oct. 5-11. West Japan Food Fair.

Kobe
March 4-6. 7th International Gift Show.
June 4-7. Kobe International Home Fair.
Aug. 25-27. 8th International Gift Show.
Sept. 24-27. WASTEC '92.
Oct. 15-18. Kobe Import Fair.
Nov. 20-23. Expo Jibs '92.

Kyoto
June 11-13. Semicon Kansai.

Nagoya
April 9-13. Chubu Pack.
June 13-16. Factory Automation Show '92.
Nov. 13-16. Plastic Industry Fair.

Osaka
March 3-5. World Fashion Trade Fair.
March 31-April 1. World Fashion Collection.
April 24-29. 20th Osaka International Trade Fair.
Oct. 23-26. 6th Japan International Food. Engineering & Industry Show.
Nov. 4-6. TECHTEXTIL Asia.
Nov. (planned). Osaka Imported Car Show.

Sapporo

April 23-26. High-Tech Hokkaido '92.

September (planned). Living & housing fair.

November (planned). Sapporo CG (computer graphics) '92.

Tokyo

Jan. 29-Feb. 1. JAPANTEX Show—Japan interior fabrics.

Feb. 5-6. Tokyo Sports Show '92.

Feb. 11-16. Tokyo International Boat Show.

Feb. 12-14. U.S. Solo Apparel Show.

Feb. 12-15. INTEROFFICE 92—8th International Office Environment and Intelligent Building Show.

Feb. 24-26. International Jewelry Tokyo '92.

February (planned). Tokyo International Book Fair.

March 3-6. Meat Industry Fair '92.

March 10-12. Sports Medicine/Rehabilitation Equipment Exhibition and Seminar.

March 10-14. FOODEX Japan '92.

March 10-14. HOTERES Japan 92—International Hotel and Restaurant Show.

March 10-14. Leisure Innovation '92.

March 17-19. Dental Equipment Show.

March 25-28. Study U.S.A. Exhibition.

March 27-30. Self Service Fair.

April 6-9. Communications Tokyo '92.

April 22-25. Microcomputer Show.

April 24-29. Tokyo International Good Living Show.

May 9-10. Camping and R.V. Show.

May 19-22. High-Tech Materials Exhibition.

May 19-22. International Food Machinery Exhibition.

May 20-23. Lifestyle Europe Exhibition.

May 20-23. Business Show

July 24. Fine Process Technology Japan.

July 9-11. International Modern Hospital Show.

July 14-17. Industrial Measuring and Metrology Show.

Sept. 4-6. Japan D.I.V. Show.

Sept. 12-13. Japan Pharmaceutical Association—Congress of Pharmaceutical Sciences.

Sept. 16-18. Microwave U.S.A. '92.

Sept. 16-19. Data Show

Sept. 24-25. Matchmaker—Sporting goods, physical fitness and recreation equipment.

Sept. 26-29. Sports Japan '92 (fall)

Sept. 30-Oct. 2. Software Systems U S.A. '92.

Oct. 13-16. Analytical Instruments Show.

Oct. 14-17. Caterex Japan '92— 14th Japan Food Catering and Equipment Exhibition.

Oct. 14-17. Japan Home Show '92.

Oct. 27-Nov. 4. International Machine Tool Show.

Nov. 11-12. Tokyo Sports Show '92.

Nov. 11-14. HOSPEX Japan 92—17th International Hospital Engineering Exhibition.

Nov. 16-19. Scientific Instruments Show.

Nov. 22-25. Japan Food Service Show.

Dec. 3-6. International Furniture Fair Tokyo.

Yokohama

April 22-24. Supercomputing Japan '92.

Kenya

March 6-8. Education and Training Exhibition.

June 17-29. Computer Exhibition.

Sept. 29-Oct. 3. Nairobi International Show.

Korea

Seoul

Feb. 12-15. Communication Networks Korea '92.

March 13-16. Korea International Fishing Tackle Show '92

March 13-16. Korea International Golf Show '92.

March 13-17. Korea International Factory Automation System Exhibition '92.

March 24-26. International Electronics Production Exhibition Conference/Semiconductor International Exhibition Korea '92.

March 24-27. International Exhibition for Environmental Pollution Control Measuring Testing Equipment '92.

April 2-6. Seoul International

Lighting Show '92.

April 2-6. Seoul International Total Interior Show '92.

April 16-20. Seoul International Chemical Plant Exhibition '92.

April 16-22. Korea International Exhibition for Computers, Office Automation and Related Equipment '92.

April 22-25. Korea International Leather and Fur Exhibition '92.

May 4-10. Seoul International Machine Tool Show '92.

May 20-24. Korea International Electronic Parts and Equipment '92.

June 4-8. Korea International Plastics, Rubber, Ceramics Show '92.

June 8-11. Industrial Pulp and Paper Exhibition for Korea '92.

June 17-21. Seoul International Kitchen Show '92.

June 17-21. Seoul International Sanitary Show '92.

June 17-21. Korea International Sports and Leisure Industries Exhibition incorporating Boat Show '92.

June 24-28. ROKAF Aerospace Symposium and Exhibition.

July 1-5. Korea International Safety and Security Exhibition

Aug. 22-26. Korea International Transportation, Handling Equipment and Storage System Exhibition '92.

Sept. 1-5. Korea International CAD/CAM & Graphics Exhibition '92.

Sept. 18-22. Seoul International Supermarket Show '92.

Sept. 19-23. International Factory Automation, Precision Instruments Show '92.

Oct. 15-20. Korea Electronics Show '92.

Oct. 19-21. Seoul Visit USA Travel Trade Show '92.

Oct. 28-31. Korea International Welding Show '92.

Oct. 28-31. Korea International Metal Working Show '92.

Nov. 7-11. Korea Auto Parts and Accessories Exhibition '92.

Dec. 11-15. Seoul International Instrumentation Exhibition '92.

Kuwait
Kuwait City

Jan. 8-17. Perfumes and Cosmetics Exhibition.

Jan. 8-17. 9th Modern House Exhibition.

Jan. 24-Feb. 8. Lebanese Trade Exhibition.

Feb. 2-7. INFO '92 Exhibition (computers and business equipment).

Feb. 26-March 3. Kuwait International Trade Fair.

March 17-23. ELECTRO '92 Exhibition.

March 18-26. Kuwait Fashion Exhibition.

Aug. 19-28. Educational Instruments Exhibition.

Dec. 2-11. Watches and Gifts Exhibition.

Dec. 2-11. Children's World Exhibition.

Dec. 9-18. Arabic Books Exhibition.

Luxembourg

March 7-15. 28th EUROPLEINAIR. Leisure and open-air.

March 12-15. 18th Antiques and Fine Arts Exhibition, together with the 11th Luxembourg Book Festival.

April 11-12. International Dog Show.

April 26-29. 6th Europe-Meubles. Furniture Show Belgium Luxembourg.

May 23-31. 58th (Spring) Luxembourg International Fair. Consumer goods.

Sept. 18-20. OEKO-Fair. Ecological products.

Sept. 18-21. Euro JICSA. European Kitchen and Bath Convention.

Oct. 3-11. 59th (Autumn) Luxembourg International Fair. Construction materials, household appliances, business equipment audio-visual equipment, advertismg gifts.

Oct. 17-18. Kruse International. Collector Car Show and Auction.

October (no definite date). International Trade Fair for Police Equipment.

Nov. 10-12. VSAT Conference and European Satellite Users' Show (4th Annual Conference and Exhibition).

Nov. 19-21. University and Professional Training Information Show.

Contact Commerce Department Desk Officer for Luxembourg at (202) 377-5373

Malawi

Blantyre

June 3-8. 5th Malawi International Trade Fair.
Contact Commerce Deparment Desk Officer for Malawi at (202) 377-5148.

Malaysia

March 11-15. Woodwork '92. 3rd Malaysian International Forestry, Timber Processing and Woodworking Exhibition.

April 27-30. DSA '92. 3rd Defense Services Asia Exhibition and Conference.

June 24-28. ITM '92. 6th Malaysian International Trade Fair of Industrial Development Technology Machinery and Equipment.

July 27-30. TECHNOBUILD '92.

Aug. 20-23. GARMENTEX '92. 4th Malaysian International Textile, Garment, Equipment and Materials Exhibition.

Aug. 20-23. Shoemach and Leather '92. 3rd Malaysian International Shoe and Leather Processing Machinery, Equipment and Materials Exhibition.

Oct. 6-11. MIF '92. Malaysia International Fair.

November (exact dates still to be decided). BOATEX '92. International Exhibition of Boats, Pleasure Crafts, and Auxiliary Equipment.

Mexico

Guadalajara, Jalisco

Jan. 14-18. Spring-Summer Expo Fashion.

Jan. 30-Feb. 1. Computers Expo.

Feb. 3-5. Exporter Wholesale Trade Show.

Feb. 11-13. Publicity Trade Show.

Feb. 20-23. Furniture Trade Show.

March 3-6. Packaging Material Exhibition.

March 3-6. Dairy Industry Show.

March 4-7. Office/School Furniture and Stationery.

March 5-8. Medical Equipment Exhibition.

March 22-24. Store Fittings Exhibition.

April 1-4. Textile Machinery Fabrics and Supplies.

April 2-5. Garden Industry Show.

May 11-16. Retail Show.

May 20-23. Electronic Equipment Conference and Expo.

May 23-26. Autumn-Winter Footwear Show.

June 3-7. Auto Show.

June 4-7. Books and School Supplies Expo.

June 17-21. Contemporary National Art Fair.

June 18-21. Gift Expo.

July 10-12. Furniture Suppliers Exhibition.

July 21-25. Autumn-Winter Fashion Show.

Aug. 5-8. Furniture Manufacturers Trade Show.

Aug. 17-19. First Ibero-American Conference on Bar Codes for Industry and Commerce.

Aug. 19-22. Metalworking Manufacturing and Equipment Show.

Aug. 27-30. Candy Show.

Aug. 27-30. Interior Design and Home Furnishing Expo.

Sept. 3-5. Footwear Suppliers Exhibition.

Sept. 9-11. Informatic and Telecommunication Expo.

Sept. 12-14. Automotive Parts and Spare Equipment Exhibition.

Sept. 19-20. Beauty Congress and Trade Show.

Sept. 20-22. National Hardware Show.

Sept. 28-Oct. 2. Jewelry and Silver Exposition.

Oct. 7-10. Sporting Goods and Recreation Expo.

Oct. 7-11. Industrial Equipment Exhibition.

Oct. 17-20. Spring-Summer Footware Show.

Oct. 28-Nov. 8. Retail Show.

Nov. 18-22. Builders Show.

Nov. 28-Dec. 6. International Book Fair.

Monterrey

Feb. 27-29. Mexican Association of Automobile Distributors.

April 22-25. Petroleum Expo.

April 30-May 3. Mexico Hardware Show.

Aug. 6-9. EXI-MUEBLE (furniture).

Sept. 22-24. USA Tech (industrial).

Morocco

Casablanca

Jan. 30-Feb. 2. Food Expo.

Feb. 11-15. Mechanical/Metallurgical/Electrical

Show.

Feb. 24-March 1. Textile and Leather Show.

April 14-19. Agriculture Show.

May 5-9. Sea Show.

May 21-26. Plastic/Processing/Packaging Show.

June 3-6. Tourism Show.

Oct. 1-6. Building and Con struction Show.

Oct. 22-25. Medical Expo.

Mozambique
Maputo

Aug. 28-Sept. 6.
Mozambique International Trade Fair (FACIM). *Contact Commerce Department Desk Officer for Mozambique a (202) 377-5148.*

Namibia
Windhoek

May 6-10. 2nd Annual Namibia International Trade Fair.

Oct. 3-9. 34th Annual Windhoek Show—oriented toward local companies. Contact: Mrs. Alet Halbich Windhoek Show Society, P.O. Box 1733, Windhoek, Namibia tel. 264-61-224728, fax 264-61 -22707.

Netherlands
Amsterdam

Jan. 6-9. HORECAVA 92— Hotel and restaurant equipment exhibition.

Jan. 20-25. LANDBOUW '92—Agricultural equipment show.

Feb. 6-15. Commercial vehicles exhibition.

March 7-15. HISWA '92— boat show.

March 25-April 5. Housewares Show.

*April30-May5.*FESPA'92— Screenpriting exhibition.

May 6-8. MCWORLD EXPO '92.

May 19-22. INTERCLEAN—industrial cleaning equipment exhibition.

Sept. 1-4. ENVIRO AMSTERDAM— Waste management, environment technology exhibition.

Sept. 1-4. AQUATECH 92—water technology exhibition.

Sept. 14-20. FIRATO 92— Consumer electronics show.

Oct. 5-9. EFFICIENCY BEURS '92—Office, information and communication technology exhibition.

Nov. 3-5. Holland Offshore '92.

Nov. 3-5. METs '92—Marine equipment show.

Nov. 3-5. PETROTECH '92— Refining and petrochemical exhibition.

Nov. 3-6. EUROCOMM '92— telecommunications exhibition.

Nov. 20-25. Caravan and Camping RAI '92.

Utrecht

Jan. 19-22. KARWEI '92— Do-It-Yourself Show.

Feb. 18-22. VSK '92— Plumbing heating, and air conditioning show.

March 8-12. Consumer Goods Spring Fair.

March 16-21. Techni Show '92— Industrial production technology show.

March 29-31. National Franchising Show.

April 6-10. HETInstrument Healthcare, Scientific, and Industrial Instruments show.

*May6-9.*EuropeSoftware'92.

May 17-20. ROKA—International food exhibition.

Sept. 6-9. International furniture show.

Sept. 6-10. Consumer Goods Fall Fair.

*Sept. 13-17.*INTERDECOR '92— Carpet and household textiles show.

Sept. 22-25. VIV—Intensive animal production show.

Oct. 5-10. AANDRIJFTECHNIEK '92—Power transmission engineering show.

Oct. 12-16. Machevo Food Engineering '92.

Oct. 12-16. Machevo Process Equipment '92.

Dec. 8-12. INTERSURFACE 92— Surface treatment protection, and corrosion prevention exhibition.

New Zealand
Auckland

March 6-8. Personal Investment

*March6-8.*Franchising 1992.

March 6-8. Destinations (holiday and travel show).

March 15-17. Autumn Gift Fair.

March 31-April 2. Computerworld.

April 30-May 2. Computing

'92— Auckland.
May 20-23. EMEX—engineering machinery and machine tools (includes Control' 92, Materials Handling '92, and Woodex '92).
June 13-16. Hospitality '92.
June 20-22. Pharmacy.
June 21-24. "50 Plus Lifestyle." *July 16-20.* Motor Show.
Aug. 4-6. APEX (advertising, marketing services).
Aug. 9-12. Food Service '92.
Aug. 12-16. IMTEC Boat Show.
Sept. 23-27. New Zealand Home Show.
Oct. 4-6. Christmas Stocking Fair.
Nov. 3-5. Foodtech.
Nov. 10-12. Macworld Expo (Apple computers and accessories).

Christchurch
March 14-16. Destinations (holiday and travel show).
June 9-11. Business Expo.
Sept. 13-15. South Island Gift Fair.
Oct. 1-3. Computing '92—Christchurch.
Oct. 16-18. Christchurch Home Show.

Hamilton
June 11-13. National Agricultural Fieldays.

Wellington
Aug. 12-14. Computing '92—Wellington.

Nigeria
Kaduna
Feb. 21-March 1. Kaduna International Trade Fair.

Lagos
April 7-10. Oil, gas, and petroleum exhibition.
May. Computers, telecommunications, and office equipment.

Norway
Oslo
Jan. 9-12. Reiseliv '92 (Norway's 5th international travel fair and conference).
Feb. 4-8. Storhusholdning '92 (Norway's 11th international hotel, restaurant, institutional, and catering exhibition and conference).
Feb. 22-25. Oslo Fashion Week (spring fashions).
March 13-22. Sjoen for Alle (Oslo's international boat show).
May 12-15. Moderne Emballering (modern packaging exhibition).
Aug. 29-Sept. 1. Oslo Fashion Week (winter fashions).
Sept. 14-18. Kontor '92 (office furniture and business machines).
Sept. 29-Oct. 3. The Technical Fair (machine tools).

Stavanger
Aug. 25-28. Offshore Northern Seas '92—ONS '92, with official U.S. pavilion (10th international offshore oil and gas equipment exhibition and conference).

Trondheim
Aug. 11-15. Nor-Fishing '92 (14th international fishing equipment exhibition and conference).

Oman
Feb. 19-28. Muscat International Trade Fair—consumer and industrial.
April 1-10. EID Festival—consumer fair.
June 9-19. EID Fair consumer fair.
Sept. 9-16. Autumn Fair—consumer and industrial.
Oct. 6-30. ELECOM—electronics and office automation (consumer and industrial).
Dec. 14-18. Gift and Fashion Show—consumer.
All events are held at the Oman Exhibition Centre, Seeb Airport, near Muscat. Contact: Hassan Mosafer, Operations Manager P. O. Box 1117, Seeb Airport, tel (968)510900, telex 5511 exhibit on; fax (968) 510055.

Panama
David, Province of Chiriqui
March 13-22. David International Trade Fair.

Panama City
March 11-16. Expocomer '92.
May 20-24. Fiaga (agricultural).
Aug. 25-30. Beautiful Homes.
Sept. 10-13. Office '92.
November. Expoauto (exact date not yet set).

Paraguay

Asuncion

Around mid-July. International Cattle and Agro-Industry Fair. *Contact: Asociacion Rural del Paraguay, Calle Antequera 651, Asuncion, Paraguay.*

Peru

Lima

Nov. 16-22. IX Agrotec (international trade fair for the agriculture, cattle, agroindustrial, and fishing industries).

Philippines

Manila

Jan. 16-19. Asia footwear and leather fair.
March 2-6. Transcom.
March 6-10. Ideal home fair.
March 12-15. Safety and Security Asia '92 (with U.S. Pavilion).
April 21-24. Asia Watersports.
May 1-5. Agri-Aqua—livestock and technology.
May 24-29. Buildex.
June 5-10. Health, sports and fitness fair.
June 17-21. Sights and Sounds Asia.
June 27-July 5. Defense and security fair.
July 1-4. Expochem Asia '92 (with U.S. Pavilion).
July 22-26. Franchising Philippines.
Aug. 6-9. Telecomex Asia '92 (with U.S. Pavilion).
Aug. 12-16. Electronica—audiovideo-hifi; and Pro Video light and sound expo.
Aug. 25-28. Asia Food Expo.

Aug. 26-29. Phil Telecom.
Sept. 4-9. Office World International.
Sept. 18-23. Food and beverage fair.
Sept. 30-Oct. 4. Machinetech.
Sept. 30-Oct. 4. Garmentex.
Sept. 30-Oct. 4. Machine/Pacprint.

Portugal

Aveiro

Nov. 21-25. EXPOMAR (Fishing and Naval Industry).

Lisbon

Jan. 8-12. BTL (Travel Market).
Jan. 22-26. FILEME (Office Automation, Equipment, Furniture.
Jan. 24-26. OPTITECNICA (Optical Equipment).
Feb. 6-9. INTERMODA/EXPOWEAR EXPOFASHION (Fashion).
Feb. 20-23. CERAMEX (Decorative Arts and Housewares).
March 6-15. NAUTICAMPO (Camping, Boating and Sport).
March 25-29. BRINCA *(Toys,* Didactical Material).
April 8-12. SK (Building Stone, Ceramics, Timber And Cork).
April 22-26. LARTECNICA (Housewares, Electrical Household Appliances).
May 6-10. TECNOFIL (Technology and Innovation).
May 6-10. FILTECNICA (Metalworking).
May 7-10. Franchising.

May 20-24. SIMAC (Building and Construction).
May 20-24. FILSOL (Alternative Sources of Energy).
June 4-7. FIL (Lisbon International Fair).
Sept. 10-13. INTERMODA/EXPOWEAR/EXPOFASHION (Fashion).
Sept. 22-27. VIDAUDIO (Sound and Audiovisual Equipment).
Oct. 6-11. INTERCASA (Furniture and Lighting).
Oct. 22-25. INFORPOR (Informatics).
Nov. 4-8. FILTRANS (Transportation).
Nov. 30-Dec. 8. MOTOEXPO (Two Wheels International Show).
Nov. 30-Dec. 8. AUTOCASIAO (Used Vehicles Market).

Oporto

Jan. 5-8. PORTEX '92 (Fashion).
Jan. 16-18. MOCAP 28 (Shoe Industry).
Jan. 23-25. FORUM DAS PME'S (Small/Medium-Size Firms).
Feb. 14-23. CAMPISPORT '92 (Camping/Sports).
March 4-8. EXPORT HOME '92 (Furniture).
March 12-15. FEPA '92 (stationery/toys).
March 21-29. VISOM '92 (Audiovisual/Photography).
April 8-12. ALIMENTACAO '92/ALITEC '92 (Food/Food Processing Equipment).
April 8-12. VINIPOR '92/

ENOTECNICA (Wine/ Wine Processing Equipment). *April 25-May 3.* EXPOMOVEL '92 (Furniture). *May 22-31.* PORTUGAL '92 (Automobile). *June 5-8.* AMBIENTE '92 (Environment). *June 18-20.* MOCAP '29 (Shoe Industry). *July 14* PORTEX '93 (Fashion). *Sept. 2-6.* CERANOR '92 (Ceramics, Decorating Articles). *Sept. 16-20.* FIP '92 (International Fair). *Sept. 16-20.* PORTOJOIA (Jewelry). *Sept. 16-20.* NORMEDICA '92 (Health). *Oct. 1-5.* HABITAT '92 (Home and Garden Furniture). *Oct. 1-5.* ENEREN '92 (Renewable Energy). *Oct. 8-11.* INFORMATICA '92 (Data Processing). *Oct. 22-25.* FIMAP/ FERRALIA '92 (Wood/ Wood Processing Equipment). *Nov. 4-8.* SUBCONTRATO/ PORTUGAL METAL/SIMIEX. METALOMECANICA '92 (Metal and Metalworking Machinery). *Nov. 18-21.* PORTEX LAR '92 (Textiles). *Dec. 10-13.* MAQUITEX '92 (Textile Equipment).

Romania

Bucharest
May 28-June 4. TIBCO '92 (consumer goods fair). *Oct. 8-15.* TIB '92 (Bucharest International Fair).

Saudi Arabia

Dhahran
Jan. 15-21. 11th Annual Motor Show. *April 19-23.* Oil, Gas and Energy Technologies Show. Oct. 11-15. Energex Show. *Oct. 25-30.* Computer Communication Show. *Nov. 8-12.* Petrochemicals, Plastics, Plastipack. *Nov. 22-26.* Regional Building Exhibition.

Jeddah
Jan. 16-24. Ideal Home '92 Show. *Feb. 2-6.* Middle East Education Training, Computing and Business Equipment. *Sept. 13-18.* Jeddah International Trade Fair. *Nov. 7-13.* Holiday, Fashion & Child World Show. *Nov. 22-26.* Jeddah Building Industries Show. *Dec. 6-11.* Jeddah Motor Show.

Riyadh
Jan. 26-30. Saudi Communications and Computer. *Feb. 16-21.* Riyadh International Trade Fair. *Oct. 4-8.* Saudi Agriculture. *Oct. 24-29.* Arabian Security Equipment & Technology Exhibition (ASTEX).

Nov. 8-12. Saudi Medicare and Dentistry. *Nov. 24-30.* Riyadh Motor Show.

Senegal

Dakar
Nov. 26-Dec. 7. Tenth International Trade Fair. Contact the Commerce Department Desk Officer for Senegal at (202) 377-4388.

Singapore

Feb. 25-March 1. Asian Aerospace '92. *April 7-10.* Food and Hotel Asia '92. *May 5-8.* Asian International Gift Fair '92. *June 2-5.* Communicasia '92. *Sept. 23-26.* Internepcon/ Semiconductor. *Oct. 15-18.* Singapore Informatics *Nov. 30-Dec. 3.* Offshore Southeast Asia '92. Contact: American Embassy, Singapore One Colomba Court, Unit 5-12, Singapare 0617: tel. (65) 338 972, fax (65) 338 5010.

South Africa

Cape Town (Cape Province)
March 18-21. Clothing/Machinery and Textile Fair. *May 27-June 6.* Design for Living. *Oct. 2-11.* National Motor Show. *Dec. 11-16.* International Boat Show.

Durban (Natal)
May. Royal Agricultural Show.
June 9-12. Nattrex. Natal Transport.
August. Computex.

Germiston (Transvaal)
April 1-6. Aviation Africa '92.

Johannesburg (Transvaal)
Feb. 24-28. PAKPROCESS/ PRINTEXPO. International Packaging and Printing Exhibition.
Feb. 24-28. FOODPRO Exhibition.
March 7-9. Sarcda Easter Show Giftware Show.
March 10-13. ELECTREX.
March 10-13. S.A. Industrial Fair.
April 1-15. Rand Show.
May 20-23. S.A. Computer Faire.
June 21-24. Fabssa. Food and Beverage.
June 21-24. FKESA. Food Equipment.
July 16-19. RETAILEX.
July 18-21. JEWELLEX.
July 29-31. Networking Expo (Lan).
Aug. 1-5. Christmas Trade Show.
Aug. 8-10. SASGAM. SA Sports Goods.
Aug. 24-29. INTERBOU. International SA Building and Construction.
Sept. 14-18. Electra Mining.
Oct 2-11. WASTEX.
Dec. 11-16. International Boat Show.

Spain

Barcelona
Jan. 18-21. PIELESPANA— leather fashion show.
Jan. 20-22. GAUDI-HOMBRE— Men's wear.
Jan. 20-22. GAUDIMUJER— Ladies wear.
Jan. 21-25. FIB—Barcelona's international fair.
Feb. 12-15. Muestra de Maquinaria Para la Confeccion-textile machinery.
March 7-12. Alimentaria— food and food technologies.
March 22-24. SPORT— sports fair.
April 24-28. EXPOMOVIL— Automotion and transportation equipment.
June. INFORMAT—data processing.
August. GAUDI-HOMBRE— Men's wear.
August. GAUDIMUJER— ladies wear.
Sept. 14-20. SONIMAG consumer electronics show.
Oct. 3-7. EXPOHOGAR— housewares.
Oct. 13-16. EXPOTRONICA—professional electronics.
Oct. 24-28. BARNAJOYA— jewelry
October. Salon Internacional del Caravaning—Camping and outdoor equipment. *November.* FER—recreation show.
Nov. 28-Dec. 6. Salon Nautico Internacional—nautical show.

Bilbao
April 1-4. AMBIENTE— installations international fair.
Sept. 23-26. FERROFORMA—international hardware show.
Oct. 21-28. BIEMH—machine tools.
Nov. 10-14. SINAVAL— Naval maritime and offshore.
Nov. 10-14. EUROFISHING—fishing industry.

Madrid
Jan. 17-21. INTERGIFT— international gift show.
Jan. 29-Feb. 2. FITUR— travel and tourism show.
Feb. 13-17. IBERJOYA— jewelery show
Feb. 13-18. ARCO art show.
Feb. 20-23. IMAGENMODA— ladies fashion show.
March 3-6. SICUR—security show.
March 14-22. Salon Internacional del Bricolage— Do-it-yourself show.
March 28-30. EXPOCALZADO— footwear.
April. IBERPIEL—furs and leather show.
April 8-12. MOGAR—furniture show.
April 22-26. ExpMusica musical instruments, theatrical lighting, and professional sound.
*April 24-27. EXPO/ OPTICA— international optics, optometry, and prothesic audiometric show.
May 4-8. BROADCAST—

radio and television equipment.

June 15-19. TEM—municipal equipment and techniques.

June 15-19. TRAFFIC—Traffic safety.

June 17-20. LIBER—book show.

Sept. 4-6. FIDEC—sports show.

Sept. 17-20. IMAGENMODA— ladies fashion show.

Sept. 18-22. INTERGIFT—international gift show.

October. IBERPIEL—furs and leather show.

Oct. 3-5. EXPOCALZADO—footwear.

Oct. 15-18. TECNOCLEAN— cleaning, maintenance and conservation techniques.

Oct. 27-31. MATELEC—electrical equipment for rural electrification installations.

Nov. 13-20. SIMO office equipment and computers.

Palma de Mallorca

Sept. 16-20. Baleares nautica—nautical show.

Valencia

Jan. 14-18. TEXTILHOGAR—home textiles.

Jan. 23-25. FIMI children's and young people's wear.

Feb. 8-12. DIPA—stationery.

Feb. 13-18. FEJU—toy fair.

Feb. 28-March 2. FIVAC—

hunting and fishing.

March 3-7. CEVISAMA—Glass and ceramics industry.

March 25-28. EXPOFRIO—refrigeration and climatization.

March 25-28. MIACOP—bakery products.

March 26-30. INTERATE—modern art.

April 3-8. CEIVDER—glass ceramics, and decoration.

April 3-8. FIAM—illumination show.

April 3-8. HABITAT—Interior designing.

May 28-31. ExpoFARMACIA—pharmaceutical specialties.

May. MUNDOBELLEZA/DROGUEXPO—Cosmetics and home cleaning products.

June 10-14. INDUTRANS— Industrial vehicles and *ATV* transportation.

June 11-15 Feria Internacional de la Joyeria—Jewelry show.

July 9-11. FIMI—children's and young people's wear.

Sept. 28-Oct. 3. FIM—furniture show.

October. MERCAFILM—films, *TV*, audiovisual.

Oct. 14-17. EUROAGRO—agriculturak

Oct. 15-18. IBERFLORA ornamental horticulture.

October. SIF—franchising.

Nov. 4-7. VINCI—innovation and industrial cooperation.

November. INDUFERIAS—equipment for amusement

and recreational facilities.

Dec. 26-Jan. 3. FIV—international fair.

Zaragoza

Feb. 14-18. SMOPYC—public works, construction and mining machinery.

April 3-9. FIMA—farm machinery.

Swaziland

Manzini

Sept. 4-13. Swaziland Trade Fair. *Contact the Commerce Department Desk Officer for Swaziland at (202) 377-5148.*

Sweden

Goteborg

Jan. 31-Feb. 9. International Boat Show.

March 4-8. AUTO—Car Maintenance and Servicing.

March 18-22. TUR '92-Travel and Tourism.

March 31-April 3. Industrial Maintenance.

April 18-21. Education and Human Resource Development.

April 27-30. CHEMISTRY—Lab. Analysis.

May 11-15. ELFACK—Electrical Installations and Control Equipment.

May 11-15. ELKRAFT—Power Generation and Power Distribution.

Sept. 18-27. International Consumer Goods Fair.

Oct. 6-9. Office Equipment Including Data Communications.

Oct. 20-23.

INTERFOOD—Hotel and Restaurant Equipment and Food.
Nov. 3-6. Interior Design For Offices and Public Premises.
Nov. 17-20. Environment/ Ecology—Pollution Control.

Sollentuna
Jan. 30-Feb. 2. FORMEX— Giftware, Glassware, and Handicrafts
Feb. 14-16. CARAVAN 92— Campers and Trailers.
March 31-April 3. DATA 92—Computers and Telecom.
Aug. 13-16. International Textile Show.
September. CASE EXPO— Computer Software Development.

Stockholm
Jan 21-26. NORDIC Building '92.
Jan. 21-26. International Trade Fair—Water Heating. and Sanitation.
Feb. 5-9. International Furniture Fair.
Feb. 15-18. International Fashion Fair.
Feb. 28-March 8. Stockholm International Boat Show.
March 17-20. Storage and Transportation.
March 31-April 3. LEISURE 92— Sports and Recreation.
April. EP 92—Electronics Production.
Sept. 3-6. International Fashion Fair.
Oct. 12-17. Scandinavian Technial Fairs—Working

Environment, Subcontracting, and Technical Week.
Nov. 3-6. BANK '92.
Nov. 11-13. UNIX '92.
Nov. 12-15. Satellite TV.
Dec. 2-4. MEDICINE '92.

Switzerland
Basel
Jan. 21-29. IFM 92—International fair of logistics.
Feb. 21-March 1. Swiss Industries Fair.
April 2-9. European Watch, Clock and Jewelry Fair. (space fully booked).
April 27-30. MAINTENANCE 91— International exhibition and conference for maintenance.
May 5-8. WORLDDIDAC 92— International education and training exhibition.
Sept. 8-12. ORBIT 92—International exhibition for communication, office organization, and information technology.
Oct. 6-9. M.U.T. 92—European exhibition for environmental technology, with Congress on environmental technology and rcsearch.

Bern
March 18-23. Logic '92.
Aug. 16-19. ORNARIS— international trade fair for consumer goods.

Geneva
Jan. 17-26. International commercial vehicles show.
Jan. 23. Visit USA seminar.
March 5-15. International

motor show.
April 3-12. International exhibition of inventions and new techniques.
April 29-May 2. International fair for books and the press.
April 29-May 3. Mondlingua Geneva—International fair for languages and cultures.
May 5-7. EIBTM '92—European incentive & business travel & meetings exhibition.
Oct. 14-17. Air Forum '92.

Lausanne
April 28-May 1. Computer '92.

Montreux
March 23-26. Space Commerce '92.
June 10-13. NAB radio conference.
Oct. 27-29. Travel trade workshop.

St. Gallen
Oct. 8-18. OLMA—Swiss agricultural and dairy farming fair.

Zurich
Jan. 12-15. ORNARIS—international trade fair for consumer goods.
Jan. 21-22. Visit USA seminar.
Jan. 29-31. Computer Graphics
Feb. 17-22. Industrial Handling '92.
March 10-12. Semicon Europa '92.
June 10-13. Logic '92 computer show.

Aug. 26-31. FERA—International TV, radio and hifi show.

Oct. 20-24. MICROTECNIC '92

Nov. 3-6. IFAS '92—International medical and hospital exhibition.

Syria
Damascus

Late August-mid-September. Damascus International Fair. Contact: American Embassy, 2 Al Mansour Str., Abou Roumaneh, P.O. Box 29, Damascus. Syria; tel. (963) (11) 332814/332315/ 714108, telex 411919 USDAMA, fax (963) (11) 71 8687.

Taiwan
Taipei

Jan. 17-22. Taipei International Book Exhibition.

Feb. 17-21. Taipei International Furniture Show.

Feb. 27-March 1. Taipei International Telecommunications Show. *March 6-10.* Taipei Electronics.

March 16-20. Taipei International Gift and Stationery (Spring).

March 25-29. Taipei International Sporting Goods.

April 4-10. Taipei International Industrial Machinery Show

April 16-20. Taipei International Cycle Show.

April 24-27. Taipei International Footwear and Leather Goods

May 7-10. Taipei International Hardware, Houseware, and Building Materials Show.

May 7-10. SOFTEX Taipei '92.

May 15-19. Taipei International Auto Show.

May 25-29. Taipei International Food Industry Show

June 5-9. COMPUTEX Taipei '92.

July 14-19. The Best of Taiwan Products Show.

Aug. 15-19. Taipei Computer Application Show.

Aug. 26-31. Taipei International Fair.

Sept. 12-16. Taipei International Jewelry and Timepiece Show

Sept. 21-25. Taipei International Toy Show.

Oct. 7-13. Taipei International Electronics Show.

Oct. 28-Nov. 1. Taipei International Gift and Stationery (autumn).

Nov. 6-9. Taipei International Medical Equipment and Pharmaceuticals Show.

Thailand
Bangkok

Jan. 15-18. PAK-EX 91— The International Exhibition for Packaging Machinery, Packaging Material, Converting Equipment, Food Packaging and Related Machinery, Accessories and Services.

Jan. 16-19. ASIA REALBUILD 92— 4th Asia International Exhibition and Conference on Real Estate

Condominiums, Housing and Golf Courses.

Jan. 16-19. Boat Show and Sports Recreation 92—international boat show, water sports, leisure equipment, and fishing equipment exhibition.

Jan. 28-31. Bank Asia 92— International Banking Equipment Exhibition and Conference.

Jan. 28-31. Telecom Infotech Asia 92—3rd events in a series accompanied by an international conference focusing on telecommunication development in Thailand.

Feb. 11-14. Signal Asia 92— military communications.

Feb. 20-23. ELENEX Thailand 92—2nd International Electric and Electronic Engineering, Power Generation, Supply, and Distribution Exhibition.

Feb. 20-23. ARICON Thailand 92—air conditioning, ventilation, heating, and refrigeration.

Feb. 20-23. Lighting Thailand 92—lighting equipment, fixtures, fittings, and technology.

Feb. 26-28. ASIACOMM 92—4th International Telecommunications and Information Technology Trade Exhibition for Thailand and Indochina.

Feb. 26-28. Computer and Infoasia 92—International Computer and Information Technology Trade Exhibition.

Feb. 27-March 1. Chemical

Thailand 92—2nd International Petrochemical and Chemical Process Engineering and contracting exhibition.

Feb. 27-March 1. Instrument Thailand 92—2nd International Instrumentation, Control, Measurement, Testing Laboratory and Analytical Technology Exhibition.

Feb. 2 7-March 1. Oct 92—International Oil and Gas Exploration and Production Exhibition Thailand.

March 2-5. OA/Business/Stationery 92—3rd Thailand Business Equipment and Services Trade Fair.

March 26-29. Garments, Textiles and Fabrics Asia 92—garments, fabrics and textiles machinery, and technology trade.

April 2-5. Architect 35 92—construction and decoration equipment, materials and supplies trade.

April 2-5. Housing and Property #10 92—10th Housing, Property and Better Living Products Trade Fair.

April 2-5. Golf and Resort #3 92—3rd Thailand Golf Courses, Golf Goods, and Resorts Trade Fair.

April 2-5. Health and Sport #1—Sporting goods, health products, fitness equipment, and servIces.

April 25-May 3. Boat Show 92—5th Thailand Boats and Water Sports Equipment

Trade Fair.

April 25-May 3. Bangkok motor show.

May 2-5. GFT '92.

May 2-5. GARMENTECH Asia '92—4th International Clothing Machinery Trade Exhibition.

May 2-5. THAITEX '92—textile machinery.

May 2-5. FABRICASIA '92—fabric and yam.

May 16-19. INTERMOULD Thailand '92—mould and die technology.

May 16-19. INTERPLASTTHAILAND '92—plastics and rubber industry.

May 21-24. FOODEX 92—food, drink, confectionary, and catering equipment.

May 21-24. HOTELEX 92—hotel, restaurant and kitchen equipment, laundry equipment, and hotel electronics (including safety and security electronic systems).

May 28-June 1. INTERMACH '92—metal workings, machine and hand tools, plastics, rubber, and general industrial machinery.

June 18-21. Thailand Port 92—The Thailand International Airport, Port, and Transportation Development Exhibition.

June 18-21. ENTECH ASEAN '92.—products related to environmental and pollution control.

June 25-28. PHARMEX Asia '92—pharmaceutical/medi-

cal and hospital equipment.

July 1-3. CATT: Computer-Aided Technologies for Thailand 92— CAD-CAM-CIM-AEC-GIS technologies and applications.

July 2-5. Furniture and Woodtech 92—woodworking machinery and furniture production supply trade.

Aug. 4-7. Thai Telecom 92—Thailand International Telecommunication and Information Technology Trade Exhibition and Conference.

Aug. 6-10. Auto and Accessories 92—motorcar workshops and service station equipment, automobile spare parts, and accessories.

Aug. 6-10. AUTOQUIP Assembly and Engineering 92—equipment and technology for car and truck assembly and components manufacturing.

Aug. 27-30. PPP THAI 92—printing, packaging, and plastic processing.

September. Packprint Asia 92— packaging and printing technology.

September. THAIPLAS — PLASTICS and rubber technology.

Sept. 3-6. Technobuild '92 construction machinery and equipment, technology for the building trade, and municipal services.

Sept. 10-13. Infomatic and Telematic 92—computer and infommation technology, telecommunications, and office automation.

Sept. 10-13. Food and Hotel

Thailand 92—hotel, catering equipment, and food exhibition and culinary arts competition.

Sept. 17-20. THAI BEX 92— Thailand International Building and Construction Exposition.

Sept. 17-20. Building Services Thailand 92—building services technology, products, and service trade.

Sept. 17-20. AEC Thailand 92— International Exposition for Automation and Computerization in the Architectural, Engineering, and Construction Industry.

Sept. 17-20. THAIPRINT/ PACK 92—printing and packaging industry.

October. THAI LABTECH 92— laboratory and research equipment exhibition.

October. Thai Instrumex 92— instrumentation and electronics.

Oct. 1-4. BUILDTECH 92— building and construction equipment and materials.

Oct. 1-4. Safety and Security 92—safety and security technology, equipment, services, and supplies.

Oct. 1-4. INDEC 92—interior decoration and furnishing materials.

Oct. 1-4. Housing and Property #11 92—housing property and better living products.

Oct. 1-4. Golf and Resort #4 92—golf courses, golf goods, and resort.

Oct. 1-4. Health and Sport #2 92—sporting goods, health products, fitness equipment, and services.

Oct. 8-11. Thai Apparel and Knitting 92—apparel, textile, knitting, and weaving.

Oct. 10-14. PROPAK Asia 92— food processing and packaging technology.

Oct. 10-21. Toys and Gifts 92— toys and gifts.

November. Sports Expo 92— sport instruments, manufacturing equipment, and sporting goods.

Nov. 5-9. THAI METALEX 92— machine tools and metalworkings.

Nov. 19-22. Fire, Safety, and Security 92—safety, security, and fire equipment and technology.

Nov. 19-22. Hospitaltec 92— medical/hospital equipment and supplies.

Nov. 19-22. Leather and Footwear Asia 92—footwear machinery tanning machinery, chemical and leather trade.

Nov. 19-22. Police Asia 92— military security and police equipment and technology.

Nov. 26-29. Business 92— business equipment and services trade fair.

Nov. 26-29. IT Trade 92— information technology, materials and supplies.

Nov. 26-29. Industry Asia 92— industrial technology, materials and supplies.

Dec. 5-13. Home Show 92— home products and house-

hold appliances.

Dec. 10-13. Optical 92—optical instrumentation technology, optolaser technology, opthalmic optics, eye wear, and optical accessories.

Dec. 10-13. Photo and Sound 92—audio visual equipment and photographic technology.

Dec. 10-13. Education and Career 92—Thailand International Exhibition and Seminar on Academic Institutions, Vocational Training, Educational Tools, and Career Development.

Trinidad & Tobago
Port of Spain
Oct. 14-18. Caribbean Expo '92.

Tunisia
Nabeul
April 17-May 3. Nabeul International Fair.

Sfax
June 17-28. Sfax International Fair.

Sousse
July 25-Aug. 13. Sousse International Fair.

Tunis
Feb. 7-10. Leather goods.
End February-Early March. Book fair.
April 20-22. Industrial subcontracting.
May 13-16. Textiles and clothing.
September. Medical equipment.

Oct. 5-14. Tunis International Fair.
October. Audiovisual and video equipment.
November. Chemicals and plastics.
November. New technologies.
December. Home furniture and kitchen equipment.
Contact the Commerce Department Desk Officer for Tunisia at (202) 377-2515.

Turkey

Ankara
May 28-31. ANKOMAK 92— construction, building machinery and technology.
Sept. 8-13. TAGRO 92— International agricultural machinery and technology fair.
Oct. 14-18. Turkey Build '92.
Oct. 22-26. Expo Design '92.

Istanbul
Jan. 9-12. Construction '92.
Jan. 11-15. Energy '92.
Jan. 22-26. Machinery Mechanics, Electricity '92.
Jan. 22-26. Office Data 92— telecommunication, computer office machinery, equipment.
Feb. 5-8. ISOHA 92—International heating, refrigeration, ventilation, and natural gas technology fair.
Feb. 5-9. Packaging '92.
Feb. 5-9. Plastics and Rubber '92.
Feb. 19-23. Catering 92— food and beverage.
Feb. 20-23. Footwear.
March 4-8. BUKOMA 92—

office equipment, automation, computers, and information technology fair.
March 17-22. Boat show '92.
March 25-29. MAKTEK 92—Plastic and metalworking machine tools, hand tools.
April 8-12. OPTIK 92—optics fair.
April 15-19. Textile machinery fair.
April 22-26. Medicine '92.
April 25-29. Woodworking machinery.
Oct. 21-25. Kitchen/bathroom '92.
Oct. 21-25. EDEXIM 92—International educational equipment and supplies fair.
Oct. 28-Nov. 1. Hotel/restaurant equipment and supplies.
Nov. 5-8. Environmental technology '92.
Nov. 11-15. ELEKTRONIK 92—electric and electronic fair.
Nov. 18-22. Communication '92.
Dec. 8-13. Motor show '92.
Dec. 17-28. Plumbing heating, ventilating, and airconditioning.

Izmir
May 7-10. COMPTEK '92— computers.
Aug. 26-Sept. 10. Izmir International Trade Fair (general)—U.S. Pavilion.
Oct. 14-18. GIDA 92—food, food packaging and catering.

Uganda
Jan. 26. Liberation Day Trade

Fair.
For information about this event, contact the Commerce Department's Uganda Desk Officer on tel. (202) 377-4564.

United Arab Emirates

Abu Dhabi
Feb. 14-18. Gulf Ideal Home Exhibition.

Dubai
Jan. 7-10. Education.
Jan. 12-15. Electricity.
Jan 12-16. World or Concrete
Jan. 26-30. International Defence, Police, and Civil Security Systems.
Feb. 9-12. ARABGAS and Oil.
Feb. 16-20. Made in the U.S.
Feb. 19-22. Travel, Tourism, and Duty Free Show.
Feb. 28-March 1. Watersport and Powerboat Show.
April 6-10. Environment.
May 4-7. Middle East Agriculture.
Sept. 14-17. Middle East Maritime and Offshore Service Industries.
Sept. 14-18. Woman '92.
Sept. 27-Oct. 1. Index"92.
Oct. 11-15. Arab Water Technology.
Oct. 21-24. MOTEXHA.
Oct. 21-24. Overseas Property and Investment Exhibition.
Nov. 2-5. Office of the Future.
Nov. 14-17. Food.
Nov. 23-26. Arab Industrial

Machinery.
Nov. 23-26. Arab Plast.

Sharjah
Nov. 15-19. 2nd Regional Building, Interior Design, and Maintenance Exhibition.

United Kingdom
Birmingham
Jan. 19-22. MIDEX—furniture exhibition.
Jan. 19-22. International hardware and housewares.
Feb. 2-6. International spring
Feb. 15-23. Boat, caravan, and leisure show.
Feb. 16-18. Premier collections exhibition.
Feb. 25-2 7. Wasteman/Wastetech—waste management and cleansing exhibition.
Feb. 25-28. International handling and storage—IHSE '92.
March 10-12. CADCAM International Show.
March 15-17. International Recycling, Technology, and Service Exhibition.
March 24-25. Recreation Management Exhibition—RECAM.
March 24-26. Nepcon Europe—electronics production and text.
April 7-10. The Which Computer? Show.
April 7-10. Communications '92.
May 6-15. International Exhibition of machine tools and manufacturing technology (MACH '92)
May 11-14. International fluid power exhibition

(IFPEX).
May 31-June 5. International packaging exhibition (PAKEX). *June 16-18.* International safety and health exhibition and conference (ROSPA).
June 16-18. Health care exhibition.
June 19-20. British Dental Association annual conference and exhibition.
June 23-25. International solid handling and processing exhibition (INTERBULK).
June 23-25. Networks '92.
June 23-26. International chemical and process engineering show and conference (EUROCHEM).
June 23-26. Rubbcrex Exhibition.
June 24-28. Green Show.
July 5-9. International Autumn Fair.
July 20-24. Electrotech '92 (electrical and power generation).
Aug. 9-12. Autumn Premier Collections.
Oct. 2-4. National Franchise Exhibition.
Oct. 24-Nov. 1. Motor Show.
Nol. 10-12. International Water and Effluent Treatment Exhibition.
Nov. 24-26. INTERPHEX—International pharmaceutical. Cosmetic, Toiletry, Perfumery, and Allied Industries Exhibition.

Farnborough
Sept. 1-8. Farnborough Air Show.

Glasgow
March 5-8. Green Show.
April 29-30. Laboratory Scotland Exhibition.
Nov. 25-26. Waste and Waste Treatment Exhibition.

Harrogate
Feb. 3-6. International Brewing Technology Conference and Exhibition.
Feb. 13-15. Science and Technology Education Exhibition.
March 24-26. LIQUIDEX—Handling, Storage, Processing of Liquids Exhibition.
May 19-21. EQUOEOOD—food processing and manufacturing exhibition.
Oct. 13-15. National Association of Theatre Nurses Conference and Exhibition.

Kenilworth
July 6-9. Royal International Agricultural Show.

London
Jan. 1-12. International Boat Show.
Jan. 11-15. STATINDEX—Stationery Industry Exhibition.
Jan. 20-25. HOTELYMPIA— International Hotel and Catering Exhibition.
Jan. 25-29. British International Toy and Hobby Fair.
Feb. 16-18. The London Show (spring fashion).
Feb. 16-19. Junior Fashion Fair.
Feb. 16 -19. IMBEX—Inter-

national Men's and Boy's Wear Exhibition.

March 4-5. Packaging Plus Show.

March 22-24. London International Book Fair.

March 30-April 3. IFSEC—International Fire and Security Exhibition and Conference.

April 22-24. British Electronics Week.

April 24-26. Spring National Franchise Exhibition.

April 25-29. International Food and Drink Exhibition.

May 12-14. International Environment Exhibition.

May 12-14. International Water Technology Exhibition world water.

May 12-14. CESIO—International Surfactants Exhibition

May 17-21. International Interior and Retail Designs.

June 21-22. International Beauty and Professional Beauty Exhibition.

Aug 23-25. Exhibition of Sports and leisure.

Sepf. 6-10. Capital Gift Fair.

Sept. 6-10. International Watch, Jewelry and Silver Trades Fair.

Sept. 8-10. The London Show (fashion-fall).

Oct. 13-15. Laboratory Exhibition and Conference.

Oct. 20-22. London Heating and Ventilating Show.

Manchester

Jan. 6-9. Fluoropolymers Symposium and Exhibition.

Feb. 19-20. Water and Indus-

trial Waste Management Exhibition.

March 4-5. Instrumentation Show.

April 1-2. Laboratory Manchester Exhibition.

April 1-2. CHEMSPEC—Speciality, Performance, and Effect Chemicals Exhibition.

Nottingham

June 10-11. Waste and Waste Treatment Exhibition.

Uruguay

Prado

Aug. 15-29 (tentative). Prado International Agro-Industrial and Commercial Fair.

Contact: Commercial Attache, American Embassy Montevideo, Attn: Econ. Unit 4510, APO AA 34035, tel. (5982) 23-60-61, fax (5982) 48-86-11.

U.S.S.R.

Moscow

Jan. 16-22. CONSUMEXPO 92—consumer goods.

Feb. 14-20. equipment and furniture for schools and universities.

Feb. 14-28. EXCLIMSTROY 92—construction in regions with severe climatic conditions on permafrost grounds.

March 11-17. Labor Security.

March 12-18. PHARMBIOPROM '92 equipment and processes in chemicopharmaceutical and microbiological production.

April 10-16. OPTICA 92—optics.

May 20-27. NEFTEGAS '92 equipment for the oil and gas

industry. *June 19-25.* Aluminum '92.

June 19-25. Sport 92—sporting goods and equipment.

June 19-25. Bank and Office 92—bank and office equipment.

June 20-26. Meteorology '92.

June 20-26. Greenhouse '92.

June 20-26. Farmers and agricultural equipment.

July 22-29. Electro '92 electrotechnical equipment and power transmission lines.

Sept. 16-23. Chemistry '92.

Oct. 22-28. Informatika 92—computers and informatics.

Oct. 22-28. Advertising '92.

Nov. 25-Dec. 2. Auto Industry '92.

Nov. 25-Dec. 2. Furniture '92.

Nov. 25-Dec. 2. Furniture Processing Equipment.

Jan. 27-31. Computer Graphics.

Feb. 27-March 4. MERA 92— processing equipment.

April 3-12. Moscow Aeroengine '92.

April 22-26. COMTECH 92— computers.

April 25-30. Bank and Communication Equipment.

May 25-30. EXPOCOM '92.

June 15-19. Made in USA.

Aug. 27-30. Automobile Fair.

Aug. 31-Sept. 4. ConsumElectronica '92.

Venezuela

Valencia

April 7-12. XVII International Fair of Venezuela.

Yugoslavia

Belgrade

March 2-8. Consumer Goods.
March 3-6. MEDIPHARM (Medical and Pharmaceutical).
March 17-21. Tourism, Sport and Nautical Equipment.
March 27-April 1. Automotive Fair.
May 11-16. Technical Fair.
Sept. 8-11. Leather and Footwear.
Sept. 8-11. PROTECTION '92
Sept. 8-11. SOLAR '92
Oct. 6-9. FASHION IN THE WORLD.
Oct. 22-27. Educational Equipment; Graphic and Paper Industry; Video and Hi-Fi Equipment.
Oct. 22-28. Book Fair.
Nov. 9-15. Furniture and Interior Decoration.
Dec. 14. New Technologies.

Ljubljana

Aug. 31-Sept. 6. VINQ 91—Wine and Wine Equipment.
Oct. 5-9. Modern Electronics 91.
Dec. 1-6. SKI EXPO 90 (Winter Sports, Tourism).

Novi Sad

May 16-24. Agricultural Fair.
Sept. 2-6. Autumn Fair.
Oct. 14-18. Hunting, Fishing, Sports and Tourism.

Sarajevo

Feb. 3-7. International Spring Fashion Fair.
Feb. 24-28. Construction Fair; Wood Fair.

March 16-19. Tourism and Sports.
Nov. 2-6. Plastics and Rubber.

Skopje

March 17-22. Upholstery.
April 7-10. MEDICINA 91 (Medical and Pharmaceutical, Dentistry).
Sept. 29-Oct. 2 SKSMESA 91 (Tobacco and Machinery; AgroIndustrial Fair).
Oct. 18-23. TEHNOMA 91 (Metals, Non-Metals, Electronics, Civil Engineering).

Zagrebacki

Feb. 25-28. Leather, Footwear and Clothing.
April 21-26. Modern Packaging.
May 16-20. Biam (Machine Tools, Welding, Material Protection).
May 26-30. MEDICINE AND TECHNOLOGY.
Sept. 14-20. International Fal Fair (With U.S. Pavilion).
Oct. 20-24. INTERBIRO-INFORMATIKA (Informatics, Telecom and Office Equipment).

Zambia

Ndola

July 1-7. Zambia International Trade Fair. *Contact: Ms. Necia L. Quast, Economic/Commercial Officer, U.S. Embassy, P.O. Box 31617, Lusaka, Zambia; tel. 260-01-228595, fax 260-01-251578, telex ZA 21970.*

Zimbabwe

Bulawayo

April 28-May 3. International Trade Fair.
Sept. 2-10. OAU All-Africa Trade Fair.

Harare

Aug. 24-29. Harare Agricultural Show.
Contact the Commerce Department Desk Officer for Zimbabwe at (202) 377-5148.

Appendix B

1992 World Commercial Holidays

Virtually every day in 1992 will be a holiday somewhere in the world, with business and government offices closed while employees watch parades, pray, or perhaps enjoy a quiet holiday at home with their family. Seasoned business travelers build their schedules around these holidays, because the alternative can be a frustrating day wasted in a hotel room while the local people, from the top executives on down, observe their traditional holiday rituals.

For many years, the most comprehensive and reliable source of information on commercial holidays around the world has been *Business America*. We get our information from U.S. Foreign Service posts all over the world, whose sources in turn are the local government offices that actually promulgate the holidays.

The following pages list, alphabetically by country, the hundreds of commercial holidays around the world each year that will close business and government offices for a day or more. Major regional holidays that are observed in many countries are included, as well as any other pertinent information.

Many commercial holidays occur on different calendar dates from year to year. Holidays and even weekends often vary from country to country, and from region to region.

In cases where holidays fall on Saturday or Sunday, commercial establishments may be closed the preceding Friday or following Monday.

For many countries, such as those in the Moslem world, holiday dates can be only approximated because the holidays are based on actual lunar observation and exact dates are announced only shortly before they occur. Note that references to the Moslem holidays often vary in spelling and dates, and that businesses in many Moslem countries are closed on Fridays.

Although U.S. holidays are not listed in this schedule, they should also be considered when appointments are made with U.S. Foreign Commercial Service officers abroad.

This calendar is intended as a working guide only. Corroboration of dates is suggested in final business travel planning.

ALGERIA—Jan. 1 (New Year's), April 4 (Aid-El-Fitr), May 1 (Labor Day), June 11 (Aid-El-Adha), June 19 (Revolutionary Recovery Day), July 2 (Awal Mouharrem), July 5 (Independence Day), July 11 (Achoura), Sept. 9 (El-Mawlid-EnNabaoui), Nov. 1 (Revolution Day).

As in other Muslim countries, the Islamic holidays listed above depend upon the sighting of the moon, and thus could vary by one calendar day.

ANGOLA—Jan. 1 (New Year's), Feb. 4 (Beginning of Liberation), March 27 (Victory or Carnival Day), May 1 (Workers' Day), Sept. 17 (Memorial Day for A. Neto), Nov. 11 (Independence Day), Dec. 10 (MPLA Day), Dec. 25 (Family Day).

ARGENTINA—Jan. 1 (New Year's), April 17 (Good Friday), May 1 (Labor Day), May 25 (Revolution Day), June 8 (Sovereignty Day), June 20 (Flag Day), July 9 (Independence Day), Aug. 17 (Death of San Martin), Oct. 12 (Columbus Day), Dec. 25 (Christmas).

AUSTRALIA—Jan. 1 (New Year's), April 17 (Good Friday), April 20 (Easter Monday), April 25 (ANZAC Day), June 8 (Queen's Birthday), Dec. 25 (Christmas), Dec. 26 (Boxing Day).
Regional holidays: Jan. 27 (Australia Day), Canberra; March 16 (Canberra Day), Canberra; Oct. 5 (Labor Day), Canberra.

AUSTRIA—Jan. 1 (New Year's), Jan. 6 (Epiphany), April 20 (Easter Monday), May 1 (Labor Day), May 28 (Ascension), June 8 (Whit Monday), June 18 (Corpus Christi), Aug. 15 (Assumption), Oct. 26 (Flag Day), Nov. 1 (All Saints), Dec. 8 (Immaculate Conception), Dec. 25 (Christmas), Dec. 26 (St. Stephen's Day).

BAHAMAS—Jan. 1 (New Year's), April 17 (Good Friday), April 20 (Easter Monday), June 5 (Labor Day), June 8 (Whit Monday), July 10 (Independence Day), Aug. XX (Emancipation Day), Oct. 12 (Discovery Day), Dec. 25 (Christmas), Dec. 26 (Box-

ing Day).

BAHRAIN—Jan. 1 (New Year's), April 3-5 (Eid Al Fitr), June 10-12 (Eid Al Adha), July 1 (Islamic New Year), July 10-12 (Ashura), Sept. 9 (Prophet's Birthday), Dec. 16 (National Day).
Islamic holidays are based on the lunar month, and the exact date may vary by one or two days.

BANGLADESH—Feb. 20 (Shab-E-Barat), Feb. 21 (Martyrs' Day), March 26 (Independence Day), April 1 (Shab-E-Qdr), April 3 (Jumat-Ul-Wida), April 5-7 (Eid-Ul-Fitr), April 14 (Bengali New Year's), April 18 (Buddha Purnima), May 1 (May Day), June 12-14 (Eid-Ul-Azha), July 11 (Muharram), Oct. 7 (Durgah Puja), Sept. 10 (Eid-E-Miladdun Nabi), Nov. 7 (National Integrity Day), Dec. 16 (Victory Day), Dec. 25 (Christmas).
The Bangladesh government will officially announce 1992 holidays in late December 1991. Muslim religious holidays are dependent on the appearance of the moon and the exact date will be announced shortly before they occur.

BELGIUM—Jan. 1 (New Year's), April 20 (Easter Monday), May 1 (Belgian Labor Day), May 28 (Ascension), June 8 (Whit Monday), July 21 (Belgian Independence Day), Aug. 15—observed on

Aug. 17 (Assumption), Nov. 1—observed on Nov. 2 (All Saints), Nov. 11 (Veterans' Day), Dec. 25 (Christmas).
Regional holidays: July 11—observed on July 13 (Flanders region); Sept. 27—observed on Sept. 28 (Wallonia region).

BELIZE—Jan. 1 (New Year's), March 9 (Baron Bliss Day), April 17 (Good Friday), April 20 (Easter Monday), May 1 (Labor Day), May 24—celebrated May 25 (Commonwealth Day), Sept. 10 (Battle of St. George's Caye), Sept. 21 (Independence Day), Oct. 12—celebrated Oct. 15 (PanAmerican Day), Nov. 19 (Garifuna Settlement Day), Dec. 25 (Christmas), Dec. 26 (Boxing Day).

BOLIVIA—Jan. 1 (New Year's), March 2-3 (Carnival), April 17 (Good Friday), May 1 (Bolivian Labor Day), June 18 (Corpus Christi), Aug. 6 (Bolivian Independence Day), Nov. 2 (All Saints), Dec. 25 (Christmas).
Regional holidays: Feb. 10 (Oruro's Local Day), April 5 (Tarija's Local Day), May 25 (Chuquisaca's Local Day), July 16 (La Paz' Local Day), Sept. 24 (Santa Cruz' and Pando's Local Day), Nov. 10 (Potosi's Local Day), Nov. 18 (Beni's Local Day),

BOTSWANA—Jan. 1 (New Year's), Jan. 2 (Public Holiday), April 17 (Good Friday), April 18 (Public Holiday),

April 20 (Easter Monday), May 28 (Ascension), July 20 (President's Day), July 21 (Public Holiday), Sept. 30 (Botswana Day), Oct. 1 (Public Holiday), Dec. 25 (Christmas), Dec. 26 (Boxing Day).

BRAZIL—Jan. 1 (New Year's), Jan. 20 (San Sebastian Day), March 2-3 (Carnival), March 4—half day (Ash Wednesday), April 17 (Good Friday), April 21 (Tiradentes' Day), May 1 (Labor Day), June 18 (Corpus Christi), June 24 (St. John's Day), July 2 (Bahia Independence Day), July 16 (N.S. Do Carmo Receife), Sept. 7 (Independence Day), Oct. 12 (N. Sra. Aparecida), Nov. 2 (All Souls), Dec. 8 (Immaculate Conception), Dec. 25 (Christmas). *Ash Wednesday is not listed on the official Brazilian calendar, but it is traditionally proclaimed as a holiday a few days before the date.*

BULGARIA—Jan. 1 (New Year's), March 3 (Liberation Day), May 1-2 (Labor Day), May 25 (Cyril and Methodius Day), Sept. 9—tentative (Liberation from Fascism), Dec. 25 (Christmas).

BURMA—Jan. 4 (Independence Day), Feb. 12 (Union Day), March 2 (Peasants' Day), March 18 (Full Moon of Tabaung), March 27 (Armed Forces Day), April 14-15 (Thingyan—Water Festival), April 16 (Burmese New Year), May 1 (Workers' Day), May 16 (Full Moon of Kason), July 14 (Full Moon of Waso), July 19 (Martyrs' Day), Oct. 11 (Full Moon of Thadingyut), Nov. 19 (National Day), Dec. 16 (Karen New Year), Dec. 25 (Christmas).

CAMEROON—Jan. 1 (New Year's), Feb. 11 (Youth Day), March 27 (Good Friday), date to be announced (End of Ramadan), May 1 (Labor Day), May 7 (Ascension), May 20 (National Day), to be announced, 70 days after End of Ramadan (Fete du Mouton), Aug. 15 (Assumption), Dec. 25 (Christmas).

CANADA—Jan. 1 (New Year's), April 17 (Good Friday), April 20 (Easter Monday), May 18 (Victoria Day—most businesses in the province of Quebec are open), July 1 (Canada Day), Sept. 7 (Labor Day), Oct. 12 (Thanksgiving Day), Nov. 11 (Remembrance Day—all businesses closed until after 11:00 a.m.), Dec. 25 (Christmas), Dec. 26 (Boxing Day). *In the Province of Quebec, commercial businesses are open after 1:00 p.m. on holidays. In Canada, national holidays are established by federal statute, which provides that when a holiday falls on a Saturday or Sunday, it is observed on the following Monday.*

CHAD—Jan. 1 (New Year's), April 5-6 (Aid-El-Fitr), April 20 (Easter Monday), May 1 (Labor Day), May 25 (African Liberation Day), June 11 (Aid-El-Adha), Aug. 11 (Chad Independence Day), Sept. 9 (Maouloud-El-Nebi), Nov. 28 (Proclamation of the Republic), Dec. 1 (Freedom/Democracy Day), Dec. 25 (Christmas). *Muslim holidays are based on the lunar calendar, and the exact dates may vary.*

CHILE—Jan. 1 (New Year's), April 17 (Good Friday), May 1 (Labor Day), May 21 (Combate Naval de Iquique), June 18 (Corpus Christi), June 29 (Sts. Peter & Paul), Aug. 15 (Assumption), Sept. 11 (Official Holiday), Sept. 18 (Independence Day), Sept. 19 (Day of the Army), Oct. 12 (Columbus Day), Nov. 1 (All Saints), Dec. 25 (Christmas).

CHINA—Jan. 1 (New Year's), Feb. 4-6 (Spring Festival), May 1 (International Labor Day), Oct. 1-2 (National Day).

COLOMBIA—Jan. 1 (New Year's), Jan. 6 (Epiphany), March 23 (St. Joseph's Day), April 16 (Holy Thursday), April 17 (Good Friday), May 1 (Labor Day), May 25 (Ascension), June 15 (Corpus Christi), June 22 (Feast of the Sacred Heart), June 29 (Sts. Peter & Paul), July 20 (Independence Day), Aug. 7 (Battle

of Boyaca), Aug. 17 (Assumption), Oct. 12 (Columbus Day), Nov. 2 (All Saints), Nov. 16 (Independence of Cartegena) Dec. 8 (Feast of Immaculate Conception), Dec. 25 (Christmas).
From Dec. 26 through Jan. 1 (Folklore Festival), offices are open only from 8:00 a. m. to 1:00 p.m.
Regional holidays: March 2–3 (Carnival), Barranquilla.

COSTA RICA—Jan. 1 (New Year's), March 19 (St. Joseph's Day), April 11 (Juan Santamaria), April 16 (Holy Thursday), April 17 (Good Friday), May 1 (Labor Day), June 18 (Corpus Christi), June 29 (Sts..Peter & Paul), Sept. 15 (Independence Day), Oct. 12 (Columbus Day), Dec. 8 (Immaculate Conception), Dec. 25 (Christmas).

CYPRUS—Jan. 1 (New Year's), Jan. 6 (Epiphany), March 9 (Clean Monday—start of Lent), March 25 (Greek Independence Day), April 1 (Eoka Day), April 24 (Good Friday), April 25 (Holy Saturday), April 27 (Easter Monday), May 1 (Labor Day), Aug. 3 (Makarios Memorial Day), Aug. 15 (Assumption), Oct. 1 (Cyprus Independence Day), Oct. 28 (OHI Day), Dec. 24 (Christmas Eve), Dec. 25 (Christmas), Dec. 26 (Boxing Day).
Regional holidays: The Turkish Cypriot community will celebrate the following holidays in

1992: Jan. 1 (New Year's), April 4 (Ramazan Bayram), April 23 (Opening of the Turkish Grand National Assembly), May 19 (Turkish Youth Day), June 11 (Kurban Bairam), July 20 (Peace and Freedom Day), Aug. 30 (Turkish Victory Day), Sept. 9 (Birthday of the Prophet), Oct. 29 (Turkish Republic Day), Nov. 15 (Republic Day of Northern Cyprus).

CZECHOSLOVAKIA—Jan. 1 (New Year's), April 20 (Easter Monday), May 1 (Labor Day), May 8 (Liberation Day), July 5 (Cyril and Methodius Day), Oct. 28 (Republic Day), Dec. 24-26 (Christmas).
The Czech Republic will observe July 6 (Jam Bus), and the Slovak Republic will observe Nov. 1 (Reconciliation Day).

DENMARK—Jan. 1 (New Year's), April 16 (Maundy Thursday), April 17 (Good Friday), April 20 (Easter Monday), May 15 (Prayer Day), May 28 (Ascension), June 8 (Whit Monday), June 5 half-day (Constitution Day), Dec. 25 (Christmas), Dec. 26 (Second Christmas Day).
June 4 (Constitution Day), Dec. 24 and Dec. 31 are traditional half-day holidays and most businesses and banks will be closed.

DOMINICAN REPUBLIC—Jan. 1 (New Year's), Jan. 6 (Epiphany), Jan. 21 (Nuestra Sra. de la Altagracia), Feb. 27 (Dominican Independence Day), April 17 (Good Friday),

May 1 (Dominican Labor Day), June 18 (Corpus Christi), Sept. 24 (Dia de Ntra. Sra de las Mercedes), Dec. 25 (Christmas).

ECUADOR—Jan. 1 (New Year's), Feb. 26-27 (Carnival), April 17 (Good Friday), May 1 (Labor Day), July 24 (Bolivar's Birthday), Aug. 10 (Independence Day), Oct. 9 (Independence of Guayaquil), Oct. 12 (Columbus Day), Nov. 2 (All Souls), Nov. 3 (Independence of Cuenca), Dec. 25 (Christmas).

EGYPT—Jan. 1 (New Year's), April 5-7 (Ramadan Bairam), April 25 (Sinai Liberation Day), April 27 (Sham El Nessim), May 1 (Labor Day), June 11 - 12 (Kurban Bairam), July 23 (National Day), Oct. 6 (Armed Forces Day).
The exact dates for Islamic holidays cannot be fixed in advance, as they are determined by actual sighting of the moon.

EL SALVADOR—Jan. 1 (New Year's), April 16 (Holy Thursday), April 17 (Good Friday), May 1 (Labor Day), Aug. 3-6 (San Salvador Feasts), Sept. 15 (Independence Day), Oct. 12 (Columbus Day), Nov. 2 (All Souls), Nov. 5 (Anniversary of First Cry of Independence), Dec. 25 (Christmas).

ETHIOPIA—Jan. 7 (Ethiopian Christmas) Jan. 20 (Ethiopian Epiphany), March

2 (Victory of Adwa), April 5 (Id Al-Fitr), April 6 (Victory Day), April 24 (Good Friday), April 26 (Easter Sunday), May 1 (International Labor Day), June 12 (Id Al-Adha), Sept. 11 (Ethiopian New Year), late September (Birthday of Mohammed, subject to lunar calendar).

FIJI—Jan. 1 (New Year's), April 17 (Good Friday), April 18 (Easter Saturday), April 20 (Easter Monday), June 2 (Ratu Sir Lala Sukuna), June 15 (Queen's Birthday), July 27 (Constitution Day), Sept. 7 (Prophet Mohammed's Birthday), Oct. 12 (Fiji Day), Oct. 26 (Diwali), Nov. 16 (Prince Charles' Birthday), Dec. 25 (Christmas), Dec. 26 (Boxing Day).

FINLAND—Jan. 1 (New Year's), Jan. 6 (Epiphany), April 17 (Good Friday), April 20 (Easter Monday), May 1 (May Day), May 28 (Ascension), June 6 (Whitsun Eve), June 19 (Midsummer's Eve), June 20 (Midsummer's Day), Oct. 31 (All Saints), Dec. 6 (Independence Day), Dec. 24 (Christmas Eve), Dec. 25 (Christmas), Dec. 26 (Second Christmas Day).

FRANCE—Jan. 1 (New Year's), April 20 (Easter Monday), May 1 (Labor Day), May 8 (Veterans' Day—World War II) May 28 (Ascension), June 8 (Whiti Pentecost Monday), July 14 (Bastille

Day/French National Day), Aug. 15 (Assumption), Nov. 1 (All Saints), Nov. 11 (Armistice Day—World War I), Dec. 25 (Christmas).

GERMANY—Jan. 1 (New Year's), April 17 (Good Friday), April 20 (Easter Monday), May 1 (Labor Day), May 28 (Ascension), June 8 (Whit Monday), Oct. 3 (Day of German Unity), Nov. 18 (Repentance Day), Dec. 25 (Christmas), Dec. 26 (Second Day of Christmas).
Regional holidays: Jan. 6 (Epiphany), Baden-Wuerttemberg and Bavaria; May 21 (Waeldchestag), Hesse; June 18 (Corpus Christi), Baden-Wuerttemberg, Bavaria, Northrhine-Westphalia, Rhineland Palatinate, Hesse, and Saarland; Aug. 15 (Assumption), Bavaria; Nov. 1 (All Saints), Baden-Wuerttemberg, Bavaria, Northrhine-Westphalia, Rhineland-Palatinate, and Saarland.

GHANA—Jan. 1 (New Year's), March 6 (Independence Day), April 17 (Good Friday), April 20 (Easter Monday), May 1 (Labor/May Day), June 4 (Uprising Day), July 1 (Republic Day). Dec. 25 (Christmas), Dec. 26 (Boxing Day), Dec. 31 (Revolution Day).

GREECE—Jan. 1 (New Year's), Jan. 6 (Epiphany), March 9 (Clean Monday) March 25 (Greek Indepen-

dence Day), April 24 (Good Friday), April 26 (Easter Sunday), April 27 (Easter Monday), May 1 (May Day), Aug. 15 (Assumption), Oct. 28 (OXI Day), Dec. 25 (Christmas), Dec. 26 (Boxing Day).
Regional holidays: March 7 (Dodecanese Accession Day), Rhodes; Oct. 4 (Liberation of Xanthi), Xanthi; Oct. 26 (St. Dimitrios Day), Thessaloniki.

GRENADA—Jan. 1 (New Year's), Feb. 7 (Independence Day), April 17 (Good Friday), April 20 (Easter Monday), May 1 (Labor Day), June 8 (Whit Monday), June 18 (Corpus Christi), Aug. 5-6 (Emancipation Day), Oct. 25 (Thanksgiving Day) Dec. 25 (Christmas), Dec. 26 (Boxing Day).
This list is a projection based on Grenada's 1991 holiday schedule, and the actual dates and holidays may vary. Also, the dates for the Carnival holidays are not included in this listing.

GUATEMALA—Jan. 1 (New Year's), April 16 (Holy Thursday), April 17 (Good Friday), April 18 (Holy Saturday), April 19 (Easter), May 1 (Labor Day), June 30 Army Day), Aug. 15 (Assumption), Sept. 15 (Independence Day), Oct. 20 (Revolution Day), Nov. 1 (All Saints), Dec. 24—from noon (Christmas Eve), Dec. 25 (Christmas), Dec. 31—from noon (New Year's Eve).
When an official holiday falls on

a Sunday the following Monday is observed by several labor unions, the banking system, and government agencies.

GUINEA—Jan. 1 (New Year's), April 3 (Declaration of Second Republic), early April (End of Ramadan—exact date to be announced, depending on sighting of the moon), May 1 (Labor Day), mid-June (Tabaski—exact date to be announced depending on sighting of the moon), Aug. 15 (Assumption), Oct. 2 (Independence Day), end of August (Prophet Mohammed's Birthday—exact date to be announced, depending on sighting of the moon), Dec. 25 (Christmas).

GUYANA—Jan. 1 (New Year's) Feb. 24 (Republic Anniversary), March iO (Phagwah), April 17 (Good Friday), April 20 (Easter Monday), May 1 (Labor Day) June 12 (Eid-Ul-Azah), July 6 (Caribbean Day), Aug. 3 (Freedom Day), Sept. 10 (Youm-Un-Nabi), Oct. 26 (Deepavali) Dec. 25 (Christmas), Dec. 26 (Boxing Day). *The dates given for Eid-Ul-Azah (June 12) and Youm-Un-Nabi (Sept. 10) are tentative, as these Muslim holidays depend on sighting of the moon and their elact dates will not be known until a few days prior to the holidays.*

HONDURAS—Jan. 1 (New Year's), April 14 (Pan American Day), April 16 (Holy Thursday), April 17 (Good Friday), May 1 (Labor Day), Sept. 15 (Independence Day), Oct. 3 (Francisco Morazan's Day), Oct. 12 (Columbus Day), Oct. 21 (Armed Forces Day), Dec. 25 (Christmas).

HONG KONG Jan. 1 (New Year's), Feb. 4-6 (Lunar New Year's Holiday), April 17 (Good Friday), April 20 (Easter Monday) June 5 (Dragon Boat Festival), June 15 (Monday following Queen's Birthday) Aug. 31 (Liberation Day), Oct. 5 (Day following Chung Yeung Festival), Dec. 25 (Christmas). *Six local holidays falling on Saturday are not included in this listing.*

HUNGARY—Jan. 1 (New Year's), March 15 (1848 Revolution Day), April 20 (Easter Monday), May 1 (Labor Day), Aug. 20 (St. Stephen's Day), Oct. 23 (Republic Day), Dec. 25 (Christmas), Dec. 26 (Boxing Day).

ICELAND—Jan. 1 (New Year's), April 16 (Maundy Thursday), April 17 (Good Friday), April 20 (Easter Monday), April 23 (First Day of Summer), May 1 (Labor Day), May 28 (Ascension), June 8 (Whit Monday), June 17 (Icelandic National Day), Aug. 3 (Bank Holiday), Dec. 24 (Christmas Eve), Dec. 25 (Christmas), Dec. 31 (New Year's Eve).

INDIA—Jan. 1 (New Year's), Jan. 26 (Republic Day), March 2 (Maha Shivratri) March 19 (Holi), April 5 (Idu'l Fitr), Aprii 15 (Mahavir Jayanti), April 17 (Good Friday), May 16 (Buddha Purnima), June 12 (Idu'l Zuha—Bakrid), July 11 (Muharram), Aug. 15 (Independence Day), Aug. 21 (Janmashtami), Sept. 10 (Milad-Un-Nabi), Oct. 2 (Mahatma Gandhi's Birthday), Oct. 5 (Dussehra), Oct. 25 (Diwali), Nov. 10 (Guru Nanak's Birthday), Dec. 25 (Christmas). *Regional holidays to be observed in Western India: April 4 (Gudi Padva), April 14 (Ambedkar Jayanti), May 1 (Maharashtra Day), May 4 (Shivaji Jayanti), Aug. 31 (Ganesh Chaturthi). Regional holidays to be observed in Madras: Jan. 15 (Pongal) Jan. 16 (Thiruvalluvar Day), Jan. 1 (Uzhavar Thirunal), April 1 (Annual Closing of Bank Accounts), April 4 (Telugu New Year's Day), April 13 (Tamil New Year's Day), May 1 (May Day), Sept. 30 (Half-Yearly Closing of Bank Accounts), Oct. 5-6 (Ayuda Pooja), Oct. 25 (Deepavali). Federal Government offices are closed on Saturdays.*

INDONESIA—Jan. 1 (New Year's), Feb. 1 (Ascension of Mohammed), March 5 (Saka New Year 1914—Hindu, Bali), April 5-6 (Idul Fitri 1412), April 17 (Good Friday) May 16 (Waisak—Buddha, Bali), May 28 (Ascension of Christ), June 11 (Idul Adha 1412H—Haj New Year), July 2 (1st Muharam—Moslem New Year 1413H), Aug. 17 (Independence Day), Sept. 9 (Mohammed's Birthday), Dec. 25 (Christmas).

IRELAND Jan. 1 (New Year's), March 17 (St. Patrick's Day), April 17 (Good Friday), April 20 (Easter Monday), June 1 (June Bank Holiday), Aug. 3 (August Bank Holiday), Oct. 26 (October Bank Holiday), Dec. 25 (Christmas), Dec. 26 (St. Stephen's Day).

ISRAEL—April 18 (Passover—first day), April 24 (Passover—last day), May 7 (Independence Day), June 7 (Pentecost—Shavuot), Sept. 28-29 (Rosh Hashana—Jewish New Year), Oct. 7 (Yom Kippur—Day of Atonement), Oct. 12 (Succot—Feast of Tabernacles), Oct. 19 (Simhat Tora—Rejoicing of the Law).

ITALY—Jan. 1 (New Year's), Jan. 6 (Epiphany), April 20 (Easter Monday), April 25 (Anniversary of the Liberation), May 1 (Labor Day), Aug. 15 (Assumption), Dec. 8 (Immaculate Conception), Dec. 25 (Christmas), Dec. 26 (St. Stephen's Day).
Regional holidays: June 24 (St. John's Day), Florence, Genoa; June 29 (Sts. Peter & Paul), Rome; July 15 (St. Rosalia's Day), Palermo; Sept. 19 (St. Gennaro's Day), Naples; Dec. 7 (St. Ambrogio's Day), Milan.

When an Italian holiday falls on a Saturday, offices and stores are closed to the public.

JAMAICA—Jan. 1 (New Year's), March 4 (Ash Wednesday), April 17 (Good Friday), May 23 (Labor Day—will be observed on Monday, May 25), Aug. 3 (Independence Day), Oct. 19 (National Heroes' Day), Dec. 25 (Christmas), Dec. 26 (Boxing Day—will be observed Monday, Dec. 28).

JAPAN—Jan. 1 (New Year's), Jan. 15 (Adult's Day), Feb. 11 (National Foundation Day), March 20 (Vernal Equinox Day), April 29 (Greenery Day), May 3 (Constitution Day—to be observed on Monday, May 4), May 5 (Children's Day), Sept. 15 (Respect for the Aged Day), Sept. 23 (Autumnal Equinox Day), Oct. 10 (Sports Day), Nov. 3 (Culture Day), Nov. 23 (Labor Thanksgiving Day), Dec. 23 (Emperor's Birthday). *In addition to government holidays, most Japanese companies and government offices traditionally close for several days during the New Year's holiday season. In 1991-92, New Year's will be observed from Dec. 28 through Jan. 3. In 1992-93, New Year's will be observed from Dec. 29 through Jan. 5. Although it depends on the individual company, many are likely to observe limited hours during "Golden Week" (April 29-May 5), and the "Festival of Souls"* *for several days in mid-August (usually Aug. 14-16).*

JORDAN—Jan. 31 (Prophet Mohammad's Ascension Day), April 26 (Easter), April 2-3* (Id Al-Fitr), May 25 (Independence Day), June 10 (Great Arab Revolt and Army Day), June 11-12* (Id Al-Adha), June 30* (Islamic New Year), Aug. 11 (King Hussein's Accession to the Throne), Sept. 22 (Prophet Mohammad's Birthday), Nov. 14 (King Hussein's Birthday).
The Islamic religious holidays listed above are determined by sighting of the moon and the exact dates may vary slightly from those given.

KENYA—Jan. 1 (New Year's), April 17 (Good Friday), April 20 (East Monday), May 1 (Labor Day), June 1 (Madaraka Day), Oct. 20 (Kenyatta Day), Dec. 25 (Christmas).

KOREA—Jan. 1-2 (New Year's), Feb. 3-5 (Lunar New Year's), March 1 (Independence Movement Day), March 10 (Labor Day), May 5 (Children's Day), June 6 (Memorial Day), July 17 (Constitution Day), Aug. 15 (Independence Day), Sept. 10-12 (Korean Thanksgiving Days), Oct. 3 (National Foundation Day), Dec. 25 (Christmas).

KUWAIT—Jan. 1-3 (New Year's), Jan. 31-Feb. 1 (Ascension), Feb. 25 (National Day), Feb. 26-27 (Liberation Holiday), April 3-5 (Eid Al-Fitr), June 9 (Waqfa), June 10-13 (Eid Al-Adha), July 1-3 (Islamic New Year), Sept. 9-11 (Prophet's Birthday).

LEBANON—Jan. 1 (New Year's), Feb. 9 (St. Maron's Day), April 4* (Feast of Ramadan—Al-Fitr), April 17 (Good Friday—Western), April 19 (Easter Monday—Western), April 24 (Good Friday—Eastern), April 26 (Easter Monday—Eastern), May 1 (Lebanese Labor Day), June 11 * (Feast of Al-Adha), July 1* (Moslem New Year—Al Hijra), July 10* (Feast of Al-Ashura), Aug. 15 (Assumption), Sept. 9* (Prophet's Birthday), Nov. 1 (All Saints), Nov. 22 (Independence Day), Dec. 25 (Christmas).
*The Islamic religious holidays listed above are determined by sighting of the moon and the exact dates may vary slightly from those given.

LIBERIA—Jan. 1 (New Year's), Feb. 11 (Armed Forces Day), March 11 (Decoration Day), March 15 (J.J. Roberts' Birthday), April 12 (National Redemption Day), April 17 (Good Friday), May 14 (Unification Day), July 26 (Independence Day), Aug. 25 (Flag Day), Nov. 5 (Thanksgiving Day), Nov. 29 (William V.S. Tubman's Birthday), Dec. 25 (Christmas).

LUXEMBOURG—Jan. 1 (New Year's), March 2 (Shrove Monday), April 20 (Easter Monday), May 1 (Luxembourg Labor Day), May 28 (Ascension), June 8 (Whit Monday), June 23 (Grand Duke's Birthday), Aug. 15 (Assumption), Nov. 1 (All Saints), Nov. 2 (All Souls), Dec. 25 (Christmas), Dec. 26 (Second Day of Christmas).

MADAGASCAR—Jan. 1 (New Year's), March 29 (Day Commemorating the Martyrs of the Malagasy Revolution), April 20 (Easter Monday), May 1 (Labor Day), May 24 (Ascension), June 8 (Whit Monday), June 26 (Independence Day), Aug. 15 (Assumption), Nov. 1 (All Saints), Dec. 25 (Christmas).
As in past years, Madagascar's holiday schedule will be selected during the third week of January by the Council of Ministers. The preceding list is a projection of holidays for Madagascar in 1992.

MALAYSIA—Jan. 1 (New Year), Feb. 1 (Kuala Lumpur City Day—to be observed on preceding Friday, Jan. 31), Feb. 4-5 (Chinese New Year's), April 4-5 (Hari Raya Ruasa—to be observed on preceding Friday, April 3, and following Monday, April 6, if dates remain unchanged), May 1 (Malaysian Labor Day), May 17 (Wesak Day—to be observed on following Monday,

May 18), June 6 (King's Birthday—to be observed on preceding Friday, June 5), June 11 (Hari Raya Haji), July 2 (Awal Muharram), Aug. 31 (Malaysian National Day), Sept. 9 (Prophet Muhammad's Birthday), Oct. 26 (Deepavali), Dec. 25 (Christmas).

MAURITANIA—Jan. 1 (New Year's), March 8 (Women's Day—applies to working national women only), April 3* (Id El-Fitr—End of Ramadan), May 1 (Labor Day), May 25 (Africa Day), June 11* (Id El-Adha—Tabaski), July 2* (Muslim New Year), July 10 (Armed Forces Day), Sept. 8* (Id El Maouloud El Nabi) Nov. 28 (Mauritian Independence Day), Dec. 12 (Anniversary of the Restructuring of CMSN).

MEXICO—Jan. 1 (New Year's), Feb. 5 (Anniversary of Mexican Constitution), March 21 (Benito Juarez' Birthday), April 16 (Holy Thursday), April 17 (Good Friday), May 1 (Mexican Labor Day), May 5 (Anniversary of the Battle of Puebla), Sept. 16 (Mexican Independence Day), Oct. 12 (Dia de la Raza and Columbus Day), Nov. 2 (All Souls), Nov. 20 (Anniversary of the Mexican Revolution), Dec. 25 (Christmas).

MOROCCO—Jan. 1 (New Year's), Jan. 11 (National Day), March 3 (Feast of the Throne), April 4-5* (Aid El Fitr), May 1 (Labor Day), May 23 (National Day), June 11-12* (Aid El Adha), July 2* (Moslem New Year), July 9 (King's Birthday), Aug. 14 (Ouad Addahab Day), Aug. 20 (National Day), Sept. 10-11* (Prophet's Birthday), Nov. 6 (Green March Day), Nov. 18 (Independence Day). *Religious holidays that are based on the lunar calendar and may fall one day earlier or later than the date shown; the government of Morocco usually grants two days for these holidays.

MOZAMBIQUE—Jan. 1 (New Year's), Feb. 3 (Day of Mozambican Heroes), April 7 (Womens' Day), May 1 (Workers' Day), June 25 (Independence Day), Sept. 7 (Lusaka Agreement), Sept. 25 (Revolution Day), Nov. 10 (Maputo City Day), Dec. 25 (Christmas).

NEPAL Jan. 30 (Martyrs' Day), Feb. 19 (National Democracy Day), March 2 (Shivaratri), March 8 (Women's Day—half-holiday for women only), April 12 (Ramnavami), April 13 (New Year's Day), May 2 (Mothers' Day), July 14 (Teachers' Day), Aug. 13 (Janai Purnima), Aug. 21 (Krishnashtami), Aug. 28 (Fathers' Day), Aug. 30 (Teej—for women only), Sept. 1 (Rishi Panchami—for women only), Sept. 27 (Ghatasthapana), Oct. 3-11 (Dasain Festival), Oct. 25-27 (Tihar Festival), Dec. 29 (King Birendra's Birthday). Regional holidays: March 18 (Fagu), hill districts; March 19 (Holi), Terai districts; April 2 (Ghode Jatra), Kathmandu Valley; Aug. 14 (Gai Jatra), Kathmandu Valley; Sept. 10 (Indra Jatra), Kathmandu Valley. All dates after April 13 are tentative as the official list of holidays will not be published until March 1992, and several Or the religious holidays are based on the lunar calendar. Saturdays are regular holidays. Government offices are open on Sunday. Fridays are half-holidays.

NETHERLANDS—Jan. 1 (New Year's), April 17 (Good Friday), April 20 (Easter Monday), April 30 (Queen's Birthday), May 5 (Liberation Day), May 28 (Ascension), June 8 (Whit Monday), Dec. 25 (Christmas).

NETHERLANDS ANTILLES AND ARUBA—Jan. 1 (New Year's), March 2 (Carnival Monday), April 17 (Good Friday), April 20 (Easter Monday), April 30 (Queen's Birthday) May 1 (Labor Day), May 28 (Ascension), Dec. 25 (Christmas), Dec. 26 (Boxing Day). Regional holidays: March 18 (Flag Day), Aruba; July 2 (Flag Day), Curacao; Sept. 6 (Flag Day), Bonaire; Nov. 11 (Flag Day), St. Maarten; Nov. 16 (Flag Day), St. Eustatius; Dec. 4 (Flag Day), Saba. On the following Jewish holidays, all Jewish establishments are closed: Sept. 28 (Rosh Hashanah), Oct. 7 (Yom Kippur).

NEW ZEALAND—Jan. 1-2 (New Year's), Feb. 6 (Waitangi Day), April 13 (Good Friday), April 17 (Easter Monday), April 20 (Easter Monday), April 25 (ANZAC Day), June 1 (Queen's Birthday), Oct. 26 (Labor Day), Dec. 25 (Christmas), Dec. 26 (Boxing Day). Regional holidays: Jan. 20 (Wellington Anniversary Day), Jan. 27 (Auckland Anniversary Day), Nov. 13 (Christchurch Anniversary Day).

NIGERIA—Jan. 1 (New Year's), April 17 (Good Friday), April 20 (Easter Monday), May 1 (Workers' Day), Oct. 1 (National Day), Dec. 25 (Christmas), Dec. 26 (Boxing Day). This list is a projection based on Nigeria's 1991 holiday schedule, and the actual dates and holidays may vary. Nigeria also observes the Muslim holidays of Eid-el-Fitr, Eid-el-Kahir, and Eid-el-Malud, the dates for which are based on the lunar calendar and announced shortly before they occur.

NORWAY—Jan. 1 (New Year's), April 16 (Holy Thursday), April 17 (Good Friday), April 20 (Easter Monday), May 1 (Labor Day), May 17 (Constitution Day), May 28 (Ascension), June 8 (Whit Monday), Dec. 25 (Christmas), Dec. 26 (Second Christmas Day).

OMAN—Feb. 24 (Ascension), April 4-5 (Eid Al-Fitr), June 11-16 (Eid Al-Adha), July 1 (Islamic New Year), Sept. 2 (Birth of the Prophet), Nov. 18-19 (National Day). *The preceding dates are approximations, because the exact dates are determined by locally-observed phases of the moon.*

PAKISTAN—March 23 (Pakistan Day), April 4-6* (Eid-Ul-Fitr), May 1 (May Day), July 11-13* (Eid-Ul-Azha), July 10-11 * (Ninth and Tenth of Moharram), Aug. 14 (Independence Day), Sept. 6 (Defense of Pakistan Day), Sept. 10* (EidI-Milad-Un-Nabi), Sept. 11 (Death Anniversary of the Quaid-E-Azam), Nov. 9 (Iqbal Day), Dec. 25 (Birthday of QuaidE-Azam).
The Muslim religious holidays listed above are determined by the sighting of the moon and the eIact dates may vary slightly from those given.

PANAMA—Jan. 1 (New Year's), Jan. 9 (Mourning Day), March 3 (Carnival), April 17 (Good Friday), May 1 (Labor Day), Nov. 3 (Independence Day—Panama from Colombia), Nov. 10 (The Uprising of Los Santos), Nov. 28 (Independence Day—Panama from Spain), Dec. 8 (Mother's Day). *In the event that a legal Panamanian holiday falls on a Sunday, the employees shall receive the following Monday off by way of compensation.*

PARAGUAY—Jan. 1 (New Year's), Feb. 3 (St. Blas, Patron of Paraguay), March 1 (Heroes' Day), April 16 (Holy Thursday), April 17 (Good Friday), May 1 (Labor Day), May 15 (Independence Day), June 12 (Chaco Armistice), Aug. 15 (Founding of the City of Asuncion), Dec. 8 (Virgin of Caacupe), Dec. 25 (Christmas).

PERU—Jan. 1 (New Year's), April 16 afternoon (Holy Thursday), April 17 (Good Friday), May 1 (Labor Day), June 24 afternoon (Countryman's Day), June 29 (Sts. Peter & Paul), July 28-29 (Independence Day), Aug. 30 (St. Rose of Lima), Oct. 8 (Battle of Angamos), Nov. 1 (All Saints), Dec. 8 (Immaculate Conception), Dec. 25 (Christmas).

PHILIPPINES—Jan. 1 (New Year's), April 9 (Heroism Day), April 16 (Maundy Thursday), April 17 (Good Friday), May 1 (Labor Day), June 12 (Independence Day), Aug. 30 (National Heroes' Day), Nov. 1 (All Saints), Nov. 30 (Bonifacio Day), Dec. 25 (Christmas), Dec. 30 (Rizal Day). *Regional holidays: June 24 (Manila Day); Aug. 19 (Quezon City Day).*

POLAND Jan. 1 (New Year's), April 20 (Easter Monday), May 1 (Labor Day), May 3 (Constitution Day), June 18 (Corpus Christi), Aug. 15 (Assumption of the Virgin Mary), Nov. 1 (All Saints), Nov. 11 (National Independence Day), Dec. 25 (Christmas), Dec. 26 (Boxing Day).

PORTUGAL Jan. 1 (New Year's), March 3 (Carnival), April 17 (Good Friday), April 25 (Liberty Day), May 1 (May Day), June 10 (Portugal Day), June 13 (St. Anthony's Day), June 18 (Corpus Christi), Aug. 15 (Assumption) Oct. 5 (Portuguese Republic Day), Nov. i (All Saints), Dec. 1 (Portuguese Independence Day), Dec. 8 (Immaculate Conception), Dec. 25 (Christmas).

ROMANIA—Jan. 1-2 (New

Year's), May 1 (Labor Day), Dec. 1 (National Day), Dec. 25 (Christmas).

SAUDI ARABIA—April 3-7 (Id-Al-Fitr/Ramadan), June 13 (Id-Al-Adha/Hajj or Pilgrimage to Mecca).
The dates of Id-Al-Fitr and Id-Al-Adha are only approximate, since the actual dates are declared by the Palace upon the sighting of the moon or at the beginning of the month, just a few days before the holiday is to begin.

SENEGAL Jan. 1 (New Year's), April 4 (Senegalese Independence Day), April 20 (Easter Monday or Paques), May 1 (Senegalese Labor Day), May 24 (Ascension), June 8 (Whit Monday or Pentecost), June 11 (Tabaski or Eid-UI Kabir), July 11 (Tamxarit/Yawmal Achoura/ Muslim New Year's), Aug. 15 (Assumption), Sept. 10 (Maouloud/Birth of the Prophet), Nov. 1 (All Saints), Dec. 25 (Christmas). The dates of Eid-UI Fitre, Eid-UI Kabir, Tamxarit, and Maouloud are lunar Muslim holidays which are subject to change.

SIERRA LEONE—Jan. 1 (New Year's), April 3 (Eid Ul Fitri), April 17 (Good Friday), April 20 (Easter Monday), April 27 (Independence Day), June 10 (Eid Ul Adha), Sept. 9 (Moulid Um Nabi), Dec.

25 (Christmas), Dec. 26 (Boxing Day).
The dates for the religious holidays Eid Ul-Fitri, Eid Ul-Adha, and Moulid Um Nabi are tentative; the exact dates will be determined by lunar sighting shortly before they occur.

SINGAPORE—Jan. 1 (New Year's), Feb. 4-5 (Chinese New Year's), April 13 (Good Friday), April 6 (Hari Raya Puasa), April 17 (Good Friday), May 1 (Singapore Labor Day), May 18 (Vesak Day), June 11 (Hari Raya Haji), Aug. 10 (Singapore National Day), Oct. 24 (Deepavali), Dec. 25 (Christmas).

SOUTH AFRICA—Jan. 1 (New Year's), April 6 (Founder's Day), April 17 (Good Friday), April 20 (Family Day), May 1 (Workers' Day), May 28 (Ascension), May 30-31 (Republic Day), Oct. 10 (Kruger Day), Dec. 16 (Day of the Vow), Dec. 25 (Christmas), Dec. 26 (Day of Goodwill).

SPAIN—Jan. 1 (New Year's), Jan. 6 (Epiphany), April 17 (Good Friday), May 1 (Labor Day), Aug. 15 (Assumption), Oct. 12 (National Day), Dec. 8 (Immaculate Conception), Dec. 25 (Christmas).
Regional holidays: March 19 (St. Joseph), Bilbao and Madrid; April 16 (Holy

Thursday), Bilbao and Madrid; April 20 (Easter Monday), Barcelona and Bilbao; May 2 (Community Day), Madrid; May 15 (St. Isidro), Madrid, June 8 (Whit Monday), Barcelona; July 31 (St. Ignatius), Bilbao; Aug. 21 (Semana Grande Day), Bilbao; Sept. 11 (Catalonia Day), Barcelona; Sept. 24 (La Merced), Barcelona; Nov. 2 (All Saints), Bilbao; Nov. 9 (Our Lady of Almudena), Madrid; Dec. 7 (Constitution Day), Madrid; Dec. 26 (St. Stephen), Barcelona.

SRI LANKA—Jan. 15 (Tamil Thai Pongal Day), Jan. 19 (Duruthu Full Moon Poya Day), Feb. 4 (National Day), Feb. 17 (Navam Full Moon Poya Day). March 2 (Maha Sivarathri Day), March 18 (Medin Full Moon Poya Day), April 5 (Ramazan Festival Day), April 12 (Day prior to Sinhala and Tamil New Year's) April 13 (Sinhala and Tamil New Year'sj, April 16 (Bak Full Moon Poya Day), April 17 (Good Friday), May 1 (May Day), May 16 (Wesak Full Moon Poya Day), May 17 (Day following Wesak Full Moon Poya Day), May 22 (National Heroes' Day), June 12 (Hadji Festival Day), June 14 (Poson Full Moon Poya Day), June 30 (Special Bank Holiday), July 14 (Esala Full Moon Poya Day), Aug. 12 (Nikini Full Moon Poya Day), Sept. 10 (Holy Prophet's

Birthday), Sept. 11 (Binara Full Moon Poya Day), Oct. 11 (Vap Full Moon Poya Day), Oct. 25 (Deepavali Festival Day), Nov. 9 (11 Full Moon Poya Day), Dec. 9 (Unduvap Full Moon Poya Day), Dec. 25 (Christmas), Dec. 31 (Special Bank Holiday).

SWAZILAND—Jan. 1 (New Year's), April 17 (Good Friday), April 20 (Easter Monday), April 19 (King Mswati III's Birthday), April 25 (National Flag Day), May 28 (Ascension), July 22 (Public Holiday), August/September (Reed Dance—exact date to be announced), Dec. 25 (Christmas), Dec. 26 (Boxing Day), December/January (Incwala—exact date to be announced).

SWEDEN—Jan. 1 (New Year's) Jan. 6 (13th Day of Christmas), April 17 (Good Friday), April 20 (Easter Monday), May 1 (First of May), May 28 (Ascension), June 8 (Whitsun), June 20 (Midsummer), Oct. 31 (All Saints), Dec. 25 (Christmas), Dec. 26 (Boxing Day).

SWITZERLAND—Jan. 1-2 (New Year's and Baerzelistag Days), April 17 (Good Friday), April 20 (Easter Monday), May 28 (Ascension), June 8 (Whit Monday), Aug. 1 (Swiss National Day), Dec. 25 (Christmas), Dec. 26

(Boxing Day).

SYRIA—Jan. 1 (New Year's), March 8 (Revolution Day), March 21 (Mothers' Day), April 4-6 (Al-Fitr), April 17 (Independence Day), May 1 (Labor Day), May 6 (Martyrs' Day), June 11-15 (Al-Adha), July 2 (Moslem New Year), Sept. 10 (Prophet's Birthday), Oct. 6 (Tishreen War), Dec. 25 (Christmas).
The exact dates of Moslem religious holidays are determined by lunar sighting and may vary from the dates given above.

TAIWAN—Jan. 1-2 (New Year's), Feb. 3-6 (New Year's Eve and Spring Festival), March 29 (Youth Day), April 4 (Women's and Children's Day), April 5 (Festival of Sweeping of the Tombs), June 5 (Dragon Boat Festival), Sept. 11 (Mid-Autumn Festival), Sept. 28 (Confucius' Birthday), Oct. 10 (Double Ten Day), Oct. 25 (Taiwan Restoration Day), Oct. 31 (President Chiang Kai-Shek's Birthday), Nov. 12 (Dr. Sun Yat-Sen's Birthday), Dec. 25 (Constitution Day).

THAILAND—Jan. 1 (New Year's), Feb. 18 (Magha Puja Day), April 6 (King Rama 1 Memorial and Chakri Day), April 13-14 (Songkran Day), May 5 (Coronation Day), May 14 (Plowing Ceremony Day), May 16 (Visakha Puja Day), July 14 (Asalha Puja

Day), July 15 (Buddhist Lent), Aug. 12 (Her Majesty the Queen's Birthday), Oct. 23 (Chulalongkorn Day), Dec. 5 (His Majesty the King's Birthday), Dec. 10 (Constitution Day), Dec. 31 (New Year's Eve).

TOGO—Jan. 1 (New Year's), Jan. 13 (National Liberation Day), Jan. 24 (Economic Liberation Day), April 20 (Easter Monday), April 27 (Independence Day), May 1 (Labor Day), May 28 (Ascension), June 8 (Pentecost), June 21 (Martyrs Day), Aug. 15 (Assumption), Nov. 1 (All Saints), Dec. 25 (Christmas).
Ramadan and Tabaski are variable Muslim holidays whose dates will be determined by sighting of the moon.

TRINIDAD AND TOBAGO—Jan. 1 (New Year's), April 17 (Good Friday), April 20 (Easter Monday), June 7 (Whit Monday) June 18 (Corpus Christi), June 19 (Labor Day), Aug. 1 (Emancipation Day), Aug. 31 (Independence Day), Sept. 24 (Republic Day), Dec. 25 (Christmas), Dec. 26 (Boxing Day).
In addition to the above, the Hindu and Muslim festivals of Divali and Eid-Ul-Fitr are celebrated, but the dates are normally published a few days in advance of the public holiday. Carnival will be celebrated on

*March 2-3; these are not offi-
cial holidays but most businesses
and government offices remain
closed.*

TUNISIA—Jan. 1 (New
Year's), March 20 (Indepen-
dence Day), March 21 (Youth
Day), April 5-6 (Aid Esseghir
El-Fitr), April 9 (Martyr's
Day), May 1 (Labor Day),
June 11-12 (Aid El-Kebir-El
Idha), July 2 (Ras El Am El
Hijri), July 25 (Republic Day),
Aug. 13 (Women's Day),
Sept. 9 (Mouled), Nov. 7
(Memorial).
*The dates for Tunisian religious
holidays listed above are ap-
proximate and actual dates will
be determined by the lunar
calendar.*

TURKEY—Jan. 1 (New
Year's), April 3-6 (Sugar
Holiday—from 1:00 p.m. on
April 3), April 23 (National
Sovereignty and Children's
Day), May 19 (National
Sovereignty and Children's
Day), June 10-14 (Sacrifice
Holiday—from 1:00 p.m. on
June 10), Aug. 30 (Victory
Day), Oct. 28-29 (Turkish
Independence Day—from
1:00 p.m. on Oct. 28).

UGANDA—Jan. 1 (New
Year's), Jan. 26 (Liberation
Day), April 17 (Good Friday),
April 20 (Easter Monday),
May 1 (Labor Day), May—
exact date to be announced
(Idd-El-Fitr), June—exact
date to be announced (Mar-

tyrs' Day), July 3 (Independence Day), Oct. 9 (Inde-
pendence Day), Dec. 25
(Christmas), Dec. 26 (Boxing
Day).
*The exact dates of the religious
holidays listed above will depend
upon the sighting of the moon.*

UNITED ARAB EMIR-
ATES Jan. 1 (New Year's),
Jan. 31 (Ascension), April 4-6
(Eid Al-Fitr) June 10 (Waqfa
Arafat), June 11-13 (Eid Al-
Adha), July 1 (Islamic New
Year), Aug. 6 (Sh. Zayed Ac-
cession Day), Sept. 9
(Prophet's Birthday), Dec. 2-
3 (National Day), Dec. 25
(Christmas).
*The exact dates of the religious
holidays depend upon the
sighting of the moon.*

UNITED KINGDOM—
Jan. 1 (New Year's), April 17
(Good Friday), April 20
(Easter Bank Monday), May
4 (May Day), May 25 (Spring
Holiday), Aug. 31 (Summer
Bank Holiday), Dec. 25
(Christmas), Dec. 26 (Boxing
Day).
*Regional holidays in Northern
Ireland: March 17 (St. Patrick's
Day), April 21 (Easter Tues-
day), July 13-14 (Orangeman's
Day).*
*Regional holidays in Scotland:
Jan. 2 (Bank Holiday), April
13 (Spring Holiday), May 18
(Victoria Day), Aug. 3 (Bank
Holiday), Sept. 21 (Autumn
Holiday). Scotland does not
observe April 20 (Easter Bank*

*Holiday), May 25 (Spring
Holiday), and Aug. 31 (Summer Bank Holiday).*

URUGUAY—Jan. 1 (New
Year's), Jan. 6 (Three Kings'
Day), March 2-3 (Carnival),
April 16-17 (Holy Week),
May 1 (Uruguayan Labor
Day), May 18 (Battle of Las
Piedras), June 19 (Birthday of
Artigas), Aug. 25 (Uruguayan
Independence Day), Oct. 12
(Columbus Day), Nov. 2 (Dia
de Los Difuntos), Dec. 25
(Christmas).

U.S.S.R.—Jan. 1 (New
Year's), March 8 (International Women's Day), May
1-2 (International Labor
Day), May 9 (Victory Day-
WWII).
*It is quite probable that the
Republics that have comprised
the U.S.S.R. will legislate different holidays for 1992 than
those celebrated under commu-
nism. However, this has not yet
been done. Holidays on the
preceding list are those that the
U.S. Embassy in Moscow be-
lieves might continue to exist in
at least some of the Republics.
The Embassy has been told that
1991 was the last year for Oct.
7 (Revolution Day) and Nov.
7-8 (October Revolution Day).
It is probable that new holidays
will be created during 1992.
Business officials should check
before they travel.*

VENEZUELA—Jan. 1
(New Year's), Jan. 6

(Epiphany), March 3 (Carnival), March 19 (St. Joseph), April 16 (Maundy Thursday) April 17 (Good Friday), May 1 (Labor Day), June 1 (Ascension), June 15 (Corpus Christi), June 24 (Battle of Carabobo). June 29 (Sts. Peter & Paul), July 24 (Bolivar's Birthday), Oct. 12 (Columbus Day), Nov. 5 (All Saints), Dec. 7 (Immaculate Conception), Dec. 25 (Christmas).

Regional holidays: Feb. 3 (Sucre's Birthday), Cumana; March 10 (Varga's Birthday), La Guaira- Oct. 24 (Urdaneta's Birthday), Maracaibo; Nov. 18 (Virgin of Chiquinquira) Maracaibo. Religious hoiidays are observed by the banking sector in accordance with the following National Banking Council regulations: holidays falling on Tuesday or Wednesday are observed the previous Monday; those falling on Thursday or Friday, the following Monday.

YEMEN—Jan. 1 (New Year's), Feb. 11* (Prophet's Ascent to Heaven in the month of Rajab), April 2-5* (Eid Al-Fitr), May 1 (Labor Day), May 22 (Unification Day), June 11-15* (Eid Al-Adha), July 3* (Islamic New Year), Sept. 11 * (Prophet's Birthday), Sept. 26 (Former North Yemen Revolution Day), Oct. 14 (Former South Yemen Revolution Day),

Nov. 30 (Former South Yemen Independence Day). *These holidays are dependent upon lunar observation, and the exact dates will be announcced later.*

YUGOSLAVIA—Jan. 1-2 (New Year's), May 1-2 (May Day), July 4 (Fighters' Day), Nov. 29-Dec. 1 (Day of the Republic).
According to the Yugoslav holiday law, when either day of a two-day holiday falls on a Sunday (Nov. 29), the next working day becomes a holiday (Dec. 1).
Regional holidays observed only in respective republics: Jan. 7 (Orthodox Christmas), Serbia and perhaps Macedonia; March 28 (Serbian State Day); April 27 (Slovenian Liberation Day); July 7 (Serbian Uprising Day); July 13 (Montenegrin Uprising Day); July 22 (Slovenian Uprising Day); July 27 (Croatian and Bosnian Uprising Day); Aug. 2 (Macedonian Uprising Day 1903); Oct. 11 (Macedonian Uprising Day); Nov. 1 (Slovenian and Croatian Day of the Dead); Nov. 25 (Bosnian State Day). This list is based on last year's and is tentative; most dates have not been confirmed by the other Republics.

ZAIRE—Jan. 1 (New Year's), Jan. 4 (Day of the Martyrs for Independence). May 1 (Labor Day), June 24 (Anniversary of New Constitution), June

30 (Independence Day), Aug. 1 (Parents' Day), Oct. 14 (Youth Day/President's Birthday), Nov. 17 (Armed Forces Day), Nov. 24 (Anniversary of the Regime), Dec. 25 (Christmas).
If the government of Zaire issues a decree, holidays falling on Saturdays or Sundays will be observed on the preceding Friday.

ZAMBIA—Jan. 1 (New Year's), March 12 (Youth Day), April 17 (Good Friday), April 18 (Holy Saturday), May 1 (Labor Day), May 25 (African Freedom Day), July 6 (Heroes' Day), July 7 (Unity Day), Aug. 3 (Farmers' Day), Oct. 24 (Independence Day), Dec. 25 (Christmas).

Appendix C

State Offices That Provide Export Assistance

For some time, governors have guided and stimulated economic development and job creation in their states. In the past 10 years, this activism extended beyond state and national borders. Today, many governors lead overseas trade missions that are an important part of state economic development programs.

President Bush told the National Governors' Association that governors "are becoming our economic envoys and ambassadors of democracy. You are a new force in restoring American international competitiveness and expanding world markets for American goods and services."

Most states have trade programs that serve as catalysts and brokers in the international arena. States provide technical assistance—from seminars on the "how to's" of trade, to individual exporter counseling, to dissemination of specific trade leads. They promote joint ventures, seek foreign investment, and encourage international travel to the United States.

Forty-one states maintain offices in 24 different countries. Seven states have export finance programs. Others provide information on non-state sources of financing.

The top international trade officials in the 50 states, the District of Columbia, and Puerto Rico are listed below, with their addresses and telephone numbers.

Alabama
Alabama Development Office
Fred Denton, Dir., Int'l Mktg.
State Capitol
Montgomery, Ala. 36130
(205) 263-0048

Alaska
State of Alaska
Governor's Office of Intl. Trade
Director
3601 C St., Ste. 798
Anchorage, Alaska 99503
(907) 561-5585

Arizona
Arizona Dept. of Commerce
Peter Cunningham, Intl. Trade
Dir.
3800 N. Central

Phoenix, Ariz. 85012
(602) 280-1371

Arkansas
Ark. Industrial Dev. Commission
Charles Sloan, Mkting. Dir.
#1 State Capitol Mall
Little Rock, Ark. 72201
(501) 682-1121

California
Calif. State World Trade Commission
Robert DeMartini, Dir., Export Dev.
1121 L St., Ste. 310
Sacramento, Calif. 95814
(916) 324-5511

Colorado
Colo. Intl. Trade Office
Morgan Smith, Dir.
1625 Broadway, Ste. 680
Denver, Colo. 80202
(303) 892-3850

Connecticut
Conn. Dept. Econ. Devel.
Int'l. Division
Matthew J. Broder, Dir.
865 Brook St.
Rocky Hill, Conn. 06067-3405
(203) 258-4256

Delaware
Delaware Dev. Office
Business Dev. Office
Donald Sullivan, Dir.
P.O. Box 1401

Dover, Del. 19903
(302) 739-4271

District of Columbia
D.C. Office of Intl. Business
Rosa Whitaker, Dir.
1250 I St.
Ste. 1003
Washington, D.C. 20005
(202) 727-1576

Florida
Florida Dept. of Commerce
Bureau of Intl. Trade and Dev.
Tom Slattery, Dir.
331 Collins Building
Tallahassee, Fla. 32399-2000
(904) 488-6124

Georgia
Georgia Dept. of Industry and
Trade
Kevin Langston, Dir.
285 Peachtree Center Ave.
Stes. 1000 and 1100
P.O. Box 1776
Atlanta, Ga. 30301-1776
(404) 656-3571

Hawaii
State of Hawaii
Dept. of Bus. and Econ. Dev.
Trade and Ind. Dev. Branch
Dennis Ling, Chief
P.O. Box 2359
Honolulu, Hawaii 96804
(808) 548-7719

Idaho
Division of Intl. Business
David P. Christensen, Admin-
istrator
Idaho Dept. of Commerce
700 W. State St.
Boise, Idaho 83720
(208) 334-2470

Illinois
Ill. Dept. of Commerce and
Community Affairs
Nan K. Hendrickson, Mgr.,
Intl. Business Div.
310 S. Michigan Ave.,
Ste. 1000
Chicago, 111. 60604
(312) 814-7164

Indiana
Indiana Dept. of Commerce
Maria Mercedes Plant,
Dir. of Intl. Trade
Business Dev. Div.
One N. Capitol, Ste. 700
Indianapolis, Ind. 46204-2288
(317) 232-8845

Iowa
Iowa Dept. of Econ. Dev.
Michael Doyle, Bureau Chief,
Intl. Mkting. Div.
200 E. Grand Ave.
Des Moines, Iowa 50309
(5 1 5) 242-4743

Kansas
Kansas Dept. of Commerce
Trade Development Div.
Jim Beckley, Dir.
400 SW 8th St., Ste: 500
Topeka, Kans. 66603
(913) 296-4027

Kentucky
Ky. Cabinet for Econ. Dev.
Michael Hayes, Dir., Office of
Intl. Mkting.
Capital Plaza Tower
Frankfort, Ky. 40601
(502) 564-2170

Louisiana
Office of Intl. Trade, Finance
and Devel.

William Jackson, Dir.
P.O. Box 94185
Baton Rouge, La. 70804-9185
(504) 342-4320

Maine
Maine State Dev. Office
Lynn Wachtel, Commissioner
State House, Station 59
Augusta, Maine 04333
(207) 289-2656

Maryland
Md. Office of Intl. Trade
(MOIT)
Eric Feldman, Exec. Dir.
7th Floor, World Trade Center
401 E. Pratt St.
Baltimore, Md. 21202
(301) 333-8180

Massachusetts
Mass. Office of Intl. Trade
Gwen Pritchard, Exec. Dir.
100 Cambridge St., Ste. 902
Boston, Mass. 02202
(617) 367-1830

Michigan
Mich. Dept. of Commerce
Gene Ruff, Actg. Dir.,
World Trade Services Div.
P.O. Box 30225
Lansing, Mich. 48909
(517) 373-1054

Minnesota
Minn. Trade Office
Director
1000 World Trade Center
30 E. 7th St.
St. Paul, Minn. 55101
(612) 297-4227

Mississippi
Miss. Dept. of Econ. & Com-

munity Dev.
Elizabeth Cleveland, Dir., Export Office
P.O. Box 849
Jackson, Miss. 39205
(601) 359-3618

Missouri
Missouri Dept. of Commerce
Intl. Business Office
Robert Black, Dir.
P.O. Box 118
Jefferson City, Mo. 65102
(314) 751-4855

Montana
Mont. Dept. of Commerce
Business Dev. Div.
Matthew Cohn, Dir., Intl. Trade Office
1429-9th Ave.
Helena, Mont. 59620
(406) 444-4380

Nebraska
Nebraska Dept. of Econ. Devel.
Steve Buttress Dir.
301 Centennial Mall S.
Lincoln Neb. 68509
(402) 471-4668

Nevada
(State of) Nevada
Commission on Econ. Dev.
Julie Wilcox, Dir.
Las Vegas Mail Room Complex
Las Vegas, Nev. 89158
(702) 486-7282

New Hampshire
(State of) New Hampshire
Dept. of Resources and Econ. Dev.
William Pillsbury, Dir. Office
of Industrial Trade
P.O. Box 856
Concord, N.H. 03301
(603) 271-2591

New Jersey
(State of) N.J. Div. of Intl. Trade
Philip Ferzen, Dir.
P.O. Box 47024
153 Halsey St., 5th Floor
Newark, N.J. 07102
(201) 648-3518

New Mexico
(State of) New Mexico
Economic Dev. and Tourism Dept.
Trade Division
Roberto Castillo, Dir.
1100 St. Francis Dr.,
Joseph M. Montoya Bldg.
Santa Fe, N.M. 87503
(505) 827-0307

New York
N.Y. State Dept. of Commerce
Dept. of Econ. Dev.
Intl. Trade Div.,
Stephen Koller, Dir.
15 15 Broadway
New York, N.Y. 10036
(212) 827-6200

North Carolina
N.C. Dept. of Econ. and Community Dev.,
Intl. Division
Richard (Dick) Quinlan, Dir.
430 N. Salisbury St.
Raleigh, N.C. 27611
(919) 733-7193

North Dakota
N.D. Econ. Devel. Commission
L.R. Minton, Dir.
Liberty Memorial Bldg.
State Capital Grounds
Bismarck, N.D. 58505
(701) 224-2810

Ohio
Ohio Dept. of Dev.
Intl. Trade Division
Dan Waterman, Dep. Dir.
77 S. High St., 29th Floor
Columbus, Ohio 43215
(614) 466-5017

Oklahoma
Oklahoma Dept. of Commerce
Gary H. Miller, Dir.
6601 Broadway Extension
Oklahoma City, Okla. 73116
(405) 841-5217

Oregon
Oregon Econ. Devel. Dept.,
Intl. Trade Division
Glenn Ford, Dir.
One World Trade Center
121 SW Salmon, Ste. 300
Portland, Ore. 97204
(503) 229-5625

Pennsylvania
Pa. Dept. of Commerce
Office of Intl. Dev.
Paul Haugland, Dir.
433 Forum Bldg.
Harrisburg, Pa. 17120
(717) 787-7190

Puerto Rico
P.R. Department of Commerce
Jorge Santiago, Secy.
P.O. Box 4275
San Juan, P.R. 00905
(809) 725-7254

Rhode Island
R.I. Dept. of Econ. Dev.

Intl. Trade Div.
Christine Smith, Dir.
7 Jackson Walkway
Providence, R.I. 02903
(401) 277-2601 x47

South Carolina
S.C. State Dev. Board
Frank Newman, Assoc. Dir.,
Intl. Business Division
P.O. Box 927
Columbia, S.C. 29202
(803) 737-0403

South Dakota
S.D. Governor's Office of
Econ. Dev.,
Export, Trade & Mktg. Div.
David Brotzman, Dir.
Capitol Lake Plaza
Pierre, S.D. 57501
(605) 773-5735

Tennessee
Tenn. Export Office
Ms. Leigh Wieland, Dir.
320 6th Ave. N.
7th Floor
Nashville, Tenn. 37219-5308
(615) 741-5870

Texas
Texas Dept. of Commerce
Office of Intl. Trade
Deborah Hernandez, Mgr.
P.O. Box 12728, Capitol Sta.
816 Congress
Austin, Tex. 78711
(512) 320-9439
The Department maintains export assistance centers in a number of Texas cities.

Utah
Utah Dept. of Community &
Econ. Devel.

Dan Mabey,
Actg. Dir., Intl. Dev.
Ste. 200
324 S. State St.
Salt Lake City, Utah 84111
(801) 538-8736

Vermont
(State of) Vermont
Agency of Dev. and Community Affairs
Ron Mackinnon, Commissioner
Pavillion Office Bldg.
109 State St.
Montpelier, Vt. 05602
(802) 828-3221

Virginia
Va. Dept. of Econ. Dev.
Stuart Perkins, Dir.,
Export Dev.
1021 East Cary St.
Richmond Va. 23206
(804) 371-8242

Washington
Wash. State Dept. of Trade and
Econ. Dev.
Importing/Exporting Office
Paul Isaki, Dir.
2001 Sixth Ave. 26th Floor
Seattle, Wash. 98121
(206) 464-7143

West Virginia
Governor's Office of Community and Ind. Dev.
Stephen Spence, Dir., Intl. Division
Room 517, Building #6
1900 Washington St. E.
Charleston, W. Va. 25305
(304) 348-2234

Wisconsin
Wis. Dept. of Development
Bureau of Intl. Dev.
Ralph Graner, Dir.
P.O. Box 7970
123 W. Washington Ave.
Madison, Wis. 53707
(608) 266-9487

Wyoming
(State of) Wyoming
Office of the Governor
Richard Lindsey, Dir.
Capitol Building
Cheyenne, Wyo. 82002
(307) 777-6412

Appendix D

Department of Commerce
Listing of Country Desk Officers

The area code for telephoning these desk officers from outside Washington, DC is 202. Letters should be addressed to the individual at his or her room number, U.S. Department of Commerce, Washington, DC 20230.

Country	Desk Officer	Phone (202)	Room
Afghanistan	Stanislaw Bilinski	377-2954	2029B
Albania	Elizabeth Brown/EEBIC *	377-2645	6043
Algeria	Jeffrey Johnson	377-4652	2039
Angola	Stephen Lamar	377-5148	3317
Anguilla	Robert Dormitzer	377-2527	3021
Argentina	Randy Mye	377-1548	3021
Aruba	Thomas Wilde	377-2527	3020
ASEAN	George Paine	377-3875	2308
Antigua/Barbuda	Robert Dormitzer	377-2527	3021
Australia	Simone Altfeld	377-3875	2308
Austria	Philip Combs	377-2920	3029
Bahamas	Mark Siegelman	377-2527	3021
Bahrain	Claude Clement	377-5545	2039
Bangladesh	Stanislaw Bilinski	377-2954	2029B
Barbados	Robert Dormitzer	377-2527	3021
Belgium	Simon Bensimon	377-5373	3046
Belize	Robert Dormitzer	377-2527	3021
Benin	Reginald Biddle	377-4388	3317
Bermuda	Robert Dormitzer	377-2527	3021
Bhutan	Stanislaw Bilinski	377-2954	2029B
Bolivia	Laura Zeiger	377-2521	3029
Botswana	Stephen Lamar	377-5148	3317
Brazil	Roger Turner/ Larry Farris	377-3871	3017

*EEBIC (Eastern Europe Business Information Center)

Country	Desk Officer	Phone (202)	Room
Brunei	Alison Lester	377-3875	2308
Bulgaria	Elizabeth Brown/EEBIC	377-2645	6043
Burkina Faso	Philip Michelini	377-4388	3317
Burma (Myanmar)	George Paine	377-3875	2308
Burundi	Jeffrey Hawkins	377-5148	3317
Cambodia	Hong-Phong B. Pho	377-3875	2308
Cameroon	Jeffrey Hawkins	377-5148	3317
Canada	Kathleen Keim/ Joseph Payne	377-3101	3033
Cape Verde	Philip Michelini	377-4388	3317
Caymans	Robert Dormitzer	377-2527	3020
Central Africa Rep.	Jeffrey Hawkins	377-5148	3317
Chad	Jeffrey Hawkins	377-5148	3317
Chile	Randy Mye	377-1548	3017
Colombia	Laurie MacNamara	377-1659	3025
Comoros	Chandra Watkins	377-4564	3317
Congo	Jeffrey Hawkins	377-5148	3317
Costa Rica	Theodore Johnson	377-2527	3020
Cuba	Mark Siegelman	377-2527	3021
Cyprus	Ann Corro	377-3945	3044
Czechoslovakia	Shelley Galbraith/EEBIC	377-2645	6043
Denmark	Maryanne Lyons	377-3254	3413
D'Jibouti	Chandra Watkins	377-4564	3317
Dominica	Robert Dormitzer	377-2527	3021
Dominican Rep.	Mark Siegelman	377-2527	3021
East Caribbean	Robert Dormitzer	377-2527	3021
Ecuador	Laurie McNamara	377-1659	3025
Egypt	Thomas Sams	377-4441	2039
El Salvador	Theodore Johnson	377-2527	3020
Equatorial Guinea	Jeffrey Hawkins	377-5148	3317
Ethiopia	Chandra Watkins	377-4564	3317
European Community	Charles Ludolph	377-5276	3036
Finland	Maryanne Lyons	377-3254	3413
France	Kelly Jacobs/ Elena Mikalis	377-8008	3042

Country	Desk Officer	Phone (202)	Room
Gabon	Jeffrey Hawkins	377-5148	3317
Gambia	Reginald Biddle	377-4388	3317
Germany	Vellzar Stanoyevitch/	377-2434	3409
	Brenda Fisher/	377-2435	3409
	Joan Kloepfer	377-2841	3409
Ghana	Reginald Biddle	377-4388	3317
Greece	Ann Corro	377-3945	3044
Grenada	Robert Dormitzer	377-2527	3021
Guadeloupe	Robert Dormitzer	377-2527	3021
Guatemala	Theodore Johnson	377-2527	3021
Guinea	Philip Michelini	377-4388	3317
Guinea-Bissau	Philip Michelini	377-4388	3317
Guyana	Robert Dormitzer	377-2527	3021
Haiti	Mark Siegelman	377-2527	3021
Honduras	Theodore Johnson	377-2527	3020
Hong Kong	JeNelle Matheson	377-3583	2317
Hungary	Russell Johnson/EEBIC	377-2645	6043
Iceland	Maryanne Lyons	377-3254	3037
India	John Simmons/	377-2954	2029B
	John Crown/		
	Tim Gilman		
Indonesia	Karen Goddin	377-3875	2308
Iran	Claude Clement	377-5545	2039
Iraq	Thomas Sams	377-4441	2039
Ireland	Boyce Fitzpatrick	377-5401	3039
Israel	Kate FitzGerald-Wilks	377-4652	2039
Italy	Noel Negretti	377-2177	3045
Ivory Coast	Philip Michelini	377-4388	3317
Jamaica	Mark Siegelman	377-2527	3021
Japan	Ed Leslie/	377-2425	2318
	Cantwell Walsh/		
	Eric Kennedy		
Jordan	Corey Wright	377-2515	2039
Kenya	Chandra Watkins	377-4564	3317
Korea	Ian Davis/	377-4957	2327
	Dan Duvall		
Kuwait	Corey Wright	377-2515	2039

Country	Desk Officer	Phone (202)	Room
Laos	Hong-Phong B. Pho	377-3875	2308
Lebanon	Corey Wright	377-2515	2039
Lesotho	Stephen Lamar	377-5148	3317
Liberia	Reginald Biddle	377-4388	3317
Libya	Claude Clement	377-5545	2039
Luxembourg	Simon Bensimon	377-5373	3046
Macao	Rosemary Gallant	377-3583	2317
Madagascar	Chandra Watkins	377-4564	3317
Malawi	Stephen Lamar	377-5148	3317
Malaysia	Alison Lester	377-3875	2308
Maldlves	Stanislaw Bilinski	377-2954	2029B
Mali	Philip Michelini	377-4388	3317
Malta	Robert McLaughlin	377-3748	3049
Martinique	Robert Dormitzer	377-2527	3021
Mauritania	Philip Michelini	377-4564	3317
Mauritius	Chandra Watkins	377-4564	3317
Mexico	Elise Pinkow/ Andrew Lowry/ Ingrid Mohn	377-4464	3028
Mongolia	Rosemary Gallant	377-3583	2317
Montserrat	Robert Dormitzer	377-2527	3314
Morocco	Claude Clement	377-5545	2039
Mozambique	Stephen Lamar	377-5148	3317
Namibia	Emily Solomon	377-5148	3317
Nepal	Stanislaw Bilinski	377-2954	2029B
Netherlands	Boyce Fitzpatrick	377-5401	3039
Netherlands Antilles	Robert Dormitzer	377-2527	3021
New Zealand	Simone Altfeld	377-3975	2308
Nicaragua	Theodore Johnson	377-2527	3021
Niger	Philip Michelini	377-4388	3317
Nigeria	Reginald Biddle	377-4388	3317
Norway	James Devlin	377-4414	3037
Oman	Claude Clement	377-5545	2039
Pacific Islands	Karen Goddin	377-3875	2308
Pakistan	Cheryl McQueen	377-2954	2029B
Panama	Theodore Johnson	377-2527	3020
Paraguay	Randy Mye	377-1548	3021
People's Rep. of China	Christine Lucyk	377-3583	2317

Country	Desk Officer	Phone (202)	Room
Peru	Laura Zeiger	377-2521	3029
Philippines	George Paine	377-3875	2308
Poland	Michael Arsenault/ Mary Moskaluk/EEBIC	377-2645	6043
Portugal	Ann Corro	377-3945	3044
Puerto Rico	Mark Seigelman	377-2527	3021
Qatar	Claude Clement	377-5545	2039
Romania	Lynn Fabrizio/EEBIC	377-2645	6043
Rwanda	Jeffrey Hawkins	377-5148	3317
Sao Tome & Principe	Jeffrey Hawkins	377-5138	3317
Saudi Arabia	Jeffrey Johnson	377-4652	2039
Senegal	Philip Michelini	377-4388	3317
Seychelles	Chandra Watkins	377-4564	3317
Sierra Leone	Reginald Biddle	377-4388	3317
Singapore	Alison Lester	377-3875	2308
Somalia	Chandra Watkins	377-4564	3317
South Africa	Emily Solomon	377-5148	3317
Spain	Mary Beth Double	377-4508	3045
Sri Lanka	Stanislaw Bilinski	377-2954	2029B
St. Barthelemy	Robert Dormitzer	377-2527	3021
St. Kitts-Nevis	Robert Dormitzer	377-2527	3021
St. Lucia	Robert Dormitzer	377-2527	3021
St. Martin	Robert Dormitzer	377-2527	3021
St. Vincent-Grenadines	Robert Dormitzer	377-2527	3021
Sudan	Chandra Watkins	377-4564	3317
Suriname	Robert Dormitzer	377-2527	3021
Swaziland	Stephen Lamar	377-5148	3317
Sweden	James Devlin	377-4414	3037
Switzerland	Philip Combs	377-2920	3039
Syria	Corey Wright	377-2515	2039
Taiwan	Laura Scogna/ Dan Duvall	377-4957	2308
Tanzania	Stephen Lamar	377-5148	3317
Thailand	Jean Kelly	377-3875	2308
Togo	Reginald Biddle	377-4564	3021
Trinidad & Tobago	Robert Dormitzer	377-2527	3021
Tunisia	Corey Wright	377-2515	2039
Turkey	Noel Negretti	377-2177	3045

Country	Desk Officer	Phone (202)	Room
Turks & Caicos Islands	Mark Siegelman	377-2527	3021
Uganda	Chandra Watkins	377-4564	3317
United Arab Emirates	Claude Clement	377-5545	2039
United Kingdom	Robert McLaughlin	377-3748	3045
Uruguay	Mark Siegelman	377-1495	3021
USSR	Susan Lewenz/ Leslie Brown/ Linda Nemac	377-4655	3318
Venezuela	Herbert Lindow	377-4303	3029
Vietnam	Hong-Phong B. Pho	377-3875	2308
Virgin Islands (UK)	Robert Dormitzer	377-2527	3020
Virgin Islands (US)	Mark Siegelman	377-2527	3021
Yemen, Rep. of	Corey Wright	377-2515	2039
Yugoslavia	Jeremy Keller/EEBIC	377-2645	6043
Zaire	Jeffrey Hawkins	377-5148	3317
Zambia	Stephen Lamar	377-5148	3317
Zimbabwe	Stephen Lamar	377-5148	3317

Listing of ITA Industry Desks

INDUSTRY	CONTACT	PHONE (202) 377-
Abrasive Products	Presbury, Graylin	5157
Accounting	Chittum, J Marc	0345
Adhesives/Sealants	Prat, Raimundo	0128
Advertising	Chittum, J Marc	3050
Aerospace Financing Issues	Jackson, Jeff	0222
Aerospace Industry Analysis	Walsh, Hugh	0678
Aerospace Market Development	Bowie, David C	4222
Aerospace-Space Programs	Pajor, Peter	8228
Aerospace Trade Policy	Bath, Sally	4222
Aerospace (Trade Promo)	White, John C	2835
Agribusiness (Major Proj)	Beii, Richard	2460
Agricultural Chemicals	Maxey, Francis P	0128
Agricuitural Machinery	Wiening, Mary	4708
Air Couriers	Elliott, Frederick	3734
Air Conditioning Eqpmt	Hoiley, Tyrena	3509
Air, Gas Compressors	McDonald, Edward	0680
Air, Gas Compressors (Trade Promo)	Zanetakos, George	0552
Air Poliution Control Eqpmt	Jonkers, Loretta	0564
Aircraft & Aircraft Engines	Driscoll, George	8228
Aircraft–Aircraft Engines (Trade Promo)	White, John C	2835
Aircraft Auxiliary Equipment	Driscoll, George	8228
Aircraft Parts (Market Support)	Driscoll, George	8228
Aircraft Parts/Aux Eqpmt (Trade Promo)	White, John C	2835
Airlines	Johnson, C William	5071
Airport Equipment	Driscoll, George	8228
Airport Equipment (Trade Promo)	White, John C	2835
Airports, Ports, Harbors (Major Proj)	Piggot, Deboorne	3352
Air Traffic Control Equip	Driscoll, George	8228

INDUSTRY	CONTACT	PHONE (202) 377-
Alcoholic Beverages	Kenney, Cornelius	2428
Alum Sheet, Plate/Foil	Cammarota, David	0575
Alum Forgings, Electro	Cammarota, David	0575
Aluminum Extrud Alum Rolling	Cammarota, David	0575
Analytical Instruments	Podolske, Lewis	3360
Analytical Instruments (Trade Promo)	Manzolillo, Franc	2991
Animal Feeds	Janis, William V	2250
Apparel	Dulka, William	4058
Apparel (Trade Promo)	Molnar, F	2043
Asbestos/Cement Prod	Pitcher, Charles	0132
Assembly Equipment	Abrahams, Edward	0312
Audio Visual Equipment (Trade Promo)	Beckham, Reginald	5478
Audio Visual Services	Siegmund, John	4781
Auto Parts/Suppliers (Trade Promo)	Reck, Robert	5479
Auto Industry Affairs	Keitz, Stuart	0554
Air Transport Services	Johnson, C William	5071
Avionics Marketing	Driscoll, George	8228
Bakery Products	Janis, William V	2250
Ball Bearings	Reise, Richard	3489
Basic Paper & Board Mfg	Smith, Leonard 5	0375
Bauxite, Alumina, Prim Aium	Cammarota, David	0575
Beer	Kenney, Neii	2428
Belting–Hose	Prat, Raimundo	0128
Beryllium	Duggan, Brian	0575
Beverages	Kenney, Cornelius	2428
Bicycles	Vanderwolf, John	0348
Biotechnology	Arakaki, Emily	3888
Biotechnology (Trade Promo)	Gwaltney, G P	3090
Boat Building (Major Proj)	Piggot, Deboorne	3352
Boats, pleasure	Vanderwolf, John	0348
Books	Lofquist, Wiiliam S	0379
Books (Trade Promo)	Kimmel, Ed	3640
Brooms & Brushes	Harris, John	1178
Breakfast Cereal	Janis, William V	2250
Building Materials & Construction	Pitcher, Charles B	0132
Business Forms	Bratland, Rose Marie	0380
CAD/CAM	McGibbon, Patrick	0314
Cable TV	Plock, Ernest	4781
Canned Food Products	Hodgen, Donald A	3346
Capital Goods (Trade Prom)	Morse, Jerry	5907

INDUSTRY	CONTACT	PHONE (202) 377-
Carbon Black	Prat, Raimundo	0128
Cellular Radio Telephone Equip	Gossack, Linda	4466
Cement	Pitcher, Charles	0132
Cement Plants (Major Proj)	White, Barbara	4160
Ceramics (Advanced)	Shea, Moira	0128
Ceramics Machinery	Shaw, Eugene	3494
Cereals	Janis, William V	2250
Chemicals (Liaison & Policy)	Kelly, Michael	0128
Chemical Plants (Major Proj)	Haraguchi, Wally	4877
Chemicals & Allied Products	Kamenicky, Vincent	0128
Chinaware	Corea, Judy	0311
Civil Aircraft Agreement	Bath, Sally	4222
Civil Aviation Policy	Johnson, C William	5071
Coal Exports	Yancik, Joseph J	1466
Cobalt	Cammarota, David	0575
Cocoa Products	Petrucco-Littleton	5124
Coffee Products	Petrucco-Littleton	5124
Commercial Aircraft (Trade Policy)	Bath, Sally	4222
Commercial Lighting Fixtures	Whitley, Richard A	0682
Commercial/Indus Refrig Eqpmt	Hoiley, Tyrena	3509
Commercial Printing	Lofquist, William S	0379
Commercialization of Space (Market)	Bowie, David C	8228
Commercialization of Space (Services)	Plock, Ernest	4781
Composites, Advanced	Manion, James	5157
Computer and DP Services	Atkins, Robert G/ Inoussa, Mary C	4781 5820
Computer Industry	Miles, Timothy O	2990
Computers (personal)	Woods, R Clay	3013
Computers (Trade Promo)	Fogg, Judy A	4936
Computer Consulting	Atkins, Robert G	4781
Confectionery Products	Kenney, Cornelius	2428
Construction	MacAuley, Patrick	0132
Construction Machinery	Heimowitz, Leonard	0558
Consumer Electronics	Fleming, Howard	5163
Consumer Goods	Boyd, Hayden	0337
Containers & Packaging	Cooperthite, Kim	5159
Cosmetics (Trade Promo)	Kimmel, Ed	3640
Cutlery	Corea, Judy	0311
Dairy Products	Janis, William V	2250
Data Base Services	Inoussa, Mary C	5820

INDUSTRY	CONTACT	PHONE (202) 377-
Data Processing Services	Atkins, Robert G	4781
Desalination/water Reuse	Greer, Damon	0564
Direct Marketing	Ellion, Frederick	3734
Distilled Spirits	Kenney, Neil	2428
Disk Drives	Kader, Victoria	0571
Dolls	Corea, Judy	0311
Drugs	McIntyre, Leo	0128
Durable Consumer Goods	Ellis, Kevin	1176
Earthenware	Corea, Judy	0311
Education Facilities (Major Proj)	White, Barbara	4160
Educational/Training	Francis, Simon	0350
Electric Industrial Apparatus Nec	Whitley, Richard A	0682
Elec/Power Gen/Transmission & Dist Eqt (Trade Promo)	Brandes, Jay	0560
Electrical Power Plants (Major Proj)	Dollison, Robert	2733
Electrical Test & Measuring	Hall, Sarah	2846
Electricity	Sugg, William	1466
ElectroOptical Instruments (Trade Promo)	Manzolillo, Franc	2991
ElectroOptical Instruments	Podolske, Lewis	3360
Electronic Components	Scott, Robert	2795
Electronic components/ Production & Test Equip (Trade Promo)	Burke, Joseph J	5014
Electronic Database Services	Inoussa, Mary C	5820
Elevators, Moving Stairways	Wiening, Mary	4708
Employment Services	Francis, Simon	0350
Energy (Commodities)	Yancik, Joseph J	1466
Energy, Renewable	Rasmussen, John	1466
Engineering/Construction Services (Trade Promo)	Ruan, Robert	0359
Entertainment Industries	Siegmund, John	4781
Entertainment Ind.	Plock, Ernes t	4781
Explosives	Maxey, Francis P	0128
Export Trading Comp anies	Muller, George	5131
Fabricated Metal Construction Materials	Williams, Franklin	0132
Farm Machinery	Wiening, Mary	4708

INDUSTRY	CONTACT	PHONE (202) 377-
Fasteners (Industrial)	Reise, Richard	3489
Fats and Oils	Janis, William V	2250
Fencing (Metal)	Shaw, Robert	0132
Ferroalloys Products	Presbury, Graylin	5158
Ferrous Scrap	Sharkey, Robert	0606
Fertilizers	Maxey, Francis P	0128
Fiber Optics	McCarthy, James	4466
Filters/Purifying Eqmt	Jonkers, Loretta	0564
Finance & Management Industries	Candilis, Wray O	0339
Fisheries (Major Proj)	Bell, Richard	2460
Flexible Mftg Systems	McGibbon, Patrick	0314
Flour	Janis, William V	2250
Flowers	Janis, William V	2250
Fluid Power	McDonald, Edward	0680
Food Products Machinery	Shaw, Eugene	3494
Food Retailing	Kenney, Cornelius	2428
Footwear	Byron, James	4034
Forest Products	Smith, Leonard S.	0375
Forest Products, Domestic Construction	Kristensen, Chris	0384
Forest Products (Trade Policy)	Hicks, Michael	0375
Forgings Semifinished Steel	Bell, Charles	0609
Fossil Fuel Power Generation (Major Proj)	Dollison, Robert	2733
Foundry Eqmt	Comer, Barbara	0316
Foundry Industry	Bell, Charles	0609
Fruits	Hodgen, Donald	3346
Frozen Foods Products	Hodgen, Donald	3346
Fur Goods	Bryon, James	4034
Furniture	Enright, Joe	3459
Gallium	Cammarota, David	0575
Games & Children's Vehicles	Corea, Judy	5479
Gaskets/Gasketing Materials	Reise, Richard	3489
General Aviation Aircraft	Walsh, Hugh	4222
Gen Indus Mach Nec, Exc 35691	Shaw, Eugene	3494
General Industrial Machinery	Harrison, Joseph	5455
Generator Sets/Turbines (Major Proj)	Dollison, Robert	2733
Germanium	Cammarota, David	0575
Glass, Fiat	Williams, Franklin	0132
Glassware	Corea, Judy	0311
Gloves (work)	Byron, James	4034

INDUSTRY	CONTACT	PHONE (202) 377-
Giftware (Trade Promo)	Beckham, Reginald	5478
Grain Mill Products	Janis, William V	2250
Greeting Cards	Bratland, Rose Marie	0380
Grocery Retailing	Kenney, Neil	2428
Ground Water Exploration & Development	Greer, Damon	0564
Hand Saws, Saw Blades	Shaw, Eugene	3494
Hand/Edge Tools Ex Mach TI/Saws	Shaw, Eugene	3494
Handbags	Byron, James	4034
Hard Surfaced Floor Coverings	Shaw, Robert	0132
Hardware (Export Promo)	Johnson, Charles E	3422
Health	Francis, Simon	0350
Heat Treating Equipment	Comer, Barbara	0316
Heating Eqmt Ex Furnaces	Hoiley, Tyrena	3509
Helicopters	Walsh, Hugh	4222
Helicopters (Market Support)	Driscoll, George	8228
High Tech Trade, U.S. Competitiveness	Hatter, Victoria L	3913
Hoists, Overhead Cranes	Wiening, Mary	4708
Home Video	Plock, Ernest	4781
Hose & Belting	Prat, Raimundo	0128
Hotel & Restaurants/Equip (Trade Promo)	Kimmel, Edward K	3640
Hotels And Motels	Sousane, J Richard	4582
Household Appliances	Harris, John M	1178
Household Appliances (Trade Promo)	Johnson, Charles E	3422
Household Furniture	Enright, Joe	3459
Housewares (Export Promo)	Johnson, Charles E	3422
Housing Construction	Cosslett Patrick	0132
Housing & Urban Development (Major Proj)	White, Barbara	4160
Hydro Power, Plants (Major Proj)	Healey, Mary Alice	4333
Industrial Controls	Whitley, Richard A	0682
Industrial Drives/Gears	Reise, Richard	3489
Industrial Gases	Kostalas, Antonios	0128
Industrial Organic Chemicals	McIntyre, Leo	0128
Industrial Process Controls	Podolske, Lewis	3360
Industrial Robots	McGibbon, Patrick	0314
Industrial Sewing Machines	Holley, Tyrena	3509

INDUSTRY	CONTACT	PHONE (202) 377-
Industrial Structure	Davis, Lester A	4924
Industrial Trucks	Wiening, Mary	4608
Information Services	Inoussa, Mary C	5820
Information Industries	Crupe, Friedrich R	4781
Inorganic Chemicals	Kamenicky, Vincent	0128
Inorganic Pigments	Kamenicky, Vincent	0128
Insulation	Shaw Robert	0132
Insurance	McAdam, Bruce	0346
Intellectual Property Rights (Services)	Siegmund, John E	4781
International Commodities	Siesseger, Fred	5124
International Major Projects	Thibeault, Robert	5225
Investment Management	Muir, S Cassin	0349
Irrigation Equipment	Greer, Damon	0564
Irrigation (Major Proj)	Bell, Richard	2460
Jams & Jellies	Hodgen, Donald A	3346
Jewelry	Harris John	1178
Jewelry (Trade Promo)	Beckham, Reginald	5478
Jute Products	Tasnadi, Diani	5124
Kitchen Cabinets	Wise, Barbara	0375
Laboratory Instruments	Podolske, Lewis	3360
Laboratory Instruments (Trade Promo)	Manzolillo, Franc	2991
Lasers (Trade Promo)	Manzolillo, Franc	2991
Lawn & Garden Equip	Vanderwolt, John	0348
Lead Products	Larrabee, David	0575
Leasing: Eqmt & Vehicles	Shuman, John	3050
Leather Tanning	Byron, James E	4034
Leather Products	Byron, James E	4034
Legal Services	Chittum, J Marc	0345
LNG Plants (Major Proj)	Thomas, Janet	4146
Local Area Networks	Spathopoulos, Vivian	0572
Logs, Wood	Hicks, Michael	0375
Luggage	Byron, James	4034
Lumber	Wise, Barbara	0375
Machine Tool Accessories	McGibbon Patrick	0314
Magazines	Bratland, Rose Marie	0380
Magnesium	Cammarota, David	0575
Major Projects	Thibeault, Robert	5225
Management Consulting	Chittum, J Marc	0345

INDUSTRY	CONTACT	PHONE (202) 377-
Manifold Business Forms	Bratland, Rose Marie	0380
Man-made Fiber	Dulka, William	4058
Margarine	Janis, William V	2250
Marine Recreational Equipment (Trade Promo)	Beckham, Reginald	5478
Marine Insurance	Johnson, C William	5012
Maritime Shipping	Johnson, C William	5012
Materials, Advanced	Cammarota, David	0575
Mattresses & Bedding	Enright, Joe	3459
Meat products	Hodgen, Donald A	3346
Mech Power Transmission Eqmt	Reise, Richard	3489
Medical Facilities (Major Proj)	White, Barbara	4160
Medical Instruments	Fuchs, Michael	0550
Medical Instruments & Equip (Trade Promo)	Keen, George B	2010
Mercury, Fluorspar	Manion, James J	5157
Metal Building Products	Williams, Franklin	0132
Metal Cookware	Corea, Judy	0311
Metal cutting Machine Tools	McGibbon, Patrick	0314
Metal Forming Machine Tools	McGibbon, Patrick	0314
Metal Powders	Duggan, Brian	0575
Metals, Secondary	Brueckmann, Al	0606
Metalworking	Mearman, John	0315
Metalworking Eqmt Nec	McGibbon, Patrick	0314
Millwork	Wise, Barbara	0375
Mineral Based Construction Materials (Clay, Concrete, Gypsum, Asphalt, Stone)	Pitcher, Charles B	0132
Mining Machinery	McDonald, Edward	0680
Mining Machinery (Trade Promo)	Zanetakos, George	0552
Mobile Homes	Cosslett Patrick	0132
Molybdenum	Cammarota, David	0575
Monorails (Trade Promo)	Wiening, Mary	4708
Motion Pictures	Siegmund, John	4781
Motor Vehicles	Warner, Albert T	0669
Motorcycles	Vanderwolf, John	0348
Motors, Electric	Whitley, Richard A	0682
Music	Siegmund, John	4781
Musical Instruments	Corea, Judy	0311
Mutual Funds	Muir, S Cassin	0349
Natural Gas	Gillett, Tom	1466
Natural, Synthetic Rubber	McIntyre, Leo	0128

INDUSTRY	CONTACT	PHONE (202) 377-
Newspapers	Bratland, Rose Marie	0380
Nickel Products	Presbury, Graylin	0575
Non-alcoholic Beverages	Kenney, Cornelius	2428
Noncurrent Carrying Wiring Devices	Whitley, Richard A	0682
Nondurable Goods	Simon, Les	0341
Nonferrous Foundries	Duggan, Brian	0610
Nonferrous Metals	Manion, James J	0575
Nonmetallic Minerals Nec	Manion, James J	0575
Nonresidential Constr	MacAuley, Patrick	0132
Nuclear Power Plants/Machinery	Greer, Damon	0681
Nuclear Power Plants (Major Proj)	Dollison, Robert	2733
Numerical Controls For Mach Tools	McGibbon, Patrick	0314
Nuts, Edible	Janis, William V	2250
Nuts, Bolts, Washers	Reise, Richard	3489
Ocean Shipping	Johnson, C William	5012
Office Furniture	Enright, Joe	3459
Oil & Gas Development & Refining (Major Proj)	Thomas, Janet	4146
Oil & Gas (Fuels Only)	Gillett, Tom	1466
Oil Field Machinery	McDonald, Edward	0680
Oil Field Machinery (Trade Promo)	Miles, Max	0679
Oil Shale (Major Proj)	Thomas, Janet	4146
Operations & Maintenance	Chittum, J Marc	0345
Organic Chemicals	McIntyre, Leo	0128
Outdoor Lighting Fixtures	Whitley, Richard A	0682
Outdoor Power Equip (Trade Promo)	Johnson, Charles E	3422
Packaging & Containers	Copperthite, Kim	0575
Packaging Machinery	Shaw, Eugene	2204
Paints/Coatings	Prat, Raimundo	0128
Paper	Smith, Leonard S	0375
Paper & Board Packaging	Smith, Leonard S	0375
Paper Industries Machinery	Abrahams, Edward	0312
Pasta	Janis, William V	2250
Paving Materials (Asphalt & Concrete)	Pitcher, Charles	0132
Pectin	Janis, William V	2250
Pens/Pencils, etc.	Corea, Judy	0311
Periodicals	Bratland, Rose Marie	0380
Pet Food	Janis, William V	2250
Pet Products (Trade Promo)	Kimmel, Ed	3640
Petrochemicals	McIntyre, Leo	0128

INDUSTRY	CONTACT	PHONE (202) 377-
Petrochem, Cyclic Crudes	McIntyre, Leo	0128
Petrochemicals Plants (Major Proj)	Haraguchi, Wally	4877
Petroleum, Crude & Refined Products	Gillett, Tom	1466
Pharmaceuticals	McIntyre, Leo	0128
Pipelines (Major Proj)	Thomas, Janet	4146
Photographic Eqmt & Supplies	Watson, Joyce	0574
Plastic Construction Products (Most)	Williams, Franklin	0132
Plastic Materials	Shea, Moira	0128
Plastic Products	Prat, Raimundo	0128
Plastic Products Machinery	Shaw, Eugene	3494
Plumbing Fixtures & Fittings	Shaw, Robert	0132
Plywood/Panel Products	Wise, Barbara	0375
Point-of-Use Water Treatment	Greer, Damon	0564
Pollution Control Equipment	Jonkers, Loretta	0564
Porcelain Electrical Supplies	Whitley, Richard A	0682
Potato Chips	Janis, William	2250
Pottery	Corea, Judy	0311
Poultry Products	Hodgen, Donald A	3346
Power Hand Tools	Abrahams, Edward	0312
Precious Metal Jewelry	Harris, John M	1178
Prefabricated Buildings (Wood)	Cosslett, Patrick	0132
Prefabricated Buildings (Metal)	Williams, Franklin	0132
Prepared Meats	Hodgen, Donald A	3346
Pretzels	Janis, William V	2250
Primary Commodities	Siesseger, Fred	5124
Printing & Publishing	Lofquit, William S	0379
Printing Trade Services	Bratland, Rose Marie	0380
Printing Trades Mach/Eqmt	Kemper, Alexis	5956
Process Control Instruments	Podolske, Lon	3360
Process Control Instruments (Trade Promo)	Marcolillo, Franc	2991
Pulp And Paper Mills (Major Proj)	White, Barbara	4160
Pulpmills	Stanley, Gary	0375
Pumps, Pumping Eqmt	McDonald, Edward	0680
Pumps, Valves, Compressors (Trade Promo)	Zanetakos, George	0552
Radio & TV Broadcasting	Siegmund, John	4781
Radio & TV Communications Eqmt	Gossack, Linda	2872
Recorded Music	Siegmund, John	4781
Recreational Eqmt (Trade Promo)	Beckham, Reginald	5478
Refractory Products	Duggan, Brian	0575
Renewable Energy Eqpmt	Garden, Les	0556

INDUSTRY	CONTACT	PHONE (202) 377-
Residential Lighting Fixtures	Whitley, Richard A	0682
Retail Trade	Margulies, Marvin J	5086
Rice Milling	Janis, William V	2250
Roads, Railroads, Mass Trans (Major Proj)	Smith, Jay L	4642
Robots	McGibbon, Patrick	0314
Roofing, Asphalt	Pitcher, Charles	0132
Roller Bearings	Reise, Richard	3489
Rolling Mill Machinery	Comer, Barbara	0316
Rubber	Prat, Raimundo	0128
Rubber Products	Prat, Raimundo	0128
Saddlery & Harness Products	Byron, James	4034
Safety & Security Equip (Trade Promo)	Umstead, Dwight	8410
Space Services	Plock, Ernest	5620
Satellites & Space Vehicles (Marketing)	Bowie, David C	8228
Satellites, Communications	Cooper, Patricia	4466
Science & Electronic (Trade Promo)	Moose, Jake	4125
Scientific Instruments (Trade Promo)	Manzolillo, Franc	2991
Scientific measurement Control Eqmt	Podolske, Lewis	3360
Screw Machine Products	Reise, Richard	3489
Screws, Washers	Reise, Richard	3489
Security & Commodity Brokers	Fenwick, Thomas R	0347
Security Management Svcs.	Chittum, J Marc	0345
Semiconductors (except Japan)	Scott, Robert	2795
Semiconductors, Japan	Nealon, Marguerite	8411
Semiconductor Prod Eqmt & Materials	Hall, Sarah	2846
Service Industries (Uruguay Round)	Dowling, Jay	1134
Services Data Base Development	Atkins, Robert G	4781
Services, Telecom	Shefrin, Ivan	4466
Shingles (Wood)	Wise, Barbara	0375
Silverware	Harris, John	1178
Sisal Products	Manger, Jon	5124
Small Arms, Ammunition	Vanderwolf, John	0348
Snackfood	Janis, William V	2250
Soaps, Detergents, Cleaners	McIntyre, Leo	0128
Software	Hyikata, Heidi	0572
Software (Trade Promo)	Fogg, Judy	4936

INDUSTRY	CONTACT	PHONE (202) 377-
Solar Cells/Photovoltaic Devices	Garden, Les	0556
Solar Eqmt Ocean/Biomass/ Geothermal	Garden, Les	0556
Soy Products	Janis, William V	2250
Space Commercialization (Equipment)	Bowie, David C	8228
Space Commercialization (Services)	Plock, Ernest	5820
Space Policy Development	Pajor, Peter	8228
Special Industry Machinery	Shaw, Eugene	3494
Speed Changers	Reise, Richard	3489
Sporting & Athletic Goods	Vanderwolf, John	0348
Sporting Goods (Trade Promo)	Beckham, Reginald	5478
Steel Industry Products	Bell, Charles	0608
Steel Industry	Brueckmann, Al	0606
Steel Markets	Bell, Charles	0608
Storage Batteries	Larrabee, David	5124
Sugar Products	Tasnadi, Diana	5124
Supercomputers	Streeter, Jonathan	0572
Superconductors	Chiarado, Roger	0402
Switchgear & Switchbo ard Apparatus	Whitley, Richard A	0682
Tea	Janis, William V	2250
Technology Affairs	Shykind, Edwin B	4694
Telecommunications	Stechschulte. Roger	4466
Telecommunications (Major Proj)	Paddock, Richard	4466
Telecommunications (Trade Promo)	Rettig, Theresa E	2952
Telecommunications (Network Equip)	Henry, John	4466
Telecommunications (military communications equip)	Mocenigo, Anthony	4466
Teletext Services	Inoussa, Mary C	5820
Textile Machinery	McDonald, Edward	0680
Textiles	Dulka, William A	4058
Textiles (Trade Promo)	Molnar, Ferenc	2043
Timber Products (Tropical)	Tasnadi, Diana	5124
Tin Products	Manger, Jon	5124
Tires	Prat, Raimundo	0128
Tools/Dies/Jigs/Fixtures	McGibbon, Patrick	0314
Tourism (Major Proj)	White, Barbara	4160
Tourism Services	Sousane, J Richard	4582
Toys	Corea, Judy	0311
Toys & Games (Trade Promo)	Becham, Reginald	5478

INDUSTRY	CONTACT	PHONE (202) 377-
Trade Related Employment	Davis, Lester A	4924
Transborder Data Flows	Inoussa, Mary C	5820
Transformers	Whitley, Richard A	0682
Transportation Industries	Alexander, Albert	4581
Tropical Commodities	Tasnadi, Diana	5124
Trucking Services	Sousane, J Richard	4581
Tungsten Products	Manger, Jon	5124
Turbines, Steam	Greer, Damon	0681
Uranium	Sugg, William	1466
Value Added	Atkins, Robert G	4781
Telecommunications Serv		
Valves, Pipe Fittings (Except Brass)	Reise, Richard	3489
Vegetables	Hodgen, Donald A	3346
Video Services	Plock, Ernest	5820
Videotex Services	Inoussa, Mary C/	5820
	Siegmund, John	4781
Wallets, Billfords, Flatgoods	Byron, James	4034
Warm Air Heating Eqmt	Holley, Tyrena	3509
Wastepaper	Stanley, Gary	0375
Watches	Harris, John	1178
Water and Sewerage	Healey, Mary Alice	4643
Treatment Plants (Major Proj)		
Water Resource Eqmt	Greer, Damon	0564
Water Supply & Distribution	Greer, Damon	0564
Welding/Cutting Apparatus	Comer, Barbara	0316
Wholesale Trade	Margulis, Marvin	3050
Wine	Kenney, Cornelius	2428
Windmill Components	Garden, Les	0556
Wire & Wire Products	Breuckmann, Al	0606
Wire Cloth, Industrial	Reise, Richard	3489
Wire Cloth	Williams, Franklin	0132
Wood Containers	Hicks, Michael	0375
Wood Preserving	Hicks, Michael	0375
Wood Products	Smith, Leonard S	0375
Wood Working Machinery	McDonald, Edward	0680
Writing Instruments	Corea, Judy	0311
Yeast	Janis, William V	2250

Appendix E

INTERNATIONAL TRADE ADMINISTRATION
U.S. and Foreign Commercial Service Overseas Posts

ALGERIA
American Embassy
Algiers
SCO Andrew Tangalos
Tel: 01 1-213-2-60-18-63
Fax: 011-213-2-60-18-63
U.S. Dept of State (Algiers)
Washington, D.C. 20521-6030

ARGENTINA
American Embassy
Buenos Aires
SCO Ralph Fermoselle
Tel: 011-54-1-773-1063
Fax: 011-54-1-775-6040
Unit 4326
APO AA 34034

AUSTRALIA
American Consulate
General
Sydney
SCO Michael Hand
Tel: 011-61-2-261-9200
Fax: 011-61-2-261-8148
Unit 11024
APO AP 96554-0002

American Consulate
Brisbane
FCSN Keith Sloggett
Tel: 011-61-7-831-1345
Fax: 011-61-7-832-6247

Unit 11018
APO AP 96553-0002

American Consulate General
Melbourne
FCSO Daniel Young
Tel: 011-61-3-526-5900
Fax: 011-61-3-510-4660
Unit 11011
APO AP 96551-0002

American Consulate General
Perth
FCSN Marion Shingler
Tel: 011-61-9-221-1177
Fax: 011-61-9-325-3569
Unit 11021
APO AP 96553-0002

AUSTRIA
American Embassy
Vienna
SCO Benjamin Brown
Tel: 011-43-222-31-55-11
Fax: 011-43-222-34-12-61
APO AE 09108

BARBADOS
American Embassy
Bridgetown
SCO Richard Ades
(contact via Miami D.O.)
Tel: 1-809-436-4950
Fax: 1-809-426-2275

Box B FPO AA 34054

BELGIUM
American Embassy
Brussels
SCO Jerry Mitchell
Tel: 011-32-2-513-3830
Fax: 011-32-2-512-6653
PSC 82 Box 002
APO AE 09724-1015

US Mission to the
European Communities
Brussels
SCO James Blow
Tel: 011-32-2-513-3830
Fax: 011-32-2-513-1228
PSC 82 Box 002
APO AE 09724

BRAZIL
American Embassy
Brasilia
SCO Kevin Brennan
Tel: 011-55-61-223-0120
Fax: 011-55-61-225-3981
Unit 3502
APO AA 34030

American Consular Agency
Belem
FCSN Raymundo Teixiera
Tel: 011-55-91-223-0800
Fax: 011-55-91-223-0413

Unit 3500
APO AA 34030

American Consular Agency
Belo Horizonte
FCSN Jose Mauricio de
Vasconcelos
Tel: 011-55-31-335-3250
Fax: 011-55-31-335-3054
Unit 3505
APO AA 34030

American Consulate General
Rio De Janeiro
FCSO Walter Hage
Tel: 011-55-21-292-7117
Fax: 011-55-21-240-9738
APO AA 34030

American Consulate General
Sao Paulo
FCSO Arthur Alexander
Tel: 011-55-853-2011
Fax: 011-55-853-2744
APO AA 34030

CAMEROON
American Consulate
Douala
FCSN Jean Sumo
Tel: 011-237-425-331
Fax: 011-237-427-790
U.S. Dept. of State (Douala)
Washington, D.C. 20251-
2530

CANADA
American Embassy
Ottawa
SCO Robert Marro
Tel: 1-613-238-5335
Fax: 1-613-233-8511
P.O. Box 5000
Ogdensburg, N.Y. 13669

American Consulate General
Calgary
FCSO Randall Labounty
Tel: 1-403-265-2116
Fax: 1-403-264-6630
Suite 1050
615 Macleod Trail, SE.
Calgary, Alberta, Canada
T2G 4T8

American Consulate General
Halifax
FCSN Richard Vinson
Tel: 1-902-429-2482
Fax: 1-902-423-6861
Suite 900, Cogswell Tower
Halifax, Nova Scotia, Canada
B3J 3KI

American Consulate General
Montreal
FCSO Geoffrey Walser
Tel: 1-514-398-9695
Fax: 1-514-398-07 11
P.O. Box 847
Champlain, N. Y. 12919-
0847

American Consulate General
Toronto
FCSO Dan Wilson
Tel: 1-416-595-5413
Fax: 1-416-595-5419
P.O. Box 135
Lewiston, N.Y. 14092

American Consulate General
Vancouver
FCSO Stephen Wasylko
Tel: 1-604-685-3382
Fax: 1-604-685-5285
P.O. Box 5002
Point Roberts, Wash. 98281-
5002

CHILE
American Embassy
Santiago
SCO Ricardo Villalobos
Tel: 011-56-2-671-0133
Fax: 011-56-2-697-2051
Unit 411 1
APO AA 34033

CHINA
American Embassy
Beijing
SCO Tim Stratford
Tel: 011-86-1-532-3831
Fax: 01 1-86-1-532-3297
PSC 461 Box 50
FPO AP 96521-0002

American Consulate General
Guangzhou
FCSO Dennis Barnes
Tel: 011-86-20-677-842
Fax: 011-86-20-666-409
PSC 461 Box 100
FPO AP 96521-0002

American Consulate General
Shanghai
FCSO Nora Sun
Tel: 011-86-2 1-433-2492
Fax: 011-86-21-433-1576
PSC 461 Box 200
FPO AP 96521-0002

American Consulate General
Shenyang
FCSO (vacant)
Tel: 011-86-24-220-057
Fax: 011-86-24-290-074
PSC 461 Box 45
FPO AP 96521-0002

COLOMBIA
American Embassy
Bogota
SCO Arthur Trezise

Tel: 011-57-1-232-6550
Fax: 011-57-1-285-7945
Unit 5 120
APO AA 34038

COSTA RICA
American Embassy
San Jose
SCO Judith Henderson
Tel: 011-506-20-3939
Fax: 011-506-31-4783
Unit 2508
APO AA 34020

COTE D'IVOIRE
American Embassy
Abidjan
SCO Catherine Houghton
Tel: 011-225-21-4616
Fax: 011-225-22-3259
U.S. Dept of State (Abidjan)
Washington, D.C. 20521-2010

CZECHOSLOVAKIA
American Embassy
Prague
SCO Robert Shipley
Tel: 011-42-2-536-641 or
532-470
Fax: 011-42-2-532-457 or
537-534
Unit 25402
APO AE 09213-5630

American Consulate General
Bratislava (Commercial Section
to open spring 1992)
FCSN

DENMARK
American Embassy
Copenhagen
SCO Stephen Helgesen
Tel: 011-45-31-42-31-44

Fax: 011-45 -31-42-01-75
APO AE 09176

DOMINICAN REPUBLIC
American Embassy
Santo Domingo
SCO Richard Ades (contact
via Miami D.O.)
Tel: 1-809-541-2171
Fax: 1-809-688-4838
Unit 5515
APO AA 34041

ECUADOR
American Embassy
Quito
SCO Jere Dabbs
Tel: 011-593-2-561-404
Fax: 011-593-2-504-550
Unit 5334
APO AA 34039-3420

American Consulate General
Guayaquil
FCSN Francisco Von
Buchwald
Tel: 011-593-4-323-570
Fax: 011-593-4-324-558
APO AA 34039

EGYPT
American Embassy
Cairo
SCO Norman Glick
Tel: 011-20-2-354-1583
Fax: 01 1-20-2-355-8368
Unit 64900 Box 11
FPO AE 09839-4900

American Consulate General
Alexandria
FCSN Hanna Abdelnour
Tel: 011-20-3-482-1911
Fax: 011-20-3-482-9 199
Unit 64904
APO AE 09839-4904

FINLAND
American Embassy
Helsinki
SCO Maria Andrews
Tel: 011-358-0-171-821
Fax: 01 1-358-0-635-332
APO AE 09723

FRANCE
American Embassy
Paris
SCO Melvin Scarls
Tel: 011-3 3-1-4296-1202
Fax: 011-33-1-4266-4827
APO AE 09777

US Mission to the OECD
Paris
SCO Robyn Layton
Tel: 01 1-33-1-4524-7437
Fax: 011-33-1-4524-7410
APO AE 09777

American Consulate General
Bordeaux
FCSN (vacant)
Tel: 011 -33-56-52-65-95
Fax: 011-33-56-5 1-60-42
APO AE 09777

American Consulate General
Lyon
FCSN Alain Beullard
Tel: 011 -33-78-24-68-49
Fax: N/A
APO AE 09777

American Consulate General
Marseille
FCSN Igor Lepine
Tel: 011-33-91-54-92-00
Fax: N/A
APO AE 09777

US Commercial Office
Nice
FCSN Reine Joguet
Tel: 011-33-93-88-89-55
Fax: N/A
APO AE 09777

American Consulate General
Strasbourg
FCSN Jacqueline Munzlinger
Tel: 011-33-88-35-3 1-04
Fax: N/A
APO AE 09777

GERMANY
American Embassy
Bonn
SCO John Bligh
Tel: 011 -49-228-339-2895
Fax: 011-49-228-334-649
Unit 21701 Box 370
APO AE 09080

US Embassy Office
Berlin
FCSO James Joy
Tel: 011-49-30-251-0244
Fax: 011-49-30-251-0246
APO AE 09235

US Commercial Office
Duesseldorf
FCSN Barbara Ernst
Tel: 011-49-211-596-798
Fax: 011-49-211-594-897
c/o Amembassy Bonn
Unit 21701 Box 370
APO AE 09080

American Consulate General
Frankfurt
FCSO Donald Businger
Tel: 011-49-69-7535-2453
Fax: 011-49-69-748-204
APO AE 09213

Amercian Consulate General
Hamburg
FCSO Hans Amrhein
Tel: 011-49-40-41 17-1304
Fax: 011-49-40-410-6598
APO AE 09215-0002

American Consulate General
Munich
FCSO Edward Ruse
Tel: 011-49-89-2888-748
Fax: 011-49-89-285-261
APO AE 09108

American Consulate General
Stuttgart
FCSO Camille Sailer
Tel: 011-49-711-246-5 13
Fax: 011-49-711-236-4350
APO AE 09154

GREECE
American Embassy
Athens
SCO John Priamou
Tel: 011-30-1-723-9705
Fax: 011-30-1-721-8660
PSC 108 Box 30
APO AE 09842

GUATEMALA
American Embassy
Guatemala
SCO Robert Fraser
Tel: 011-502-2-348-479
Fax: 011-502-2-317-373
Unit 3306
APO AA 34024

HONDURAS
American Embassy
Tegucigalpa
SCO Eric Weaver
Tel: 011-504-32-3120
Fax: 011-504-32-0027

Unit 2923
APO AA 34022

HONG KONG
American Consulate General
Hong Kong
SCO Thomas L. Boam
Tel: 011-852-521-1467
Fax: 011-852-845-9800
PSC 464 Box 30
FPO AP 96522-0002

HUNGARY
American Embassy
Budapest
SCO Gary Gallagher
Tel: 011-36-1-122-8600
Fax: 011-36-1-142-2529
APO AE 09213-5270

INDIA
American Embassy
New Delhi
SCO James Moorhouse
Tel: 011-91-11-600-651
Fax: 011-91-11-687-2391
U.S. Dept. of State (New Delhi)
Washington, D.C. 20521-9000

American Consulate General
Bombay
FCSO Dorothy Lutter
Tel: 011-91-22-828-0571
Fax: 011-91-22-822-0350
U.S. Dept. of State (Bombay)
Washington, D.C. 20521-6240

American Consulate General
Calcutta
FCSN Nargiz Chatterjee
Tel: 011-91-33-44-3611
Fax: 011-91-33-28-3823

U.S. Dept. of State (Calcutta)
Washington, D.C. 20521-6250

American Consulate General
Madras
FCSO Rajendra Dheer
Tel: 011-91-44-475-947
Fax: 011-91-44-825-0240
U.S. Dept. of State (Madras)
Washington, D.C. 20521-6260

INDONESIA
American Embassy
Jakarta
SCO Theodore Villinski
Tel: 011-62-21-360-360
Fax: 011-62-21-385-1632
Box 1
APO AP 96520

American Consulate General
Medan
FCSN Zulhava Luthfi
Tel: 011-62-61-322-200
Fax: N/A
APO AP 96520

American Consulate General
Surabaya
FCSN Midji Kwee
Tel: 011-62-31-67100
Fax: N/A
APO AP 96520

IRELAND
American Embassy
Dublin
SCO Gene Harris
Tel: 011-353-1-288-4569
Fax: 011-353-1-608-469
U.S. Dept. of State (Dublin)
Washington, D.C. 20521-5290

ISRAEL
American Embassy
Tel Aviv
SCO Mike Mercurio
Tel: 011-972-3-654-338
Fax: 011-972-3-658-033
PSC 98 Box 100
APO AE 09830

ITALY
American Embassy
Rome
SCO Emilio Iodice
Tel: 011-39-6-4674-2202
Fax: 011-39-6-4674-2113
PSC 59
APO AE 09624

American Consulate General
Florence
FCSN (vacant)
Tel: 011-39-55-211-676
Fax: 011-39-55-283-780
PSC 59 Box F
APO AE 09624

American Consulate General
Genoa
FCSN Erminia Lezzi
Tel: 011-39-10-282-741
Fax: 011-39-10-290-027
PSC 59 Box G
APO AE 09624

American Consulate General
Milan
FCSO Peter Alois
Tel: 01 1-39-2-498-2241
Fax: 011-39-2-481-4161
PSC 59 Box M
APO AE 09624

American Consulate General
Naples
FCSN Christiano Sartorio
Tel: 011-39-81-761-1592

Fax: 011-39-81-761-1869
PSC 59 Box N
FPO AE 09624

JAMAICA
American Embassy
Kingston
SCO Richard Ades (contact
via Miami D.O.)
Tel: 1-809-929-4850
Fax: 1-809-929-3637
U.S. Dept. of State (Kingston)
Washington, D.C. 20521-3210

JAPAN
American Embassy
Tokyo
SCO George Mu
Tel: 01 1-81-3-3224-5000
Fax: 011-81-3-3589-4235
Unit 45004 Box 204
APO AP 96337-0001

American Consulate
Fukuoka
FCSN Yoshihiro Yamamoto
Tel: 011-81-92-751-9331
Fax: 011-81-92-27 1-3922
Box 10
FPO AP 98766

Representative Office
Nagoya
FCSO Todd Thurwatcher
Tel: 011-81-52-203-4011

Fax: 011-81-52-201-4612
c/o U.S. Embassy Tokyo
Unit 45004, Box 280
APO AP 96337-0001

American Consulate General
Osaka-Kobe
FCSO Patrick Santillo
Tel: 011-81-6-315-5953

Fax: 011-81-6-361-5978
Unit 45004 Box 239
APO AP 96337

American Consulate General
Sapporo
FCSN Kenji Itaya
Tel: 011-81-11-641-1115
Fax: 011-81-11-641-0911
APO AP 96503

KENYA
American Embassy
Nairobi
SCO Richard Benson
Tel: 011-254-2-334-141
Fax: 011-254-2-340-838
Unit 64100 Box 51
APO AE 09831-4100

KOREA
American Embassy
Seoul
SCO Peter Frederick
Tel: 011-82-2-732-2601
Fax: 011-82-2-739-1628
Unit 15550
APO AP 96205-0001

KUWAIT
American Embassy
Kuwait
SCO Robert Connan
Tel: 011-965-242-4151
or 244-8073
Fax: 011-965-244-7692
Unit 69000 Box 10
APO AE 09880-9000

MALAYSIA
American Embassy
Kuala Lumpur
SCO Paul Walters
Tel: 011-60-3-248-9011
Fax: 011-60-3-242-1866
APO AP 96535-5000

MEXICO
American Embassy
Mexico City
SCO Roger Wallace
Tel: 011-52-5-211-0042
Fax: 011-52-5-207-8938
PO Box 3087
Laredo, Tex. 78044-3087

American Consulate General
Guadalajara
FCSO Americo Tadeu
Tel: 011-52-36-25-0321
Fax: 011-52-36-26-3576
PO Box 3088
Laredo, Tex. 78044-3088

American Consulate General
Monterrey
FCSO Dawn Cooper-Bahar
Tel: 011-52-83-452-120
Fax: 011-52-83-42-5172
PO Box 3098
Laredo, Tex. 78044-3098

MOROCCO
American Consulate General
Casablanca
SCO Sam Starrett
Tel: 011-212-26-45-50
Fax: 011-212-22-02-59
PSC 74 Box 024
APO AE 09718

American Embassy
Rabat
FCSN Asma Daimoussi
Tel: 011-212-7-622-65
Fax: 011-212-7-656-61
APO AE 09718

NETHERLANDS
American Embassy
The Hague
SCO Michael Hegedus
Tel: 011-31-70-310-9417

Fax: 011-31-70-363-2985
PSC 71 Box 1000
APO AE 09715

American Consulate General
Amsterdam
FCSO Bert Engelhardt
Tel: 011-31-20-664-8111
Fax: 011-31-20-675-2856
APO AE 09159

NEW ZEALAND
American Consulate General
Auckland
SCO Bobette Orr
Tel: 011-64-9-303-2038
Fax: 011-64-9-366-0870
PSC 467 Box 99
FPO AP 96531-1099

American Embassy
Wellington
FCSN Janet Coulthart
Tel: 011 -64-4-722-068
Fax: 011-64-4-781-701
PSC 467 Box I
FPO AP 96531-1001

NIGERIA
American Embassy
Lagos
SCO Frederic Gaynor
Tel: 011-234-1-616-477
Fax: 011-234-1-619-856
U.S. Dept. of State (Lagos)
Washington, D.C. 20521-
8300

American Consulate General
Kaduna
FCSN Mathias Mgbeze
Tel: 011-234-62-201-070
Fax: N/A
U S. Dept. of State (Kaduna)
Washington, D.C. 20521-
2260

425

NORWAY
American Embassy
Oslo
SCO Scott Bozek
Tel: 011-47-2-44-85-50
Fax: 011-47-2-55-88-03
PSC 69 Box 0200
APO AE 09707

PAKISTAN
American Consulate General
Karachi
SCO George Kachmar
Tel: 011-92-21-518-180
Fax: 011-92-21-568-1381
Unit 62400 Box No 137
APO AE 09814-2400

American Consulate General
Lahore
FCSN Shalla Malik
Tel: 011-92-42-870-221
Fax: N/A
Unit 62216
APO AE 09812-2216

PANAMA
American Embassy
Panama
SCO Carlos Poza
Tel: 011-507-27-1777
Fax: 011-507-27-1713
Unit 0945
APO AA 34002

PERU
American Embassy
Lima
SCO Richard Lenahan
Tel: 011-51-14-33-0555
Fax: 011-51-14-33-4687
Unit 3780
APO AA 34031

PHILIPPINES
American Embassy

Manila
SCO Jonathan Bensky
Tel: 011-63-2-818-6674
Fax: 011-63-2-818-2684
APO AP 96440

POLAND
American Embassy
Warsaw
SCO Joan Edwards
Tel: 011-48-22-21-45-15
Fax: 011-48-22-21-63-27
APO AE 09213-5010

PORTUGAL
American Embassy
Lisbon
SCO Miguel Pardo de Zela
Tel: 011-351-1-726-6600
Fax: 011-351-1-726-8914
PSC 83 Box FCS
APO AE 09726

American Consulate
Oporto
FCSN Adolto Coutinho
Tel: 011-351-2-63094
Fax: 011-351-2-600-2737
APO AE 09726

ROMANIA
American Embassy
Bucharest
SCO Kay Kuhlman
Tel: 011-40-0-10-40-40
Fax: 011-40-0-11-84-47
APO AE 09213-5260

SAUDI ARABIA
American Embassy
Riyadh
SCO Dirck Teller
Tel: 011-966-1-488-3800
Fax: 011-966-1-48 8-3237
Unit 61307
APO AE 09038-1307

American Consulate General
Dhahran
FCSO Danny Devito
Tel: 011-966-3-891-3200
Fax: 011-966-3-89 1-8332
Unit 66803
APO AE 09858-6803

American Consulate General
Jeddah
FCSO Mike Frisby
Tel: 011-966-2-667-0040
Fax: 011-966-2-665-8106
Unit 6211 2
APO AE 09811-2112

SINGAPORE
American Embassy
Singapore

SCO George Ruffner
Tel: 011-65-338-9722
Fax: 011-65-338-5010
FPO AP 96534-0006

SOUTH AFRICA
American Consulate General
Johannesburg
SCO L. Richard Jackson
Tel: 011-27-11-331-3937
Fax: 011-27-11-331-6178
U.S. Dept. of State
(Johannesburg)
Washington, D.C. 20521-2500

American Consulate General
Cape Town
FCSN Sylvia Frowde
Tel: 011-27-21-21-4280
Fax: 011-27-21-254-151
U.S. Dept. of State (Cape Town)
Washington, DC 20521-2480

SPAIN
American Embassy
Madrid
SCO Robert Kohn
Tel: 011-34-1-577-4000
Fax: 011-34-1-575-8655
PSC 61 Box 0021
APO AE 09642

American Consulate General
Barcelona
FCSO Ralph Griffin
Tel: 011-34-3-319-9550
Fax: 011-34-3-319-5621
PSC 64
APO AE 09646

SWEDEN
American Embassy
Stockholm
SCO Harrison Sherwood
Tel: 011-46-8-783-5346
Fax: 011-46-8-660-9181
U.S. Dept. of State
(Stockholm)
Washington, D.C. 20521-
5750

SWITZERLAND
American Embassy
Bern
SCO Arthur Reichenbach
Tel: 011-41-31-43-73-41
Fax: 011-41-31-43-73-36
U.S. Dept. of State (Bern)
Washington, D.C. 20521-
5110

US Mission to GATT
Geneva
SCO Andrew Grossman
Tel: 011-41-22-749-5281
Fax: 011-41-22-749-48 85
U.S. Dept. of State (Geneva)
Washington, DC 20521-
5120

American Consulate General
Zurich
FCSN Paul Frei
Tel: 011-41-1-552-070
Fax: 011-41-1-383-9814
U.S. Dept. of State (Zurich)
Washington, D.C. 20521-
5130

THAILAND
American Embassy
Bangkok
SCO Herbert Cochran
Tel: 011-66-2-253-4920
Fax: 011-66-2-255-2915
APO AP 96546

TRINIDAD & TOBAGO
American Embassy
Port of Spain
SCO Richard Ades (contact
via Miami D.O.)
Tel: 1-809-622-6371
Fax: 1-809-622-9583
U.S. Dept. of State (Port of
Spain)
Washington, D.C. 20521-
3410

TURKEY
American Embassy
Ankara
SCO Dave Katz
Tel: 011-90-4-126-5470
Fax: 011-90-4-167-1366
PSC 93 Box 5000
APO AE 09823

American Consulate General
Istanbul
FCSO Russell Smith
Tel: 011-90-1-151-3602
Fax: 011-90-1-152-2417
PSC 97 Box 0002
APO AE 09827-0002

American Consulate General
Izmir
FCSN Berrin Erturk
Tel: 011-90-51-149-426
Fax: 011-90-51-130-493
APO AE 09821

UNITED ARAB
EMIRATES
American Consulate General
Dubai
SCO Paul Scogna
Tel: 011-971-4-378-584
Fax: 011-971-4-375-121
U.S. Department of State
(Dubai)
Washington, D.C. 20521-
6020

American Embassy
Abu Dhabi
FCSO Sam Dhir
Tel: 011-971-2-345-545
Fax: 011-971-2-33 1-374
U.S. Dept. of State (Abu
Dhabi)
Washington, D.C. 20521-
6010

UNITED KINGDOM
American Embassy
London
SCO Kenneth Moorefield
Tel: 011-44-71-499-9000
Fax: 011-44-71-491-4022
PSC 801 Box 33
FPO AE 09498-4033

U.S.S.R.
American Embassy
Moscow
SCO James May
Tel: 011-7-095-255-4848
Fax: 011-7-095-230-2101
APO AE 09721

American Consulate General
St. Petersburg
FCSO Douglas Wake
Tel: 011-7-812-274-8235
Fax: N/A
APO AE 09723

VENEZUELA
American Embassy
Caracas
SCO Bob Taft
Tel: 011-58-2-285-2222
Fax: 011-58-2-285-0336
Unit 4958
APO AA 34037

YUGOSLAVIA
American Embassy
Belgrade
SCO Peter Noble
Tel: 011-38-11-645-655
Fax: 011-38-11-645-096
APO AE 09213-5070

American Consulate General
Zagreb
FCSN Djuro Njers
Tel: 011-38-41-444-800
Fax: 011-38-41-440-235
APO AE 09213-5080

TAIWAN
Unofficial, commercial, and other relations with Taiwan are conducted through an unofficial instrumentality, the American Institute in Taiwan (AIT), which has offices in Taipei and Kaoshiung. Contact AIT at American Trade Center, Room 3207, International Trade Building, Taipei World Trade Center, 333 Keelung Road, Section I, Taipei 10548 Taiwan, tel. 886-2-7201550; telex 23890 U.S. Trade, fax 886-2-7577162

Appendix F

INCOTERMS 1990
Understanding International Terms of Sale

In Chapter 14, under PRICING THE PRODUCT, we discussed Terms of Sale—words which define when and under what conditions buyers and sellers are responsible for certain costs and risks.

Exporters have always been troubled by the fact that certain abbreviations used in international trade could mean different things to buyers and sellers. In 1919, a draft version of American Foreign Trade Definitions was set up and used until 1941 when it was extensively revised by The Chamber of Commerce of the U.S., The National Council of American Importers, and the National Foreign Trade Council.

In 1936, a similar set of definitions called INCOTERMS, (INTERNATIONAL COMMERCIAL TERMS) was adopted by the International Chamber of Commerce headquartered in Paris. Several extensive revisions were made in 1953, 1967, 1976, 1980 and most recently in 1990.

For decades, the American Foreign Trade Definitions of 1941 were the terms most frequently used by American exporters and most overseas buyers agreed with them. In recent years however, new modes and techniques of transportation and documentation have demanded more precise definitions of trade terms. At the present time, most foreign trade specialists agree that INCOTERMS 1990 are the most authoritative and definitive, and recommend that U.S. traders use them in place of the 1941 American Definitions.

Please note there are 13 INCOTERMS in use in the 1990 listing. The text presented here describes only 12. The description of the 13th term, "Delivered Duty Paid," (DDP) is almost the same as the 12th term, "Delivered Duty Unpaid," (DDU). The obvious difference between the two is that under DDP the seller will provide import clearance, i.e., the import license, and pay taxes, fees, and import duties.

For more detailed descriptions and illustrations of INCOTERMS 1990, an excellent book is available. It is called *A Guide To INCOTERMS 1990,* and is published by the ICC Publishing Corporation, 156 Fifth Avenue, Suite 820, New York, NY 10010. Order it under their number 461/90, and specify language wanted since it is available in English, French, German, Spanish and Italian.

INCOTERMS 1990

The Seller and the Buyer are the two Parties to the International Transaction. They will make use of a contract of sale to determine the quantity, and quality of the goods being offered, along with the price that is being paid. The contract of sale will also address the manner in which payment is to be made to the Seller.

The Trade Terms as defined in the **Incoterms 1990** will deal with questions that relate to the delivery of the goods, and should be clearly incorporated as part of the contract of sale. The selected Trade Term would address the following:

1. Who clears the goods for export or import?
2. Who pays the cost of loading/unloading of the goods?
3. Who pays for the cost of transportation?
4. At what point does the "risks" of loss or damage transfer from the Seller to the Buyer?
5. Who should arrange for cargo insurance to protect against "risks?"

The Trade Terms will deal specifically with the costs of carriage and the risks to goods. They do *not* deal with property rights, the transfer of property rights, nor do they deal with the transfer of title of the goods. The transfer of ownership of the goods and other property rights would be separately addressed in the contract of sale.

FOUR BASIC LETTER GROUPS OF TRADE TERMS

SELLER'S COST/RISK	COMMENTS; SELLER'S COST/RISK
LETTER GROUP "E"	
EXW	The Seller minimizes his risk by only making the goods available at his premises.
LETTER GROUP "F"	
FCA	Main Carriage *not* paid by the Seller. Seller clears for export.
FAS	Main Carriage *not* paid by the seller. Seller *does not* clear goods for export.
FOB	Main Carriage *not* paid by the Seller. Seller clears for export.

LETTER GROUP "C"

CFR

> Main Carriage paid by the Seller *without* assuming the risk of the carriage. Seller clears goods for export.

CIF

> Main Carriage paid by the Seller *without* assuming the risk of the carriage. Also, Seller arranges and pays cost of insurance to named point *without* assuming the risk to the point.

CPT

Same as CFR.

CIP

Same as CIF.

LETTER GROUP "D"

DAF

> Seller's cost/risk is maximized. Seller makes goods available upon arrival at named destination.

DES

Same as above—ocean freight only.

DEQ

Same as above—ocean freight only. Seller also assumes customs clearance.

DDU

> Similiar to DAF only Seller responsible for delivery to final named destination (beyond the frontier or place of import clearance). Duty unpaid.

DDP

> Same as DDU only Seller also assumes the cost and responsibility of customs clearance.

INCOTERMS 1990

Clear the Goods for Export: On export shipments from the United States, the Seller will usually (by the selected **Incoterm 1990** Trade Term or by separate agreement) assume the responsibilities of the Exporter; field number two on this form. Also identified in field number thirty four which requires a federal identification (tax) number.

The Exporter of Record ships (exports) the goods in compliance with the Export Administration Regulations. Compliance includes applying for "validated" licenses (when necessary), and providing the data for the completion of the Shipper's Export Declaration (S.E.D.).* Frequently, the foreign Buyer is not in a position to accept and fulfill the responsibilities of an Exporter from the U.S., and therefore, the Trade Term *Ex Works* should be avoided.

The Exporter of Record will also be held responsible for the payment of the Harbor Maintenance Fee (HMF) which is assessed on ocean exports from U.S. ports. U.S. Customs (who collects this fee) considers the name of the Exporter as it appears on the S.E.D. as the Party responsible for the payment of the fee.

*See sample of the Shipper's Export Declaration included in this appendix

FORM 503 WHSE. NO. 0852
APPERSON BUSINESS FORMS, INC.
(800) 438-0162 (1-1-88)

U.S. DEPARTMENT OF COMMERCE • BUREAU OF THE CENSUS - INTERNATIONAL TRADE ADMINISTRATION

FORM **7525-V** (1-1-88)

SHIPPER'S EXPORT DECLARATION

OMB No. 0607-0018

1a. EXPORTER (Name and address including ZIP code)		
ZIP CODE	2. DATE OF EXPORTATION	3. BILL OF LADING/AIR WAYBILL NO.

b. EXPORTER'S EIN (IRS) NO.	c. PARTIES TO TRANSACTION ☐ Related ☐ Non-related

4a. ULTIMATE CONSIGNEE

b. INTERMEDIATE CONSIGNEE

5. FORWARDING AGENT

A. N. DERINGER
727 Honeyspot Road
Stratford, Connecticut 06497

6. POINT (STATE) OF ORIGIN OR FTZ NO.	7. COUNTRY OF ULTIMATE DESTINATION

8. LOADING PIER (Vessel only)	9. MODE OF TRANSPORT (Specify)	
10. EXPORTING CARRIER	11. PORT OF EXPORT	
12. PORT OF UNLOADING (Vessel and air only)	13. CONTAINERIZED (Vessel only) ☐ Yes ☐ No	

14. SCHEDULE B DESCRIPTION OF COMMODITIES,
15. MARKS, NOS, AND KINDS OF PACKAGES   (Use columns 17—19)

D/F (16)	SCHEDULE B NUMBER (17)	CHECK DIGIT	QUANTITY - SCHEDULE B UNIT(S) (18)	SHIPPING WEIGHT (Kilos) (19)	VALUE (U.S. dollars, omit cents) (Selling price or cost if not sold) (20)

21. VALIDATED LICENSE NO./GENERAL LICENSE SYMBOL	22. ECCN (When required)

23. Duly authorized officer or employee	The exporter authorizes the forwarder named above to act as forwarding agent for export control and customs purposes.

24. I certify that all statements made and all information contained herein are true and correct and that I have read and understand the information for preparation of this document, set forth in the "Correct Way to Fill Out the Shipper's Export Declaration." I understand that civil and criminal penalties, including forfeiture and sale, may be imposed for making false or fraudulent statements herein, failing to provide the requested information or for violation of U.S. laws on exportation (13 U.S.C. Sec. 305; 22 U.S.C. Sec. 401; 18 U.S.C. Sec. 1001; 50 U.S.C. App. 2410).

Signature

Title

Date

Confidential - For use solely for official purposes authorized by the Secretary of Commerce (13 U.S.C. 301 (g)).

Export shipments are subject to inspection by U.S. Customs Service and/or Office of Export Enforcement.

25. AUTHENTICATION (When required)

The "Correct Way to Fill Out the Shipper's Export Declaration" is available from the Bureau of the Census, Washington, D.C. 20233.

Sample Shipper's Export Declaration

TRANSFER OF RISK

All **Incoterms** 1990 are based on the principle that the risk of loss or damage to the goods transfers from the Seller to the Buyer when the Seller has fulfillled his *delivery* obligation. This would be item "A 4." of the ten main headings of Seller/Buyer obligations (illustrated on page 6 of this program). "A 5." of FOB, CFR and CIF further specifies that the risk transferred when the goods "passed the ship's rail at the port of *shipment.*"

The Trade Terms connect the transfer of the risk with the delivery of the goods and not with other circumstances, such as passing of ownership or the time of the conclusion of the contract. Neither Incoterms nor the CISG (Convention on the International Sale of Goods) deal with the transfer of title to the goods or other property rights with respect to the goods.

The passing of risk for loss of or damage to the goods concerns the risk of fortuitous events (accidents), and does not include lossor damage caused by the Seller or Buyer; ie, through inadequate packing or marking of the goods. Therefore, even if damage occurs subsequent to the transfer of the risk, the Seller may still be responsible if the damage could be attributed to the fact that the goods were not delivered in conformity with the contract (Items "A 1." and "A 9." make reference to these circumstances. Also, item "A 5." of the Terms starts with the phrase "subject to the provision of B 5.". This means that there are exceptions to the main rule which may result in a premature passing of risk because the Buyer failed to fulfill his obligations.

Obligations of Sellers and Buyers

The Incoterms 1990 define the obligations of the Sellers and Buyers. The definitions are structured to list these obligations in ten main headings and express the position of each of the Parties in respect to the headings. All ten headings are not necessarily applicable to all of the Incoterms.

Seller's Responsibilities	Buyer's Responsibilities
A 1. Provision of goods in conformity with the contract	B 1. Payment of the Price
A 2. Licenses, authorizations and formalities	B 2. Licenses, authorizations and formalities
A 3. Contract of carriage and Insurance	B 3. Contract of Carriage
A 4. Delivery	B 4. Taking delivery
A 5. Transfer of risks	B 5. Transfer of risks
A 6. Division of costs	B 6. Division of costs
A 7. Notice to the Buyer	B 7. Notice to the Seller
A 8. Proof of Delivery, transport document or equivalent electronic message	B 8. Proof of Delivery, transport document or equivalent electronic message
A 9. Checking, packaging marking	B 9. Inspection of goods
A 10. Other Obligations	B 10. Other Obligations

Herman J. Maggiori

SPANISH LINE

SHIPPER/EXPORTER	DOCUMENT NUMBER
Name of the Seller	FORWARDERS REFERENCE
	EXPORTERS REFERENCE

CONSIGNEE	FORWARDER
(Note: To be a freely negotiable document, the bill of lading would be consigned as follows:) **To Order**	
	COUNTRY OF ORIGIN

NOTIFY PARTY	ALSO NOTIFY AND/OR ADDITIONAL ROUTING INSTRUCTIONS

INTERMODAL ORIGIN & CARRIER	TRANSSHIPMENT PORT VESSEL-VOY

VESSEL/VOY	PORT OF LOADING/TERMINAL
FOREIGN PORT OF UNLOADING	INTERMODAL DESTINATION & CARRIER

EXCESS VALUE DECLARATION $ .... (SEE CLAUSE 23 PRINTED ON BACK PAGE)

MARKS AND NUMBERS	NO OF PKGS TYPE OF PKG	DESCRIPTION OF GOODS	GROSS WEIGHT	MEASUREM(
		Title Documents: Ocean Bills of Lading (Contracts of Cariage) that can be issued in original form, can be prepared as a "title" documents, and therefore, denote ownership to the goods shipped. The consignee would be shown as "To Order". Transfer of ownership would be accomplished when the original(s) are properly endorsed by the Shipper/Exporter (Seller). The Party who then holds the properly endorsed original(s) bill of lading, has title to the goods shipped The Incoterms 1990 do not deal with the transfer of property, or title documents.		

(CONDITIONS CONTINUED FROM REVERSE SIDE)
In accepting this Bill of Lading the Shipper, the Consignee and the Owner of the goods agree to be bound by all of its stipulations and conditions, whether written, printed or stamped on the front or back hereof, any local customs of privileges to the contrary notwithstanding. In agreement, the Shipper specifically approves the clauses on the front and on the back of this Bill of Lading

THE SHIPPER

IN WITNESS WHEREOF, the master or Agent of said vessel has affirmed to THREE (3) ORIGINAL Bills of Lading, all of the tenor and date, one of which being accomplished the others to stand void.

Note: The phrase to the left states that "Three (3) original Bills of Lading were issued.

by _____

AGENTS

DATED AT

B/L No. ___ Mo. ___ Day ___ Yr ___

7.

Sample Ocean Bill of Lading

ACL Datafreight Receipt

SHIPPER/EXPORTER (COMPLETE NAME AND ADDRESS)	BOOKING NO.	DATA FREIGHT RECEIPT NO.
	EXPORT REFERENCES	
CONSIGNEE (COMPLETE NAME AND ADDRESS)	FORWARDING AGENT. F.M.C. NO.	
	POINT AND COUNTRY OF ORIGIN OF GOODS	
NOTIFY (COMPLETE NAME AND ADDRESS)	ALSO NOTIFY — ROUTING & INSTRUCTIONS	

PRE-CARRIAGE BY*	PLACE OF RECEIPT*	
VESSEL	FLAG PORT OF LOADING	LOADING PIER/TERMINAL
PORT OF DISCHARGE	PLACE OF DELIVERY*	TYPE OF MOVE

MRKS & NOS/ CONTAINER NOS	NO. OF PKGS	PARTICULARS FURNISHED BY SHIPPER / DESCRIPTION OF PACKAGES AND GOODS	GROSS WEIGHT	MEASUREM...

Example of: Proof of Delivery, Transport Document, or Equivalent Electronic Message

The **Express** Ocean Bill of Lading contains the same basic conditions of carriage as the standard ocean bill of lading. The Express Bill allows for straight consignments only, and therefore, can not be issued as a "title" document. Note that on the face of this document there is no mention of the issuance of an "original" bill of lading (one of the conditions that must be present before a ocean bill can be issued as a title document). Carriers transmit the information contained on the face of this document electronically to the port or place of carrier delivery.

*APPLICABLE ONLY WHEN THIS RECEIPT COVERS THROUGH TRANSPORTATION

SHIPPERS DECLARED VALUE $_____ SUBJECT TO EXTRA FREIGHT			FREIGHT PAYABLE AT
	PRE	COL	
			RECEIVED by ACL for shipment between above mentioned ports, pre- and carriage where stated above to be arranged by ACL subject to all the terms conditions of the ACL bill of lading, which are incorporated herein by refere...
...D VALOREM FREIGHT AS PER CLAUSE 6 OF B/L			PLACE AND DATE OF ISSUE
NUMBER	DATE		FOR ACL

8.

Sample Express Ocean Bill of Lading (electronic proof of delivery document)

Cargo Insurance: The Incoterms will indicate at what point the risks of loss of or damage to the goods transfers from the Seller to the Buyer. While either of the Parties will be at risk, they are not necessarily obligated by the specific Incoterm to protect against the risks. However, it is well advised that the Party at risk take the steps necessary to eliminate any potential loss of or damage to the goods. This is most commonly accomplished through the proper placement of *all risk* cargo insurance. Also, proper cargo insurance will protect the goods against the limits of carrier's liability that are standard to most transport documents.

Either the Seller or the Buyer should arrange for the proper cargo insurance. The following cost charts have addressed the payment for cargo insurance in all instances. When not an actual obligation in accordance with the selected term, the cost chart will indicate who is at risk, and therefore, who should place and pay for the insurance.

CARGO INSURANCE

When the Seller has the obligation to obtain and pay for cargo insurance under the Incoterms CIF and CIP (Item A 3 (b) under the ten basic obligations within the terms for Sellers and Buyers), insurance is based on "minimum cover" as set forth in the Institute Cargo Clauses drafted by the Institute of London Underwriters. Minimum cover could also follow any other similiar set of clauses.

In practice, however, "all risk" insurance (Institute Clause A) is preferred to less extended cover (Institute Clauses B or C), since the minimum cover is only appropriate when the risk of loss of or damage to the goods in transit is more or less confined to casualties affecting both the means of conveyance and the cargo, such as those resulting from collisions, strandings and fire. In such cases, even the minimum cover would protect the Buyer against the risk of having to pay compensation to a shipowner for his expenses in salvaging the ship and cargo (General Average conditions).

But minimum cover is not suitable to manufactured goods, because of the risk of theft, pilferage or improper handling or custody of the goods. Therefore, extended coverage is usually taken out as a protection against such risks (Institute Clause A is then advisable). The Buyer should stipulate in the contract of sale that deals with CIF or CIP Terms the requirement for extended coverage beyond the "minimum." The Buyer may also request in the contract cover that is *not* included in Clause A; ie, insurance against war, riots, civil commotions, strikes or other labor disturbances. This again would be addressed by the Buyer separately, and at an additional expense. The total cost of insurance on a sigle consignment that calls for "all risks—cargo and war " would be calculated using separate premium rates for the two factors.

INCOTERMS 1990

Clear the Goods for Import: includes applying for import licenses, payinc import duties, taxes and fees. A Seller's responsibility has been substantially increased when he assumes these obligations.

"Delivered Ex Ship (Named Port)" brings the goods and the Seller's responsibility to the named port, *on board* the vessel, available for clearance by the Buyer. The next "D"term, "Delivered Ex Quay (Duty Paid) (Named Port of Destination)" brings the goods (and the Seller's risk) to the named quay (wharf) available to the Buyer, and *cleared for import.* A major increase in the risks and responsibilities on the part of the seller.

Although all Customs Authorities throughout the trading world are different, many of their functions are the same. They will determine the admissability of merchandise into their country, determine the dutiable status of the merchandise being entered into their country, and collect any duty or taxes on the goods being entered. For instance, the U.S. Customs Service looks towards the "Importer of Record" as indicated on Customs form 7501 (illustrated) as the Party responsible for the payment of *duty, taxes, and fees* on goods entered into the Customs Territory of the United states. Field eleven on the form identifies the Importer of Record, and field twelve refers to the Importer's federal tax number (EIN). U.S. Customs will collect the duty, taxes, and *Harbor Maintenance Fee* (along with User's Fees) from the Importer of Record.

From the above, it is noted that there is a significant difference between delivering goods to a specified point and providing the goods *cleared for import* at a named point.

Herman J. Maggiori

| DEPARTMENT OF THE TREASURY UNITED STATES CUSTOMS SERVICE | ENTRY SUMMARY |

Sample Customs Form 7501

Who Pays for the Cost? Seller or Buyer?

Trade Term: EX WORKS (Named Place)

Comments: The Seller fulfills his obligation to deliver when he has made the goods available at his premises (ie, works, factory, warehouse, etc.) to the Buyer. He is not responsible for loading the goods or clearing the goods for export. The Buyer bears all costs and risks in taking the goods from the Seller's premises to the desired destination. This term should not be used when the Buyer (directly or indirectly) can not fulfill the formalities of export.

Mode of Transportation: All modes of Transport

Cost Headings of Transportation/Handling	Seller	Buyer
1. Loading at Seller's Warehouse		X
2. U.S. Inland Freight/Cartage		X
3. Arrange Contract of Carriage/Dispatch		X
4. Export Documentation (U.S.)		X
5. U.S. Customs Clearance (Shipper's Export Declaration, etc.)		X
6. Export Charges (Including Payment of Harbor Maintenance Fee)		X
7. Loading at Carrier's Terminal		X
8. Arrange Transportation Equipment		X
9. Cargo Insurance for Transportation		X
10. International Freight		X
11. Unloading at Foreign Terminal		X
12. Trade Documentation in country of Transit/Importation		X
13. Customs Clearance in Foreign Country		X
14. Import charges		X
15. Foreign Carriage to Buyer's Warehouse		X
16. Unloading at Buyer's Warehouse		X

Other specific costs should be addressed separately as part of the contract of sale between the Seller and Buyer.

Who Pays for the Cost? Seller or Buyer?

Trade Term: FREE CARRIER (Named Terminal)

Comments: The Seller fulfills his obligation to deliver when he has hande(over the goods, cleared for export, into the charge of the carrier named by the Buyer at the named place or point. When, according to commercial practice, the Seller's assistance is required in making the contract with the carrier, the Seller may act at the Buyer's risk and expense.

Mode of Transportation: All modes of Transport

Cost Headings of Transportation/Handling	Seller	Buyer
1. Loading at Seller's Warehouse	X	
2. U.S. Inland Freight/Cartage	X	
3. Arrange Contract of Carriage/Dispatch	X	
4. Export Documentation (U.S.)	X	
5. U.S. Customs Clearance (Shipper's Export Declaration, etc.)	X	
6. Export Charges (Including Payment of Harbor Maintenance Fee)	X	
7. Loading at Carrier's Terminal		X
8. Arrange Transportation Equipment		X
9. Cargo Insurance for Transportation		X
10. International Freight		X
11. Unloading at Foreign Terminal		X
12. Trade Documentation in country of Transit/Importation		X
13. Customs Clearance in Foreign Country		X
14. Import charges		X
15. Foreign Carriage to Buyer's Warehouse		X
16. Unloading at Buyer's Warehouse		X

Other specific costs should be addressed separately as part of the contract of sale between the Seller and Buyer.

Who Pays for the Cost? Seller or Buyer?

Trade Term: FREE ALONGSIDE SHIP "FAS" (Named Port of Shipment)

Comments: The Seller fulfills his obligation to deliver when the goods have been placed alongside the vessel on the quay or in lighters at the named port of shipment. The Buyer has to bear all costs and risks of loss or damage to the goods from that moment. The Buyer must clear the goods for export.

Mode of Transportation: Ocean Shipments Only

Cost Headings of Transportation/Handling	Seller	Buyer
1. Loading at Seller's Warehouse	X	
2. U.S. Inland Freight/Cartage	X	
3. Arrange Contract of Carriage/Dispatch		X
4. Export Documentation (U.S.)		X
5. U.S. Customs Clearance (Shipper's Export Declaration, etc.)		X
6. Export Charges (Including Payment of Harbor Maintenance Fee)		X
7. Loading at Carrier's Terminal		X
8. Arrange Transportation Equipment		X
9. Cargo Insurance for Transportation		X
10. International Freight		X
11. Unloading at Foreign Terminal		X
12. Trade Documentation in country of Transit/Importation		X
13. Customs Clearance in Foreign Country		X
14. Import charges		X
15. Foreign Carriage to Buyer's Warehouse		X
16. Unloading at Buyer's Warehouse		X

Other specific costs should be addressed separately as part of the contract of sale between the Seller and Buyer.

Who Pays for the Cost? Seller or Buyer?

Trade Term: FREE ON BOARD "FOB" (Named Port of Shipment)

Comments: The Seller fulfills his obligation to deliver when the goods have passed over the ship's rail at the named port of shipment. Therefore, the Buyer has to bear all costs and risks of loss or damage to the goods from that point. The Seller clears the goods for export. When the ship's rail serves no practical purpose, such as in the case of roll-on/roll-off or container traffic, the FCA term would be more appropiate.

Mode of Transportation: Ocean Shipments Only

Cost Headings of Transportation/Handling	Seller	Buyer
1. Loading at Seller's Warehouse	X	
2. U.S. Inland Freight/Cartage	X	
3. Arrange Contract of Carriage/Dispatch	X	
4. Export Documentation (U.S.)	X	
5. U.S. Customs Clearance (Shipper's Export Declaration, etc.)	X	
6. Export Charges (Including Payment of Harbor Maintenance Fee)	X	
7. Loading at Carrier's Terminal	X	
8. Arrange Transportation Equipment		X
9. Cargo Insurance for Transportation		X
10. International Freight		X
11. Unloading at Foreign Terminal		X
12. Trade Documentation in country of Transit/Importation		X
13. Customs Clearance in Foreign Country		X
14. Import charges		X
15. Foreign Carriage to Buyer's Warehouse		X
16. Unloading at Buyer's Warehouse		X

Other specific costs should be addressed separately as part of the contract of sale between the Seller and Buyer.

Who Pays for the Cost? Seller or Buyer?

Trade Term: COST AND FREIGHT "CFR" (Named Port of Destination)

Comments: The Seller must pay for the costs and freight necessary to bring the goods to the named port of destination. But the risk of loss of or damage to the goods, as well as any additional costs due to events after the time the goods have been delivered on board the vessel, is transferred to the Buyer when the goods pass the ship's rail in the port of shipment.

The Seller clears the goods for export.

Mode of Transportation: Ocean Shipments Only

Cost Headings of Transportation/Handling	Seller	Buyer
1. Loading at Seller's Warehouse	X	
2. U.S. Inland Freight/Cartage	X	
3. Arrange Contract of Carriage/Dispatch	X	
4. Export Documentation (U.S.)	X	
5. U.S. Customs Clearance (Shipper's Export Declaration, etc.)	X	
6. Export Charges (Including Payment of Harbor Maintenance Fee)	X	
7. Loading at Carrier's Terminal	X	
8. Arrange Transportation Equipment	X	
9. Cargo Insurance for Transportation		X
10. International Freight	X	
11. Unloading at Foreign Terminal	X	
12. Trade Documentation in country of Transit/Importation		X
13. Customs Clearance in Foreign Country		X
14. Import charges		X
15. Foreign Carriage to Buyer's Warehouse		X
16. Unloading at Buyer's Warehouse		X

Other specific costs should be addressed separately as part of the contract of sale between the Seller and Buyer.

Who Pays for the Cost? Seller or Buyer?

Trade Term: COST, INSURANCE AND FREIGHT "CIF" (Named Port of Destination

Comments: The Seller has the same obligations as under CFR but with the addition that he has to procure marine insurance against the Buyer's risk of loss of or damage to the goods during the carriage. The Seller contracts for insurance and pays the insurance premium. The Seller clears the goods for export. Note that the Buyer assumes the risk for the goods when the goods pass the ship's rail at the port of *loading*.

Mode of Transportation: Ocean Shipments Only

Cost Headings of Transportation/Handling	Seller	Buyer
1. Loading at Seller's Warehouse	X	
2. U.S. Inland Freight/Cartage	X	
3. Arrange Contract of Carriage/Dispatch	X	
4. Export Documentation (U.S.)	X	
5. U.S. Customs Clearance (Shipper's Export Declaration, etc.)	X	
6. Export Charges (Including Payment of Harbor Maintenance Fee)	X	
7. Loading at Carrier's Terminal	X	
8. Arrange Transportation Equipment	X	
9. Cargo Insurance for Transportation	X	
10. International Freight	X	
11. Unloading at Foreign Terminal	X	
12. Trade Documentation in country of Transit/Importation		X
13. Customs Clearance in Foreign Country		X
14. Import charges		X
15. Foreign Carriage to Buyer's Warehouse		X
16. Unloading at Buyer's Warehouse		X

Other specific costs should be addressed separately as part of the contract of sale between the Seller and Buyer.

Who Pays for the Cost? Seller or Buyer?

Trade Term: CARRIAGE PAID TO "CPT" (Named Place of Destination)

Comments: The Seller pays the freight for the carriage of the goods to the named destination. The risk of loss of or damage to the goods, as well as any additional costs due to events occurring after the time the goods have been delivered to the carrier, is transferred from the Seller to the Buyer when the goods have been delivered into the custody of the carrier. A "carrier" is anyone who performs or undertakes to procure the performace of carriage. The Seller clears the goods for export.

Mode of Transportation: All modes of Transport

Cost Headings of Transportation/Handling	Seller	Buyer
1. Loading at Seller's Warehouse	X	
2. U.S. Inland Freight/Cartage	X	
3. Arrange Contract of Carriage/Dispatch	X	
4. Export Documentation (U.S.)	X	
5. U.S. Customs Clearance (Shipper's Export Declaration, etc.)	X	
6. Export Charges (Including Payment of Harbor Maintenance Fee)	X	
7. Loading at Carrier's Terminal	X	
8. Arrange Transportation Equipment	X	
9. Cargo Insurance for Transportation	X	
10. International Freight	X	
11. Unloading at Foreign Terminal		X
12. Trade Documentation in country of Transit/Importation		X
13. Customs Clearance in Foreign Country		X
14. Import charges		X
15. Foreign Carriage to Buyer's Warehouse		X
16. Unloading at Buyer's Warehouse		X

Other specific costs should be addressed separately as part of the contract of sale between the Seller and Buyer.

Who Pays for the Cost? Seller or Buyer?

Trade Term: CARRIAGE AND INSURANCE PAID TO "CIP" (Named Place of Destination)

Comments: The Seller has the same obligations as under CPT but with the addition that the Seller has to procure cargo insurance against the Buyer's risk of loss or of damage to the goods during the carriage. The Seller contracts for the insurance and pays the premium. The Seller clears the goods for export.

Mode of Transportation: All modes of Transport

Cost Headings of Transportation/Handling	Seller	Buyer
1. Loading at Seller's Warehouse	X	
2. U.S. Inland Freight/Cartage	X	
3. Arrange Contract of Carriage/Dispatch	X	
4. Export Documentation (U.S.)	X	
5. U.S. Customs Clearance (Shipper's Export Declaration, etc.)	X	
6. Export Charges (Including Payment of Harbor Maintenance Fee)	X	
7. Loading at Carrier's Terminal	X	
8. Arrange Transportation Equipment	X	
9. Cargo Insurance for Transportation	X	
10. International Freight	X	
11. Unloading at Foreign Terminal		X
12. Trade Documentation in country of Transit/Importation		X
13. Customs Clearance in Foreign Country		X
14. Import charges		X
15. Foreign Carriage to Buyer's Warehouse		X
16. Unloading at Buyer's Warehouse		X

Other specific costs should be addressed separately as part of the contract of sale between the Seller and Buyer.

Who Pays for the Cost? Seller or Buyer?

Trade Term: DELIVERED AT FRONTIER "DAF" (Named Place)

Comments: The Seller fulfills his obligation to deliver when the goods have been made available, cleared for export, at the named point and place at the frontier, but before the customs border of the adjoining country. The term "frontier" may be used for any frontier including that of the country of export, and therefore, it is important to define the exact point. The term is primarily intended when goods are to be carried by rail or road.

Mode of Transportation: All modes of Transport

Cost Headings of Transoortation/Handling	Seller	Buver
1. Loading at Seller's Warehouse	X	
2. U.S. Inland Freight/Cartage	X	
3. Arrange Contract of Carriage/Dispatch	X	
4. Export Documentation (U.S.)	X	
5. U.S. Customs Clearance (Shipper's Export Declaration, etc.)	X	
6. Export Charges (Including Payment of Harbor Maintenance Fee)	X	
7. Loading at Carrier's Terminal	X	
8. Arrange Transportation Equipment	X	
9. Cargo Insurance for Transportation	X	
10. International Freight	X	
11. Unloading at Foreign Terminal	X	
12. Trade Documentation in country of Transit/Importation		X
13. Customs Clearance in Foreign Country		X
14. Import charges		X
15. Foreign Carriage to Buyer's Warehouse		X
16. Unloading at Buyer's Warehouse		X

Other specific costs should be addressed separately as part of the contract of sale between the Seller and Buyer.

Who Pays for the Cost? Seller or Buyer?

Trade Term: DELIVERED EX SHIP "DES" (Named Port of Destination)

Comments: The Seller fulfills his obligation to deliver when the goods have been made available to the Buyer on board the ship uncleared for import at the named port of destination. The Seller has to bear all of the costs and risks involved in bringing the goods to the named port of destination.

Mode of Transportation: Ocean Shipments Only

Cost Headings of Transportation/Handling	Seller	Buyer
1. Loading at Seller's Warehouse	X	
2. U.S. Inland Freight/Cartage	X	
3. Arrange Contract of Carriage/Dispatch	X	
4. Export Documentation (U.S.)	X	
5. U.S. Customs Clearance (Shipper's Export Declaration, etc.)	X	
6. Export Charges (Including Payment of Harbor Maintenance Fee)	X	
7. Loading at Carrier's Terminal	X	
8. Arrange Transportation Equipment	X	
9. Cargo Insurance for Transportation	X	
10. International Freight	X	
11. Unloading at Foreign Terminal		X
12. Trade Documentation in country of Transit/Importation		X
13. Customs Clearance in Foreign Country		X
14. Import charges		X
15. Foreign Carriage to Buyer's Warehouse		X
16. Unloading at Buyer's Warehouse		X

Other specific costs should be addressed separately as part of the contract of sale between the Seller and Buyer.

Who Pays for the Cost? Seller or Buyer?

Trade Term: DELIVERED EX QUAY (DUTY PAID) (Named Port of Destination)

Comments: The Seller fulfills his obligation to deliver when he has made the goods available to the Buyer on the quay (wharf) at the named port of destination, cleared for importation. The Seller has to bear all risks and costs including duties, taxes and other charges of delivering the goods to the named port. There are deviations, if the Seller wants the Buyer to pay duties and taxes; ie, "Delivered Ex Quay–Duty Unpaid".

Mode of Transportation: Ocean Shipments Only

Cost Headings of Transportation/Handling	Seller	Buyer
1. Loading at Seller's Warehouse	X	
2. U.S. Inland Freight/Cartage	X	
3. Arrange Contract of Carriage/Dispatch	X	
4. Export Documentation (U.S.)	X	
5. U.S. Customs Clearance (Shipper's Export Declaration, etc.)	X	
6. Export Charges (Including Payment of Harbor Maintenance Fee)	X	
7. Loading at Carrier's Terminal	X	
8. Arrange Transportation Equipment	X	
9. Cargo Insurance for Transportation	X	
10. International Freight	X	
11. Unloading at Foreign Terminal	X	
12. Trade Documentation in country of Transit/Importation	X	
13. Customs Clearance in Foreign Country	X	
14. Import charges	X	
15. Foreign Carriage to Buyer's Warehouse		X
16. Unloading at Buyer's Warehouse		X

Other specific costs should be addressed separately as part of the contract of sale between the Seller and Buyer.

Who Pays for the Cost? Seller or Buyer?

Trade Term: DELIVERED DUTY UNPAID (Named Place of Destination)

Comments: The Seller fulfills his obligations to deliver when the goods have been made available at the named place in the country of importation. The Seller has to bear the costs and risks involved in bringing the goods thereto (excluding duties, taxes and other official charges payable upon importation as well as the costs and risks of carrying out customs formalities). The Buyer has to pay any additional costs and bear any risks caused by his failure to clear the goods for import in time.

Mode of Transportation: All modes of Transport

Cost Headings of Transportation/Handling	Seller	Buyer
1. Loading at Seller's Warehouse	X	
2. U.S. Inland Freight/Cartage	X	
3. Arrange Contract of Carriage/Dispatch	X	
4. Export Documentation (U.S.)	X	
5. U.S. Customs Clearance (Shipper's Export Declaration, etc.)	X	
6. Export Charges (Including Payment of Harbor Maintenance Fee)	X	
7. Loading at Carrier's Terminal	X	
8. Arrange Transportation Equipment	X	
9. Cargo Insurance for Transportation	X	
10. International Freight	X	
11. Unloading at Foreign Terminal	X	
12. Trade Documentation in country of Transit/Importation		X
13. Customs Clearance in Foreign Country		X
14. Import charges		X
15. Foreign Carriage to Buyer's Warehouse	X	
16. Unloading at Buyer's Warehouse		X

Other specific costs should be addressed separately as part of the contract of sale between the Seller and Buyer.

Appendix G

Additional Sources and Reading

In addition to the sources noted in individual chapters in the text, those listed in this appendix will provide the exporter with much additional information necessary for various operations within the export department as well as for furthering his/her knowledge of many aspects of international trade.

NATIONAL TRADE ESTIMATE REPORT, 1989, published by the Office of the U.S. Trade Representative, it documents significant foreign barriers to U.S. exporters. This report covers the most important barriers affecting goods, services, investment and intellectual property rights of major U.S. trading partners. It includes import policies; standards, testing, labeling and certification; government procurement; export subsidies; intellectual property protection; services barriers; investment barriers; and other barriers.

If feasible, quantitative estimates of foreign practices' impact upon the volume of U.S. exports are also included. Information on actions being taken to eliminate any act, policy or practice identified in the report are also listed.

The report is available for reference in most Department of Commerce libraries.

OPERATION OF THE TRADE AGREEMENTS PROGRAM, 41st Report, 1989, Published by the United States International Trade Commission (USITC Publication 2317), it is available free by writing to the USITC, Washington, D. C. 20436. The report covers all the trade agreement in which the U. S. participates and the activities of the USITC related to them.

THE OMNIBUS TRADE AND COMPETITIVENESS ACT OF 1988 (Public Law 100-418, signed by President Ronald Regan, August 23, 1988). The act calls for a free and open multilateral trading system and seeks better ways to open foreign markets to U. S. exporters. In addition, the act provides trade-negotiating authority for the President, less burdensome export controls by paring down the list of controlled technology products and reducing the number of export-license applications by 20 to 25 percent.

The act also clarifies and provides better guidance to exporters by amending the Foreign Corrupt Practices Act.

The new law also adopts and implements the Harmonized Commodity Description Coding System of Tariff Classification and replaces the Tariff Schedule of the United States. This makes the United States part of the universal coding system and places U. S. exporters on a par with its trading partners.

Of great interest to exporters is the provision in the law for the establishment of a National Trade Data Bank to collect and provide to exporters, accurate trade and economic data. The Export Promotion Data System will be part of the NTDB Committee, and will also include the Commerce Department's Commercial Information Management System (CIMS), providing data and information on markets and industrial sectors of foreign countries of greatest potential to exporters.

A full reading of the Trade Act of 1988 will disclose many other benefits accruing to the U.S. exporter.

THE EXPORT ADMINISTRATION REGULATIONS The Export Administration Regulations are issued by the Department of Commerce to enforce the Export Administration Act of 1979. In passing this legislation, the Congress listed three general policy guidelines for the use of export controls.

First, controls should be used on exports which "would make a significant contribution to the military potential of any other country or combination of countries which would prove detrimental to the national security of the United States."

Second, controls should be used "where necessary to further significantly the foreign policy of the United States or to fulfill its declared international obligations."

Third, controls should be used "where necessary to protect the domestic economy from the excessive drain of scarce materials and to reduce the serious inflationary impact of foreign demand."

Copies of the regulations can be obtained from the Department of Commerce.

THE INTERNATIONAL TRADE REPORTER, An export shipping manual published by the Bureau of National Affairs, 1231 25th Street, N.W., Washington D. C. 20037. It covers documentation requirements of every country in the world, and describes the needed documents in great detail assuring that your shipment will not run into delays or problems.

EXPORTER'S ENCYCLOPEDIA, published by Dun & Bradstreet (Dun's Marketing Services), 3 Sylvan Way, Parsippany, New Jersey 07054. Among the many excellent chapter headings are: Export Markets, Export Know-How, Communications Data, Transportation Data and Information Sources and Data.

MARINE INSURANCE by CIGNA Companies, Philadelphia, Pa. 19101. Notes and comments on ocean cargo insurance.

PORTS OF THE WORLD by CIGNA Companies, Philadelphia, Pa. 19101, describes U.S. and foreign ports detailing all facilities, services and types of cargo handled.

THE SHIPPING DIGEST, published weekly by Geyer-McAllister Publications, 51 Madison Avenue, New York, New York 10010. This is an excellent publication listing vessel sailings from all Atlantic, Gulf, Pacific Coast, Great Lakes and Canada to all foreign ports.

MAGAZINES DEVOTED TO EXPORTING:

EXPORT TODAY, published monthly by Trade Communications Inc., 733 15th Street, N.W., Suite 1100, Washington, D. C. 20005.

THE EXPORTER, published monthly by Trade Data Reports, Inc., 6 West 37th Street, New York, New York, 10018.

NORTH AMERICAN INTERNATIONAL BUSINESS, published monthly by American International Publishing Col, 401 Theodore Fremd Avenue, Rye, New York 10580.

GLOBAL TRADE MAGAZINE, published by the Global Trade Group. Information on transportation, finance and commercial services.

REPORTS:

BUSINESS INTERNATIONAL, published weekly by Business International Corporation, One Dag Hammerskjold Plaza, New York, New York 10017.

EXPORTER'S GUIDE TO FOREIGN SOURCES FOR CREDIT INFORMATION. Available from publishers of THE EXPORTER (see above).

UNIFORM CUSTOMS AND PRACTICE FOR DOCUMENTARY CREDITS, 1983 REVISION, ICC PUBLICATION NO. 400. The Uniform Customs and Practice for Documentary Credits were first published by the International Chamber of Commerce (I.C.C.) in 1933. Revised versions were issued in 1951,1962 and 1974. This latest revision was adopted by the I.C.C. in June 1983 and published as publication No. 400 and is effective October 1st, 1984.

WORLD INFORMATION SERVICES, produced by Bank of America's Economic-Policy Research Department. In three volumes: COUNTRY OUTLOOK—intelligence briefings and detailed economic data for 36 leading countries; COUNTRY OUTLOOK—intelligence briefings and detailed economic data for 36 leading countries; COUNTRY DATA FORECASTS—Statistical data tables of historical performance and 5-year forecasts of 23 economic measurements for 100 countries, to compare international trends; COUNTRY RISK MONITOR—Ranks and compares the same 100 countries for current and future business risk. Based on a common set of key economic ratios and financial criteria. Each volume includes periodic updates. Available from Bank of America, World Information Services, c/o Worldnet Management, Inc., 3187F Airway Avenue, Costa Mesa, Ca. 92626.

AN ANALYSIS OF THE EXPORT LICENSING MECHANISM. Its effect upon the competitiveness of U. S. high technology exports, by David R. Kamerschen and Roger J. Robinson. In volume 17, AKRON BUSINESS AND ECONOMIC REVIEW - Spring 1986. Available in most major libraries.

BOOKS: Publications on Cultural Aspects of International Business. (Courtesy of Business America, Department of Commerce)

DO'S AND TABOOS AROUND THE WORLD. Roger E. Axtell. John Wiley & Sons, New York. 1990.

DO'S AND TABOOS OF HOSTING INTERNATIONAL VISITORS. Roger E. Axtell. John Wiley & Sons, New York. 1990.

BIG BUSINESS BLUNDERS; MISTAKES IN MULTINATIONAL MARKETING. David A. Ricks. Dow Jones-Irwin, Homewood, Ill. 1983.

UNDERSTANDING CULTURAL DIFFERENCES: GERMANS, FRENCH, AND AMERICANS. Edward T. Hall and Mildred Reed Hall. International Cultural Press, Yarmouth, Maine. 1990.

THE CULTURAL ENVIRONMENT OF INTERNATIONAL BUSINESS. Vern Terpstra. South-Western Publishing Company, Cincinnati, Ohio. 1978.

THE GLOBAL EDGE; HOW YOUR COMPANY CAN WIN IN THE INTERNATIONAL MARKETPLACE. Sondra Snowdon, Simon and Schuster, New York 1986.

NATIONAL NEGOTIATING STYLES. Edited by Hans Binnendijk. The Foreign Service Institute, U. S. Department of State, Washington, D.C. 1987.

INTERNATIONAL NEGOTIATION: A Cross-Cultural Prospective. Glen Fisher. Intercultural press, Yarmouth, Maine. 1980.

THE TRAVELER'S GUIDE TO EUROPEAN CUSTOMS AND MANNERS. Nancy L. Braganti and Elizabeth Devine. Simon and Schuster, New York. 1984.

THE TRAVELER'S GUIDE TO LATIN AMERICAN CUSTOMS AND MAN-

NERS. Elizabeth Devine and Nancy L. Braganti. St. Martin's Press, New York 1988.

THE INTERNATIONAL BUSINESSWOMAN: A Guide to Success in the Global Marketplace. Marlene L. Rossman. Praeger Publishers, New York 1986.

THE WORLD CLASS INTERNATIONAL EXECUTIVE. Neil Chesanow. Rawson Associates, 1985. How to do business like a "Pro" around the world.

SUPER TRAVELER. Samuel Miller. Holt 1980. Trade-law legislation, international travel regulations, legal status of Americans in foreign countries.

GOING INTERNATIONAL. Lennie Copeland and Lewis Griggs, published 1985 by Random House, New York, New York.

MANAGING CULTURAL DIFFERENCES. Philip R. Harris and Robert T. Moran. Second edition published 1987 by Gulf Publishing, Houston, Texas.

BEYOND GLOBALISM. Raymond Vernon. Subtitled Remaking American Foreign Economic Policy, published 1989 by the Free Press, New York, New York.

INTERNATIONAL BUSINESS: Environments and Operations. Lee H. Radebaugh, published 1979 by Wesley Publishing Company, Reading, Massachusetts.

INTRODUCTION TO MULTINATIONAL ACCOUNTING. Frederick D. S. Choi, published 1978 by Prentice Hall.,

A STUDY OF FUTURE WORLDS. Richard A. Falk, published 1975 by The Free Press, New York, New York.

GOING METRIC. Stewart M. Brooks, published 1976 by A. S. Barnes.

PRIVATE POWER: MULTINATIONAL CORPORATIONS AND SURVIVAL OF OUR PLANET. Axel Madison, Published 1980 by W. Morrow.

THE WORLD CHALLENGE. Jean-Jacques Servan-Schreiber, published 1980 by Simon & Schuster.

INTERNATIONAL BUSINESS—Introduction & Essentials. Donald A. Ball and William H. McCullough, Jr., fourth edition 1990, BPI/Irwin Press, Homewood, Il. 60430 and Boston, Ma. 02116. (used as a university textbook).

EUROPEAN CHALLENGE: THE BENEFITS OF A SINGLE MARKET. Paolo Cecchini, 1988 in London by Wildwood House; available in the U. S. through Gower Publishing Company, Old Post Road, Brookfield, Vt. 05036.

ECONOMIC GEOGRAPHY. Joseph H. Butler, published 1980 by John Wiley and Sons, New York, New York.

Many reports and bulletins are issued on a regular basis by banks, trade associations, organizations such as the European Community and the United Nations and others. Articles of timely interest to international traders often appear in Wall Street Journal, Journal of Commerce, New York Times and other good metropolitan newspapers.

You should read all you can about what's going on around the world and how other countries are handling their economic, political and social problems. You never know when one or more of these factors might have a direct bearing on your business.

Index